CRITICAL SURVEY OF POETRY

Surrealist Poets

Editor

Rosemary M. Canfield Reisman
Charleston Southern University

SALEM PRESS
A Division of EBSCO Publishing, Ipswich, Massachusetts

Cover photo:
Aimé Césaire (© Sergio Gaudenti/Kipa/Corbis)

ISBN: 978-1-42983-654-8

CONTENTS

CONTRIBUTORS

Peter Baker
*Southern Connecticut State
University*

Franz G. Blaha
*University of Nebraska-
Lincoln*

Alvin G. Burstein
*University of Tennessee,
Knoxville*

Carole A. Champagne
*University of Maryland-
Eastern Shore*

Paul Christensen
Texas A&M University

Steven E. Colburn
Largo, Florida

J. Madison Davis
*Pennsylvania State College-
Behrend College*

William V. Davis
Baylor University

Frank Day
Clemson University

Andonis Decavalles
*Fairleigh Dickinson
University*

Lillian Doherty
University of Maryland

Lee Hunt Dowling
University of Houston

Theresa E. Dozier
*Prince George's Community
College*

Desiree Dreeuws
Sunland, California

Clara Estow
University of Massachusetts

Katherine Gyékényesi Gatto
Richmond Heights, Ohio

Daniel L. Guillory
Millikin University

Sarah Hilbert
Pasadena, California

David Harrison Horton
Patten College

Tracy Irons-Georges
Glendale, California

Maura Ives
Texas A&M University

Philip K. Jason
*United States Naval
Academy*

Jeffry Jensen
Pasadena, California

Irma M. Kashuba
Chestnut Hill College

Philip Krummrich
University of Georgia

Rebecca Kuzins
Pasadena, California

William T. Lawlor
*University of Wisconsin-
Stevens Point*

Cherie R. Maiden
Furman University

Richard A. Mazzara
Oakland University

Christina J. Moose
Pasadena, California

C. L. Mossberg
Lycoming College

Károly Nagy
Middlesex County College

Kenneth A. Stackhouse
*Virginia Commonwealth
University*

Gordon Walters
DePauw University

Shawncey Webb
Taylor University

SURREALIST POETRY

Out of the horrors of World War I came a revolution in literature, one that found its footing primarily in Paris, France. It was as if all of the values on which Western society had been built were now irrelevant. If what had transpired during World War I represented progress, logic, and reason, so the theory went, then why would any sane person continue to support the status quo in Western civilization? The French poet and theorist André Breton clarified what the new movement stood for in his *Manifeste du surrealisme* (1924; *Manifesto of Surrealism*, 1969). As he saw it, Surrealism had more than one meaning.

Breton stands tall in the history of literature for being not only the founder of Surrealism but also its leader and guiding light. Not many literary figures can take credit for dramatically altering the cultural world, but Breton is one such individual. He was born in the small Normandy town of Tinchebray. Before long, his family moved to the Atlantic coast of Brittany, where the seaside setting would help to foster his imagination. As Breton was an only child, his parents had high hopes for his success. During World War I, he worked in the neurological section of a Nantes hospital. His experiences at this hospital and at a Saint-Dizier psychiatric center during the war would influence the impressionable Breton. He saw mental illness firsthand, and felt driven to piece together a theoretical approach to what he witnessed on a daily basis. After the war, he flirted with the nihilism of Dadaism, but that movement did not have a hold on him for very long. During the early 1920's, and with the help of a few friends, Breton came to the conclusion that he had to be more positive in his approach to creativity. The despair that seemed to envelop Dadaism was not what Breton hoped to express.

SURREALISM FORGES AHEAD

Of all the movements that came into existence during the early years of the twentieth century, including Dadaism, Futurism, and Imagism, it is Surrealism that has remained the most influential. The movement owes its longevity to the theoretical discipline that Breton provided. To him, Surrealism was first and foremost an expression of liberation from all traditional cultural and societal boundaries. It also emphasized a belief in the power of the human imagination and its capacity to speak to the unconscious via wordplay and image associations. This new movement was intended to do away with the stagnation that was corroding Western culture. While such nineteenth century movements as English Romanticism and French Symbolism had called for change, Surrealism combined both art and literature in order to transform the poet into someone who would be more true to his fertile imagination, becoming one of the leading avant-garde artistic movements.

Surrealism shared its disgust for war with Dadaism, which had been given life by

Jean Arp and Tristan Tzara in Switzerland around 1916. In a sense, if not for Dadaism, there may not have been Surrealism. Both movements were strongly anti-status quo, believing that the economic and political conditions that had led to World War I had to be eliminated. In fact, the Surrealists were anti- most things. They were against the military, nationalism, capitalism, imperialism, and even art. Surrealism questioned the typical role of the artist and poet. Was the poet really the sole creator of the final product? A poem did not necessarily come into existence merely through the efforts of the poet. The crafting of a final art object gave way to something that was unpredictable. Whether the product was a collage or a sound poem, chance predicted the outcome more than anything else did.

After the end of World War I, Paris became the center of the avant-garde world, and important artists and writers came from all over to make Paris their home. Within this cauldron of creativity, Surrealism came into its own. The French poet Guillaume Apolliniere tragically died during the war in 1918, but in his short life, he introduced valuable innovations to poetry that would become part of Surrealism. His poetry was greatly influenced by painters such as Henri Rousseau, Robert Delaunay and Pablo Picasso; his 1913 collection *Alcools* (English translation, 1964) includes one of his most revolutionary poems, "Zone," which opens with the line "In the end you are weary of this ancient world" (translation by Samuel Beckett). It is often anthologized because of its startling imagery, the seeming randomness of which is both jarring and riveting. It was a poem like this that Breton would point to as an important example of what he felt poetry should accomplish.

With the publication of his first manifesto, Breton had laid the groundwork for the Surrealist movement, which would focus on creativity as a positive force. There was no room for standing still, for merely being critical of the past. Between 1924 and 1930, when Breton would publish the *Second Manifeste du surréalisme* (*Second Manifesto of Surrealism*, 1969), Surrealism had a dramatic burst of creativity among its supporters. With the rise of communist thought, both Breton and others of the movement also attempted to incorporate Marxist philosophy into Surrealism. The movement expanded into other parts of the world where communist philosophy was also gaining influence. Breton sought refuge in New York during World War II; by the time he returned to Paris in 1946, the unified movement of Surrealism no longer existed, but he still remained the inspiration for those around the world who believed in it. Even after his death in Paris in 1966, the seeds that he had planted many decades before continued to thrive in the far reaches of the world.

A LASTING IMPACT

Surrealism has not always been taken as seriously as it should. Because of its perceived eccentricities, it has at times been dismissed as no more than an insignificant prank. That characterization does a great disservice to a movement that, at its core, takes its role in society very seriously. Surrealism became more than merely a literary or artistic movement. It reached beyond into film and even interior decoration. In the end, it entered the consciousness of a vast populace, even if that populace was not truly aware of what Surrealism was. The movement found a way to enter the imagination of several nations, and it was a strong voice for change between the two world wars.

Although Surrealism was mainly identified with Breton in the 1920's, there are artists and literary figures from previous eras who can be considered to have exhibited traits of Surrealism. These figures include the English poet William Blake, the artist Hieronymus Bosch, and the American writer Edgar Allan Poe. The French Symbolist poets such as Charles Baudelaire, Arthur Rimbaud, and Gerard de Nerval can be seen as forerunners of what Surrealism would embrace. While this looking back is typical of most literary movements, Surrealism benefited from having a great theorist like Breton to put the movement into perspective.

The enthusiasm of Surrealism sparked an almost out-of-control urge to create. It challenged poets to create something of value by means of automatic writing, although many writers only produced pages of nonsense; poets of worth may have employed Surrealist attempts to tap the subconscious, but they also took the time to revise their efforts in order to confirm their value. Despite being intrigued by the thought of a free flowing of words, these poets realized that it was still necessary to edit what they wrote. The best at manipulating the automatic approach included Louis Aragon, Paul Eluard, and Federico García Lorca, while some of the best English language poets to be inspired by the movement were John Ashbery, Ted Hughes, Robert Bly, Allen Ginsberg, and James Tate. These are just a few examples of those who found Surrealism to be the key to unlocking the door to greater creativity.

Jeffry Jensen

BIBLIOGRAPHY

Conley, Katharine, and Pierre Taminiaux, eds. *Surrealism and Its Others*. New Haven, Conn.: Yale University Press, 2006. Takes an in-depth look at why members of the Surrealist movement were so passionate about their work, as well as the theories behind it.

Matthews, J. H. *Surrealist Poetry in France*. Syracuse, N.Y.: Syracuse University Press, 1969. A critical history of the Surrealist movement.

Montagu, Jemima. *The Surrealists: Revolutionaries in Art and Writing, 1919-35*. London: Tate, 2002. An exploration of a movement that set out to make a difference.

Peyre, Henri. "The Significance of Surrealism." *Yale French Studies* 31 (1964): 23-36. Discusses the continued impact of Surrealism on the literary world.

Rosemont, Franklin. "Surrealism, Poetry, and Politics." *Socialist Review* 28, no. 1 (2001): 54-63. Makes clear the Surrealist position that poetry is a power that can change society.

RAFAEL ALBERTI

Born: Puerto de Santa María, Spain; December 16, 1902
Died: Puerto de Santa María, Spain; October 28, 1999

PRINCIPAL POETRY

Marinero en tierra, 1925
La amante, 1926
El alba del alhelí, 1927
Cal y canto, 1929
Sobre los ángeles, 1929 (*Concerning the Angels*, 1967)
Consignas, 1933
Verte y no verte, 1935 (*To See You and Not to See You*, 1946)
Poesía, 1924-1938, 1940
Entre el clavel y la espada, 1941
Pleamar, 1944
A la pintura, 1945 (*To Painting*, 1997)
Retornos de lo vivo lejano, 1952
Baladas y canciones del Paraná, 1954 (*Ballads and Songs of the Parana*, 1988)
Poesías completas, 1961
Rafael Alberti: Selected Poems, 1966 (Ben Belitt, translator)
The Owl's Insomnia, 1973
Alberti tal cual, 1978

OTHER LITERARY FORMS

Although Rafael Alberti (ol-BEHR-tee) established his reputation almost entirely on the basis of his poetry, he became involved in drama after emigrating to Argentina, writing plays of his own and adapting Miguel de Cervantes' *El cerco de Numancia* (wr. 1585, pb. 1784; *Numantia: A Tragedy*, 1870) for the modern stage in 1944.

Alberti's most notable achievement in prose, a work of considerable interest for the student of his poetry, was his autobiography, *La arboleda perdida* (1942; *The Lost Grove*, 1976). In addition, he was a talented painter and supplied illustrations for some of his later volumes.

ACHIEVEMENTS

Rafael Alberti had at once the ill luck and the singular good fortune to flourish during Spain's second great literary boom. Despite his acknowledged worth, he was overshadowed by several of his contemporaries—in particular, by Federico García Lorca. Although Alberti's name is likely to come up in any discussion of the famous *generación del 27*, or Generation of '27, he generally languishes near the end of the list. On the other hand, the extraordinary atmosphere of the times did much to foster his talents; even among the giants, he earned acceptance and respect. He may occasionally have been lost in the crowd, but it was a worthy crowd.

His *Marinero en tierra* (sailor on dry land) won Spain's National Prize for Literature in 1925, and throughout his long career, his virtuosity never faltered. Always a difficult poet, he never gave the impression that his obscurity stemmed from incompetence. His political ideology—Alberti was the first of his circle to embrace communism openly—led him to covet the role of "poet of the streets," but Alberti will be remembered more for his poems of exile, which capture better than any others the poignant aftermath of the Spanish Civil War.

Ultimately, Alberti stands out as a survivor. Many of his great contemporaries died in the civil war or simply lapsed into a prolonged silence. Despite his wholehearted involvement in the conflict, Alberti managed to persevere after his side lost and to renew his career. He continued to publish at an imposing rate, took up new activities, and became a force in the burgeoning literary life of Latin America, as evidenced by his winning of the Cervantes Prize, the Spanish-speaking world's highest literary honor, in 1983. Consistent in his adherence to communism, he received the Lenin Prize for his political verse in 1965. Oddly enough, then, Alberti emerges as a constant—an enduring figure in a world of flux, a practicing poet of consistent excellence during six decades.

BIOGRAPHY

Rafael Alberti was born near Cádiz in Andalusia, and his nostalgia for that region pervades much of his work. His genteel family had fallen on hard times, and Alberti's schoolmates made him painfully aware of his inferior status. In 1917, the family moved to Madrid, where Alberti devoted himself to painting in the cubist manner, attaining some recognition. Illness forced him to retire to a sanatorium in the mountains—a stroke of luck, as it happened, for there he subsequently met such luminaries as García Lorca, Salvador Dalí, and Luis Buñuel and began seriously to write poetry. He won the National Prize for *Marinero en tierra* and thereby gained acceptance into the elite artistic circles of the day. Personal difficulties and an increasing awareness of the plight of his country moved Alberti to embrace communism. In 1930, he married María Teresa León, also a writer, and together they founded the revolutionary journal *Octubre* in 1934.

Alberti's new political credo enabled him to travel extensively and to encounter writers and artists from all parts of Europe and the Americas. After participating actively in the civil war, he emigrated to Argentina in 1940. There, he began to write for the theater, gave numerous readings, and resumed painting. Hard work and fatherhood—his daughter Aitana was born in 1941—preserved Alberti from embittered paralysis, and his production of poetry never slackened. Indeed, many of his readers believe that he reached his peak in the late 1940's.

In 1964, Alberti moved to Rome, where he lived until 1977, when he was finally able to return to Spain, after almost thirty-eight years in exile. He was welcomed by more than three hundred communists carrying red flags as he stepped off the airliner. "I'm not coming with a clenched fist," he said, "but with an open hand." He enjoyed a resurgence of popularity after his return and proceeded to run for the Cortes, giving poetry readings instead of speeches, and won. Alberti resigned his seat after three months to devote himself to his art. He became a well-respected literary figure in his last two decades in Spain; the lost Andalusian had returned home. He died there on October 28, 1999, from a lung ailment; he was ninety-six years old.

ANALYSIS

Throughout his long career, Rafael Alberti proved to be a remarkably versatile poet. His facility of composition enabled him to shift smoothly from fixed forms to free verse, even within the confines of a single poem. Whether composing neomedieval lyrics, Baroque sonnets, or Surreal free verse, he always managed to be authentic. His deep emotions, sometimes obscured by his sheer virtuosity, found expression in all modes. His technical skill did not allow him to stagnate: Commentators on Alberti agree in their praise of his astonishing technical mastery. He might continue in the same vein for three volumes, but he would invariably break new ground in the fourth. His massive corpus of poetry comprises a remarkable array of styles, themes, and moods.

Although he was a natural poet with little formal training, Alberti always kept abreast of current developments in his art—indeed, he kept himself in the vanguard. He associated with the best and brightest of his time and participated in their movements. When the luminaries of Spain reevaluated Luis de Góngora y Argote, Alberti wrote accomplished neo-Baroque poetry; when Dalí and Buñuel were introducing Surrealism in Spanish art and film, Alberti adapted its principles to Spanish poetry; when most of the intellectuals of Spain were resisting General Franciso Franco and embracing communism, Alberti was the "poet of the streets." He remained withal a genuine and unique lyric voice. Even his political verses are not without poetic merit—an exception, to be sure. Alberti changed by adding and growing, never by discarding and replacing; thus, he became a richer talent with each new phase of his creative development.

Alberti's poetry is suffused with nostalgia. The circumstances of his life decreed that he should continually find himself longing for another time, a distant place, or a lost friend, and in his finest poems, he achieves an elegiac purity free of the obscurity and self-pity that mar his lesser works. From first to last, the sadness for things lost remains Alberti's great theme, one he explored more fully than any other poet of his generation.

Alberti was a poet who could grow without discarding his past. The youthful poet who composed marvelous lyrics persisted in the nostalgia of exile; the angry poet of the streets reasserted himself in diatribes against Yankee imperialism in Latin America. At ease in all forms and idioms, forever the Andalusian in exile, always growing in his art and his thought, Alberti wrote a staggering number of excellent poems. In the vast treasure trove of twentieth century Spanish poetry, he left a hoard of pearls and sapphires—hidden at times by the rubies and the emeralds, but worthy nevertheless.

MARINERO EN TIERRA

The doyens of Spanish letters received *Marinero en tierra* with immediate enthusiasm, and the young Alberti found himself a de facto member of the Generation of '27, eligible to rub elbows with all the significant writers of the day. Although Alberti seems to have been happy in the mid-1920's, his early volumes glow with poignant nostalgia for the sea and the coasts of his native Andalusia. He expresses his longing in exquisite lyrics in the medieval tradition. Ben Belitt, introducing his translations collected in *Selected Poems*, confesses that he could find no way to render these lyrics in English. They depend entirely on a native tradition, the vast trove of popular verses from Spain's turbulent Middle Ages. Alberti's genius is such that the poems have no savor of pedantry or preciosity. Luis Monguió, in his introduction to Belitt's translations, suggests that "it is far from unlikely that they are being sung in the provinces today by many in complete ignorance of their debt to Rafael Alberti." The notion is a tribute both to the poet and to the tradition he understood so well.

The verses themselves may seem enigmatic, but only because the modern reader is accustomed to probe so far beneath the surface. One of the best of them, "Gimiendo" ("Groaning"), presents the plaint of a sailor who remembers that his shirt used to puff up in the wind whenever he saw the shore. The entire poem consists of only six brief lines; there is only one image, and only one point. That single image conveys a feeling close to the hearts of those born within smell of the sea—a need unfulfilled for Alberti. He speaks for all seafarers who are marooned inland, the sailors on land.

"Pradoluengo," an aubade in the same style, is only seven lines long and conveys an equally simple message. The beloved to whom the poem is addressed is told that the cocks are crowing, that "we need cross only river waters, not the sea," and is urged to get up and come along. With all the richness of the genre, Alberti hints at a wealth of erotic possibilities and natural splendors. Only William Butler Yeats, in modern English poetry, matches this exquisite simplicity and feeling for tradition.

CAL Y CANTO

As noted above, Alberti took a leading role in the Góngora tricentennial of 1927, and many of the poems in *Cal y canto* owe much to the Baroque model. Here, Alberti reveals a new facet of his technical mastery, particularly in his handling of the sonnet, perhaps the most difficult of forms. "Amaranta," a sonnet that frequently appears in anthologies, shows how completely Alberti was able to assimilate the poetics of Góngora and to adapt them to the twentieth century. The octave describes, in ornate and lavish terms, the beauty of Amaranta; as with Góngora, the very exuberance of the description disquiets the reader. Her breasts, for example, are polished "as with the tongue of a greyhound." The sestet conceals the scorpion sting so often found in Góngora's conclusions: Solitude, personified, settles like a glowing coal between Amaranta and her lover. In this poem, Alberti displays his affinity with Góngora in two respects: an absolute control of his idiom and an obscurity that has deprived both poets of numerous readers. As Alberti himself remarked in his autobiography, "this was painterly poetry—plastic, linear, profiled, confined."

CONCERNING THE ANGELS

Concerning the Angels differs sharply from Alberti's previous work. Bouts of depression and a loss of faith in his former ideals drove him to abandon nostalgia and to confront despair. Suddenly, all the joy and tender sorrow of his early work is gone, replaced by anguish and self-pity. The revolution in content corresponds to a rebellion in form: Free verse prevails as more appropriate to the poet's state of mind than any traditional order. Alberti does not despair utterly, as Monguió indicates, but the overall tone of the collection is negative.

"Tres recuerdos del cielo" ("Three Memories of Heaven"), a tribute to the great Romantic poet Gustavo Adolfo Bécquer, constitutes a noteworthy exception to the depressing tone of the volume. Here, Alberti displays the subtlety and tenderness that characterize his work at its most appealing. Evoking a condition of being before time existed, Alberti recaptures the tenuous delicacy of Bécquer, the sense of the ineffable. The meeting between the lovers, for example, takes place in a world of clouds and moonlight: "When you, seeing me in nothingness/ Invented the first word." Alberti imitates Bécquer masterfully, at the same time finding a new way to express his own nostalgia.

"Three Memories of Heaven," however, is atypical of the collection. Virtually all the other poems treat of "angels" and ultimately of a world turned to wormwood and gall. "El ángel desengañado" ("The Angel Undeceived") debunks the ideals of the younger Alberti, particularly in its desolate conclusion: "I'm going to sleep./ No one is waiting for me." "El ángel de carbón" ("Angel of Coals") ends no less grimly: "And that octopus, love, in the shadow:/ evil, so evil." Several of the poems offer a kind of hope, but it is a wan hope, scarcely better than despair. Like the T. S. Eliot of "The Hollow Men," however, Alberti maintains his poetic control, even with the world withering away around him.

TO SEE YOU AND NOT TO SEE YOU

Two pivotal events in Alberti's life helped him out of this quagmire: meeting his future wife and becoming a communist. The political commitment, while it did little to benefit his poetry, provided him with a set of beliefs to fill the void within. Of his proletarian verse, one can say only that it is no worse than most political poetry. Like his friend and contemporary Pablo Neruda, Alberti mistook a sincere political commitment for an artistic imperative; like Neruda, he eventually returned to more personal themes, although he never wholly abandoned doctrinaire verse.

Even at the height of his political activism, however, Alberti was capable of devoting his gifts to the elegy; the death of Ignacio Sánchez Mejías in the bullring moved him to write the sonnet series that makes up *To See You and Not to See You* in 1935. The same tragedy also inspired Federico García Lorca to compose one of the most famous poems in the Spanish language, "Llanto por Ignacio Sánchez Mejías" ("Lament for Ignacio Sánchez Mejías"). A comparison of the two poems reveals the radical differences between these two superficially similar poets. García Lorca chants compellingly, "At five in the afternoon," evoking the drama of the moment and the awful immediacy of the bull. Alberti reflects on the bull's calfhood, its callow charges as it grew into the engine of destruction that destroyed Sánchez Mejías. García Lorca goes on to convey, in muted tones, his sense of loss. Alberti expresses that sense of loss in terms of distance: As his friend dies in the bullring, Alberti is sailing toward Romania on the Black Sea. The memory of the journey becomes permanently associated with the loss of the friend and thus a redoubled source of nostalgia.

IN GARCÍA LORCA'S SHADOW

As usual, García Lorca enjoys the fame, and Alberti is lost in his shadow. No doubt García Lorca's elegy speaks more clearly and more movingly; it probably *is* better than its counterpart. Alberti himself admired the "Lament for Ignacio Sánchez Mejías" without reservation. The pattern, however, is only too familiar: Alberti, so like García Lorca in some ways, found himself outmatched at every turn while his friend and rival was still alive. Alberti wrote exquisite medieval lyrics, but García Lorca outdid him with the *Romancero gitano* (1928; *The Gypsy Ballads*, 1953). Alberti captured the essence of Andalusia, but the public identified Andalusia with García Lorca. Alberti wrote a noble and moving elegy for Ignacio Sánchez Mejías, but his rival composed such a marvelous lament that Alberti's has been neglected.

All this is not to imply conscious enmity between the two poets. Alberti had cause to envy his contemporary's fame, and his bitterness at playing a secondary role may have been reflected in *Concerning the Angels*. Indeed, although Alberti gave many indications, in verse and prose, of his profound regard for García Lorca, his relationship with the poet of Granada represents an analogue to the dilemma of his literary life. The competition must have stimulated him, but, because his poetry was less accessible and less dramatic in its impact, he tended to be eclipsed. After the Spanish Civil War, Alberti emigrated to Argentina, mourning his slain and dispersed comrades, including García Lorca, who was senselessly gunned down at the outset of the hostilities. The war poems in the Alberti canon compare favorably with any on that subject, not least because his lively imagination enabled him to look beyond the slaughter.

ENTRE EL CLAVEL Y LA ESPADA

For all his faith, the poet soon found himself across the Atlantic, listening to reports of World War II, picking up the pieces. Somehow he managed to recover and to emerge greater than ever. A poem from his first collection published outside Spain, *Entre el clavel y la espada* (between sword and carnation), sounds the keynote of his renewed art:

> After this willful derangement, this harassed
> and necessitous grammar by whose haste I must live,
> let the virginal word come back to me whole and
>   meticulous,
> and the virginal verb, justly placed with its rigorous
>   adjective.

The poem, written in Spain, anticipates the purity of Alberti's poetry in exile. The poet forgot neither the horrors he had seen nor his love for his homeland.

Another elegy deserves mention in this context. Written after news of the death of the great poet Antonio Machado, "De los álamos y los sauces" (from poplar and willow) captures the plight of Alberti and his fellow exiles in but a few lines. The man in the poem is caught up "in the life of his distant dead and hears them in the air." Thus, Alberti returns grimly to his leitmotif, nostalgia.

RETORNOS DE LO VIVO LEJANO

With his return to his nostalgic leitmotif, Alberti reached his full potential as a poet during the 1940's and 1950's. He poured forth volume after volume of consistently high quality. *Retornos de lo vivo lejano* (returns of the far and the living), a book wholly devoted to his most serviceable theme, may well be the finest volume of his career. The poems are at once accessible and mysterious, full of meaning on the surface and suggestive of unfathomed depths.

"Retornos del amor en una noche de verano" ("Returns: A Summer Night's Love") recalls in wondrous imagery the breathlessness of a time long past. For example, two pairs of lips, as they press together, become a silent carnation. "Retornos de Chopin a través de unas manos ya idas" ("Returns: Chopin by Way of Hands Now Gone") evokes some of the poet's earliest memories of his family. After many years, the poet is reunited with his brothers by an act of imagination, supported by the memory of Frédéric Chopin's music as played by the poet's mother. This is the quintessential Alberti, the master craftsman and the longing man in one.

TO PAINTING

Amid the melancholy splendor of his poems of exile, Alberti distilled a curious volume entitled *To Painting*. In contrast to all that Alberti lost in exile, painting stands as a rediscovered treasure, and the Alberti of the early 1920's comes face to face with the middle-aged émigré. The collection includes sonnets on the tools of painting, both human and inanimate; free-verse meditations on the primary colors; and poems on various painters, each in a style reminiscent of the artist's own. Beyond its intrinsic value, the volume reveals much about the mutual attraction of the two arts.

"BALLAD OF THE LOST ANDALUSIAN"

A poem from *Ballads and Songs of the Parana*, deserves special mention. "Balada del Andaluz perdido" ("Ballad of the Lost Andalusian"), as much as any single poem, reflects Alberti's self-image as a poet in exile. Written in terse, unrhymed couplets, it tells of a wandering Andalusian who watches the olives grow "by the banks of a different river." Sitting alone, he provokes curious questions from the Argentine onlookers on the opposite bank of the river, but he remains a mystery to them. Not so to the reader, who understands the pathos of the riderless horses, the memory of hatred, the loneliness. The final question admits of no answer and in fact needs none: "What will he do there, what is left to be done/ on the opposite side of the river, alone?"

OTHER MAJOR WORKS

PLAYS: *El hombre deshabitado*, pb. 1930; *El trébol floride*, pb. 1940; *El adefesio*, pb. 1944; *El cerco de Numancia*, pr. 1944 (adaptation of Miguel de Cervantes' play).
NONFICTION: *La arboleda perdida*, 1942 (*The Lost Grove*, 1976).

BIBLIOGRAPHY

Gagen , Derek . " *Marinero en tierra* : Alberti's first 'Libro organico de poemas'?" *Modern Language Review* 88, no. 1 (January, 1993): 91. Alberti's *Marinero en tierra* is examined in detail.

Havard, Robert. *The Crucified Mind: Rafael Alberti and the Surrealist Ethos in Spain*. London: Tamesis Books, 2001. A biographical and historical study.

Herrmann, Gina. *Written in Red: The Communist Memoir in Spain*. Urbana: University of Illinois Press, 2009. This work examining memoirs of Communists in Spain contains a chapter on Maria Teresa León and Alberti.

Jiménez-Fajardo, Salvador. *Multiple Spaces: The Poetry of Rafael Alberti*. London: Tamesis Books, 1985. A critical analysis of Alberti's poetic works. Includes bibliographic references.

Manteiga, Robert C. *Poetry of Rafael Alberti: A Visual Approach*. London: Tamesis Books , 1978 . A study of Alberti's literary style. Text is in English with poems in original Spanish. Includes bibliographic references.

Nantell, Judith. *Rafael Alberti's Poetry of the Thirties*. Athens: University of Georgia Press, 1986. This study puts Alberti's work in historical and social context by analyzing the influences from a turbulent decade in which civil war erupts, ignites a European conflagration, and ends in societal crises. The author discusses political poems that are not as memorable as his earlier works but deserve recognition for their artistic as well as social value.

Soufas, C. Christopher. *The Subject in Question: Early Contemporary Spanish Literature and Modernism*. Washington, D.C.: Catholic University of America Press, 2007. This overview of Spanish literature and modernism contains a chapter examining the poetry of Alberti and Luis Cernuda.

Ugarte, Michael. *Shifting Ground: Spanish Civil War Exile Literature*. Durham, N.C.: Duke University Press, 1989. Examination of the importance of Spanish exile literature during and after the civil war. The second section of the book explores the intellectual diaspora of the civil war, and an analysis of Alberti's *The Lost Grove* is featured prominently.

Philip Krummrich
Updated by Carole A. Champagne and Sarah Hilbert

VICENTE ALEIXANDRE

Born: Seville, Spain; April 26, 1898
Died: Madrid, Spain; December 14, 1984

<small>PRINCIPAL POETRY</small>
Ámbito, 1928
Espadas como labios, 1932 (*Swords as if Lips*, 1989)
La destrucción o el amor, 1935 (*Destruction or Love: A Selection*, 1976)
Pasión de la tierra, 1935, 1946
Sombra del paraíso, 1944 (*Shadow of Paradise*, 1987)
Mundo a solas, 1950 (*World Alone*, 1982)
Nacimiento último, 1953
Historia del corazón, 1954
Mis poemas mejores, 1956
Poesías completas, 1960
Picasso, 1961
En un vasto dominio, 1962
Presencias, 1965
Retratos con nombre, 1965
Poemas de la consumación, 1968
Poems, 1969
Poesía superrealista, 1971
Sonido de la guerra, 1972
Diálogos del conocimiento, 1974
The Caves of Night: Poems, 1976
Twenty Poems, 1977
A Longing for Light: Selected Poems of Vicente Aleixandre, 1979
A Bird of Paper: Poems of Vicente Aleixandre, 1981
Primeros poemas, 1985
Nuevos poemas varios, 1987
El mar negro, 1991
En gran noche: Últimos poemas, 1991
Noche cerrada, 1998

<small>OTHER LITERARY FORMS</small>
Vicente Aleixandre (o-lehk-SON-dreh) published a great number of prologues, critical letters, memoirs, and evocations of friends and literary figures, many of them later included or rewritten for his major prose work, *Los encuentros* (1958; "the encoun-

ters"). Aleixandre also made several speeches on poetry and poets, later published in pamphlet or book form.

ACHIEVEMENTS

After receiving the Nobel Prize in Literature in 1977, Vicente Aleixandre stated that the prize was "a response symbolic of the relation of a poet with all other men." In Aleixandre's own estimation, winning the Nobel was his only worthy achievement. All other influences on the development of poetry were insignificant compared with the poet's call to speak for his fellow humans.

The extent of Aleixandre's influence is considerable, however, even if he denied its importance. He was a member of the Royal Spanish Academy (1949), the Hispanic Society of America, the Academy of the Latin World, Paris, the Royal Academy of Fine Arts of San Telmo, Málaga, the Spanish American Academy of Bogotá, and the Academy of Arts and Sciences of Puerto Rico, and, as of 1972, an honorary fellow of the American Association of Spanish and Portuguese.

All these honors recognize Aleixandre's lifelong devotion to the production of a unified body of poetry. A member of the celebrated Generation of '27, which included Jorge Guillén, Pedro Salinas, Federico García Lorca, Rafael Alberti, and Gerardo Diego, Aleixandre was one of the central figures of Spanish Surrealism. Although influenced by André Breton and his circle, the Spanish Surrealists developed to a great extent independently of their French counterparts. While French Surrealism is significant for its worldwide impact on the arts, it produced a surprisingly small amount of lasting poetry. In contrast, Spanish Surrealism—both in Spain and, with notable local variations, in Latin America—constitutes one of the richest poetic traditions of the twentieth century, a tradition in which Aleixandre played a vital role.

BIOGRAPHY

Vicente Aleixandre Merlo was born on April 26, 1898, in Seville, Spain, the son of Cirilo Aleixandre Ballester, a railway engineer, and Elvira Merlo García de Pruneda, daughter of an upper-middle-class Andalusian family. Married in Madrid, Aleixandre's parents moved to Seville, the base for his father's travels with the Andalusian railway network. Four years after Aleixandre's birth, the family moved to Málaga, remaining there for seven years, spending their summers in a cottage on the beach at Pedregalejo a few miles from the city.

Aleixandre seems to have been very happy as a boy in Málaga, where he attended school, frequented the movie theater across the street from his house (he particularly liked the films of Max Linder), and read the Brothers Grimm and Hans Christian Andersen. Happy memories of Málaga and the nearby sea appear frequently in Aleixandre's poetry: He calls them "ciudad del paraíso" (city of paradise) and "mar del paraíso" (sea of paradise), respectively.

In 1911, the family moved to Madrid, where Aleixandre continued his studies at Teresiano School, but he found the strict requirements for the bachelor's degree tedious and preferred reading the books in his grandfather's library: classical and Romantic works and detective novels, especially those by Sir Arthur Conan Doyle. Aleixandre frequently visited the National Library, where he read novels and drama from Spain's Golden Age to the Generation of '98. During the summer of 1917, his friend Dámaso Alonso loaned him a volume by Rubén Darío, a book that, Aleixandre said, revealed to him the passion of his life—poetry. The next year, he discovered the works of Antonio Machado and Juan Ramón Jiménez, as well as the Romantic world of Gustavo Adolfo Bécquer, and his interest in poetry was firmly established.

At the age of fifteen, Aleixandre began to study law and business administration, finishing the two programs in 1920. He became an assistant professor at the School of Commerce of Madrid and worked at night editing a journal of economics in which he published several articles on railroads. In 1921, he left his teaching post to work for the railway company, but when, in 1925, he suffered an attack of renal tuberculosis, he dropped all professional and social activities, dedicating himself to his poetry, reading, and traveling with his family through Portugal, France, England, and diverse regions of Spain.

Aleixandre's first poems appeared in *Revista de occidente* (journal of the West) in 1926, and two years later his first collection, *Ámbito* (ambit) was published. In 1929, he discovered Sigmund Freud, James Joyce, and Arthur Rimbaud, and, although he suffered a relapse into his tubercular condition in 1932, this period of his life was very productive, resulting in three collections published between 1932 and 1935.

After the removal of a diseased kidney in 1932, Aleixandre retired to Miraflores de la Sierra to convalesce, but in 1933, he returned to Madrid. Carlos Bousoño reports that during this year, Aleixandre read French translations of the German Romantic writers Ludwig Tieck and Novalis, as well as *Les Romantiques allemands* (1933; a translation of Ricarda Huch's *Blüthezeit der Romantik*, 1899; "the German Romantics"). He completed this new spiritual phase with the lyric poetry of William Shakespeare, John Keats, Percy Bysshe Shelley, and William Wordsworth. In 1934, Aleixandre's mother died, and he again traveled through England, France, and Switzerland. During the years of the Spanish Civil War (1936-1939), Aleixandre was isolated from political turmoil, spending much of the time in convalescence after renewed bouts of illness. The death of his father in 1939 brought him even closer to his sister Concepción.

Aleixandre's work reflects his psychological and physiological state as vitally passionate and chronically sick, and as a calm, patient, and creative man. His poetic production was sustained over a lifetime, although a great many years passed between his published collections. In his own words, "The poet dies only when the man dies. And then, his poetry lives forever."

ANALYSIS

In the work of Vicente Aleixandre's first period, the poet is interested primarily in terrible mythic elements of nature without people; he is chaotic, delirious, and grotesque. His is a kind of rebellion against the middle class that hems him in, but he is not yet aware that to save himself from its oppression he must transform his blind, ineffective rebellion into a conscious, efficient one. In his middle period, although Aleixandre continues to take refuge in myth to escape the horrible realities of the day, he faces them as he recalls his family and past, realizing that he cannot remain aloof from history, politics, and other realities when people believe in him. Finally, in his later work, the poet becomes academic, literary, cultured, and decorative. Gradually, finding historical and telluric man and his own dialectical reality, Aleixandre identifies with the public, and the amorous solidarity of the man and poet with all creation is complete.

The idea that love equals death is the leitmotif of almost all of Aleixandre's poetry; it appears most clearly in his recurring images of the sea. In addition to repressed sexuality, a neurotic and somewhat limited group of fantasies recur throughout his oeuvre, many of them associated with the sea. His early years in Málaga impressed the sea on his consciousness, so that it became for him a symbol of youth, equated in turn with innocence, happiness, and his mother (in psychoanalytic dream interpretation, the sea often symbolizes the mother). His desire to return and merge with that happiness and all it represents implies his death as an individual, as he is absorbed by a larger unit. Intrauterine life, being premortal (except to the Roman Catholic Church), is easily equated with postmortal life—life before birth equals life after death.

The sea occupies a high place in Aleixandre's poetic scale of values. Among the 336 poems of his *Poesías completas*, the sea appears 182 times; moreover, it is used as a central theme in sixteen poems. The sea, a recurring symbol or archetype that integrates all of Aleixandre's characteristic themes, represents primitive, instinctive life, true values lost by modern civilized humans and maintained by simple sea creatures, a constant interplay between Thanatos and Eros, and a variety of sensual, erotic states involving repressed sexuality. Often Aleixandre juxtaposes the sea with images of forest, beach, teeth, tongue, birds, sun, moon, and breast. The sea in Aleixandre's poetry is pathognomonic in its psychological connotations, rooted in the painful dynamic of Aleixandre's own life, although at times it evokes a happy, innocent childhood, much as the gypsy symbolized the childhood of Federico García Lorca. Aleixandre disguises the relationship between the symbol and its meaning at unconscious levels; he distorts and represses it so that the symbols may lend themselves to many interpretations, which only psychoanalysis can fully reveal.

Indeed, a catharsis comparable to psychological analysis is accomplished by Aleixandre's poetry, except that here the patient ministers to himself; for example, unconscious forces account for the breast motif associated with the sea, one of Aleixandre's most constant neurotic projections. Throughout his poems, Aleixandre uses the sea as a surface on which to project his images, according to which it takes on various hues, colors, and attributes. It can be an "unstable sea," an "imperious sea," or a "contained sea," and it serves as the principal, though not the exclusive, vehicle for the projection of neurotic fantasies in which the poet employs symbols to convey meaning he might consciously wish to suppress. Aleixandre's sea imagery irrationally yet imaginatively challenges the reader's preconceptions, as the poet attempts deliberately or otherwise to recapture an unconscious knowledge and create a unity of perception.

Aleixandre's interest in Freudian analysis made him particularly receptive to Surrealism, yet he never accepted the "pure" Surrealism of Breton. Breton defined Surrealism as a psychic automatism through which he proposed to express the real functioning of thought without control by reason and beyond all aesthetic or moral norms, revealing the relationship between the real and the imaginary. For Breton, perception and representation are products of the dissociation of a single original faculty which the eidetic image recognizes and which is to be found in the primitive and the child. The distinction between the subjective and the objective lost its value as the poet sought to engage in a kind of automatic writing. Aleixandre rejected the notion of automatic writing, but in his preoccupation with the subconscious and his powerful, irrational imagery, he introduced Surrealism to Spanish poetry, where it found extremely fertile soil.

ÁMBITO

Ámbito, Aleixandre's first collection, is related to the much later volume, *Shadow of Paradise*. *Ámbito*, composed of seven sections and eight "Nights" (including an initial and final "Night" and one "Sea"), contains classical and Gongoristic forms—not unexpected at the time, since the collection was composed partly during the tercentenary of Luis de Góngora y Argote, when Baroque formalism ruled the day. Nature is everywhere; although there is a faint reflection of the cosmic force, the poet is largely descriptive and objective in a somewhat traditional way. Here, he contemplates nature, while in later works he would seek to possess it and be one with it. Written during his first serious illness, the book sensually examines the fleeting aspects of time. Within his own boundary—the limits of his sickroom, where he lived a solitary existence—he waxed both tender and uncontrollably passionate. However, *Ámbito*'s formal beauty, pleasure in the contemplation of nature, desire for perfection, and joy in life reflect both Juan Ramón Jiménez and Jorge Guillén more than the later Aleixandre. The poetry deals with the world of the senses, classic and cold at times but also warm and romantic. The elusive imagery resembles the reverberations of a musical instrument. The poet employs traditional ballad form instead of the free verse that he later came to use almost exclusively, and his ten- and six-syllable lines reveal his great sense of rhythm. In this volume of youthful love, Aleixandre delicately renders his love affair with nature, a love whose equations frequently resist logical interpretation.

SWORDS AS IF LIPS

Begun in the summer of 1929, Aleixandre's second collection, *Swords as if Lips*, concerns the central themes of life, death, and love—themes that the poet, in his moment of inspiration and suffering, views from a new perspective. An epigraph from Lord Byron, to the effect that the poet is "a babbler," serves notice that the volume eschews conventional "meaning." The work as originally presented was filled with poetic transpositions and capriciously arranged punctuation to help Aleixandre release what he considered his "interior fire." His intention was not to induce a Surrealistic trance but to create a voluntary pattern of unusual images. Aleixandre, in his somewhat illogically and incoherently developed poetic structures, does not know exactly what theme he will develop. The diffuse emotion he creates in this confused and disturbed work gives rise to apparent indecision for the poet, which transfers to the reader. His liberty of form allows Aleixandre to cover a variety of subjects in a dream atmosphere that hovers between sensation and thought. *Swords as if Lips*, in its examination of reality, petrifies it—or, as one critic phrases it, indulges in the immobilization of the moment. Aleixandre's bittersweet imagery of dead roses, coals of silence (because they lack life-giving flame), and other signs of loss and decay suggests a desire to embrace the reality of death.

DESTRUCTION OR LOVE

If *Swords as if Lips*, despite its striking images, lacks imaginative coherence, Aleixandre's third collection, *Destruction or Love*, is an undisputed masterpiece. Here, in fifty-four poems divided into six parts, the poet offers a visionary transfiguration of the world in flux, a world of mystery and darkness whose basic fabric is erotic love. Aleixandre's universe is a place of cosmic and human passion, of frustrated and desperate clamor, and of unchained telluric forces that often prove fatal to humans, absorbing them and destroying them. In Aleixandre's vision, people can obtain love only by destroying themselves and fusing with the cosmos, for human love is fleeting, and a final fusion with the earth will prove to be the most enduring love of all. Aleixandre excludes the life beyond and salvation. Absorbed in the living unity of nature, he acclaims a love without religious connotations. Aleixandre stresses the idea that the unity of the world includes humanity's works and its civilization, but they remain peripheral to the primary, instinctive life. Perhaps love can save people from society's mask—for love fuses all things, animal, vegetable, and mineral, into one substance—but to achieve fusion, people must give up their limiting structures. Thus, the title of the volume is intended to signify not a choice between mutually exclusive alternatives (either destruction or love) but rather an identification (as when the subtitle of a book is introduced by the word "or").

In *Destruction or Love*, the animal and the vegetable worlds constantly interact with the thoughts and feelings of the poet. In virgin forests, ferocious beasts surround "man," who seeks fruitlessly to find himself, half glimpsing his salvation in an identification with nature in all its forms and thus affirming rather than denying love for all creation. Animals, the forest, and the sea live in intimate union with elementary forces of nature, and tender, small animals exist with large, destructive ones: the beetle and the scorpion with the cobra, the eagle, lions, and tigers. Thus, the tiger is an elastic fire of the forest, and the eagles resemble the ocean. Like other aspects of nature, such as the ocean, the moon, or the heavens, these animals may be virginal and innocent or terrible and destructive. In this vision of nature as a physical whole in which violence and love are complementary forces, everything attacks, destroys, and loves everything and, in so doing, loves, attacks, and destroys itself. Life is death. The limits between flora and fauna dissolve into a new unity; the sea's fish appear to be birds; foam is hair; a body becomes an ocean; a heart becomes a mountain; man may be metal or a lion. Like the mystic poets of old—who had to die in order to find eternal life—Aleixandre offers a mystic fusion or death with the sea and the maternal earth.

SHADOW OF PARADISE

Shadow of Paradise, begun in 1939 and finished in November, 1943, created a sensation among young poets even before its publication in book form; when it finally appeared in 1944, it won a wide and enthusiastic readership among the literary youth of the day. Here, Aleixandre returns to the innocent world of infancy, to a paradise beyond Original Sin and knowledge, to be one with the heavens and the creatures of the dawn. He evokes a Garden of Eden where he may find lost happiness to escape the evil world of humanity, its folly and malignity. The poet narcissistically reinvents his own reality, remembers it, or perhaps imaginatively re-creates the world of childhood before the horrifying and inevitable loss of innocence. In his universe of serenity, order, and beauty, however, Aleixandre implies an awareness of the historical world, in which humans must play their role. The tension between paradise and history is always just beneath the surface.

Shadow of Paradise is divided into six parts. Of its fifty-two poems, only a dozen have a definite metric form, but through them all there are patterns of association among rhythms of different kinds. The verse lines are of varying length, including hendecasyllables, pentasyllables, hexameters, exciting combinations of anapestic lines, and irregular meters. Avoiding monotony in his rhythmical movements by means of this prodigality of expression, Aleixandre uses exclamations, interrogatives, and an almost musical progression of scales to form a polyphonic richness. His fetish for rhythmic simplicity extends to his use of adjectives, which he occasionally employs adverbially and, rarely, in double or triple combination. Often his naked nouns convey his precise tone or mood; on other occasions, for special effect, he ends a poetic line with a verb; infrequently, he employs gerundives experimentally.

HISTORIA DEL CORAZÓN

Of Aleixandre's later collections, the most important is *Historia del corazón* (history of the heart). Many underlying crosscurrents of thought and emotion can be found in this volume, but its central theme is the need for human solidarity and compassion for the victims of injustice. *Historia del corazón* reveals a dramatic change in Aleixandre's conception of humanity. Here, no longer creatures of telluric forces, humans are defined by the dolorous round of daily experience. Likewise, Aleixandre's conception of poetry has changed: The poet, a man, becomes all humans, destined to live and die, without the assurance of paradise or eternal life, in a world where death is always present. Nevertheless, the poet proclaims, it is not necessary to live desperate, solitary lives; he sings for all humankind of fleeting time, social love, and human solidarity. The poet recognizes that he is aging, but without despair, and empathizes with his neighbor, who must also stoically face the end.

OTHER MAJOR WORKS

SHORT FICTION: *Prosas completas*, 2002.

NONFICTION: *Los encuentros*, 1958; *Epistolario*, 1986 (with José Luis Cano).

CHILDREN'S LITERATURE: *Vicente Aleixandre para niños*, 1984 (illustrated by Concha Martinez).

MISCELLANEOUS: *Obras completas*, 1977 (2 volumes).

BIBLIOGRAPHY

Cabrera, Vicente, and Harriet Boyer, eds. *Critical Views on Vicente Aleixandre's Poetry.* Lincoln, Nebr. : Society of Spanish and Spanish-American Studies, 1979. Criticism and interpretation of Aleixandre's addresses, essays, lectures, and poetry. Includes selected poems in English translation.

Daydí-Tolson, Santiago. "Light in the Eyes: Visionary Poetry in Vicente Aleixandre." In *Contemporary Spanish Poetry: The Word and the World*, edited by Cecile West-Settle and Sylvia Sherno. Madison, N.J.: Fairleigh Dickinson University Press, 2005. Notes that the poet's work was filled with light and sensual descriptions of what he had observed, and that the poet's blindness in the 1970's severely affected his work.

_____, ed. *Vicente Aleixandre: A Critical Appraisal.* Ypsilanti, Mich.: Bilingual Press, 1981. A critical study of Aleixandre's work with a biographical introduction, extensively annotated bibliography, index, and Aleixandre's Nobel Prize acceptance lecture.

Harris, Derek. *Metal Butterflies and Poisonous Lights: The Language of Surrealism in Lorca, Alberti, Cernuda, and Aleixandre.* Anstruther, Fife, Scotland: La Sirena, 1998. History and criticism of Surrealism in Spanish literature, including the works of Aleixandre. Includes bibliography.

_____. "Prophet, Medium, Babbler: Voice and Identity in Vicente Aleixandre's Surrealist Poetry." In *Companion to Spanish Surrealism*, edited by Robert Havard. Rochester, N.Y.: Tamesis, 2004. Discusses Surrealism in Aleixandre's poems.

Ilie, P. *The Surrealist Mode in Spanish Literature*. Ann Arbor: University of Michigan Press, 1968. A study of Surrealism in Spanish literature. Includes bibliographic references.

Murphy, Daniel. *Vicente Aleixandre's Stream of Lyric Consciousness*. Lewisburg, Pa.: Bucknell University Press, 2001. Criticism and interpretation of Aleixandre's poetics, with bibliographical citations and index.

Schwartz, Kessel. *Vicente Aleixandre*. New York: Twayne, 1970. An introductory biography and critical analysis of selected works by Aleixandre.

Soufas, C. Christopher. *The Subject in Question: Early Contemporary Spanish Literature and Modernism*. Washington, D.C.: Catholic University of America Press, 2007. One chapter examines the geographies of presence in the poetry of Aleixandre and Jorge Guillén. Information on modernism in Spanish literáture provides a context for understanding Aleixandre's works.

Richard A. Mazzara

GUILLAUME APOLLINAIRE

Born: Rome, Italy; August 26, 1880
Died: Paris, France; November 9, 1918
Also known as: Wilhelm Apollinaris; Guillelmus Apollinaris de Kostrowitzki

<small>PRINCIPAL POETRY</small>

Le Bestiaire, 1911 (*Bestiary*, 1978)
Alcools: Poèmes, 1898-1913, 1913 (*Alcools: Poems, 1898-1913*, 1964)
Calligrammes, 1918 (English translation, 1980)
Il y a, 1925
Le Guetteur mélancolique, 1952
Tendre comme le souvenir, 1952
Poèmes à Lou, 1955
Œuvres poétiques, 1956

<small>OTHER LITERARY FORMS</small>

Besides poetry, Guillaume Apollinaire (ah-pawl-ee-NEHR) wrote a number of prose works. Among the most significant of his short stories and novellas are *L'Enchanteur pourrissant* (1909; "the putrescent enchanter"), published by Henry Kahnweiler and illustrated with woodcuts by André Derain; *L'Hérésiarque et Cie.* (1910; *The Heresiarch and Co.*, 1965), a contender for the Prix Goncourt; and *Le Poète assassiné* (1916; *The Poet Assassinated*, 1923). They are contained in the Pléiade edition, *Œuvres en prose* (1977), edited by Michel Décaudin.

Apollinaire collaborated on numerous plays and cinema scripts. His best-known individual works in these genres are two proto-Surrealist plays in verse: *Les Mamelles de Tirésias* (pr. 1917; *The Breasts of Tiresias*, 1961), first published in the magazine *SIC* in 1918, and *Couleur du temps* (the color of time; pr. 1918), which first appeared in the *Nouvelle Revue française* in 1920. They are available in the Pléiade edition of *Œuvres poétiques*. Apollinaire also published a great deal of art criticism and literary criticism in journals, newspapers, and other periodicals. In 1913, the articles published before that year were collected in *Peintres cubistes: Méditations esthétiques* (*The Cubist Painters: Aesthetic Meditations*, 1944). In 1918, *Mercure de France* published his famous manifesto "L'Esprit nouveau et les poètes" ("The New Spirit and the Poets"), which later appeared, along with many other articles, in *Chroniques d'art, 1902-1918* (1960), edited by L. C. Breunig. This collection has been translated into English as *Apollinaire on Art: Essays and Reviews, 1902-1918* (1972).

ACHIEVEMENTS

After Guillaume Apollinaire, French poetry was never the same again. Writing at the end of the long Symbolist tradition, a tradition very apparent in his early works, Apollinaire moved into a new perception of the world and of poetry. In the world of his mature verse, spatial and temporal relations are radically altered. Apollinaire's was one of the first voices in French poetry to attempt to articulate the profound discontinuity and disorientation in modern society. At the same time, however, his works reflect hope, frequently ecstatic, in the promise of the future.

Apollinaire's sense of radical discontinuity was reflected in his formal innovations, analyzed in considerable depth by Jean-Claude Chevalier in *Alcools d'Apollinaire* (1970). Immediately before the publication of *Alcools*, Apollinaire went through the volume and removed all punctuation, a device that he continued to use in most of his later works. His most notable poems, such as "Zone," "Liens" ("Chains"), and "Les Fenêtres" ("Windows"), use free verse with irregular rhyme and rhythm; his most startling works are the picture poems of *Calligrammes*, a form that he falsely claimed to have invented. They consist of verses arranged to give both a visual and an auditory effect in an effort to create simultaneity.

Like the cubists and other modern painters who sought to go beyond the traditional boundaries of space and time, Apollinaire desired to create the effect of simultaneity. This ambition is evident in "Zone," with its biographical, geographical, and historical discontinuity. In this single poem, the poet leaps from his pious childhood at the Collège Saint-Charles in Monaco to the wonders of modern aviation and back to the "herds" of buses "mooing" on the streets of Paris. Perhaps his most obvious achievement in simultaneity, though less profound, is in "Lundi rue Christine" ("Monday in Christine Street"), which records overheard bits of conversation in a "sinistre brasserie," a low-class café-restaurant that Apollinaire had frequented as early as 1903.

The friend and collaborator of many important painters during the exciting years in Paris just before World War I, Apollinaire began associating with artists when he met Pablo Picasso in 1904, after which he frequented the famous Bateau-Lavoir on the rue Ravignan with Max Jacob, André Derain, Maurice Vlaminck, Georges Braque, and others. After 1912, he moved into the world of art criticism, not always appreciated by the artists themselves, as critic Francis Steegmuller has noted. Not unrelated to this interest was Apollinaire's tumultuous liaison with Marie Laurencin from 1907 to 1912. He frequently inspired works and portraits by artists, including Laurencin, Henri Rousseau, and Picasso. Apollinaire's own works further testify to his links with painters: *Bestiary* was illustrated by Raoul Dufy, and "Windows" was the introductory poem to the catalog of the Robert Delaunay exhibit in 1912. His poems often parallel the work of the painters in their spirit of simultaneity; in their subjects, such as the *saltimbanques* of Picasso; and in their moods, such as those of Marc Chagall's dreamworld and inverted figures.

After 1916, Apollinaire became the *chef d'école*, the leader of a new generation of poets and painters. Among them were Pierre Reverdy, Philippe Soupault, Jean Cocteau, André Breton, and Tristan Tzara. His own works appeared in the most avant-garde journals: Reverdy's *Nord-Sud*, Picabia's *391*, and Albert Birot's *SIC*. His lecture "The New Spirit and the Poets" called poets to a new prophetic vision, imploring them to create prodigies with their imagination like modern Merlins. Like Paul Claudel, Apollinaire regarded the poet as a creator. The modern poet, he believed, must use everything for his (or her) creation: new discoveries in science, in the subconscious and the dreamworld, and in the cinema and visual arts.

The Surrealists, in their desire to revolutionize art and literature, saw in Apollinaire their precursor. It was he who coined the word *surréaliste*, in the preface to his drama in verse *The Breasts of Tiresias*. In it, he explains that an equivalent is not always an imitation, even as the wheel, though intended to facilitate transportation, is not a reproduction of the leg. Apollinaire conveys his message with a lighthearted tone, employing incongruous rhythms, parody, and sexual imagery. This is essentially the technique he employs in his most avant-garde poetry, and *The Breasts of Tiresias* echoes poems from "Ondes" ("Waves," the first part of *Calligrammes*) such as "Zone," "Le Brasier" ("The Brazier"), "Les Fiançailles" ("The Betrothal"), and "Le Larron" ("The Thief"). Thus, Apollinaire indicated the path to follow in revolutionizing poetry, although much of his work was in some respects traditional. Like Victor Hugo, he served subsequent poets chiefly as a guide rather than as a model, but it was his "esprit nouveau" that gave considerable impetus to a new form of modern poetry.

BIOGRAPHY

Born in Rome on August 26, 1880, Guillaume Albert Wladimir Alexandre Apollinaire de Kostrowitzky was an illegitimate child; in "The Thief," he says that his "father was a sphinx and his mother a night." In reality, his mother was a Polish adventurer of noble ancestry, Angelique Kostrowicka, known in Paris mostly as "Olga." His father's identity has never been definitively ascertained. The most plausible supposition points to Francesco Flugi d'Aspermont, who was from a noble Italian family that included many prelates. This theory is based on the careful investigation of biographer Marcel Adéma. Apollinaire's mysterious and involved parentage haunted the poet throughout his life, leaving unmistakable marks on his character and works.

Apollinaire received his only formal education at the Collège of Saint-Charles in Monaco and the Collège Stanislas at Cannes, from 1890 to 1897, where he acquired a solid grounding in religious and secular knowledge. Although his Catholic training was to remain firmly implanted in his memory and is evident in his poetry, he moved away from any outward adherence to religious beliefs after 1897. In 1899, he arrived in Paris, his home for most of the next nineteen years of his life and the center and inspiration of his literary activity. First, however, he made a significant trip to Germany's Rhineland in 1901, as tutor to Gabrielle, the daughter of the viscountess of Milhau. There, he met and fell in love with Annie Playden, Gabrielle's English governess. This ill-fated romance and the beauty of the Rhineland inspired many of Apollinaire's early poems, which were later published in *Alcools*.

Apollinaire's return to Paris coincided with the beginning of friendships with artists and writers such as André Salmon, Alfred Jarry, Max Jacob, and especially Picasso. In 1903, he began his collaboration on many periodicals, which he continued throughout his lifetime. Most of his prose and poetry was first published in such journals, many of which—such as *Le Festin d'Esope* and *La Revue immoraliste*—were of very short duration. His works appeared under several pseudonyms, of which "Apollinaire" was the most significant. Others included "Louise Lalame," "Lul," "Montade," and "Tyl." In 1907, he met Marie Laurencin, an artist, whose talent Apollinaire tended to exaggerate. Their liaison continued until 1912 and was an inspiration and a torment to both of them. During this period, Apollinaire was deeply marked by the false accusation that he was responsible for the theft of the *Mona Lisa* from the Louvre. A series of six poems in *Alcools*, "À la Santé" ("At the Santé") describes his brief stay in the prison of La Santé in Verlainian imagery.

The year 1912 marked Apollinaire's break with Laurencin and his definite espousal of modern art, of which he became a staunch proponent. During the two years preceding World War I, he gave lectures and wrote articles on modern art and prepared *Alcools* for publication. The beginning of the war, in 1914, was to Apollinaire a call to a mission. Although not a French citizen until the year 1916, he embraced with great enthusiasm his *métier de soldat* as an artilleryman and then as an infantryman, according an almost mystical dimension to his military service. His poetry of these first two years reveals the exaltation of war and the idealization of two women, "Lou" (Louise de Coligny-Châtillon) and Madeleine Pagès, to whom he was briefly engaged.

Wounded in the head in 1916, Apollinaire required surgery and was then discharged from the service. He returned to the world of literature and art with numerous articles, lectures, two plays, and a volume of poetry, *Calligrammes*. In May of 1918, he married Jacqueline Kolb ("Ruby"), the "jolie rousse" ("pretty redhead") of the last poem in *Calligrammes*. The marriage was of short duration, however, as Apollinaire died of Spanish influenza on November 9 of the same year.

ANALYSIS

In his poetic style, Guillaume Apollinaire might be characterized as the last of the Symbolists and the first of the moderns. He is considered a revolutionary and a destroyer, yet the bulk of his work shows a deep influence of traditional symbolism, especially biblical, legendary, and mythical. Very knowledgeable in Roman Catholic doctrine from his years with the Marianists at Monaco and Cannes, he uses extensive biblical imagery: Christ, the Virgin Mary, and the Holy Spirit in the form of a dove.

Robert Couffignal has analyzed Apollinaire's religious imagery in detail and considers his comprehension of the Bible to be "a cascade of superficial weavings." Scott Bates sees the Last Judgment, with its apocalyptic implications, as central to Apollinaire's works. The concept of messianism and the advent of a new millennium is evident in both the early works and the war poems, which predict a new universe. In the Symbolist tradition, the poet is the seer of the new kingdom.

Many of Apollinaire's symbols are from the realm of legend and myth. Rosemonde, the idealized woman of the Middle Ages, is present in several poems, though she appears also as a prostitute. In "Merlin et la vielle femme" ("Merlin and the Old Woman"), the medieval seer foreshadows Apollinaire's vision of the future. Ancient mythology is the source for Orpheus, under whose sign *Bestiary* is written. Orpheus is also the symbol of Christ and the poet, as is Hermès Trismègiste. Ancient Egypt appears in frequent references to the Nile, the Israelites in bondage, and Pharaoh, the image of the poet himself. The fantastic abounds in Apollinaire's works: ghosts, diabolic characters, and phantoms, as found, for example, in "La Maison des Morts" ("The House of the Dead") and especially in the short stories.

Much of Apollinaire's early symbolism is directed toward the quest for self-knowledge; his choice of the name Apollinaire is a clue to his search. Though it was the name of his maternal grandfather and one of the names given to him at baptism, he seems to have chosen it for its reference to Apollo, the god of the sun. Indeed, solar imagery is central to his poetry, and the introductory poem of *Alcools*, "Zone," ends with the words "Soleil cou coupé" ("Sun cut throat"). Bates argues that the violent love-death relationship between the sun and night, with its corresponding symbolism, is as crucial to the interpretation of Apollinaire as it is to a reading of Gérard de Nerval or Stéphane Mallarmé. Along with love and death is death and resurrection. Apollinaire chooses the phoenix as a sign of rebirth and describes his own psychological and poetic resurrection in "The Brazier" and "The Betrothal," poems that he regarded as among his best. Fire seems to be his basic image, with its multiple meanings of passion, destruction, and purification.

Passion as a flame dominated Apollinaire's life and poetry. Of the many women whom he loved, five in particular incarnated his violent passion and appear in his work: Playden and Laurencin in *Alcools*; Lou, Madeleine, and Jacqueline in *Calligrammes* and in several series of poems published after his death. Apollinaire is capable of expressing tender, idealistic love, as in the "Aubade chantée à Lætare un an passé" ("Aubade Sung to Lætare a Year Ago") section of the "La Chanson du mal-aimé" ("The Song of the Poorly Loved") and in "La Jolie Rousse" ("The Pretty Redhead"), which closes *Calligrammes*. In most cases, Apollinaire is the *mal-aimé*, and as he himself says, he is much less the poorly beloved than the one who loves poorly. His first three loves ended violently; his last was concluded by his death. Thus, the death of love is as important as its first manifestation, which for him resembles the shells bursting in the war.

Autumn is the season of the death of love, wistfully expressed in such nostalgic works as "L'Adieu" ("The Farewell") and "Automne" ("Autumn"). Because the end of love usually involved deep suffering for him, the image of mutilation is not uncommon. The beloved in "The Song of the Poorly Loved" has a scar on her neck, and the mannequins in "L'Émigrant de Landor Road" ("The Emigrant from Landor Road") are decapitated, much like the sun in "Zone." Apollinaire perceives love in its erotic sense, and in many cases he resorts to arcane symbolism, as in the seven swords in "The Song of the Poorly Loved." "Lul de Faltenin" ("Lul of Faltenin") is also typical, with its subtle erotic allusions. Such themes are more overt in Apollinaire's prose; indeed, Bates has compiled a glossary of erotic symbolism in the works of Apollinaire.

Apollinaire was both a lyric poet and a storyteller. In the lyric tradition, he writes of his emotions in images drawn from nature. His work is particularly rich in flora and fauna. *Bestiary* shows his familiarity with and affection for animals and his ability, like the fabulists, to see them as caricatures of people. *Alcools*, as the title indicates, often evokes grapes and wine; it also speaks of fir trees (in "Les Sapins") and falling leaves. "Zone" contains a catalog of birds, real and legendary. The Seine comes alive in Apollinaire's ever-popular "Le Pont Mirabeau" ("Mirabeau Bridge"). In *Calligrammes*, the poet often compares the explosion of shells to bursting buds.

Apollinaire was the author of many short stories, and he maintains a narrative flavor in his poetry. "The House of the Dead" was originally a short story, "L'Obituaire," and it reads like one. Many of the picture poems in *Calligrammes* tell a story; "Paysage" ("Landscape"), for example, portrays by means of typography a house, a tree, and two lovers, one of whom smokes a cigar that the reader can almost smell. Apollinaire's technique often involves improvisation, as in "Le Musicien de Saint-Merry" ("The Musician of Saint-Merry"). Although he claims almost total spontaneity, there are revised versions of many of his poems, and he frequently borrowed from himself, rearranging both lines and poems. In particular, Apollinaire tells stories of the modern city, imitating its new structures as Arthur Rimbaud did in his innovative patterns, and like Charles Baudelaire, Apollinaire peoples his verse with the forgotten and the poor, the prostitutes and the clowns.

Apollinaire had a remarkable sense of humor, displayed in frequent word-plays, burlesques, and parodies. The briefest example of his use of puns is the one-line poem "Chantre" ("Singer"): "Et l'unique cordeau des trompettes marines" ("and the single string of marine trumpets"). *Cordeau*, when read aloud, might be *cor d'eau*, or "horn of water," another version of a marine trumpet, as well as *corps d'eau* ("body of water") or even *cœur d'eau* ("heart of water"). The burlesque found in his short stories appears in poetry as dissonance, erotic puns, and irreverent parodies, such as in "Les Sept Epées" ("The Seven Swords") as well as in "The Thief," a poem that Bates interprets as parodying Christ. Apollinaire's lighthearted rhythm and obscure symbolism tend to prevent his verse from becoming offensive and convey a sense of freedom, discovery, and surprise.

BESTIARY

Bestiary is one of the most charming and accessible of Apollinaire's works. The idea for the poem probably came from Picasso in 1906, who was then doing woodcuts of animals. In 1908, Apollinaire published in a journal eighteen poems under the title "La Marchande des quatre saisons ou le bestiaire moderne" (the costermonger or the modern bestiary). When he prepared the final edition in 1911, with woodcuts by Raoul Dufy, he added twelve poems and replaced the merchant with Orpheus. According to mythology, Orpheus attracted wild beasts by playing on the lyre he had received from Mercury. He is the symbol of Gnosis and Neoplatonic Humanism and is also identified with Christ and poetry, in a mixture of mystical and sensual imagery.

Apollinaire himself wrote the notes to the volume and uses as its sign a δ (the Greek letter delta) pierced by a unicorn. He interprets it to mean the delta of the Nile and all the legendary and biblical symbols of ancient Egypt, also suggesting a D for Deplanche, the publisher, in addition to the obvious sexual symbolism. He added the motto "J'émerveille" ("I marvel"), thus giving a fantastic aura to the work. Roger Little sees in the volume a "delicious and malicious" wit, with metamorphoses, syncretism, pride in poetry, carnal love, and mysticism. Like all Apollinaire's early works, it is full of self-analysis. In "La Souris" ("The Mouse"), the poet speaks of his twenty-eight years as "mal-vécus" ("poorly spent").

The animals represent human foibles; the peacock, for example, displays both his best and, unbeknownst to him, his worst. They also speak of love: the serpent, the Sirens, the dove, and Orpheus himself. They point to God and things divine: the dove, the bull, or, again, Orpheus. They speak of poetry: the horse, the tortoise, the elephant, and the caterpillar. For Apollinaire, poetry is a divine gift. He concludes his notes by observing that poets seek nothing but perfection, which is God himself. Poets, he says, have the right to expect after death the full knowledge of God, which is sublime beauty.

ALCOOLS

The most analyzed and the best known of Apollinaire's works is *Alcools*, a slender volume published in 1913 with the subtitle *Poèmes, 1898-1913*. A portrait of Apollinaire, an etching by Picasso, serves as the frontispiece. Apollinaire chose fifty-five of the many poems he had written from his eighteenth to his thirty-third year and assembled them in an order that has continued to fascinate and baffle critics. Michel Décaudin says that the order in *Alcools* is based entirely on the aesthetic and sentimental affinities felt by the author, or their discrete dissonances. Very few poems have dates, other than "Rhénanes" (September, 1901, to May, 1902) and "At the Santé" (September, 1911); nevertheless, critics have succeeded in dating many, though not all, of the poems.

The poems have several centers, though not all of those from one group appear together. More than twenty were inspired by Apollinaire's trip to the Rhineland in 1901, including the nine in the cycle "Rhénanes." Several of these poems and some others, such as "The Song of the Poorly Loved," "Annie," and "The Emigrant from Landor Road," refer to his unhappy love affair with Playden. These poems and an interview with her as Mrs. Postings in 1951 by Robert Goffin and LeRoy Breunig are the only sources of information about this significant period in Apollinaire's life. Three poems, "Mirabeau Bridge," "Marie," and "Cors de chasse" ("Hunting Horns"), scattered throughout the volume, refer to Laurencin.

The poems exhibit great variety in form, tone, and subject matter. They range from the one-line "Chantre" to the seven-part "The Song of the Poorly Loved," the longest in the collection. Most of them have regular rhyme and rhythm, but "Zone" and "Vendémiaire," the first and the last, give evidence of technical experimentation. The poems range from witty ("The Synagogue") to nostalgic ("Autumn," "Hunting Horns") and from enigmatic ("The Brazier") to irreverent ("The Thief"). Critics have arranged them in various ways. Bates, for example, sees the volume as a "Dionysian-Apollonian dance of life in three major symbols: fire, shadow, alcools."

Apollinaire chose the beginning and concluding poems of the collection, "Zone" and "Vendémiaire," with great care. "Zone" is overtly autobiographical in a Romantic-Symbolist ambience, yet its instant leaps in space and time make it very modern. Also modern is the image of the city, where Apollinaire can see beauty in a poster, a traffic jam, and a group of frightened Jewish immigrants. The city is also the central focus in the concluding poem, "Vendémiaire" (the name given the month of vintage, September 22-October 21, in the revolutionary calendar), a hymn to the glory of Paris. The poet exuberantly proclaims his immortality and omnipresence: "I am drunk from having swallowed all the universe." Bates sees the end of the poem as a hymn to joy reminiscent of Walt Whitman and Friedrich Nietzsche.

The bizarre juxtapositions, the inner borrowings of lines from one poem to the next, and the absence of punctuation provoked various responses from critics. Cubists hailed Apollinaire as a great poet. Georges Duhamel, writing in the June 15, 1913, issue of *Mercure de France*, called the volume a junk shop. Critics such as Adéma, Décaudin, and Marie-Jeanne Durry analyze *Alcools* with depth and scholarship. They discover many platitudes and much mediocrity but find it redeemed by what Steegmuller identifies as a spirit of freedom.

CALLIGRAMMES

Intended as a sequel to *Alcools*, *Calligrammes* is much more unified than *Alcools*, yet its importance was seen only much later. It consists of six parts. The first part, "Waves," is the most innovative and was written before World War I in the frenzied stimulation of artistic activity in Paris. The other five contain poems inspired by the war and by the poet's love for Lou, Madeleine, and—in the final poem—his future wife, Jacqueline.

Philippe Renaud sees the difference between *Alcools* and "Waves" as one of nature rather than degree. Even the most enigmatic poems of *Alcools* follow a familiar plan, he maintains, whereas in "Waves" the reader is in unfamiliar territory, disoriented in space and time. In "Waves" one feels both the insecurity and the indefiniteness that can only be called modern art. The introductory poem, "Chains," uses the elements recommended by Apollinaire in "The New Spirit and the Poets" yet remains anchored in the past. It leaps from the Tower of Babel to telegraph wires in disconcerting juxtapositions, speaking of humankind's eternal, frustrating quest for unity. In "The Windows," the window opens like an orange on Paris or in the tropics and flies on a rainbow across space and time.

Beginning with "Waves" and throughout *Calligrammes*, Apollinaire uses what he calls ideograms, or picture poems. They are the most attractive pieces in the book, though not necessarily the most original. They became excellent vehicles for the war poems, where brevity and wit are essential. The theme of war dominates the majority of poems in *Calligrammes*. The war excited Apollinaire, promising a new universe. He experienced exhilaration as he saw shells exploding, comparing them in the poem "Merveilles de la guerre" ("Wonders of War") to constellations, women's hair, dancers, and women in childbirth. He saw himself as the poet-hero, the omnipresent seer, the animator of the universe. In "La Tête étoilée" ("The Starry Head"), his wound was a crown of stars on his head.

Apollinaire was as dependent on love as he was on air, and he suffered greatly in the solitary trenches of France. His brief romance with Lou was intense and violent, as his pun on her name in "C'est Lou qu'on la nommait" ("They Called Her Lou") indicates; instead of "Lou," the word *loup* (which sounds the same in French but means "wolf") is used throughout the poem. In his poems to Madeleine, he devours images like a starving man. The anthology ends serenely as he addresses Jacqueline, "la jolie rousse," the woman destined to be his wife, as poetry was destined to be his life. This final poem is also his poetic testament, in which he bequeaths "vast and unknown kingdoms, new fires and the mystery of flowers to anyone willing to pick them."

OTHER MAJOR WORKS

LONG FICTION: *L'Enchanteur pourrissant*, 1909; *Le Poète assassiné*, 1916 (*The Poet Assassinated*, 1923).

SHORT FICTION: *L'Hérésiarque et Cie.*, 1910 (*The Heresiarch and Co.*, 1965).

PLAYS: *Les Mamelles de Tirésias*, pr. 1917 (*The Breasts of Tiresias*, 1961); *Couleur du temps*, pr. 1918; *Casanova*, pb. 1952.

NONFICTION: *Peintres cubistes: Méditations esthétiques*, 1913 (*The Cubist Painters: Aesthetic Meditations*, 1944); *Chroniques d'art, 1902-1918*, 1960 (*Apollinaire on Art: Essays and Reviews, 1902-1918*, 1972).

MISCELLANEOUS: *Œuvres complètes*, 1966 (8 volumes); *Œuvres en prose*, 1977 (Michel Décaudin, editor).

BIBLIOGRAPHY

Adéma, Marcel. *Apollinaire*. Translated by Denise Folliot. New York: Grove Press, 1955. This is the prime source of biographical material, the bible of scholars researching the poet and his epoch.

Bates, Scott. *Guillaume Apollinaire*. Rev. ed. Boston: Twayne, 1989. This book offers detailed erudite analyses of Apollinaire's major works and informed judgments on his place in French literature and in the development of art criticism. It emphasizes the importance to the entire world of Apollinaire's vision of a cultural millennium propelled by science and democracy and implemented by poetry. Included are a chronology, a twenty-six-page glossary of references, notes, and selected bibliographies of both primary and secondary sources.

Bohn, Willard. *The Aesthetics of Visual Poetry: 1914-1928*. New York: Cambridge University Press, 1986. Chapter 3, "Apollinaire's Plastic Imagination," reveals the lyric innovations that Apollinaire brought to visual poetry with *Calligrammes*: new forms, new content, multiple figures in a unified composition, a dual sign system used to express a simultaneity, and a difficulty of reading that mirrors the act of creation. Chapter 4, "Toward a Calligrammar," offers a sophisticated structural and statistical analysis of the calligrammes to demonstrate metonymy as the principal force binding the visual tropes, whereas metaphor and metonymy occur evenly in the verbal arena.

_____. *Apollinaire and the Faceless Man: The Creation and Evolution of a Modern Motif*. Rutherford, N.J.: Fairleigh Dickinson University Press, 1991. Traces the history of Apollinaire's faceless man motif as a symbol of the human condition, from its roots in the poem "Le Musicien de Saint-Mercy" to its dissemination to the arts community through the unproduced pantomime "A quelle heure un train partira-t-il pour Paris?"

_____. *Apollinaire and the International Avant-Garde*. Albany: State University of New York Press, 1997. Chronicles the early artistic and critical reception of Apollinaire in Europe, North America, and Latin America. Especially interesting is the discussion of Argentina, exported through the Ultraism of Jorge Luis Borges, and Apollinaire's place in the revolutionary circles of Mexico.

Cornelius, Nathalie Goodisman. *A Semiotic Analysis of Guillaume Apollinaire's Mythology in "Alcools."* New York: Peter Lang, 1995. Examines Apollinaire's use of linguistic and mythological fragmentation and reordering to mold his material into an entirely new system of signs that both encompasses and surpasses the old. Chapters give close semiotic readings of four poems: "Claire de lune," "Le Brasier," "Nuit rhëane," and "Vendémaine."

Couffignal, Robert. *Apollinaire*. Translated by Eda Mezer Levitine. Tuscaloosa: University of Alabama Press, 1975. This is a searching analysis of some of Apollinaire's best-known works, including "Zone," strictly from the Roman Catholic point of view. It traces his attitude toward religion from his childhood to his death. The book contains a chronology; translations of ten texts, both poems and prose, with the author's comments; a bibliographical note; and an index.

Matthews, Timothy. *Reading Apollinaire: Theories of Poetic Language*. New York: Manchester University Press, 1987. Uses a variety of historical, biographical, and stylistic approaches to offer an accessible point of entry into often difficult texts. Matthews's detailed discussion of *Alcools* focuses heavily on "L'Adieu" and "Automne malade," which allows for a reading that may be transferred to the rest of the book. His chapter "Poetry, Painting, and Theory" offers a solid historical background that leads directly into his examination of *Calligrammes*.

Shattuck, Roger. *The Banquet Years*. Rev. ed. New York: Vintage Books, 1968. In the two long chapters devoted to Apollinaire, "The Impresario of the Avant-garde" and "Painter-Poet," the author gives a year-by-year and at times even a month-by-month account of his life, loves, friends, employment, writings, and speeches. The tone is judicial, the critical judgments fair and balanced. Includes a bibliography and an index.

Steegmuller, Francis. *Apollinaire: Poet Among the Painters*. New York: Farrar, Straus, 1963. This is an exhaustive, extremely well-documented, unbiased, and highly readable biography. Contains a preface, translations, numerous photographs and illustrations, two appendixes, notes, and an index.

Irma M. Kashuba
Updated by David Harrison Horton

LOUIS ARAGON

Born: Paris, France; October 3, 1897
Died: Paris, France; December 24, 1982

PRINCIPAL POETRY

Feu de joie, 1920
Le Mouvement perpétuel, 1925
La Grande Gaîté, 1929
Persécuté persécuteur, 1931
Hourra l'Oural, 1934
Le Crève-coeur, 1941
Brocéliande, 1942
Les Yeux d'Elsa, 1942
En Français dans le texte, 1943
Le Musée grévin, 1943
La Diane française, 1945
Le Nouveau Crève-coeur, 1948
Les Yeux et la mémoire, 1954
Le Roman inachevé, 1956
Elsa, 1959
Les Poètes, 1960
Le Fou d'Elsa, 1963
Les Chambres, 1969
Aux abords de Rome, 1981
Les Adieux, et autres poèmes, 1982

OTHER LITERARY FORMS

Louis Aragon (ah-rah-GAWN) was one of the most prolific French authors of the twentieth century, and although lyric poetry was his first medium, to which he always returned as to a first love, he also produced many novels and volumes of essays. As a young man, he participated in the Surrealist movement, and his works of this period defy classification. In addition to the exercises known as automatic writing, which had a considerable impact on his mature style in both prose and poetry, he wrote a number of Surrealist narratives combining elements of the novel (such as description and dialogue) and the essay. The most important of these, *Le Paysan de Paris* (1926; *Nightwalker*, 1970), is a long meditation on the author's ramblings in his native city and on the "modern sense of the mythic" inspired by its streets, shops, and parks.

In the 1930's, after his espousal of the Communist cause, Aragon began a series of novels under the general title of *Le Monde réel* (1934-1944), which follow the tenets of

Louis Aragon
(Library of Congress)

Socialist Realism. These are historical novels dealing with the corruption of bourgeois society and the rise of Communism. His later novels, however, beginning with *La Semaine sainte* (1958; *Holy Week*, 1961), show greater freedom of form and lack the explicit "message" characteristic of Socialist Realism; these later works incorporate an ongoing meditation on the novel as a literary form and on its relation to history and biography.

An important characteristic of Aragon's style that cuts across all his works of fiction and poetry is the use of spoken language as a model: His sentences reproduce the rhythms of speech, full of parentheses, syntactic breaks, and interjections, and his diction, especially in prose, is heavily interlarded with slang. This trait is true to some extent even of his essays, although the latter tend to be more formal to both diction and rhetorical strategy. His nonfiction works are voluminous, for he was an active journalist for much of his life, producing reviews and essays on politics, literature, and the visual arts for a variety of Surrealist and then Communist publications.

ACHIEVEMENTS

Like most writers who have taken strong political stands, Louis Aragon was, during the course of his lifetime, the object of much praise and blame that had little to do with the literary value of his work. This was especially true of his series of novels, *Le Monde réel*, which was hailed by his fellow Communists as a masterpiece and criticized by most non-Communist reviewers as contrived and doctrinaire. He was, with André Breton, one of the leaders of the Surrealist movement; his poetry after the mid-1940's combined elements of Romanticism and modernism, but his style evolved in a direction of its own and cannot be identified with that of any one school.

After his Surrealist period, during which he wrote for an intellectual elite, Aragon sought to make his work accessible to a wider public and often succeeded. The height of his popularity was achieved in the 1940's, when his poems played an important role in the French Resistance: written in traditional meters and using rhyme, so that they might more easily be sung, they became rallying cries for French patriots abroad and in occupied France. (Many of Aragon's poems have, in fact, been set to music by writers of popular songs, including Léo Ferré and George Brassens.) Beginning in the late 1950's, Aragon's work became much less overtly political, which contributed to its acceptance by non-Communist critics. At the time of his death in 1982, Aragon was considered even by his political opponents as a leading man of letters. Writers of lesser stature have been elected to the French Academy, but Aragon never applied for membership, and it is hard to imagine such an ardent advocate of commoners, who used slang liberally in his own work, sitting in judgment on the purity of the French language.

For Aragon, who wrote his first "novel" at age six (and dictated a play to his aunt before he could write), writing was like breathing, a vital activity coextensive with living. He was a novelist whose eye (and ear) for telling detail never dulled, a poet whose lyric gifts did not diminish with age.

BIOGRAPHY

Until late in life, Louis Aragon was reticent about his childhood, and many biographical notices erroneously describe it as idyllic; in fact, his family (which consisted of his grandmother, mother, and two aunts) was obsessed with a concern for appearances that caused the boy considerable pain. The illegitimate son of a prominent political figure, Louis Andrieux, who chose the name Aragon for his son and acted as his legal guardian, Aragon was reared as his mother's younger brother, and although as a boy he guessed much of the truth, it was not until his twentieth year that he heard it from his mother (at the insistence of his father, who had previously insisted on her silence). Since his maternal grandfather had also deserted the family, his mother, Marguérite Toucas-Masillon, supported them all as best she could by painting china and running a boardinghouse. According to his biographer, Pierre Daix, the circumstances of Aragon's childhood left him with an instinctive sympathy for outsiders, especially women, and a great longing to be accepted as a full member of a group. This longing was first satisfied by his friendship with André Breton and later by Aragon's adherence to the Communist Party. (Indeed, his deep need to "belong" may help to account for his unswerving loyalty to the party throughout the Stalinist era.)

Breton, whom he met in 1917, introduced Aragon to the circle of poets and artists that was to form the nucleus of the Dadaist and Surrealist movements. Horrified by the carnage of World War I (which Aragon had observed firsthand as a medic), these young people at first embraced the negative impulse of Dada, an absurdist movement founded in Zurich by Tristan Tzara. Their aim was to unmask the moral bankruptcy of the society that had tolerated such a war. Realizing that a philosophy of simple negation was ultimately sterile, Breton and Aragon broke away from the Dadaists and began to pursue the interest in the subconscious, which led them to Surrealism. Through the technique of automatic writing, they tried to suppress the rational faculty, or "censor," which inhibited free expression of subconscious impulses.

Politically, the Surrealists were anarchists, but as they became increasingly convinced that profound social changes were necessary to free the imagination, a number of them, including Aragon, joined the French Communist Party. At about the same time (1928), Aragon met the Russian poet Vladimir Mayakovsky and his sister-in-law, the novelist Elsa Triolet, at the Coupole, a Paris café. As Aragon put it, describing his meeting with Elsa many years later, "We have been together ever since" (literally, "We have not left each other's side"). In Elsa, Aragon found the "woman of the future," who could be her husband's intellectual and social equal while sharing with him a love in which all the couple's aspirations were anchored. Aragon celebrated this love in countless poems spanning forty years; some of the most ecstatic were written when the two were in their sixties. Elsa introduced Aragon to Soviet Russia, which they visited together in the early 1930's; she also took part with him in the French Resistance during World War II, publishing clandestine newspapers and maintaining a network of antifascist intellectuals. Although he followed the "party line" and tried to rationalize the Soviet pact with the Nazis, Aragon was an ardent French patriot; he was decorated for bravery in both world wars and wrote hymns of praise to the French "man (and woman) in the street," who became the heroes of the Resistance.

After the war, Aragon redoubled his activities on behalf of the Communist Party, serving as editor of the Communist newspaper *Ce Soir* and completing his six-volume novel *Les Communistes* (1949-1951). In 1954, he became a permanent member of the Central Committee of the French Communist Party, and in 1957, the Soviet Union awarded him its highest decoration, the Lenin Peace Prize. He was vilified by many of his fellow intellectuals in France for failing to criticize Stalin; not until 1966, during the much-publicized trial of two Soviet writers, Andrei Sinyavsky and Yuli Daniel, did he venture to speak out against the notion that there could be a "criminality of opinion." In 1968, he joined with the French Communist Party as a whole in condemning the Russian invasion of Czechoslovakia. Throughout his life, Aragon continued to produce a steady stream of poetry, fiction, and essays. His wife's death in 1970 was a terrible blow, but he survived it and went on to write several more books in the twelve years that were left to him.

ANALYSIS

Despite the length of Louis Aragon's poetic career and the perceptible evolution of his style in the course of six decades, there is a remarkable unity in the corpus of his poetry. This unity results from stylistic as well as thematic continuities, for even when he turned from free verse to more traditional metric forms, he managed to preserve the fluency of spoken language. In fact, his most highly structured verse has some of the qualities of stream-of-consciousness narrative. There are a variety of reasons for this. Aragon began to write as a very young boy and continued writing, steadily and copiously, throughout his life. As critic Hubert Juin has observed, Aragon never needed to keep a journal or diary because "his work itself was his journal," into which he poured his eager questions and reflections on what most closely concerned him.

This confessional impulse was reinforced and given direction in Aragon's Surrealist period by experiments with automatic writing, a technique adapted for literary use primarily by Breton and Philippe Soupault. By writing quickly without revising and by resisting the impulse to edit or censor the flow of words, the Surrealistis hoped to tap their subconscious minds and so to "save literature from rhetoric" (as Juin puts it). Literature was not all they hoped to save, moreover, for "rhetoric" had poisoned the social and political spheres as well; in liberating the subconscious, Aragon and his friends sought to break old and unjust patterns of thought and life. They also expected this powerful and hitherto untapped source to fuel the human imagination for the work of social renewal. Although Aragon repudiated the Surrealist attitude (which was basically anarchistic) when he embraced Communism as the pattern of the future, he never lost the stylistic freedom that automatic writing had fostered, nor did he become complacent about the "solution" he had found. Like his relationship with his wife, in which his hopes for the future were anchored, Aragon's Communism was a source of pain as well as of fulfillment: the deeper his love and commitment, the greater his vulnerability. Thus, poetry remained for him, as it had been in his youth, a form of questioning in which he explored the world and his relation to it.

There were, nevertheless, perceptible changes in Aragon's style during the course of his career. After the Dadaist and Surrealist periods, when he wrote mainly free verse (although there are metrically regular poems even in his early collections), Aragon turned to more traditional prosody—including rhyme—in the desire to make his verses singable. At the same time, he sought to renew and broaden the range of available rhymes by adopting new definitions of masculine and feminine rhyme based on pronunciation rather than on spelling. He also applied the notion of enjambment to rhyme, allowing not only the last syllable of a line but also the first letter or letters of the following line to count as constituent elements of a rhyme. Partly as a result of the conditions under which they were composed, Aragon's Resistance poems are for the most part short and self-contained, although *Le Musée grévin* (the wax museum) is a single long poem, and the pieces in *Brocéliande* are linked by allusions to the knights of the Arthurian cycle,

opens with a passage that might be described as expository, and although it moves from particular details to a general observation and closes with a sort of reprise, it strikes the reader as more loosely organized than it actually is. This impression results from its rhythm being that of association—the train of thought created when a person dwells on a single topic for a sustained period of time. Because the topic is unhappy love and the bitterness of rejection, the process of association takes on an obsessive quality, and although the resulting monologue is ostensibly addressed to the lover, the title suggests that neither she nor anyone else is expected to respond. The overall effect, then, is that of an interior monologue, and its power stems not from any cogency of argument (the "rhetoric" rejected by the Surrealists) but from the cumulative effects of obsessive repetition. Thus, the speaker's memories are evoked in a kind of litany ("I remember your shoulder/ I remember your elbow/ I remember your linen."); later, struck by the realization that memory implies the past tense, he piles up verbs in the *passé simple* (as in "Loved Was Came Caressed"), the tense used for completed action.

The lack of a rhetorical framework in the poem is paralleled by the absence of any central image or images. Although many arresting images appear, they are not linked in any design but remain isolated, reinforcing the sense of meaninglessness that has overwhelmed the speaker. The "little rented cars" and mirrors left unclaimed in a baggage room evoke the traveling the couple did together, which the speaker now sees as aimless. Some of the details given remain opaque because they have a private meaning that is not revealed ("Certain names are charged with a distant thunder"); others seem to be literary allusions, such as Mazeppa's ride (described in a poem by George Gordon, Lord Byron) and the bleeding trees, which to a reader who knows the works of Dante suggest that poet's "wood of the suicides." (Not until many years later did Aragon reveal that he had attempted suicide after the breakup with Cunard.)

The use of such arcane personal and literary allusions was a legacy of the Symbolist movement; as a young man, Aragon admired both Arthur Rimbaud and Stéphane Mallarmé, two of the most gifted Symbolists. The Surrealist approach to imagery evolved directly out of Symbolism in its more extreme forms, such as "Le Bateau ivre" ("The Drunken Boat") of Rimbaud and the *Chants de Maldoror* (1869) of Comte de Lautréamont. Despite its hopelessness, "Poem to Shout in the Ruins" conveys the almost hallucinatory power the Surrealists saw in imagery: its ability to charge ordinary things with mystery by appealing to the buried layers of the subconscious. "Familiar objects one by one were taking on . . . the ghostly look of escaped prisoners. . . ." The poem also suggests, however, that Aragon is not content merely to explore his subconscious; he hungers for a real connection to a real woman. In his desperate desire to prolong the liaison, he tries fitfully to make a "waltz" of the poem and asks the woman to join him, "since *something* must still connect us," in spitting on "what we have loved together." Despite its prevailing tone of negation and despair, the poem anticipates two central themes of Aragon's mature works: the belief that love between man and woman should be infinitely more than a source of casual gratification and the awareness of mortality (which the finality of parting suggests). This awareness is not morbid but tragic—the painful apprehension of death in a man whose loves and hopes were lavished on mortal existence.

"ELSA'S EYES"

"Les Yeux d'Elsa" ("Elsa's Eyes"), the opening poem in the collection of that name, is a good example of the metrically regular pieces Aragon produced in the 1940's (and continued to produce, together with free verse, until the end of his life). It is particularly characteristic in that, while each stanza has internal unity, the stanzas do not follow one another in a strictly necessary order; like those of a folk song or lyrical ballad, they offer a series of related insights or observations without logical or narrative progression. Many of Aragon's mature poems *do* exhibit such a progression (notably "Toi qui es la rose"—"You Who Are the Rose"), but in most cases it is subordinated to the kind of associative rhythm observed in "Poem to Shout in the Ruins."

The imagery of "Elsa's Eyes" is more unified than that of the earlier poem. Taking his wife's eyes as the point of departure, the poet offers a whole array of metaphors for their blueness (sky, ocean, wildflowers), brilliance (lightning, shooting stars), and depth (a well, far countries, and constellations). The last four stanzas are more closely linked than the preceding ones and culminate in an apocalyptic vision of Elsa's eyes surviving the end of the world. The poem as a whole, however, cannot be said to build to this climax; its power stems from the accumulation of images rather than from their arrangement. It should be noted that Aragon's Surrealist formation is still very much in evidence here, not only in the hallucinatory quality of his images but also in their obvious connection with subconscious desires and fears. The occasional obscurities are no longer the result of a deliberate use of private or literary allusions; Aragon was already writing with a wider public in mind. Nevertheless, he continued to evoke his own deepest desires and fears in language whose occasional ambiguity reflects the ambiguity of subconscious impulses.

A relatively new departure for Aragon in this period, the serious use of religious imagery, is reflected in the references to the Three Kings and the Mother of the Seven Sorrows in "Elsa's Eyes." Although reared a Catholic, Aragon became an atheist in his early youth and never professed any religious faith thereafter. During World War II, however, he was impressed by the courage of Christian resisters and acquired a certain respect for the faith that sustained them in the struggle against fascism. For his own part, Aragon began to use the vocabulary of traditional religion to extol his wife. Thus, for example, in "Elsa's Eyes," Elsa is described as the Mother of the Seven Sorrows, an epithet of the Virgin Mary; at the same time, Elsa is assimilated by natural forces and survives the cataclysm of the last stanza like a mysterious deity. This is partly attributable to Aragon's rediscovery, at about this time, of the courtly love tradition in French poetry, in which the lady becomes the immediate object of the knight's worship, whether as a mediatrix (who shows the way to God) or as a substitute for God himself. Repeatedly in Aragon's postwar poetry, Elsa is endowed with godlike qualities, until, in *Le Fou d'Elsa*, a virtual apotheosis takes place: The "holy fool" for whom the book is named (a Muslim, not a Christian) is convicted of heresy for worshiping a woman—Elsa—who will not be born for four centuries.

Whenever he was questioned on the subject, Aragon insisted that his aim was not a deification of Elsa but the replacement of the transcendent God of traditional religions with a "real" object, a woman of flesh and blood who could serve as his partner in building the future. Thus, Elsa's madman tells his judge, "I can say of her what I cannot say of God: She exists, because she *will be*." At the same time, the imagery of "Elsa's Eyes" clearly indicates that on some level there is an impulse of genuine worship, compounded of love, fear, and awe, in the poet's relation to his wife; he turned to the courtly tradition because it struck a deep chord in him. From the very first stanza, Elsa is identified with forces of nature, not all of which are benevolent: "Your eyes are so deep that in stooping to drink/ I saw all suns reflected there/ All desperate men throw themselves there to die." In most of the early stanzas, emphasis is laid on her grief (presumably over the effects of war), which only enhances her beauty, but the insistence on her eyes also suggests that, like God, she is all-seeing. Aragon himself often referred to his wife as his conscience, and Bernard Lecherbonnier has suggested in *Le Cycle d'Elsa* (1974) that the circumstances of Aragon's upbringing created in him, first in regard to his mother and later in regard to his wife, "an obsession with self-justification that permitted the myth of god-as-love to crystallize around the person, and in particular the eyes, of Elsa." Such an attitude is especially suggested by the final images of the poem, that of "Paradise regained and relost a hundred times" and that of Elsa's eyes shining over the sea after the final "shipwreck" of the universe.

"YOU WHO ARE THE ROSE"

An attitude of worship can also be seen in "You Who Are the Rose," from the collection *Elsa*, but it is tempered considerably by the vulnerability of the rose, the central image around which the poem is built. Its tight construction makes this a somewhat uncharacteristic poem for Aragon, yet his technique is still that of association and accumulation rather than logical or rhetorical development. As in "Poem to Shout in the Ruins," short syntactic units give the impression of spoken (indeed, in this poem, almost breathless) language. With an obsessiveness reminiscent of the earlier poem, the speaker worries over the flowering of the rose, which he fears will not bloom "this year" because of frost, drought, or "some subterranean sickness." The poem has a clear dramatic structure: The tension of waiting builds steadily, with periodic breaks or breathing spaces marked by the one-line refrain "*(de) la rose*," until the miraculous flowering takes place and is welcomed with a sort of prayer. The images that accumulate along the way, evoked by the poet in a kind of incantation designed to call forth the rose, are all subordinated to this central image of flowering, yet by their startling juxtaposition and suggestiveness, they clearly reflect Aragon's Surrealist background. Thus, the dormant plant is compared to "a cross contradicting the tomb," while two lines later its roots are "like an insinuating hand beneath the sheets caressing the sleeping thighs of winter." The use of alliteration is excessive—as when six words beginning with *gr-* appear in the space of three lines—and although this serves to emphasize the incantatory quality of the verse, to hostile critics it may look like simple bad taste. Hubert Juin, a friendly critic, freely acknowledges that a certain kind of bad taste is evident in Aragon; he ascribes it to the poet's "epic" orientation, his desire to include as much of the world as possible in his design, which precludes attention to every detail. It seems more to the point to recall that for the Surrealists, editing was a kind of dishonesty; by writing rapidly and not revising, they sought to lay bare what was most deeply buried in their psyches. What often saves Aragon from *préciosité*, or literary affectation, is the realism of this stream-of-consciousness technique. Caught up in the speaker's own anxiety or fantasy, the reader does not stop to criticize the occasional banalities and lapses of taste; he follows in the poet's wake, eager to see where the train of thought will lead.

The poignancy of "You Who Are the Rose," as of so many of Aragon's late poems, stems from the contrast between his exaggerated hopes—still virtually those of a young man—and the fact of old age, which threatens to deprive him of his wife and of his poetic voice. There is also, in some of his later work, a hint of sadness (although never of disillusionment) at the failure of Communism to fulfill its promise within his own lifetime. It is worth noting that in France the rose has long been associated with Socialist ideals; the poet's fear for his wife in "You Who Are the Rose" may be doubled by a tacit fear that the promise of Marxism will not be fulfilled. The two fears are related, moreover, because Aragon saw the harmony between husband and wife as the hope of the future, the cornerstone of a just and happy (Communist) society. His anguish is that of the idealist who rejects the possibility of transcendence: His "divinity" is mortal, like him. This helps to account for the fact that he continued to write with undiminished passion until the very end of his life, for poetry held out the only prospect of immortality in which he believed. The rose is mortal, but she has a name, and the poet can conjure with it (as his conclusion emphasizes: "O rose who are your being and your name"). What is more, Elsa Triolet was herself a writer, and in the preface to an edition combining her own and her husband's fiction, she described their mutually inspired work as the best possible memorial to their love. Aragon will probably be remembered primarily as the poet of Elsa—"Elsa's Madman," perhaps, in his anguished self-disclosure—but above all as Elsa's troubadour, an ecstatic love poet who insists on the possibility of earthly happiness because he has tasted it himself.

OTHER MAJOR WORKS

LONG FICTION: *Anicet: Ou, le panorama*, 1921; *Les Aventures de Télémaque*, 1922 (*The Adventures of Telemachus*, 1988); *Le Paysan de Paris*, 1926 (*Nightwalker*, 1970); *Les Cloches de Bâle*, 1934 (*The Bells of Basel*, 1936); *Le Monde réel*, 1934-1944 (includes *Les Cloches de Bâle*, 1934; *Les Beaux Quartiers*, 1936; *Les Voyageurs de l'impériale*, 1942; and *Aurélien*, 1944); *Les Beaux Quartiers*, 1936 (*Residential Quarter*, 1938); *Les Voyageurs de l'impériale*, 1942 (*The Century Was Young*, 1941); *Aurélien*, 1944 (English translation, 1947); *Les Communistes*, 1949-1951; *La Semaine sainte*, 1958 (*Holy Week*, 1961); *La Mise à mort*, 1965; *Blanche: Ou, L'oubli*, 1967; *Théâtre/roman*, 1974.

SHORT FICTION: *Servitude et grandeur de français*, 1945; *Le Mentir-vrai*, 1981.

NONFICTION: *Le Traité du style*, 1928; *Pour une réalisme socialiste*, 1935; *L'Homme communiste*, 1946, 1953; *Introduction aux littératures soviétiques*, 1956; *J'abats mon jeu*, 1959; *Les Deux Géants: Histoire parallèle des États-Unis et de l'U.R.S.S.*, 1962 (with André Maurois; 5 volumes; partial translation *A History of the U.S.S.R. from Lenin to Khrushchev*, 1964); *Entretiens avec Francis Crémieux*, 1964; *Écrits sur l'art moderne*, 1982.

BIBLIOGRAPHY

Adereth, M. *Aragon: The Resistance Poems*. London: Grant & Cutler, 1985. A brief critical guide to Aragon's poetry.

_____. *Elsa Triolet and Louis Aragon: An Introduction to Their Interwoven Lives and Works*. Lewiston, N.Y.: Edwin Mellen Press, 1994. An introductory biography of Triolet and Aragon and their lives together including critical analysis of their work and a bibliography.

Becker, Lucille Frackman. *Louis Aragon*. New York: Twayne, 1971. An introductory biography of Aragon and critical analysis of selected works. Includes bibliographic references.

Benfey, Christopher, and Karen Remmler, eds. *Artists, Intellectuals, and World War II: The Pontigny Encounters at Mount Holyoke College, 1942-1944*. Amherst: University of Massachusetts Press, 2006. Contains a chapter on Aragon, Gustave Cohen, and the poetry of the Resistance. Provides a general perspective on World War II literature.

Josephson, Hannah, and Malcolm Cowley, eds. *Aragon, Poet of the French Resistance*. New York: Duell, Sloan and Pearce, 1945. A study of Aragon's poetic works produced between 1939 and 1945.

Lillian Doherty

HANS ARP

Born: Strassburg, Germany (now Strasbourg, France); September 16, 1887
Died: Basel, Switzerland; June 7, 1966
Also known as: Jean Arp

<small>PRINCIPAL POETRY</small>
Die Wolkenpumpe, 1920
Der Pyramidenrock, 1924
Weisst du schwarzt du, 1930
Des taches dans le vide, 1937
Sciure de gamme, 1938
Muscheln und Schirme, 1939
Rire de coquille, 1944
Le Siège de l'air, 1946 (as Jean Arp)
On My Way: Poetry and Essays, 1912-1947, 1948
Auch das ist nur eine Wolke: Aus dem Jahren, 1920 bis 1950, 1951
Beharte Herzen, Könige vor der Sintflut, 1953
Wortraüme und schwarze Sterne, 1953
Auf einem Bein, 1955
Unsern ta[guml]lichen Traum, 1955
Le Voilier dans la forêt, 1957 (as Jean Arp)
Worte mit und ohne Anker, 1957
Mondsand, 1959
Vers le blanc infini, 1960 (as Jean Arp)
Sinnende Flammen, 1961
Gedichte, 1903-1939, 1963
L'Ange et la rose, 1965 (as Jean Arp)
Logbuch des Traumkapitäns, 1965
Jours effeuillés: Poèmes, Essais, Souvenirs, 1920-1965, 1966 (as Jean Arp; *Arp on
    Arp: Poems, Essays, Memories*, 1972)
Le Soleil recerclé, 1966 (as Jean Arp)
Gedichte, 1939-1957, 1974
Three Painter Poets, 1974

<small>OTHER LITERARY FORMS</small>

In addition to his large body of poetry, Hans Arp (orpt) wrote a substantial number of lyrical and polemical essays, in which the metaphysical basis of his thought is given its clearest and most systematic expression. These essays are collected in *On My Way* and

Dreams and Projects (1952). Arp also wrote about his fellow artists in *Onze peintres vus par Arp* (1949), a collection that helps clarify the aesthetic values that influenced his own work as a plastic artist. Arp also published two works of fiction: *Le Blanc aux pieds de nègre* (1945), a collection of short stories, and *Tres inmensas novelas* (1935), short novels written in collaboration with the Chilean poet Vicente Huidobro.

ACHIEVEMENTS

Hans Arp actually has two reputations: one as a sculptor and painter of long-standing international fame, the other as a poet. Although his reputation as a plastic artist overshadowed his work as a poet during his lifetime, he is now recognized as an important and original contributor to the twentieth century literary avant-garde. As a literary artist, Arp is best known for his association with Dada and Surrealism. Together with Tristan Tzara, Hugo Ball, Richard Hülsenbeck, Marcel Janco, and Emmy Hennings, Arp was one of the earliest and most enthusiastic supporters of the Dada movement, which began in Zurich in February of 1916. In the 1950's and 1960's he erected sculptures for Harvard University, the University of Caracas, and the UNESCO Secretariat Building, the Brunswick Technische Hochschule, and Bonn University Library. He also finished cement steles and walls for the Kunstgewerbeschule in Basel. In addition to these achievements, Arp is best known for sculptures such as *Owl's Dream* (1936), *Chinese Shadow* (1947), *Muse's Amphora* (1959), and *Shepherd's Clouds* (1953). In 1954, he won the international prize for sculpture at the Venice Biennale.

BIOGRAPHY

Hans Arp, also known as Jean Arp, was born in Strasbourg on September 16, 1887. At the time of his birth, Alsace-Lorraine, the region in which Strasbourg lies, belonged to Germany, although culturally it was tied to France, to which it presently belongs. Arp's bilingualism, his equal ease with both French and German, which was a product of the history of this region, helps to account for the confusion concerning his Christian name. As Arp explained it, when he wrote in French, he called himself Jean Arp; when he wrote in German, he called himself Hans Arp. In his view, neither name was a pseudonym—the change was made simply for convenience, as one shifts from speaking one language to the other according to the language of the auditor.

This mingled French and German heritage was also reflected in Arp's home and social environment. His father, Pierre Guillaume Arp, who operated a cigar and cigarette factory in Strasbourg, was of Danish descent. His mother, Josephine Köberlé Arp, was of French descent. At home, Arp recalled, French was spoken. In the state-operated primary and secondary schools he attended, however, standard High German was used, and taught, the Alsace-Lorraine being at the time under German annexation. With his friends he spoke the Alsatian vernacular, a dialect of different derivation from the standard German used in education and for official business.

Arp's first published poem appeared in 1902, when he was only fifteen. Like most of his earliest poetry, it was written in the Alsatian dialect, although only two years later he had completed, in standard High German, a manuscript volume of poems. This manuscript, entitled "Logbuch," was unfortunately mislaid by the publisher to whom it was sent. Three poems by Arp in German did appear the same year, however, in *Das Neue Magazin*.

About 1904, Arp's involvement with the plastic arts began in earnest. He visited Paris for the first time, and for the next five years he studied art not only at Strasbourg but also in Weimar and Paris. In 1909, Arp, having served his artistic apprenticeship at various academies, moved with his family to Weggis, on the eastern shore of Lake Lucerne in Switzerland. In the five years Arp spent at Weggis, two important developments occurred. Isolated from the influences of the academies and their avant-garde faddishness, Arp began to develop the personal aesthetic he called concrete art, which was to influence the entire course of his career. In addition, he became acquainted with other artists who, like himself, were also pursuing personal aesthetics independent of the Paris academies. During this period, Arp exhibited his work with some of these artists, including Wassily Kandinsky and Paul Klee.

In 1914, Arp returned to Paris only to discover that war had been declared. Because his German money was suddenly valueless in France, and his German citizenship unwelcome, he promptly returned to neutral Zurich. To avoid the draft, he persuaded the authorities at the German consulate that he was mentally ill. In Zurich, Arp exhibited the abstract collages and tapestries that are the earliest examples of his work extant. In November of 1915, at an exhibition of his work with his friend and fellow artist Otto Van Rees, he met his future wife, Sophie Taeuber, an artist who was a native of Zurich.

In 1916, Arp and Taeuber participated in the activities of the newly formed Dada group, which met regularly at the Cabaret Voltaire. At this time, Arp produced bas-relief sculptures and woodcuts reflecting the developing aesthetic that he termed "concrete art." Unlike the earlier geometric productions of his abstract period, these reliefs and woodcuts were composed of asymmetrical curvilinear and bimorphic forms; they were, as Arp later explained, "direct creations," truly "concrete" art, not abstract representations of already existing forms. In 1921, Arp married Taeuber, and together they collaborated on cut-paper collages and other plastic works. Arp also returned to writing poetry, producing a great number of poems in German that were collected in *Die Wolkenpumpe*, *Der Pyramidenrock*, and *Weisst du schwartz du*.

After the demise of Dada in 1924, Arp formed an increasingly close association with the Surrealist movement, and in 1926, he settled permanently in the Paris suburb of Meudon. Arp's first poem written directly in French was published in 1933, in the Surrealists' journal *Le Surréalisme au service de la révolution*, and his first collection of poems in French, *Des taches dans le vide* (splotches in space), appeared in 1937. At this time, Arp also began to create the free-form sculptures that he called concretions, and that were to bring him international acclaim as a sculptor. He also began to experiment with a new type of "torn-paper" collage; his comments on these collages have often been linked to the Surrealist technique of automatic writing. From this time on, Arp published poetry in both French and German, often translating originals from one language into the other, and in the process frequently introducing substantial changes.

In 1940, with the outbreak of World War II, the Arps fled south from Paris to Grasse to escape the German occupation, later managing to reach Zurich, in neutral Switzerland, in 1942. It was there that Taeuber met with an accidental death on January 13, 1943, sending Arp into a deep depression that lingered for many years. Some of his most moving poems are beautiful evocations of Taeuber's transforming influence on his life.

After the war, Arp's growing fame as an important modern sculptor, as well as the increasing demand for exhibitions of his plastic works, allowed him to travel widely. During this period, he visited the United States, Mexico, Italy, Greece, Jordan, Israel, and Egypt.

In 1959, Arp married Marguerite Hagenbach, who had been a friend of Taeuber in Zurich and had long admired Arp's work. In the remaining seven years of his life, Arp and Hagenbach spent part of the year at their home in Meudon and the remainder at a second home near Locarno, in southern Switzerland. On June 7, 1966, Arp died at the age of seventy-eight, while away from home, in Basel.

ANALYSIS

Hans Arp was one of the founding members of the Dada movement, which had a broad impact on both art and literature in the early twentieth century. Dada's principal target was humanity's overestimation of reason. Its aim, Arp said, was "to destroy the reasonable deceptions of man," to expose "the fragility of life and human works" through the use of Dadaist humor, which would reveal "the natural and unreasonable order" of things. The poems of Arp's first collection, *Die Wolkenpumpe* (the cloud pump), date from this period, as does "Kaspar ist Tot" ("Kaspar Is Dead"), perhaps the most famous of all Dada poems. The Dada use of humor to reorient humanity's attitude toward the world was followed by Arp in these poems, where he began to develop his decidedly personal "Arpian humor."

Dada's critique of modern humanity, however, was not entirely destructive, despite the commonly held belief that it was a totally negative response to the world. Arp's own work is one of the best testaments to this fact. To rectify modern humanity's mistaken view of its place in the universe, Arp offered the notion of a concrete art that could transform both humankind and the world. His intention was "to save man from the most dangerous of follies: vanity . . . to simplify the life of man . . . to identify him with nature."

It was through his participation in the Dada group that Arp became acquainted with the Paris Surrealists, after he and his wife moved to the Paris suburb of Meudon in 1926, Arp frequently participated in Surrealist activities and contributed to their publications.

Two important characteristics of Arp's poetry distinguish it, however, from the work of other Dada and Surrealist poets: his highly personal humor and the metaphysical philosophy that underlies all his mature work.

Arp's humor achieves its effect by combining opposites: the celestial with the terrestrial, the eternal with the transitory, the sublime with the mundane, among others. That which comes from above—the celestial, the eternal, the sublime—sustains and nourishes humanity, while that which comes from below—the terrestrial, the transitory, the mundane—confuses and intoxicates humanity. Thus, Arp's conception of humor is connected with his metaphysical philosophy, which aims to restore the lost balance of forces in humans. Arp uses humor in his work to destroy "the reasonable deceptions of man," which lead him to believe that he is "the summit of creation."

"KASPAR IS DEAD"

In Arp's view then, humor and metaphysics are not mutually exclusive, and elements of both are often present in a single work. A good example of this is the early poem "Kaspar Is Dead." The poem is written in the form of an elegy, and it begins, as is customary in the genre, with a lament for the dead. The poem then proceeds to describe the remarkable accomplishments of the deceased, which seem superhuman in character: "who will conceal the burning banner in the cloud's pigtail now . . . who will entice the idyllic deer out of the petrified bag . . . who will blow the noses of ships umbrellas beekeepers ozone-spindles and bone the pyramids." It seems as if some golden age has passed: The link between humanity and nature has been broken by the death of Kaspar. At this realization, the speaker resumes his lament, but this time it seems even more self-conscious, and it includes a note of facetiousness: "alas alas alas our good kaspar is dead. goodness gracious me kaspar is dead." In the second half of the poem, the speaker turns to more generalized metaphysical speculation: "into what shape has your great wonderful soul migrated. are you a star now or a chain of water . . . or an udder of black light?" He despairs once again at the realization that, wherever he is and in whatever form, Kaspar can no longer reestablish for humankind the broken link between itself and nature. He has ceased to be human and has thus been liberated from the tragic condition of temporal consciousness that the speaker still suffers. The speaker concludes with resignation that it is humanity itself that is obligated to reestablish a proper relationship with nature; it cannot rely on anyone or anything else to do this for it, even such a heroic figure as Kaspar.

"I AM A HORSE"

One of Arp's most successful attacks on the reasonable deceptions of humanity is a poem of his early maturity, "Ich bin ein Pferd" (in French as "Je suis un cheval" and translated into English as "I Am a Horse"). It is not humankind itself that is under attack but humanity's vain rationality. The speaker of the poem is a reasoning horse, who resembles Jonathan Swift's Houyhnhnms. Investing a subhuman creature with the proud vanity of rational humanity creates an ironic situation reminiscent of the fable, in which talking animals are used to satirize particular forms of human folly. In this poem, however, it is the human beings who behave instinctively, emotionally, and impulsively— much to the disgust of the dignified horse, who observes the action from a detached perspective.

As the poem begins, the equine speaker is riding in a crowded passenger train, and "every seat is occupied by a lady with a man on her lap"—a most unpleasant sight to the snobbish, socially respectable horse. In addition to being crowded, the compartment is unbearably hot, and all the human passengers "eat nonstop." When the men suddenly begin to whine, unbuttoning the women's bodices and clutching their breasts, wanting to be suckled, the horse alone resists this primitive, uncivilized impulse, maintaining his proud composure. However, at the end of the poem, the detachment of the speaker, his feeling of superiority relative to the weak-willed humans with whom he shares the compartment, is revealed as a mere pose that disguises the same basic impulses behind the mask of rationality, for when he neighs loudly, "hnnnnn," he thinks proudly of "the six buttons of sex appeal" on his chest—"nicely aligned like the shiny buttons of a uniform." Through the agency of a reasoning horse, Arp presents a Dadaist fable which exposes the foolish vanity and isolation that has resulted from humanity's overestimation of its greatest creation—reason.

ARP'S WORLDVIEW

Arp's work consists of more than attacks on the reasonable deceptions of humanity and satires of his vain pride. Arp devoted a substantial portion of his mature work to communicating, in poetic images and symbols, his distinctive metaphysical philosophy, which has been called variously Platonic, Neoplatonic, Romantic, and Idealist. Arp's worldview eludes these categories; it is personal and intuitive in character, not critical and systematic.

When Arp spoke about the formation of his worldview, he associated it with two particular experiences. The first was the period of isolation he spent at Weggis, which gave him the opportunity to cast aside the aesthetic of abstraction and formulate his theory of concrete art. The second experience was his meeting Sophie Taeuber, whose work and life expressed in an intuitive way, free from self-consciousness, the reorientation of human values that Arp had been seeking.

"IN SPACE"

Arp's metaphysical beliefs, transformed into poetic images and symbols, appeared with increasing frequency in his poetry in the years following Taeuber's death. One of the best of these metaphysical poems is "Dans le vide" ("In Space"), a moving, imaginative elegy written after the death of Arp's friend and fellow artist, Theo van Doesburg.

In this poem, death is treated as cause for celebration, not mourning. When the poem begins, the soul of Arp's beloved friend—after having sojourned for a time in the transitory material world below—is preparing to leap out into the unknown, the eternal realm of unbounded space above. The soul, freed from the physical body, realizes that death is a return home, not an exile. This is reinforced by the fact that he enters space, the Above, in the fetal position—which is also the crouch he assumes in order to leap into space.

Refusing to see this death as a loss, Arp focuses on the freedom his friend is now able to enjoy for the first time, as he is joyously liberated from the demands of others. Doesburg now knows neither honor nor dishonor, censure nor obligation; he dwells blissfully alone, in an eternal realm of light. Arp had already described this state of blissful eternal existence in a much earlier poem entitled "Il chante il chante" ("He Sings He Sings"). It is in later poems such as "In Space" that Arp reached the height of his powers as a highly distinctive, imaginative, and lyrical poet.

OTHER MAJOR WORKS
> LONG FICTION: *Tres inmensas novelas*, 1935 (with Vicente Huidobro).
> SHORT FICTION: *Le Blanc aux pieds de nègre*, 1945.
> NONFICTION: *Onze peintres vus par Arp*, 1949; *Dreams and Projects*, 1952; *Collected French Writings*, 1974.
> MISCELLANEOUS: *Gesammelte Gedichte*, 1963-1984 (3 volumes).

BIBLIOGRAPHY
Cathelin, Jean. *Jean Arp*. Translated by Enid York. New York: Grove Press, 1960. A short introduction to Arp's life and art, with many photographs of his artwork.
Fauchereau, Serge. *Hans Arp*. Translated by Kenneth Lyons. New York: Rizzoli, 1988. Biographical and critical introduction to Arp's artwork and poetry.
Jean, Marcel. Introduction to *Arp on Arp: Poems, Essays, Memories*, by Jean Arp. Translated by Joachim Neugroschel. New York: Viking, 1972. This introductory essay is an excellent summary of Arp's life and work, and the rest of the book consists of English translations of his collected French poetry and prose.
Last, Rex W. *German Dadaist Literature: Kurt Schwitters, Hugo Ball, Hans Arp*. New York: Twayne , 1973. This clear, thorough study of the three major German-speaking poets of the Dada movement helps to dispel the mistaken notion that it was mostly a French phenomenon after the Zurich period ended. Contains useful chronologies and succinct bibliographies.
_____. *Hans Arp: The Poet of Dadaism*. London: Wolff, 1969. Makes the criticism of Arp's poetry, most of which has been published in German, accessible to an English-speaking audience. The second half consists of translations of many of his German poems.
Lemoine, Serge. *Dada*. Translated by Charles Lynn Clark. New York: Universe Books,

1987. Introduction to Dadaism with biographical information on Arp and other artists. Includes bibliography.

Mortimer, Armine Kotin. "Jean Arp, Poet and Artist." *Dada/Surrealism* 7 (1977): 109-120. Explores the important symbiotic relationship between Arp's poetry and his visual art.

Motherwell, Robert, ed. *The Dada Painters and Poets.* 2d ed. Cambridge, Mass.: Harvard University Press, 1989. A collection of texts and illustrations by Arp and others in the Dada movement with a critical bibliography by Bernard Karpel.

Richter, Hans. *Dada: Art and Anti-Art.* Translated by David Britt. New York: Thames & Hudson, 1997. A historical and biographical account of Dada by one of the artists involved in the movement. Includes bibliographical references and index.

Rimbach, Guenther C. "Sense and Non-Sense in the Poetry of Jean Hans Arp." *German Quarterly* 37 (1963): 152-163. Argues that Arp is at root a religious poet and that the lack of reference to reality in his work is an attempt to come closer to God.

Steven E. Colburn

JOHN ASHBERY

Born: Rochester, New York; July 28, 1927

OTHER LITERARY FORMS

Although known mainly as a poet, John Ashbery has produced a number of works in various genres. *A Nest of Ninnies* (1969) is a humorous novel about middle-class American life written by Ashbery in collaboration with James Schuyler. His plays include *The Compromise: Or, Queen of the Carabou* (pr. 1956) and *Three Plays* (1978). He also produced a volume of art criticism, *Reported Sightings: Art Chronicles, 1957-1987* (1989). His Charles Eliot Norton Lectures (given at Harvard University) were collected as *Other Traditions* (2000), an engaging volume of literary criticism about six eccentric poets.

ACHIEVEMENTS

John Ashbery won three major literary awards for *Self-Portrait in a Convex Mirror:* the National Book Award in Poetry, the Pulitzer Prize, and the National Book Critics Circle Award. Ashbery is a member of the Academy of Arts and Sciences and the American Academy of Arts and Letters (since 1980) and served as chancellor for the Academy of American Poets (1988-1999). He has been honored with two Guggenheim Fellowships, two Fulbright Fellowships, and two National Endowment for the Arts grants. He won the Yale Series of Younger Poets award (1955) for *Some Trees*, Union League Civic and Arts Poetry Prize (1966), an Award in Literature from the American Academy of Arts and Letters (1969), the Shelley Memorial Award (1973), the Levinson Prize (1977), the Jersome J. Shestack Poetry Award (1983), and the Bollingen Prize from Yale University (1985). In 1982, Ashbery was awarded the Fellowship of the Academy of American Poets. In 1985, he was named a winner of both a MacArthur Prize Fellowship and a Lenore Marshall Poetry Prize. He received the Commonwealth Award in Literature (1986), the Ruth Lilly Poetry Prize (1992), the Frost Medal from the Poetry Society of America (1995), the Gold Medal for Poetry from the American Academy of Arts and Letters (1997), the prestigious Antonio Feltrinelli Prize from the Accademia Nazionale dei Lincei in Rome (1992), the Bingham Poetry Prize (1998), theWallace Stevens Award (2001), and the Griffin Poetry Prize (2008). In 2002, he was made an officer of the French Legion of Honor by presidential decree.

BIOGRAPHY

Born in Rochester, New York, in 1927, John Lawrence Ashbery grew up in rural Sodus, New York. He attended Deerfield Academy and Harvard University, where he became friends with poet Kenneth Koch. Ashbery received his B.A. from Harvard in 1949 and his M.A. from Columbia University in 1951. After leaving university life, Ashbery worked for various publishers in New York City until he moved to Paris in 1955. He remained in Paris until 1965, writing for the *New York Herald Tribune*, *Art International*, and *Art News*. From 1965 until 1972, Ashbery worked as executive editor for *Art News* in New York, before becoming a distinguished professor of writing at the Brooklyn College campus of the City University of New York. He has also taught at Harvard University. Ashbery became the Charles P. Stevenson, Jr., Professor of Languages and Literature at Bard College in 1990.

ANALYSIS

As a brief review of his biography would suggest, John Ashbery has had a considerable amount of exposure to the world of art and to the language of art criticism. Ashbery spent a full decade of his life in Paris, the art capital of Europe, where he read deeply in French poetry and immersed himself in the day-to-day life of French culture. Readers of Ashbery's poetry, then, should not be surprised to encounter references to art and occasional snatches of the French language as part of the poetic texts. For example, one of his poems is entitled "Le Livre est sur la table." There are other titles in German, Latin, and Russian, and the poetry as a whole bristles with references from every department of highbrow, middlebrow, and lowbrow culture, including cartoons ("Daffy Duck in Hollywood"), silent movies ("The Lonedale Operator"), literature ("Sonnet," "A Long Novel," and "Thirty-seven Haiku"), history ("The Tennis Court Oath"), and linguistics ("The Plural of 'Jack-in-the-Box'").

Because of its unpredictable style and subject matter, Ashbery's poetry has managed to infuriate, befuddle, amuse, delight, and instruct its readers. His work remains some of the most difficult verse produced, for he refuses to provide the reader with a poetic "reality" that is any less complex than the "reality" of the world outside poetry. Ashbery cannot be simplified or paraphrased because his work has no "content" in the ordinary sense. His poetry is "about" the act of knowing, the process of imagining, the curious associational leaps made by the human mind as it experiences any given moment in time. To read Ashbery is to be teased into a whole range of possible meanings without finally settling on a single one. Although this openness might confuse the reader at the outset, the process of reading Ashbery becomes more pleasurable on each encounter. New meanings appear, and Ashbery's voice comes to seem strangely present, as if he were intoning directly into the reader's ear. These poems are filled with little verbal cues and signals aimed directly at the reader; many of the poems depend on a complicated dialogue or interplay between the author and the reader (a technique he exploits masterfully in *Three Poems*). Thus his work is a kind of half-poetry, always requiring an active reader to make it whole. Ashbery achieves his trademark effect of apparent intimacy while simulating the very process of thought itself.

How Ashbery came to create this new kind of poetry is actually a subchapter in the general history of art and culture in the twentieth century. Certainly he benefited mightily from his study of other artists and thinkers. During his formative years in Paris, he absorbed the French language and the famous paintings of the Louvre while immersing himself in all kinds of printed matter: cheap pamphlets and paperback novels bought from the bookstalls, as well as journalistic prose (in French and English) and the rarefied language of art criticism (which he himself was producing).

In addition, it is clear that a strong line of influence connects Ashbery with writers such as Gertrude Stein, who used disjointed syntax and unorthodox grammar as part of her Surrealistic poetry. He owes a clear debt also to Wallace Stevens, who taught him how to philosophize in poetry and also how to approach subjects obliquely. Stevens, also, was a great lover of French Impressionist painting and Symbolist poetry. From W. H. Auden, who chose Ashbery's *Some Trees* for the Yale Series of Younger Poets, Ashbery learned a conversational naturalness and a lyrical or musical way of phrasing. It might be argued that Ashbery, as a literate artist, was influenced by all the great thinkers of the century, but these poetic debts seem particularly obvious, especially in the early books. He probably learned something from Ludwig Wittgenstein's idea of language as a game, just as he must have responded to Jackson Pollock's expressionist paintings, which use paint in much the same way that Ashbery uses words. Something of the sheer shock value and unpredictability of musicians such as Igor Stravinsky, John Cage, and Anton Webern must have touched him also, since Ashbery is clearly fond of similar effects in his own poems.

These debts to the artistic pioneers of the twentieth century are most obvious in Ashbery's earlier books—that is, those preceding the publication of *Three Poems*: *Some Trees*, *The Tennis Court Oath*, and *Rivers and Mountains*. All these books are relatively short and compact, typically containing one long or major poem, often positioned near the end of the volume.

Ashbery's characteristic wonder and inventiveness has proven a hallmark of the several volumes published since 1990. During that period, Ashbery wrote and published more and wrote more of the highest quality than at any other time in his career. With Ashbery, there is no limit to the possibilities inherent in human life and to the sheer fun of the mind's response to them. Regular readers of Ashbery will begin to inhabit a world that is larger, more unpredictable, and infinitely more interesting than anything they have known before.

SOME TREES

Typical of Ashbery's early poems are "The Instruction Manual" from *Some Trees* and the title poem from *Rivers and Mountains*, each of which forces the reader to perform another kind of imaginative leaping, one that is different from the mere shock of the surreal. In "The Instruction Manual," the speaker is bored with his job of writing an instruction manual on the uses of a new metal and, instead, falls into a prolonged aesthetic daydream on the city of Guadalajara, Mexico, which he has never visited. He invents this city in magical detail for the rest of the poem. In like manner, the places described on a map and the map itself become utterly indistinguishable in "Rivers and Mountains," as if Ashbery were suggesting that one's most vivid moments are those that have been rescued or resurrected by the fertile powers of the poetic imagination. Ashbery always emphasizes the primacy of the imagination. In his view, the most vivid reality occurs in the poem itself, because that is the precise point where the inner and outer (spiritual and sensory) experiences of life actually intersect.

Two more early poems bear analysis here, because they also illustrate the poetic techniques favored in many of Ashbery's later poems. "Le Livre est sur la table" and "The Picture of Little J. A. in a Prospect of Flowers" (both from *Some Trees*) are magnificent feats of imaginative power, and each operates on the same principle of aesthetic meditation. In each poem, the poet looks at reality through a work of art, or as if it were a work of art (in "The Picture of Little J. A. in a Prospect of Flowers" a photograph is the medium). The effect is largely the same, because the world is always transformed and made into a work of art by the conclusion of the poem. Stevens is probably the model for this kind of poem, exemplified by his "Thirteen Ways of Looking at a Blackbird" and "A Study of Two Pears." Other poets, particularly William Carlos Williams, Marianne Moore, and Elizabeth Bishop, were to involve themselves passionately in the writing of aesthetically oriented poems, and one can look to some of their pioneering work to explain the sureness and control of Ashbery's similar efforts.

In "Le Livre est sur la table," Ashbery offers the reader a number of aesthetic propositions to contemplate, the most important of which is the notion that beauty results from a certain emptiness or from the placement of an object in an unusual or unaccustomed position. In both instances, the viewer is forced to see the object in a new way. Ashbery again underlines the power of the imagination, giving the example of an imaginary woman who comes alive in her stride, her hair, and her breasts as she is imagined. Most important of all is the artist who creates small artistic catalysts, new and strange relationships that haunt the perceiver with their beauty. Neither the sea nor a simple birdhouse can make for innovative art but placing them together in a fundamental relationship changes them forever:

> The young man places a bird-house
> Against the blue sea. He walks away
> And it remains. Now other
> Men appear, but they live in boxes.

The men in the boxes are the nonartists, who do not realize that the newly created sea is a highlighted thing. All along, the sea has been "writing" a message (with its waves and lines), but only the "young man" (the artist) can read it.

The other "young man," or artist figure, in *Some Trees* is Ashbery himself, described in the snapshot that serves as the aesthetic focal point for the autobiographical poem "The Picture of Little J. A. in a Prospect of Flowers." This little fellow has a head like a mushroom and stands comically before a bed of phlox, but he has the makings of a poet precisely because he appreciates the value of words—especially lost words, those tip-of-the-tongue utterances and slips of the tongue, in which the speaker strains to specify clear meaning. "The Picture of Little J. A. in a Prospect of Flowers" is a typical Ashbery performance, not merely because of its high aesthetic theme but also because of its inclusion of low comedy, irony, and parody. The epigraph—taken from Boris Pasternak's autobiography *Okhrannaya gramota* (1931; *Safe Conduct*, 1945 in *The Collected Prose*

Works)—seemingly contradicts the rest of the poem in what is the first of many jokes (Dick and Jane of childhood books become Dick and Genevieve, conversing in complicated Elizabethan sentences). Childhood is full of jokes and embarrassments, like standing in front of the clicking shutter of a camera, but childhood can also be the beginning of the artist's journey: The poem ends by praising the imagination and its ability to rescue this early phase of life through the power of words. "The Picture of Little J. A. in a Prospect of Flowers" is a bittersweet portrait of a self-conscious and precocious young man who was destined to become a great artist.

THE TENNIS COURT OATH

In *The Tennis Court Oath*, the reader encounters the long quasi-epical poem entitled "Europe," a work related in overall form to T. S. Eliot's *The Waste Land* (1922) and to similar efforts by Ezra Pound, Hart Crane, and Williams. In the most general terms, "Europe" here means the accumulated cultural wealth of European history and its ability—or inability—to help the creative artist in the twentieth century. The decay, or "wasteland," of Europe is juxtaposed to or "intercut" (in film terms) with a trivial story of two travelers, Pryor and Collins, whose unheroic status stands in sharp contrast to the old order. As the poem begins, the poet registers all these complex feelings, while focusing on the shocking blueness of the morning sky, here presented surrealistically:

> To employ her
> construction ball
> Morning fed on the
> light blue wood
> of the mouth

The wrecking ball of construction crews is one of the most visible symbols of the typical cityscape, suggesting simultaneously the twin processes of destruction and re-creation. The sudden, destructive impact of the steel ball approximates the elemental power of the morning light as it, too, rearranges and alters the city and all of its facets. The bystander is left openmouthed and speechless, like the sky itself. This analysis does not fully explicate Ashbery's lines, because, like all dream imagery, they resist final explication. One can describe their suggestiveness and allusiveness, but the dream itself remains a mystery, as does this purely perceived moment of an ordinary morning in the city.

THREE POEMS

Some of the poet's greatness is evident on nearly every page of *Three Poems*, the book that many critics cite as Ashbery's masterpiece. The long, meditative work consists of three interlocking prose poems, "The New Spirit," "The System," and "The Recital," and totals 118 densely packed pages of text. Most of that text is written in prose, a highly interactive prose that constantly urges the reader forward, raises questions, voices doubts and suspicions, and generally plunges the reader headlong into a highly meditative process of thinking and reflecting. *Three Poems* is Ashbery at his most difficult and most satisfying, even though there is virtually no story or tidy paraphrase that can be made of the reading experience itself. Nevertheless, a few elusive details do emerge, and one dimly begins to realize that *Three Poems* is an oblique narrative that in general terms charts a deep relationship between two lovers, one that somehow founders, so that the narrator grows more and more self-possessed. The narrator becomes less and less likely to address the familiar "you" who is called upon again and again in the opening pages of the book. By the end, the "you" has virtually disappeared, as if the loss of love might be charted by the absence of the "you" from pages where only the "I" can finally dominate.

The form of *Three Poems* deserves some attention, because the poems are cast in the form of prose, though their imagery, tonal shifts, and complicated rhythms all suggest poetic (not prosaic) form. To complicate matters even further, Ashbery originally published the second section of the work, "The System," in the *Paris Review* in 1971, the year before the whole work appeared in the form of a book. Ashbery specifically allowed "The System" to be published as a prose work, so by titling the whole three-part composition *Three Poems*, he seems to be teasing the reader again on the simplest level and at the same time calling attention to the arbitrariness of literary labels and taxonomy. As if all those complications were not enough, Ashbery carries the joke further by inserting several poems (or at least texts that look like poems) into the longer work. What counts in the end is the sustained act of mediation and empathy with the narrator that these manipulations of typeface and marginal format will induce in the reader.

The reader, facing *Three Poems*, has a Herculean task to perform: absorbing a long, oblique narrative that requires constant reflection, analysis, and thoughtful mediation. The difficulty is an intentional by-product of Ashbery's stated goal on the first page of the book: to leave out as much as possible in order to create a newer and truer form of communication. Any love story the reader could have encountered would have finally become banal; what Ashbery gives, however, cannot grow stale. To read *Three Poems* is to invent on every page the pain and exaltation that make up the essence of a love story. In that way, the "private" person of the book remains mysterious, as all lovers essentially must remain. Thus, one cannot summarize Ashbery's love story, but one can experience it vicariously.

In "The System," the second and most difficult part of the poem, the narrator becomes utterly preoccupied with himself. In "The New Spirit," even small details of urban life were associated with something the beloved had said or done; here, however, the details and the lover have disappeared. Instead, the narrator is trapped in a kind of mental labyrinth, or "system." In one memorable passage, he imagines the members of the human race boarding a train, which is, of course, their whole life. No one has any idea where the train is going or how fast it is moving. The passengers are ignorant of their journey and—the narrator insists—ignorant of their fundamental situation. The very core of their being is ignorance, yet they fail to recognize this crucial fact. Hence, the narrator views them with contempt.

Three Poems concludes on a lighter note, literally on notes of music, which offer a kind of deliverance for the narrator, who has been trapped in the labyrinth of his doleful thoughts. "The Recital" is important because Ashbery often sees music as an analogue to poetry. Indeed, at one point, he had planned to become a musician, and music has remained a rich source of inspiration throughout his career. The power of music and its essential abstractness make a powerful appeal to the narrator, who at this juncture is exhausted by his Hamlet-like speculations. The poem ends, and with it the whole book, with a description of the power of music (and of art)—the power to inspire new beginnings and new possibilities. In a final jest, Ashbery offers the reader an ending that is actually a beginning: "There were new people watching and waiting, conjugating in this way the distance and emptiness, transforming the scarcely noticeable bleakness into something both intimate and noble." With this brilliant virtuoso effect, Ashbery concludes a poem that is at once a continuance of the great Western tradition of meditative writing (one that includes Saint John of the Cross and Sir Thomas Browne)—and a dramatically arresting rendition of how it feels to be alive in the last decades of the twentieth century. The old and the new come together in a synthesis that is as disturbing, fascinating, and elusive as the century that produced it.

Having reached a kind of artistic plateau with *Three Poems*, Ashbery's career took a new direction. In many ways, *Three Poems* occupies the kind of position in his life that *The Waste Land* did for Eliot. Both works explore psychological traumas and deeply sustained anguish; both plumb the depths of despair until a kind of spiritual nadir is reached. After Eliot completed *The Waste Land*, his work took on a new, spiritual dimension, culminating in the complex Christian poem he called *Four Quartets* (1943). Ashbery's work also changed after the publication of *Three Poems*, but he has not embraced Christian or even theistic belief; he has always insisted on a kind of agnostic or even atheistic vision of life, in which art supplants all conventional notions of divinity. Nevertheless, like Eliot, he has passed through the proverbial dark night of the soul, and his work after *Three Poems* is somehow more confident, less self-consciously experimental, and less opaque. The newer poetry is still impossible to paraphrase, but it is much more accessible and more readable (at least on first sight) than the most extravagant of the early poems, and its subject matter generally seems more central to human experience.

SELF-PORTRAIT IN A CONVEX MIRROR

All these tendencies culminate in a book that won the National Book Award, the Pulitzer Prize, and the National Book Critics Circle Award: *Self-Portrait in a Convex Mirror*. Those prizes and the book itself helped put Ashbery on the literary map, so that he could no longer be summarily dismissed as an eccentric aesthete turning out brilliant but inaccessible work. Readers began to look more closely at what Ashbery was saying and to embrace his message (however complex) as never before.

"Self-Portrait in a Convex Mirror," the title poem, is a brilliant piece of autobiographical writing that does not reveal gritty details of Ashbery's personal life so much as his opinions about art and its power to transform the artist. Self-portraits are as old as art itself, but Ashbery as an art critic and former expatriate had encountered some especially powerful examples of the genre. He must have encountered the great self-portraits of Rembrandt van Rijn and Vincent van Gogh, but the particular work that inspired this poem is a famous masterpiece of the High Renaissance, *Self-Portrait in a Convex Mirror* (1524) by Parmigianino (Girolamo Francesco Maria Mazzola), which hangs in the Kunsthistorisches Museum in Vienna. Ashbery tells the reader that he encountered Parmigianino's famous painting in the summer of 1959, during a visit to Vienna. Parmigianino's self-portrait is uniquely circular in overall form and, as the title suggests, resulted from the artist's close inspection of his visage in a convex mirror, an optical device that creates interesting distortions of scale and distance. Parmigianino's hand, for example, is grossly exaggerated and dominates the foreground of the painting, while his head seems undersized and nearly childlike. It is possible that the Italian artist's childlike appearance appealed to Ashbery because it reminded him of the snapshot of little John Ashbery that had inspired his earlier, much shorter autobiographical lyric, "The Picture of Little J. A. in a Prospect of Flowers."

It is in the nature of self-portraits, then, to conceal and reveal simultaneously—hence the appropriateness of the convex mirror, whose powers of transformation and distortion apply equally to Parmigianino and Ashbery. The poet begins the poem by quoting and paying homage to Giorgio Vasari, the first great art critic. (Ashbery too had been an art critic at the time he saw the painting in Venice.) Vasari explains the complicated arrangements that preceded Parmigianino's actual painting: the use of a barber's convex mirror and the necessity of having a carpenter prepare the circular wooden substratum of the painting. These operations are mere preliminaries, however, to the much more important work of the eyes themselves once the painting has been set up. The eyes cannot penetrate the artificial depth created by this strange mirroring device; therefore, everything that results is a kind of speculation—a word that derives from the Latin word for mirror, *speculum*, as Ashbery points out. Thus in the self-portrait one kind of "mirroring" leads to another; what one sees is not precisely what is there. To hold the paradox in the mind is to enter the world of the artist.

The argument that Ashbery then goes on to develop may perhaps be summarized by the adagelike statement that stability (or order) can be maintained in the presence of instability (or chaos). The movements of time, weather, table tennis balls, and tree branches are all potential elements for the synthesizing and harmonizing power of art, no matter if it distorts something in the process. Perhaps the greatest distortion is that of stability; the stable simply cannot be found in nature, as Isaac Newton showed through his laws of thermodynamics. It is only in the mirror of art (a symbol also favored by William Shakespeare) that stability, order, and form may thrive. Since all art is by definition artificial, then, stability also is an artifice.

Nevertheless, artistic stability is all the artist and the race of human beings can rely on to reveal meaning in an otherwise meaningless space. So Parmigianino's Renaissance painting, like all art, is applicable to all future generations, and Ashbery borrows Parmigianino's technique of mirroring until the world seems to spin around him in a merry-go-round of papers, books, windows, trees, photographs, and desks, and "real life" itself becomes a kind of trick painting. Addressing the Italian master, Ashbery admits that the "uniform substance" or order in his life derives from the Italian genius: "My guide in these matters is your self."

He goes on to quote a contemporary art critic, Sydney Freedberg, who finds the idealized beauty and formal feeling of Parmigianino's self-portrait to depend on the very chaos Ashbery had earlier described. For Freedberg this instability is a collection of bizarre, unsettling aspects of reality that somehow the painting enfolds and harmonizes.

Readers might at this point recall similar discussions—though in radically different language—by John Keats, especially in his great meditation on art, "Ode on a Grecian Urn," which asks the reader to accept art precisely because it transforms the chaos and changeability of human life. Ultimately, this process results in a complete fusion of truth (or reality) and beauty (or art), in Keats's formulation. Ashbery is not Keats, but one has to note the similar posture of the two poets, both contemplating the power of art, both commencing with an art object (the Grecian urn and the Italian self-portrait) and concluding on a note of affirmation. For Ashbery, the power of art is not only magnificent but terrifying, like a pistol primed for Russian roulette with only one bullet in the chamber. Art has the potential to "kill" our old perceptions. Some people might consider this power to be only a dream, but for Ashbery the power remains, and art becomes a kind of "waking dream" in the same unhappy world of human beings that Keats evokes in "Ode on a Grecian Urn." Even in the city, which Ashbery imagines as an insect with multifaceted eyes, art somehow survives. He envisions each person as a potential artist holding a symbolic piece of chalk, ready to begin a new self-portrait.

HOUSEBOAT DAYS

Ashbery continues with this more accessible (and essentially more affirmative) kind of poetry in *Houseboat Days*, the title poem of which likens the mind and its vast storehouse of memory to a boardinghouse that is open to everyone, taking in boarders of every possible type and description. This metaphorical way of describing the sensory, intellectual, and imaginative powers of human beings is a valuable clue for understanding another poem in the volume, one of Ashbery's wittiest and most polished performances, "Daffy Duck in Hollywood," a poem that manages to be tender, lyrical, comic, outrageous, and serious without losing its sense of direction.

An obscure opera serves as a kind of grid or structural framework for this rather free-wheeling poem. The poem begins with a stupefyingly absurd collection of mental odds and ends, the flotsam and jetsam of a highly cultured and sophisticated mind that also appreciates the artifacts of popular culture: an Italian opera, Rumford's Baking Powder, Speedy Gonzales, Daffy Duck, Elmer Fudd, the Gadsden Purchase, Anaheim(California), pornographic photographs, and the comic-strip character Skeezix. All these apparent irrelevancies are entirely relevant, because they illustrate the random nature of the mind, its identity as a stream of consciousness. However, these items are also a kind of dodge or subterfuge to block out images of a significant other, possibly a lover. Because of the odd way the mind works through the principle of association, however, these same cartoonlike images also remind the narrator of that other person.

As in so many of his other poems, Ashbery is again insisting that the only reality is the one human beings make, and he concludes by wisely noting that no one knows all the dimensions of this mental life or where the parts fit in. The goal, in Ashbery's opinion, is to keep "ambling" on; thus, each person might remain "intrigued" and open to all the extravagant invitations of life. The mind, with its interminable image making, is strangely cut off from life, but when used properly (that is, aesthetically) it can lay hold of the abundant and unanticipated gifts that always surround and endow impoverished human beings.

A WAVE

This optimistic vein is apparent in most of *A Wave* but especially in the title poem, which seems to contrast crests of positive feelings with troughs of despair. The poem is a long discursive work in which Ashbery creates variations on one essential theme: that a fundamental feeling of security (not to be confused with superficial happiness), a deep and abiding sense of the goodness of life, can, in fact, sustain the person through the pain that life inevitably brings. In this poem, human beings do have final control of their destiny because they are supported by something powerfully akin to older notions of grace or faith. Having this power or "balm," as Ashbery terms it, no one is ever really stripped of autonomy: "we cannot be really naked/ Having this explanation."

APRIL GALLEONS

This mood of sustained hope continues in the exquisitely lyrical *April Galleons*, a book that, like *Houseboat Days*, relies on the metaphor of a boat as a vehicle for psychological as well as physical travel. Included is "Ice Storm," a poem that is highly original yet somehow manages to echo Robert Frost (especially "Birches" and "Design"). As Frost did in "Birches," Ashbery describes winter ice in glittering detail. As Frost did in "Design," Ashbery questions the fate of small things that are out of their accustomed places, such as the rose he stumbles on, growing beside a path entirely out of season.

However, none of these matters disturbs him fundamentally, because he is beginning to get his "bearings in this gloom and see how [he] could improve on the distraught situation all around me, in the darkness and tarnished earth."

AND THE STARS WERE SHINING

Ashbery's wit and virtuosity are often noted by critics, yet his humanity and intelligence are equally important facets of his work. In *And the Stars Were Shining*, this fact becomes readily apparent when in many of the poems his wisdom of age is blended with a great and tender sadness and bursts of wit and vitality. The title poem harks back to the long poems of another age—Roman numerals mark its sections and its cadences recall a past era—but its direct and relaxed language brings it firmly into the late twentieth century. There are fifty-seven more poems in the volume, displaying Ashbery's characteristic wryness and filled with tragicomic snapshots of our time. The works are also philosophical, as he endeavors to find amusement as well as pain in his autumnal themed poems, including the title poem and "Token Resistance."

YOUR NAME HERE

The title of *Your Name Here* aptly hints at the volume's rambunctious, arbitrary themes and pell-mell performances: Poems include "Frogs and Gospels," "Full Tilt," "Here We Go Looby," "Amnesia Goes to the Ball," and "A Star Belched." While his poetic themes are capricious and whimsical, Ashbery's language is intricate, tightly constructed, rhythmic, and sinuous, with a serious undercurrent of memory, time, loss, angst, and desire. Thus, his tone is at once melancholic and comedic, best demonstrated in "What Is Written."

WHERE SHALL I WANDER

Ashbery is reported to have once said that his ambition was "to produce a poem that the critic cannot even talk about." Most of Ashbery's readers would probably agree that he has satisfied this ambition, although some of the poems in *Where Shall I Wander* are more accessible. For example, "Interesting People of Newfoundland" is quite easy to talk about, with its roll call of characters like Larry, who performed foolishly on street corners, and the Russian who said he was a grand duke—and may have been. Doc Hanks was a good "sawbones" when he was not completely drunk; even half drunk he could perform "decent cranial surgery." Walsh's department store had teas and little cakes and rare sherries from all over. The population was small: "But for all that/ we loved each other and had interesting times." Altogether different in conception, "Novelty Love Trot" is hardly transparent, but it musters some explicable philosophical commentary. The poet's taste in books runs to biographies and cultural studies; in music, he likes Liszt's Consolations, "though I've never been consoled/ by them." In the poet's view, for most people, religion is about going to Hell: "I'm probably the only American/

/ who thinks he's going to heaven," but first there is "the steep decline/ into a declivity."

The title of the prose piece "From China to Peru" comes from the first two lines of Samuel Johnson's *The Vanity of Human Wishes* (1749), an imitation of Juvenal's tenth satire: "Let observation with extensive view,/ Survey Mankind, from China to Peru." The vanity of the title stands out clearly in Ashbery's version as the speaker finds himself "taunted" for his dark woolen suit when he arrives at some trivial social occasion where the men appear dressed "to go off on a safari." His only recourse is to the bar, where the "unnerving" events around him make him eager for the cocktail hour. The coherence of this satire then dissolves into a typical Ashbery riff on Japan declaring war on Austro-Hungary and his failure to track down a weather report. "The Red Easel" has a rhymed counterpart in "The Bled Weasel," a *jeu d'esprit* that exemplifies the kind of opaque collection of apparently random lines that frustrates so many readers. No weasel appears in the poem but a caterpillar shows up, "Erect on its parasol," while "Glow-worms circulated/ under the trees, confirmed [whatever 'confirmed' means] by whimpering Dobermans." This frivolity collapses, appropriately, in a "crazy quilt of expired pageantry."

A WORLDLY COUNTRY

The title poem of *A Worldly Country*, written in long lines worked into couplets, tells of a city that is riotous by day, with "insane clocks" and "the scent of manure in the municipal parterre." Chickens and geese enjoy the leftover bonbons, but even though "all hell broke loose" in the day, all was calm again by evening. The poet's musings lead him to a moral: "And just as waves are anchored to the bottom of the sea/ we must reach the shallows before God cuts us free." In "Autumn Tea Leaves," it is a partial eclipse that violates the normal day, but the poet cannot discern "what is special about this helix." These phenomena raise questions: What blanket will be sufficient for a freezing night? The dancers who celebrated the celestial occasion revealed "faces/ and senses of humor." However, when it all ended, who knows how many cakes were served, "or leaves collected/ in the hollow of a stump"?

In the fifteen four-line stanzas of "Phantoum," the second line of each stanza is repeated as the first line of the next, with other patterns sneaked in as the stanzas proceed. For example, in stanza 5, the second line, "The auks were squawking, the emus shrieking," becomes line 1 of stanza 6. Little Orphan Annie's adoptive father, Daddy Warbucks, makes a guest appearance in stanza 9 ("Daddy Warbucks was sad, but kept his reasons to himself") with no appreciable gain to the plotless but amiable verses.

A line from Auden's poem "At Last the Secret Is Out" provides the title "The Hand-shake, the Cough, the Kiss," and it is tempting to interpret the secret as Auden's homosexuality. Even though nothing in the poem speaks directly to a sexual theme, stanza 3 encourages speculation: "We risked it anyway,/ out on the ice where it darkens/ and seems to whisper/ from down below. Watch out, it's the Snow Queen. . . ." The poem then evolves into the poet's reminiscences of childhood in the unnamed "port city of his birth," where he was something of a boy wonder, "the local amateur historian." Rambling thoughts about childhood and the city lead to an apparent climax to the poet's relationship with a coworker in the television industry, a man identified only as "him": "look,/ if that's all you can bring to the table, why are we here?" The speaker concludes his critique by lamenting "an academy/ where losers file past, and the present is unredeemed,/ and all fruits are in season." The poems in this volume show no fading of the wit and bright phrasing of the works first published nearly half a century earlier.

OTHER MAJOR WORKS

LONG FICTION: *A Nest of Ninnies*, 1969 (with James Schuyler).

PLAYS: *Everyman*, pr. 1951; *The Heroes*, pr. 1952; *The Compromise: Or, Queen of the Carabou*, pr. 1956; *The Philosopher*, pb. 1964; *Three Plays*, 1978.

NONFICTION: *The Poetic Medium of W. H. Auden*, 1949 (senior thesis); *Reported Sightings: Art Chronicles, 1957-1987*, 1989; *Other Traditions*, 2000; *John Ashbery in Conversation with Mark Ford*, 2003; *Selected Prose*, 2004.

TRANSLATIONS: *Melville*, 1960 (of Jean-Jacques Mayoux); *Murder in Montarte*, 1960 (of Noel Vixon); *The Deadlier Sex*, 1961 (of Genevieve Manceron); *Alberto Giacometti*, 1962 (of Jacques Dupin); *The Landscape Is Behind the Door*, 1994 (of Pierre Martory); *Giacometti: Three Essays*, 2002 (of Dupin); *The Recitation of Forgetting*, 2003 (of Franck André Jamme).

EDITED TEXT: *Best American Poetry, 1988*, 1988.

BIBLIOGRAPHY

Ashbery, John. "John Ashbery in Conversation with Mark Ford." Interview by Mark Ford. In *Seven American Poets in Conversation: John Ashbery, Donald Hall, Anthony Hecht, Donald Justice, Charles Simic, W. D. Snodgrass, Richard Wilbur*, edited by Peter Dale, Philip Hoy, and J. D. McClatchy. London: Between the Lines, 2008. Ashbery talks about his life and works, including his influences.

_____. "A Kind of Musical Spa." Interview by Craig Burnett. *Frieze* 85 (September, 2004). Ashbery identifies and discusses some of his favorite writers—Ronald Firbank, André Breton, and Frank O'Hara. He praises Guy Maddin's films and says he hated writing art criticism.

Bloom, Harold, ed. *John Ashbery: Comprehensive Research and Study Guide*. Philadelphia: Chelsea House, 2004. Overview of Ashbery's published work, discussing his form, complex linguistics, and vision.

Herd, David. *John Ashbery and American Poetry*. New York: Palgrave, 2000. Herd chronicles Ashbery's poetic career, analyzing his continuities, differences, and improvements over time.

Lehman, David. *The Last Avant-Garde: The Making of the New York School of Poets*.

New York: Doubleday, 1998. Chronicle of New York School of poets, closely tracing Ashbery's life and analyzing elements contributing to the backdrop of his poetry.

MacArthur, Marit J. *The American Landscape in the Poetry of Frost, Bishop, and Ashbery: The House Abandoned*. New York: Palgrave Macmillan, 2008. Examines the poetry of Ashbery, Robert Frost, and Elizabeth Bishop, noting that all three had the subject of the abandoned house.

Malinowska, Barbara. *Dynamics of Being, Space, and Time in the Poetry of Czesław Miłosz and John Ashbery*. New York: Peter Lang, 2000. Malinowska provides a challenging discussion of poetic visions of reality in the works of Miłosz and Ashbery. She works with Martin Heidegger's philosophy of phenomenology and applies key Heideggerian terms—Dasein, space, time, and culture—to explore the reality created by or alluded to in their writings. Jargon heavy but useful.

Milne, Ira Mark, ed. *Poetry for Students*. Vol. 28. Detroit: Thomson/Gale Group, 2008. Contains an analysis of Ashbery's "Self-Portrait in a Convex Mirror."

Shoptaw, John. *On the Outside Looking Out: John Ashbery's Poetry*. Cambridge, Mass.: Harvard University Press, 1994. Abundant and detailed information about Ashbery's life, publication history, and manuscripts make the book valuable. It offers an intriguing but perhaps overworked and insufficiently proven argument that Ashbery's elusiveness derives from his homosexuality.

Vendler, Helen. "Toying with Words." Review of *Plainsphere. The New York Times Book Review*, December 13, 2009, p. 14. Vendler reviews the collection dedicated to Ashbery's partner, David Kermani. She notes his wordplay and praises his lyric poems.

Vincent, John Emil. *John Ashbery and You: His Later Books*. Athens: University of Georgia Press, 2007. Examines *And the Stars Were Shining*, *Your Name Here*, and other later works by Ashbery.

Daniel L. Guillory; Philip K. Jason; Sarah Hilbert
Updated by Frank Day

ROBERT BLY

Born: Madison, Minnesota; December 23, 1926

OTHER LITERARY FORMS

Robert Bly has been a prolific critic, translator, and anthologist. His work in these areas complements his poetic accomplishments and was a significant influence on the internationalization of the literary community in the last third of the twentieth century. His most important works include translations of the poems of Georg Trakl, Juan Ramón Jiménez, Pablo Neruda, Tomas Tranströmer, Federico García Lorca, Jalāl al-Dīn Rūmī, Kabir, and Antonio Machado. He has also called attention to the work of other poets through anthologies: *News of the Universe: Poems of Twofold Consciousness* (1980),

The Winged Life: The Poetic Voice of Henry David Thoreau (1986), *The Rag and Bone Shop of the Heart: Poems for Men* (1993), and *The Soul Is Here for Its Own Joy: Sacred Poems from Many Cultures* (1995).

Bly's writings about the practice of poetry have been published as *Leaping Poetry: An Idea with Poems and Translations* (1975) and *American Poetry: Wildness and Domesticity* (1990). His social criticism has ranged from *A Poetry Reading Against the Vietnam War* (1966; with David Ray) to *Iron John: A Book About Men* (1990), the best seller that became a primer for the men's movement of the 1990's. It was followed by similarly controversial studies, including *The Spirit Boy and the Insatiable Soul* (1994) and *The Sibling Society* (1996).

ACHIEVEMENTS

Robert Bly is the central poet of his generation. His wide-ranging achievements in poetry, criticism, and translation, as well as his work as editor and itinerant apologist for poetry and various social causes, have made him one of the most conspicuous, ubiquitous, and controversial poets in the United States since the mid-1960's. His significance and influence extend well beyond his own work.

Bly's various accomplishments have been rewarded by a Fulbright Fellowship for translation (1956-1957), the Amy Lowell Traveling Fellowship (1964), two Guggenheim Fellowships (1965 and 1972), a Rockefeller Foundation grant (1967), and a National Institute of Arts and Letters Award (1966). In 1968, *The Light Around the Body*, his most controversial collection of poetry, won the National Book Award. Bly received the McKnight Distinguished Artist Award (2000) and the Minnesota Book Award (2002) for *The Night Abraham Called to the Stars*. In 2008, his poem "War and Childhood," won the Theodore Roethke Prize from *Poetry Northwest*.

BIOGRAPHY

Born in the small farming community of Madison, Minnesota, Robert Elwood Bly grew up, as he said, a "Lutheran Boy-god." He attended a one-room school in his early years. Upon graduation from high school, he enlisted in the U.S. Navy, where he first became interested in poetry. After the war, Bly enrolled at St. Olaf's College in Northfield, Minnesota, but after only one year there, he transferred to Harvard University. At Harvard, he read "the dominant books" of contemporary American poetry, associated with other young writers (among them John Ashbery, Frank O'Hara, Kenneth Koch, Adrienne Rich, and Donald Hall), worked on *The Harvard Advocate* (which he edited in his senior year), delivered the class poem, and graduated magna cum laude in 1950.

Having decided to be a poet and seeking solitude, Bly moved back to Minnesota; then, in 1951, still "longing for 'the depths,'" he moved to New York City, where he lived alone for several years, reading widely and writing his early poems. In 1953, he moved to Cambridge, Massachusetts, and in 1954 to Iowa City, where he enrolled in the creative writing program at the University of Iowa. His M.A. thesis consisted of a short collection of poems titled "Steps Toward Poverty and Death" (1956). Bly was married to Carolyn McLean in 1955, and in 1956, they moved to Oslo, Norway, via a Fulbright grant. In Norway, Bly sought out his family roots, read widely, and translated contemporary Norwegian poetry.

In 1957, back in Minnesota, living on the family farm, Bly continued his work as a translator. In 1958, he founded a magazine, *The Fifties* (which would become *The Sixties*, *The Seventies*, and *The Eighties*), in which he published his translations and early literary criticism. He did not publish his first book of poetry, "Poems for the Ascension of J. P. Morgan," but in 1962, he published two books: *The Lion's Tail and Eyes* (written with his friends James Wright and William Duffy), and *Silence in the Snowy Fields*, his first independent book of poetry.

By the mid-1960's, Bly was actively engaged in the anti-Vietnam War movement. He and David Ray formed a group called American Writers Against the Vietnam War, and they published an anthology titled *A Poetry Reading Against the Vietnam War* (1966). Bly attended draft card turn-ins, and he demonstrated at the Pentagon in 1967. When his second book of poems, *The Light Around the Body*—filled with his outspoken poems against the war—won the National Book Award in 1968, Bly donated the prize money to the draft resistance.

During the 1970's, Bly's interests and activities diversified considerably. He studied Sigmund Freud, Carl Jung, Eastern meditation, myths and fairy tales, philosophy, and psychology. He organized conferences on "Great Mother and New Father" culture and consciousness. Bly's poetry, social commentary, and literary criticism during this period reflected his wide-ranging interests. By this point in his career, he said, he believed that he had "gotten about half-way to the great poem."

In 1979, Bly and his wife of more than twenty-five years were divorced. In 1980, he was married to Ruth Ray; they moved to Moose Lake, Minnesota, and lived there for ten years before moving to Minneapolis in 1990.

During the 1980's and 1990's, Bly continued to work at a rapid pace, writing and publishing widely in several genres, translating, giving readings throughout the United States and overseas, and holding meetings and seminars for groups of women and men. His books during and since the 1980's document, as well as anything, the life and activities of this exceedingly visible and yet, ultimately, extremely private individual.

ANALYSIS

Since Robert Bly has habitually brought his wide-ranging interests in literary history, myth, fairy tales, philosophy, psychology, politics, social concerns, and poetry past and present into his own work, his poetry reflects these interests and is enriched by them. Furthermore, because he has been prolific and unsystematic, even at times seemingly self-contradictory, he is extremely difficult to categorize and analyze. Nevertheless, it is possible—indeed necessary—to consider Bly's poetry in terms of the series of various phases it has gone through. These phases, although they are also reflected in Bly's other writings and involvements, are most evident in his poetry.

SILENCE IN THE SNOWY FIELDS

Bly's first published book of poetry, *Silence in the Snowy Fields*, remains one of the best examples of his deepest obsession: the notion that a personal, private, almost mystical aura adheres to and inheres with the simplest things in the universe—old boards, for example, or a snowflake fallen into a horse's mane. These things, observed in the silence of contemplation and set down honestly and simply in poems, may, Bly believes, inform human beings anew of some sense of complicity, even communion, they have always had with the world, but have forgotten. Bly's focus has caused his work to be labeled Deep Image poetry. In a 1981 essay, "Recognizing Image as a Form of Intelligence," he explained the term's application to his work: "When a poet creates a true image, he is gaining knowledge; he is bringing up into consciousness a connection that has been largely forgotten." In this sense, these early poems provide the reader with the re-created experience of Bly's own epiphanic moments in the silences of "snowy fields," and they become his means of sharing such silences with his readers.

The epigraph to *Silence in the Snowy Fields*, "We are all asleep in the outward man," from the seventeenth century German mystic Jacob Boehme, points up both the structural and the thematic principles on which Bly builds his book. The three sections of the book suggest a literal and a mental journey. The second, central section, "Awakening," contains twenty-three of the forty-four poems in the book and serves as a structural and thematic transition from "Eleven Poems of Solitude," the first section, to the final section, "Silence on the Roads," which sends both book and reader, via the central "awakening," outward into the world. The solitude and contemplative silence of this first book, then, prepare both poet and reader for the larger world of Bly's work.

THE LIGHT AROUND THE BODY

The way the world impinges on private life is immediately evident in Bly's next book, *The Light Around the Body*. This is his most famous (or for some, most infamous) book. Like *Silence in the Snowy Fields*, *The Light Around the Body* shows the strong influence of Boehme (four of the five sections of the book have epigraphs from Boehme), especially in terms of the dichotomy of the inward and the outward person, the "two languages," one might argue, of Bly's first two books. If *Silence in the Snowy Fields* deals primarily with the inward being, clearly the focus of *The Light Around the Body* is on the outward being—here seen specifically in a world at war.

The Light Around the Body was published in the midst of the American obsession with the Vietnam War, and most of the poems in it are concerned with that war, directly or indirectly. The third section of the book (following sections titled "The Two Worlds" and "The Various Arts of Poverty and Cruelty") is specifically titled "The Vietnam War." This is the most definitive, the most outspoken and condemnatory group of poems—by Bly or anyone else—on the war in Vietnam. Bly reserves his harshest criticism for American involvement in the war. He does not mince words, and he names names: "Men like [Dean] Rusk are not men:/ They are bombs waiting to be loaded in a darkened hangar" ("Asian Peace Offers Rejected Without Publication").

Perhaps the most famous poem Bly has written is also his most definitive criticism of the Vietnam War. In "Counting Small-Boned Bodies," the speaker of the poem has been charged with keeping the grisly count of war casualties to be reported on the evening news. Shocked by the mounting death tolls, he finds himself trying to imagine ways to minimize these terrifying statistics. The refrain that runs through the poem is, "If we could only make the bodies smaller." The implication is that if the bodies could be made smaller, then people might, through some insane logic, be able to argue the war away. Bly's poems in *The Light Around the Body* ensure that the war will never be forgotten or forgiven.

The last two sections of *The Light Around the Body* ("In Praise of Grief" and "A Body Not Yet Born") move back "inward" from the "outward" world of the war, just as the first two sections of the book had moved "outward" from the "inward" world of *Silence in the Snowy Fields*. Since the war, however, this new inward world can never again ignore or fail to acknowledge the outward world. Therefore, Bly writes "in praise of grief" as a way of getting through, psychologically speaking, both outward and inward conflicts.

The first three poems of the fourth section of the book define a progression back toward a place of rest, calm, peace. In the third poem, the body is described as "awakening" again and finding "nourishment" in the death scenes it has witnessed. Such a psychic regeneration, which parallels the inevitable regeneration of nature after a battle, is what is needed to repair the damage the war has done if people are to be restored to full human nature. Thus, in the final section of the book, although the new body is not yet fully born, it is moving toward birth, or rebirth.

Although *The Light Around the Body* will no doubt be most often remembered for its overt antiwar poems, from the point of view of Bly's developing poetic philosophy, it is best seen as a description of the transition from the outer world back into the inner world.

SLEEPERS JOINING HANDS

The psychological movement first suggested and then begun in *The Light Around the Body* is followed further inward by Bly's next important book, *Sleepers Joining Hands*. This book contains three distinctly different sections. The first section consists of a series of short lyric poems. Beginning with "Six Winter Privacy Poems," it comes to a climax with a long poem, "The Teeth Mother Naked at Last," Bly's final, psychological response to the war in Vietnam.

The second section of *Sleepers Joining Hands* consists of an essay in which Bly documents many of the philosophical ideas and psychological themes with which he has long been obsessed and which he has addressed (and will continue to address) both in his poetry and in his criticism. Bly here summarizes his thinking in terms of Jungian psychology, father and mother consciousness, the theory of the three brains, and other ideas that he groups together as "mad generalizations." This essay, although it is far from systematic, remains an important summary of the sources of many of Bly's most important poems and ideas.

Thus, although *Sleepers Joining Hands* does not contain Bly's most important poetry, it does deal with most of the elements of the literary theory behind that poetry, and it is an extremely important book. In the central essay, Bly describes in detail the way in which "mother consciousness" has come to replace "father consciousness" during the last several centuries. Four "force fields" make up the Great Mother (or Magna Mater), which, according to Bly, is now "moving again in the psyche." The Teeth Mother, one of these force fields, attempts to destroy psychic life. She has been most evident in the Vietnam War and has caused the "inward" harm that that war has brought to the world. "The Teeth Mother Naked at Last," the climactic poem in the first section of *Sleepers Joining Hands*, like the earlier antiwar poems in *The Light Around the Body*, describes the conditions of psychic reality in terms of the presence of the Teeth Mother. It argues that once the Teeth Mother is acknowledged (made "naked at last"), she can be dealt with and responded to, and then the outward physical world can be effectively reconnected with the inward psychic or spiritual world.

"Sleepers Joining Hands," the long title poem that constitutes the collection's third section, is an elaborate and challenging poem, a kind of dream journal or a journey, with overt Jungian trappings. Thematically, it shifts back and forth between dreamed and awakened states. These thematic shifts are evidenced in the structure of the poem. The poem as a whole is a kind of religious quest based in large part on the Prodigal Son story—one of the great paradigms of the journey motif in Western culture. At the end of the poem, bringing to climax so many of his themes, Bly provides "An Extra Joyful Chorus for Those/ Who Have Read This Far" in which "all the sleepers in the world join hands."

THE MORNING GLORY

The next several books in Bly's canon consist of prose poems. Bly believes that when a culture begins to lose sight of specific goals, it moves dangerously close to abstraction, and that such abstraction is reflected in the poetry of the time. Prose poetry, then, often appears as a way of avoiding too much abstraction. Whether this theory holds up historically or not, it certainly can be made to apply in Bly's case, even if only after the fact—the theory having been invented to explain the practice. Certainly, there is ample reason to think that Bly believed that his own work, influenced by the events the world was witnessing, was moving dangerously toward "abstraction," perhaps most conspicuously so in *Sleepers Joining Hands*. For whatever reason, then, Bly turned, in the middle of his career, to the genre of the prose poem. His prose poems of this period are extremely strong work, arguably some of his strongest poetry.

The two most important collections of prose poems are *The Morning Glory* (which includes as its central section the ten-poem sequence "Point Reyes Poems," published separately the year before, and one of the most powerful sequences of poems Bly has written) and *This Body Is Made of Camphor and Gopherwood*. All these prose poems move "deeply into the visible," as the old occult saying Bly quotes as epigraph to *The Morning Glory* demands, and they are poems written "in a low voice to someone he is sure is listening," as Bly suggested they should be in his essay "What the Prose Poem Carries with It" (1977).

The Morning Glory, like *Silence in the Snowy Fields*, contains forty-four poems. It suggests of a new beginning in Bly's career. These poems follow a rather typical pattern. They begin in offhanded ways, frequently with the speaker alone outdoors, prepared, through his openness to all possibilities, for whatever he may find there. The poems, then, are journeys; they move from the known to the unknown. Even so, what can be learned from them is often difficult to analyze, especially since Bly frequently only suggests what it is or might be. Indeed, often it seems to be something that the body comes to know and only later—if at all—the mind comprehends. In this sense these are poems of preparation, and they frequently imply apocalyptic possibilities.

The Morning Glory ends with several poems that describe transformations. One of the most important of these, "Christmas Eve Service at Midnight at St. Michael's," involves the personal life of the poet, who, six months after his only brother has been killed in an automobile accident, attends a Christmas Eve service with his parents. He and his parents take Communion together and hear the Christian message. Coming so soon after his brother's death, however, the message is "confusing," since the poet knows that "we take our bodies with us when we go." The poem ends in a reverie of transfiguration in which a man (both brother and Christ), with a chest wound, flies out and off over the water like a large bird.

THIS BODY IS MADE OF CAMPHOR AND GOPHERWOOD

The basic "religious" theme begun in *The Morning Glory* is continued in *This Body Is Made of Camphor and Gopherwood*. Here Bly writes overtly religious meditations, thus picking up again the aura of the sacred that has been important in his work since the beginning. Indeed, this book immediately reminds the reader of *Silence in the Snowy Fields*, both thematically and in terms of Bly's basic source material.

There are twenty poems in *This Body Is Made of Camphor and Gopherwood*; they are divided into two thematic units. The first ten poems describe, often through dreams, visions, or dream-visions, "what is missing." Not surprisingly, given this theme, Bly frequently uses the metaphor of sleep and awakening. Indeed, the first poem in the book begins, "When I wake." This awakening is both a literal and an imaginative or metaphoric awakening, and it signals at the outset the book's chief concern.

The second section of the book is filled with intensely heightened, almost ecstatic, visionary poems. The crucial transitional poems in *This Body Is Made of Camphor and Gopherwood*—which is itself a crucial transition in Bly's canon—are "Walking to the Next Farm" and "The Origin of the Praise of God." "Walking to the Next Farm" describes the culmination of the transition "this body" has been going through as the poet, his eyes wild, feels "as if a new body were rising" within him. This new body and the energy it contains are further described and defined in the other central poem, "The Origin of the Praise of God." It begins with exactly the same words that begin several other poems in this book: "My friend, this body." This poem, in the words of Ralph J. Mills, Jr., "a visionary hymn to the body, . . . dramatizes [the] experience of the inner deity" and thus is the paradigm of the entire prose-poem sequence. By the end of the book, this visionary, mystical, yet still fully physical body is finally fully formed and is "ready to sing" both the poems already heard and the poems ahead.

THIS TREE WILL BE HERE FOR A THOUSAND YEARS

This Tree Will Be Here for a Thousand Years is a second collection of "snowy fields" poems. Bly said that it should be understood as a companion volume to *Silence in the Snowy Fields*. In this sense, then, *This Tree Will Be Here for a Thousand Years* is a specific, overt attempt on Bly's part to return to his beginnings. Just as it is a return, however, it is also a new beginning in the middle of his career. Bly is clearly a poet obsessed with a need for constant renewal, and in many ways each of his books, although taking a different direction, also retraces each earlier journey from a different vantage point.

Perhaps it is not surprising that, although *This Tree Will Be Here for a Thousand Years* is a new beginning for Bly, it is also a darker beginning, a darker journey than the journey he took in *Silence in the Snowy Fields*. Here the journey envisions its end. This, then, is the book of a man facing his mortality, his death, and walking confidently toward it. As Bly puts it in one of these poems, "there are eternities near." At the same time, there is the inevitable paradox that poems outlive the poet who has written them— and, thus, even poems that speak of death outlive the death of their speaker.

THE MAN IN THE BLACK COAT TURNS

Two later books may be seen as companions to each other: *The Man in the Black Coat Turns* and *Loving a Woman in Two Worlds*. Like *This Tree Will Be Here for a Thousand Years*, these books circle back to Bly's beginnings at the same time that they set out on new journeys. Furthermore, these books are among the most personal and private he has published, and thus they are particularly immediate and revealing.

The Man in the Black Coat Turns is divided into three sections, the central section, as in *The Morning Glory* and *This Body Is Made of Camphor and Gopherwood*, being made up of prose poems. The prose poems here, however, are different from their predecessors in being much more clearly related to Bly's personal experiences; as he says in the first of them, "Many times in poems I have escaped—from myself. . . . Now more and more I long for what I cannot escape from" ("Eleven O'Clock at Night").

More than anything else, the poems in *The Man in the Black Coat Turns* are poems about men. The dominant theme of the book is the father-son relationship. This theme and its association with the book's title is immediately, and doubly, announced at the outset of the book, in the first two poems, "Snowbanks North of the House" and "For My Son, Noah, Ten Years Old," as Bly works the lines of relationship through the generations of his own family: from his father to himself as son, then, as father, through himself to his own son, Noah. The third poem, "The Prodigal Son," places the personal family references into a larger context by relating them to the father and son in the New Testament parable. In the final poem in this first section of the book, "Mourning Pablo Neruda," Bly extends the father-son relationship again—this time to include one of his own important poetic "father figures," Pablo Neruda, a poet he has often translated.

The final section of *The Man in the Black Coat Turns* draws all these themes together in "The Grief of Men." This poem is clearly the climactic thesis piece for the whole book. There are, however, a number of important poems grouped together in this last section: "Words Rising," "A Meditation on Philosophy," "My Father's Wedding," "Fifty Males Sitting Together," "Crazy Carlson's Meadow," and "Kneeling Down to Look into a Culvert." In the last of these poems, via the account of a symbolic, ritualized sacrificial death, the poet completes his preparations for another new life.

LOVING A WOMAN IN TWO WORLDS

The poems of *Loving a Woman in Two Worlds* are, for the most part, short—almost half of them contain fewer than eight lines, and eleven of them are only four lines long. Technically speaking, however, this book contains poems in most of the forms and with most of the themes Bly has worked in and with throughout his career. In this sense, the collection is rather a tour de force. Many of these poems of *Loving a Woman in Two Worlds* are love poems, and some of them are quite explicitly sexual. The book can be read in terms of the stages of a love relationship. These are poems that focus on the female, on the male and female together, and on the way the man and the woman together share "a third body" beyond themselves, a body they have made "a promise to love."

This book thus charts another version of the "body not yet born" journey with which Bly began his poetry. In the final poem in *Loving a Woman in Two Worlds*, Bly, speaking not only to one individual, but also to all of his readers, writes, "I love you with what in me is unfinished.// . . . with what . . . is still/ changing."

SELECTED POEMS

In *Selected Poems*, in addition to poems from all of Bly's previous major collections (some of the poems have been revised, in some cases extensively), he has included some early, previously uncollected poems. A brief essay introduces each of the sectional groupings of this book. *Selected Poems*, then, is a compact, convenient collection, and it succinctly represents Bly in the many individual phases of his work.

MORNING POEMS

Bly's later collections continue to develop, without any loss of power, his distinctive vision and manner. *Morning Poems* is something of a departure, revealing a rich vein of humor and growing out of the discipline of writing a poem a day. These poems capture the speaker's amazement at newness, the splendor of reawakening, but they also do their share of mourning. In an unexpected and powerful sequence, Bly presents an imagined interchange with Wallace Stevens, a somewhat surprising father figure for Bly.

THE NIGHT ABRAHAM CALLED TO THE STARS

In *The Night Abraham Called to the Stars*, Bly employs the leaps of the ghazal, a poetic form developed in Persia and Arabia in the seventh century in which each stanza exists as an independent poem. At once seemingly and simultaneously opened to everything and closed upon themselves, these poems, with their leaping shifts of focus, underscore the great range of Bly's curiosity, his reasonable argument against reason, his quest for a mystical simplicity and unity that does not deny the power of the particular. Biblical allusions permeate this collection, as do historical references and legends. As ever, Bly oscillates between the generic and the generative.

MY SENTENCE WAS A THOUSAND YEARS OF JOY

My Sentence Was a Thousand Years of Joy continues Bly's exploration of the ghazal. The ghazal consists of a series of seemingly discontinuous tercets that thematically turn the real into the surreal and often conflate the inward world of consciousness with elements of the outward world by forcing them to collide or collapse into one another. The poem concludes with a moment of insight or illumination. Since, traditionally, the poet's name is mentioned at the end of a ghazal (usually in the penultimate line), the illumination that the poem elicits provides a eureka moment for the poet and for the reader simultaneously. As such, the ghazal, with its series of statements and questions—which often enough seem to be a series of non sequiturs—is an almost inevitable form for Bly. Indeed, it would seem to be the natural outgrowth of the kind of "leaping" poetry that has been his most conspicuous trademark since the beginning of his career.

My Sentence Was a Thousand Years of Joy consists of forty-eight ghazals, each made up of six tercets. Keeping to the tradition of the ghazal, Bly includes his own name (typically at the outset of the final tercet) in one third of these poems. In addition to satisfying the demands of the ghazal, several of the poems also make use of conspicuous patterns of repetition. For instance, each tercet of "The Blind Tobit" ends with the phrase "so many times," while in "Growing Wings," nine of the lines (exactly one half of the poem) begin with the phrase "It's all right."

Bly weaves references to numerous literary and historical figures through these poems. There are explicit references to Plato, Paul Cézanne, Neruda, Anna Akhmatova, Freud, Thoreau, Frederick Douglass, Rembrandt, Johannes Brahms, Søren Kierkegaard, Franz Kafka, Herman Melville, Johann Sebastian Bach and Robinson Jeffers, as well as many others. It is as if Bly wishes to include the whole of the world in this book and to stress the universality of these otherwise seemingly personal and private poems.

Ultimately, however, the vivid metaphors and all the allusions serve to support Bly's overarching theme of the transience of life and the need for joy even in the midst of the pain and pitfalls of existence. This theme is perhaps made most obvious in two poems ("Brahms" and "Stealing Sugar from the Castle"), both of which directly allude to a well-known passage in Saint Bede the Venerable's *Ecclesiastical History of the English People* (731). In it, Bede compares human life to the flight of a sparrow through a hall during a wintery day. The bird flies in at one door and out another, experiencing only momentary comfort and safety from the winter's storm before it vanishes into the unknown from whence it came. In these short lyrics, Bly extends the "brief moment" of the ghazal to create a "sentence" that becomes the "thousand years of joy" alluded to both in his title and in the final line of the book.

OTHER MAJOR WORKS

NONFICTION: *Leaping Poetry: An Idea with Poems and Translations*, 1975; *Talking All Morning*, 1980; *American Poetry: Wildness and Domesticity*, 1990; *Iron John: A Book About Men*, 1990; *The Spirit Boy and the Insatiable Soul*, 1994; *The Sibling Society*, 1996; *The Maiden King: The Reunion of Masculine and Feminine*, 1998 (with Marion Woodman).

TRANSLATIONS: *Twenty Poems of Georg Trakl*, 1961 (with James Wright); *Forty Poems*, 1967 (of Juan Ramón Jiménez); *Hunger*, 1967 (of Knut Hamsun's novel); *I Do Best Alone at Night*, 1968 (of Gunnar Ekelöf); *Twenty Poems of Pablo Neruda*, 1968 (with Wright); *Neruda and Vallejo: Selected Poems*, 1971; *Ten Sonnets to Orpheus*, 1972 (of Rainer Maria Rilke); *Lorca and Jiménez: Selected Poems*, 1973; *Friends, You Drank Some Darkness: Three Swedish Poets, Harry Martinson, Gunnar Ekelöf, and Tomas Tranströmer*, 1975; *The Kabir Book: Forty-four of the Ecstatic Poems of Kabir*, 1977; *Twenty Poems*, 1977 (of Rolf Jacobsen); *Truth Barriers*, 1980 (of Tomas Tranströmer); *Selected Poems of Rainer Maria Rilke*, 1981; *Times Alone: Selected Poems of Antonio Machado*, 1983; *The Half-Finished Heaven: The Best Poems of Tomas*

Tranströmer, 2001; *The Roads Have Come to an End Now: Selected and Last Poems of Rolf Jacobsen*, 2001 (with Roger Greenwald and Robert Hedin); *Horace: The Odes*, 2002 (with others; J. D. McClatchy, editor); *The Winged Energy of Delight: Selected Translations*, 2004; *The Angels Knocking on the Tavern Door: Thirty Poems of Hafez*, 2008 (with Leonard Lewisohn); *The Dream We Carry: Selected and Last Poems of Olav H. Hauge*, 2008 (with Robert Hedin).

EDITED TEXTS: *A Poetry Reading Against the Vietnam War*, 1966 (with David Ray); *News of the Universe: Poems of Twofold Consciousness*, 1980; *The Winged Life: The Poetic Voice of Henry David Thoreau*, 1986; *The Rag and Bone Shop of the Heart: Poems for Men*, 1993; *The Soul Is Here for Its Own Joy: Sacred Poems from Many Cultures*, 1995.

BIBLIOGRAPHY

Davis, William V. *Critical Essays on Robert Bly*. New York: G. K. Hall, 1992. An excellent selection of essays, reviews, and overviews of Bly's work, together with a detailed critical introduction documenting his career to the early 1990's.

_____. *Robert Bly: The Poet and His Critics*. Columbia, S.C.: Camden House, 1994. This chronological study traces the twists and turns of Bly's reputation, accounting for both the aesthetic and nonaesthetic components of critical judgments.

_____. *Understanding Robert Bly*. Columbia: University of South Carolina Press, 1988. A book-length study of Bly's poetic career, geared to an understanding of the chronological development and ongoing significance of Bly's life and work through a detailed analysis of individual poems and an in-depth consideration of each of the major books. Includes a primary and secondary bibliography and an index.

Harris, Victoria Frenkel. *The Incorporative Consciousness of Robert Bly*. Carbondale: Southern Illinois University Press, 1992. This in-depth study examines Bly's poetry in terms of his idea of universalizing poetic processes. Contains an exhaustive bibliography of work by and about Bly.

Hertzel, Laurie. "The Poet Comes Home: Reckless Youth. War protester. Translator. Men's-Movement Guru. Through It All, Robert Bly's Enduring Passion Has Been for His Poetry." *Star Tribune*, September 27, 2009, p. E1. This profile of Bly looks at his life and his love for poetry, which he says should have a quality of "wildness." Discusses his Madison home and the men's conferences that his book spawned.

Jones, Richard, and Kate Daniels, eds. *Of Solitude and Silence: Writings on Robert Bly*. Boston: Beacon Press, 1981. A miscellany of materials on Bly, including essays, memoirs, poems, notes, and documents, as well as new poems and translations by Bly. Includes an extensive primary and secondary bibliography.

Nelson, Howard. *Robert Bly: An Introduction to the Poetry*. New York: Columbia University Press, 1984. A detailed critical introduction to and analysis of Bly's career through *The Man in the Black Coat Turns*, stressing the ways in which his various theories illuminate his poems. Includes a chronology of his life, a primary and secondary bibliography, and an index.

Peseroff, Joyce, ed. *Robert Bly: When Sleepers Awake*. Ann Arbor: University of Michigan Press, 1984. A substantial collection of reviews and essays (including several previously unpublished) on Bly and his work through *The Man in the Black Coat Turns*. Includes an extensive primary and secondary bibliography but no index.

Quetchenbach, Bernard W. *Back from the Far Field: American Nature Poetry in the Late Twentieth Century*. Charlottesville: University of Virginia Press, 2000. In a lengthy chapter on Bly, the author explores Bly's concept of a true humanity, including his insistence that consciousness be linked to the environment or disaster will follow.

Sugg, Richard P. *Robert Bly*. Boston: Twayne, 1986. An introductory critical overview of Bly's work and career stressing a Jungian interpretation, through *The Man in the Black Coat Turns*. Includes a selected bibliography of primary and secondary sources and an index.

William V. Davis; Philip K. Jason
Updated by Davis

YVES BONNEFOY

Born: Tours, France; June 24, 1923

PRINCIPAL POETRY

Traité du pianiste, 1946
Anti-Platon, 1947
Du mouvement et de l'immobilité de Douve, 1953 (*On the Motion and Immobility of Douve*, 1968)
Hier régnant désert, 1958
Pierre écrite, 1965 (*Words in Stone*, 1976)
Selected Poems, 1968
Dans le leurre du seuil, 1975 (*The Lure of the Threshold*, 1985)
L'Ordalie, 1975
Rue traversière, 1977
Trois remarques sur la couleur, 1977
Poèmes, 1978
Poems, 1959-1975, 1985
Things Dying, Things Newborn: Selected Poems, 1985
Ce qui fut sans lumière, 1987 (*In the Shadow's Light*, 1991)
Début et fin de la neige, 1991
Early Poems, 1947-1959, 1991
New and Selected Poems, 1995
Le Cœur-espace, 2001
Les Planches courbes, 2001 (*The Curved Planks*, 2006)

OTHER LITERARY FORMS

Yves Bonnefoy (BAWN-foy) has distinguished himself in the fields of art criticism and literary criticism. He is also renowned for his translations of William Shakespeare's plays into French. His essays on art span the entire range from Byzantine to contemporary, from studies of the Renaissance and the Baroque to such works as Bonnefoy's *Alberto Giacometti: Biographie d'une œuvre* (1991; *Alberto Giacometti: A Biography of His Work*, 1991), on the twentieth century Italian sculptor. Bonnefoy is not simply an academic critic; some of his most moving prose writing is that which ties the experience of the artist to the interior experience of the imaginative writer. In *L'Arrière-pays* (1972; the back country), for example, he combines insightful discussions of classical Renaissance paintings with meditations on the sources of inspiration he draws from his own childhood. The title (which brings to mind *arrière-plan*, the background in a painting) allows for an extended meditation on the figures in the backgrounds of classic paintings and the feeling of well-being that Bonnefoy has experienced in his childhood and in his many travels.

This interior experience is Bonnefoy's major focus in his literary criticism as well, from the essays in *L'Improbable et autres essais* (1959, 1980; "The Improbable" and other essays) to the monograph *Rimbaud par luimême* (1961; *Rimbaud*, 1973) to the collections *Le Nuage rouge* (1977; the red cloud) and *La Présence et l'image* (1983; the presence of the image). Bonnefoy returns again and again to the idea that the images a poet uses, while in some sense unreal, are able to lead the reader to what he calls the "true place" of poetry. Thus the line "Ô Saisons, ô châteaux" (oh seasons, oh castles), which begins the famous poem by Rimbaud, becomes for Bonnefoy both a utopian dream and a reality that can be reached through language.

The philosophical issues that the poet locates in his artistic and literary researches are, in turn, fed back into his poetry, with the result that the poetry and the critical works come to mirror each other's concerns. His collection of lectures, *Lieux et destins de l'image: Un Cours de poétique au Collège de France, 1981-1993* (1999) is a compilation of his poetics.

ACHIEVEMENTS

Yves Bonnefoy is one of the most highly admired poets to reach maturity in France in the post-World War II period, and many would identify him as the most important French poet-intellectual at the turn of the twenty-first century. His early work had the character of being challenging and even hermetic, but it struck a chord with a whole generation of readers and poets. His poetry has always maintained the quality of being highly meditated and serious in purpose. While his preoccupations are philosophical—death, the existence of the loved one, the place of truth—his poetic language is highly imaged and moves equally in the realms of beauty and truth.

The close association Bonnefoy has always maintained with visual artists who are his contemporaries has given him a high prominence in the art world as well. Though he maintains a teaching position in literature, he has tended more and more in his later career to pursue his interests in art and the theory of culture. His writings on art are prized both for what they say about individual artists and for the high level of reflection they bring to the subject of creativity.

Bonnefoy's nomination to the chair of comparative studies of the poetic function at the Collège de France in 1981 confirmed his position as one of France's leading poets and intellectual figures. A regular affiliation with Yale University and visiting professorships at other American universities ensured Bonnefoy's prominence among American academic circles as well; he was awarded an honorary doctorate by the University of Chicago in 1988. He was also honored, in 1992, with an exhibition of his manuscripts and other documents at the Bibliothèque Nationale, Paris. His many other awards include the Grand Prix de Poésie from the French Academy (1981), the Grand Prix

Société des Gens de Lettres (1987), the Bennett Award from *Hudson Review* (1988), the Bourse Goncourt (1991), the Prix Balzac (1995), the Prix Del Duca (1995), the Prix National de Poésie (1996), the Masaoka Shiki International Haiku Grand Prize (2000), and the Franz Kafka Prize in 2007.

BIOGRAPHY

Yves Bonnefoy was born on June 24, 1923, in Tours, France. His mother was a nurse and later a schoolteacher; his father died when Bonnefoy was thirteen. His early life was divided between the working-class surroundings of Tours and the rural home of his maternal grandfather, a schoolteacher and natural intellectual who had a great influence on the boy, and in many ways, Bonnefoy considered his grandparents' home his own true home. He studied in Tours and at the University of Poitiers, primarily chemistry and mathematics.

Bonnefoy moved to Paris in 1943 to continue his scientific studies, but once there he found that his interests moved more toward poetry and philosophy. He sought out what remained of the Surrealist group—André Breton in particular—and although his formal association with it was brief, he formed many important friendships with young artists and poets, including Egyptian francophone Surrealist Georges Henin. Bonnefoy married, edited a review, and studied widely different subjects, eventually taking a degree by writing a thesis on Charles Baudelaire and Søren Kierkegaard. This combined interest in poetry and philosophy has remained with him during his entire career.

Bonnefoy accepted jobs in Paris as a mathematics and science teacher, escaping the draft for "compulsory labor" during World War II because the war ended before he was called. During this time, he was reading the poetry of Paul Éluard, whose influence, according to Bonnefoy, "tempered the influences of Baudelaire and [Paul] Valéry." In politics, he was a Trotskyite, and having broken away from Breton's influence, he and friends edited a journal, *La Revolution, la nuit*. He was poor during these years and benefited from his sister's influence as a secretary at the Sorbonne in that she found him a job there, which allowed him to attend lectures and apply for research grants. These, in turn, allowed him to travel. He began to publish his poems and art criticism as well. Subsequently, he earned a living teaching at universities, both in France and in the United States, becoming a professor of comparative poetics and department chair at the Collège de France in 1981.

In 1981, at the inauguration ceremony of his being named a department chair at the Collège de France, his highly publicized lecture "La Présence et l'image" (presence and the image) became a major statement for his particular style of intermixing philosophy and literature. Throughout his working career, Bonnefoy has traveled widely, especially in pursuing his growing interest in art, art history, and the theory of culture. He is recognized as one of the most important poets of his generation. In 2001, he published a collection of early Surrealist texts, *Le Cœur-espace* (heart space), and a new collection of poetry, *The Curved Planks*. In 2005, *The Curved Planks* was included among the texts of the *baccalauréat*. He published his work on Francisco de Goya's paintings *Goya, les peintures noires*, in 2006. Bonnefoy examines the relationship between prose and poetry in *La Longue Chaîne de l'ancre* (2008; the anchor's long chain).

ANALYSIS

From the beginning of his poetic career, Yves Bonnefoy's work has sounded the note of a serious pursuit of the truths that language reveals. His early divergence from the later figures of the Surrealist movement in France seems to have been provoked by what he perceived as a lack of purpose in their pursuits. For Bonnefoy, poetic language, above all, is a place or a function that grants access to the truths of existence. The path to those truths may of necessity be a difficult one, but once one is on that path, there can be no turning back. Bonnefoy is a highly original and engaging writer of criticism exploring these issues, but it has always been in his poetry that he has sought to discover their ground.

ANTI-PLATON

The early works *Anti-Platon* (against Plato) and *On the Motion and Immobility of Douve* introduce his poetry of high seriousness and announce a break from Surrealist practice. If Bonnefoy declares early his stance, it is to restore the real dimension of experience, this object here and now, against any sort of Platonic ideal. By extension, the importance of this real object leads Bonnefoy to examine the importance of this real life, here and now, in its affective dimension. Perhaps paradoxically, the importance of life emerges fully only when one confronts the actual death of someone. The poems in the second collection take up this theme; they are also the poems that established Bonnefoy as one of the most important poets of his generation.

ON THE MOTION AND IMMOBILITY OF DOUVE

The figure of Douve in Bonnefoy's second collection, *On the Motion and Immobility of Douve*, is based on a young girl of his acquaintance who died a sudden and tragic death. (He gives her name only in a later collection.) As the form in the poems alternates between highly organized quatrains and looser prose-poem utterances, so the investigation in the poems moves between the image of the dead young woman and death in general. As the sequence progresses, the speaker seeks to discover his own destiny based on an identification with the words of the young woman. In this work, death is present in the form of a person who is no longer there. She is troubling, however, because she poses the question of existence, of essence, of being. It is by means of this questioning that the poet discovers his own means of expression. More even than the torment of mourning, there seems to emerge the injunction to silence as the most accurate means of representing death.

There is a progression, then, in the poems of this collection as far as the identification of the poet with the figure of the dead woman by means of her speech. When she speaks in the first part of the collection, it is in the past tense, and she speaks of natural forces, wind and cold. The poet-speaker sees her, however, and as a result there is a separation, the separation of death. The only way to overcome this separation is by the identification involved in speaking. Changing to the present tense, the speaker says, "Douve je parle en toi" ("Douve, I speak in you"):

> Et si grand soit le froid qui monte de ton être,
> Si brûlant soit le gel de notre intimité,
> Douve, je parle en toi; et je t'enserre
> Dans l'acte de connaître et de nommer.

> (And though great cold rises in your being,
> However burning the frost of our intimacy
> Douve, I speak in you; and I enshroud you
> In the act of knowing and of naming.)

This is one of the strong moments of identification and the beginning of poetic creation, as Bonnefoy describes it in his essay "The Act and the Place of Poetry": "So Dante who has lost her, will *name* Beatrice." Over against the natural forces that are imaged here as present because of her death, the act of naming and of knowing restores a certain presence to the lost loved one. Even so, this is a first stage: Far from being consoling, it leads the poet to the point of anguish.

The central part of the collection, "Douve parle" (Douve speaks), begins with this identification in speaking, "ce cri sur moi vient de moi" ("this cry above me comes from me"). Paradoxically, in the series of poems bearing the title "Douve speaks," she finishes by saying: "Que le verbe s'éteigne" ("Let the verb be extinguished"). That which one must recognize in oneself as death surpasses the function of speech. The poet enters this region of contradiction when he says: "Je parle dans ton sang" ("I speak in your blood").

This progression reaches its completion in the injunction, which the figure of the woman makes to the speaker, to remain silent. The poem that begins "Mais que se taise" ("but that one be silent") requires silence above all of the one "Qui parle pour moi" ("who speaks for me"). In the following poems, she is even more direct, saying simply, "Tais-toi" ("remain silent; shut up"). The speaker finds himself in a place of radical transformations, during a time of anguish and of struggle: "Quand la lumière enfin s'est faite vent et nuit" ("When the light at last has become wind and night"). The figure of the dead woman has led the speaker to a privileged place of being, where the poet not only recognizes himself in his own expression but also is faced with his own anguish, his authentic attitude toward death.

HIER RÉGNANT DÉSERT

The collected edition of Bonnefoy's poetry *Poèmes* of 1978 added three important collections to the earlier work, *Hier régnant désert* (yesterday the desert reigning), *Words in Stone*, and *The Lure of the Threshold*. These collections continue to explore the areas mapped out by Bonnefoy's earlier work. The tone is serious and the subject matter highly philosophical. Death is a constant presence and is confronted continually for what it tells about existence. In *Hier régnant désert*, Bonnefoy returns again to the Douve figure, although here, at least in one poem, she is named—Kathleen Ferrier. The same contradictions between a conflicted natural universe and a tragic sense of human destiny are confronted again in the elemental terms: face, voice. Whereas to see an image of the dead young woman leads to separation, an identification with her voice allows the poet to discover his own utterance. As he says in "À la voix de Kathleen Ferrier" ("to the voice of Kathleen Ferrier"):

> Je célèbre la voix mêlée de couleur grise
> Qui hésite aux lointains du chant qui s'est perdu
> Comme si au delà de toute forme pure
> Tremblât un autre chant et le seul absolu.

> (I celebrate the voice mixed with grey color
> Which hesitates in the sung distances of what is lost
> As if beyond every pure form
> Trembled another song and the only absolute.)

This poem is more insistently philosophical than any examined hereto. The voice that is celebrated seems to have lost all contact with the merely human as it moves toward the realms of pure being.

WORDS IN STONE

Even the poems ostensibly concerned with inanimate objects bear their burden of existence, as does this short poem from *Words in Stone*, "Une Pierre" (a stone):

> Il désirait, sans connaître,
> Il a péri, sans avoir.
> Arbres, fumées,
> Toutes lignes de vent et de déception
> Furent son gîte.
> Infiniment
> Il n'a étreint que sa mort.

> (It desired, without knowing
> It perished, without having.
> Trees, smoke,

All lines of wind and of deception
Were its shelter
Infinitely
It only grasped its death.)

This deceptively simple poem about a stone carries a weight of thought and image balanced off in a skillful suspension. It may or may not carry direct reference to Jean-Paul Sartre's existential philosophy, which affirmed the stone's interiority and self-identity over time while denying these same inherent qualities to the human subject. Bonnefoy's turn on the idea here is to introject the tragic sense into the simple being of the stone. Bereft of the human qualities of knowing or having, it was at one with nature and alone to face death.

POÈMES

Bonnefoy's later poems in *Poèmes* trace a dialectic between the tragic sense of human destiny, as presented in Douve's words, and the introjected tragedy of nature examined in the poem from *Words in Stone*. The difference in the later works is in their form. From the short, often highly formal, verse of his early career, Bonnefoy here moves to a more expanded utterance. Though the poems are longer, however, there is a greater degree of fragmentation. It is as though the silence that was so important thematically in the speech of Douve has been refigured in the form of the poem itself. From the highly wrought, lapidary form of the early work has emerged a laconic style, hinting at what the speaker cannot say.

Into the atmosphere of charged philosophical speculation—in effect, a dialogue between being and nonbeing—Bonnefoy brings a new element of disjunction and, ultimately, of mystery, as in these lines from "Deux Barques" (two boats): "Étoiles, répandues./ Le ciel, un lit défait, une naissance." ("Stars, spread out./ The sky, an unmade bed, a birth.") The traditional analysis of metaphor in terms of "tenor" and "vehicle" becomes very difficult with lines such as these. How is one to decide what is the content of the statement and what is the rhetorical trapping? Here the stars could be the vehicle for an image having as its content the beginning of human life. In like manner, the heavens could be the content and the bed an image to describe the appearance of stars, with birth as an added metaphorical element. As this example makes clear, Bonnefoy's long meditations on the power of language to investigate the central issues of existence remain as intense in his later work as in his earlier poetry.

In all of Bonnefoy's work, an extremely restricted vocabulary is used to describe the conflicts between nature and human existence. Words such as "stone" and "fire," "wind" and "star," take on an elemental sense rather than being merely descriptive. These word elements are placed in the context of laconic statements, each statement offering but a hint of the overall movement in the poem. This overall movement in turn is established through the cumulative force of these elemental images placed into disjunctive and often contradictory sequences. Almost always, a mood of high seriousness is the result. The simplest language thus becomes a language of tragic dimensions. The elemental forces at work in the poem's image sequences reflect directly on the human dimension of existence. Bonnefoy places hard demands on the conceptual capabilities of his readers. He is clearly uninterested in easy sentiment or pleasing verses. His poetry presents a continual invitation to join in the struggle out of which the truths of existence emerge.

In the final poem of this collection, "L'Épars, l'indivisible" (the sparse, the indivisible), an anaphoric repetition is utilized, with the first word of most stanzas being "Oui" (yes). Under the general structuring principle of affirmation, the seemingly most opposite elements are joined. One section reads simply: "Oui, par la mort,/ Oui, par la vie sans fin" ("Yes, through death,/ Yes, through life without end"). Affirming opposites in this manner runs the risk of affirming nothing, but again the cumulative effect of the contradictions is to lead to a synthesis of values. Two sections later, the speaker states: "Oui, par même l'erreur,/ Qui va,// Oui, par le bonheur simple, la voix brisée." ("Yes, even through error,/ Which passes,// Yes, through simple happiness, the broken voice.") Bonnefoy does not seek easy resolution or unexamined pleasures. When he speaks of happiness in the same breath with a broken voice, however, the force of the image goes beyond the conceptual setting up of paradoxes. Happiness that leads to a broken voice is happiness that carries with it a strong emotion and the force of personal history. These deceptively simple images are weighted with complex and achieved emotion.

The figure of Bonnefoy the poet is closely allied to that of Bonnefoy the thinker. His researches into art, literature, and the sources of creativity in life history have always been motivated by a search for truth that can then find form and be expressed in his poetry. This is not to say that reading Bonnefoy's poetry is the equivalent of reading his essays and criticism or that the philosophical underpinnings of the works are presented in a predigested or easily digestible form. His highly imaged poems show a consistent concern for poetic image and emotion. As a result, the reality they possess is one that adds to experience. The highly wrought, imaginatively charged poems of Bonnefoy reveal the common origins of thinking and of poetry. By posing the central questions of existence, they are timeless. They are also of a pressing timeliness in that they recall the reader to being in the present.

LE CŒUR-ESPACE

Surrealism has played an important role in Bonnefoy's poetry, initially as a guide to poetical expression and subsequently as a point of departure into a poetical expression that rejects much of Surrealism. Surrealism fascinated Bonnefoy as a young poet because it proposed to dissolve the barrier between the conscious and unconscious and to make known the true reality. Surrealism, however, with its automatic writing and its lack of control of language in creation of images and its reliance on the imagined, soon began to lose its authenticity as poetical expression for him. Bonnefoy has stated that *Le Cœur-espace*, while still Surrealist in its form and content, was the poetical writing that freed him from the confines of Surrealism. While writing the text, he discovered what he refers to as a rhythm in the images that played a greater role in revealing the true than the images themselves. For Bonnefoy, language moved beyond the function of merely a tool for expressing image to become the object of his poetical questioning and expression.

Le Cœur-espace is a poetry dominated by images that in the Surrealist tradition hope to reveal that which is true, the reality beyond the reality of everyday life. Written in 1945, when Europe was in the middle of the destruction of World War II, the poetry's imagery is harsh and unsettling. It relies on fantasy and imagination. The poet is in a garden, he cries out in pain as death's branches claw his face. The gray stars of midday reign anguish on him. Appearing is a poor woman with a Gorgon head and carrying a child. Other images include pikes of wind, the earth deforming a frozen face in mirrors, and the terrible silence of the garden. These images contrast sharply with those found in Bonnefoy's later poetry.

THE CURVED PLANKS

The Curved Planks takes its name from the récit or short story "The Curved Planks" included in the collection. In this short tale, written in a repetitive, almost staccato language, Bonnefoy recounts the passage of the child to adulthood and the void that develops as the individual moves from the presence of childhood to that of adulthood. The passeur (ferryman) as the inevitable flow of time and change in a mortal's life transfers his passenger from one shore of the river to the other, from childhood to adulthood. Bonnefoy also anchors human existence in the terrestrial. The ferryman explains to the child that to be a father, one must have a house, and that he (the ferryman) is not real, but only the ferryman, the symbol or metaphor of passage.

However, while the human being cannot actually physically return to the past, the events of the past can be taken into the mind or subconscious and relived as memories or dreams. The poems of "La Pluie d'eté" ("Summer Rain") and "La Maison natale" ("The House Where I Was Born") treat past experiences of the poet as memories recalled or awakened in dreams. Images of water predominate in the poems. Just as water carries the child from childhood to adulthood in "The Curved Planks," water invades and transforms the childhood home of the poems of "The House Where I was Born." In "Summer Rain," water in the form of rain refreshes human beings: it gives brilliance and translucence to objects. Water and rain become transparent veils which alter sensory perception.

"Jeter les pierres" ("Throwing Stones"), the final group of texts of *The Curved Planks* is composed of three texts that have totally abandoned traditional poetic form for the prose form of the story or essay. However, the language of the texts is neither narrative nor explanatory in the traditional sense. It is a language of images, the language of poetry. This relationship between prose and poetry becomes one of the major areas of Bonnefoy's further research into language as means and as object.

The poems also reaffirm Bonnefoy's beliefs in the mortality of the human being, of his close ties to the earth. The poems collected under the title "Que ce monde demeure!" ("Let This World Endure!") both through their imagery and the rhythm of their verse witness the poet's joy in the terrestrial, in being and being part of the earth. Throughout the collection, the rhythm of the language plays an important role. The poetical strength of the images comes as much from their rhythm as from their portent.

LA LONGUE CHAÎNE DE L'ANCRE

La Longue chaîne de l'ancre contains a mix of genres. It addresses Bonnefoy's research and further development of his poetics after the publication of *The Curved Planks*. The major theme of the collection is the relationship between poetry and prose. He treats both the place and the act of poetry, two fields of investigation that have been of concern to him during his entire involvement with language and writing. He examines the relationship of poetry to the language of the short story and to that of theater, both of which are prose writing. Bonnefoy's language in both the "prose" writings and the poems is carried along by a rhythm that makes it fluid and enlarges the concept of the poetic such that poetry and prose subconsciously become one language.

Bonnefoy continues to employ simple images drawn from that which surrounds the human being, and this reiterates the importance of presence. He uses an image of wheel tracks in wet earth that shine slightly to define the act of writing poetry. However, for Bonnefoy, the place of poetry, of thought, of creativity remains in the subconscious. There life and thought meet. In his imagery of the anchor, its chain, and the boat to which it is attached, he attests that the boat cannot anchor in the earth for it desires and seeks another space that is the realm of dream or subconscious. The long anchor chain anchors the human spirit or consciousness in the subconscious. It is that which makes poetry, writing, painting, or any act of creativity more than merely descriptive.

OTHER MAJOR WORKS

NONFICTION: *Peintures murales de la France gothique*, 1954; *L'Improbable et autres essais*, 1959, 1980; *Rimbaud par luimême*, 1961 (*Rimbaud*, 1973); *La Seconde Simplicité*, 1961; *Miró*, 1964 (English translation, 1967); *La Poésie française et le principe d'identité*, 1967; *Un Rêve fait à Mantoue*, 1967; *Rome 1630: L'Horizon du premier baroque*, 1970; *L'Arrière- pays*, 1972; *Le Nuage rouge*, 1977; *Entretiens sur la poésie*, 1981; *La Présence et l'image*, 1983; *La Vérité de Parole*, 1988; *The Act and the Place of Poetry: Selected Essays*, 1989; *Alberto Giacometti: Biographie d'une œuvre*, 1991 (*Alberto Giacometti: A Biography of His Work*, 1991); *La Vie errante, suivi de Une autre Époque de l'écriture*, 1993; *Dessin, couleur, et lumière*, 1995; *The Lure and the Truth of Painting: Selected Essays on Art*, 1995; *Théâtre et poésie: Shakespeare et Yeats*, 1998; *Lieux et destins de l'image: Un Cours de poétique au Collège de France, 1981-1993*, 1999; *La Communauté des traducteurs*, 2000; *Le Poète et le flot mouvant des multitudes: Paris pour Nerval et pour Baudelaire*, 2003; *Shakespeare and the French Poet*, 2004; *Le Secret de la pénultième*, 2005; *Goya, les peintures noires*, 2006; *La Stratégie de l'éingme: Piero dela Francesca, la Flagellation du Christ*, 2006; *Ce qui alarma Paul Celan*, 2007; *Le Grand espace*, 2008.

TRANSLATIONS: *Une Chemise de nuit de flanelle*, 1951 (of Leonora Carrington); *I Henri IV, Jules César, Hamlet, Le Conte d'hiver, Vénus et Adonis, Le Viol de Lucrèce*, 1957-1960 (6 volumes; of William Shakespeare); *Le Roi Lear, Roméo et Juliette, Macbeth*, 1965-1983 (5 volumes; of Shakespeare); *La Tempête*, 1997 (of Shakespeare).

EDITED TEXTS: *Dictionnaire des mythologies et des religions des sociétés traditionnelles et du monde antique*, 1981 (*Mythologies*, 1991); *Greek and Egyptian Mythologies*, 1992; *Roman and European Mythologies*, 1992; *American, African, and Old European Mythologies*, 1993; *Asian Mythologies*, 1993.

MISCELLANEOUS: *La Longue Chaîne de l'ancre*, 2008 (includes poems and short stories).

BIBLIOGRAPHY

Caws, Mary Ann. *Yves Bonnefoy*. Boston: Twayne, 1984. A book-length work in English that introduces Bonnefoy's life and works to students. Bibliography.

Greene, Robert W. *Searching for Presence: Yves Bonnefoy's Writing on Art*. Amsterdam: Rodopi, 2004. Although focused on Bonnefoy's art criticism, the text deals with the notion of presence, which is also one of the main concerns of his poetics.

Grosholz, Emily. "Song, Rain, Snow: Translating the Poetry of Yves Bonnefoy." *Hudson Review* 61, no. 4 (Winter, 2009): 625-644. Examines the process of translation, presenting translations of several of his poems as examples.

Lawler, James. "'La Neige Piétinée est la seule rose': Poetry and Truth in Yves Bonnefoy." *L'Esprit Créateur* 32, no. 2 (Summer, 1992): 43-53. Analysis of his work.

Naughton, John T. *The Poetics of Yves Bonnefoy*. Chicago: University of Chicago Press, 1984. One of the few book-length studies in English devoted to Bonnefoy's poetics. Naughton's notes provide detailed information. Includes a bibliography of works by and about the poet and an index of names and titles.

Petterson, James. *Postwar Figures of "L'Ephémère": Yves Bonnefoy, Louis-René de Forêts, Jacques Dupin, André Du Bouchet*. Lewisburg, Pa.: Bucknell University Press, 2000. Discusses Bonnefoy and other postwar poets associated with the journal *L'Ephémère* (1966-1972).

Peter Baker; Gordon Walters; Christina J. Moose
Updated by Shawncey Webb

ANDRÉ BRETON

Born: Tinchebray, France; February 19, 1896
Died: Paris, France; September 28, 1966

OTHER LITERARY FORMS

André Breton (bruh-TOHN) published many experimental works during his career, some of which were written in collaboration with friends. *Les Champs magnétiques* (1921; *The Magnetic Fields*, 1985), the first Surrealist text to employ the technique of what came to be called automatic writing, was done with Philippe Soupault. *L'Immaculée Conception* (1930; immaculate conception), an attempt to simulate the thought processes of various types of insanity, was written with Paul Éluard. Among the basic Surrealist documents were several works by Breton alone, such as *Poisson soluble* (1924; soluble fish) and *Les Vases communicants* (1932; *Communicating Vessels*, 1990), which mixed lyrical elements with philosophical speculations cast in the form of prose, as well as the numerous polemical manifestos such as *Manifeste du surréalisme* (1924; *Manifesto of Surrealism*, 1969) and *Second Manifeste du surréalisme* (1930; *Second Manifesto of Surrealism*, 1969). Breton's numerous essays were also collected in three volumes: *Les Pas perdus* (1924; the lost steps), *Point du jour* (1934; *Break of Day*, 1999), and *Perspective cavalière* (1970). Convenient selections from Breton's prose in English translation have appeared in *Les Manifestes du surréalisme* (1955; *Manifestoes of Surrealism*, 1969), translated by Richard Seaver and Helen R. Lane, and *What Is Surrealism? Selected Writings* (1978), edited by Franklin Rosemont.

ACHIEVEMENTS

Above all, André Breton will be remembered as the founder and leader of the Surrealist movement. Of all the avant-garde movements that rocked the foundations of the arts at the beginning of the twentieth century, Surrealism has had perhaps the greatest and longest-lived impact. Surrealism, created in Paris in 1924 by Breton and a small group of friends, was the last inheritor of a long series of "isms," including Dadaism, German expressionism, French and Spanish cubism, Italian Futurism, and Anglo-American Imagism and Vorticism, which attempted to transform the conception of the world through artistic innovation. Under the leadership of Breton, Surrealism became the most mature expression of this developing sensibility, not only because of its relatively well developed underlying philosophy—which was both far-reaching and systematic in nature—but also because it eventually came to have the greatest international scope of all these movements and because it stimulated the production of a vast body of work of great diversity in all the major artistic genres—poetry, fiction, drama, philosophy, painting, sculpture, and film.

BIOGRAPHY

André Breton was born on February 19, 1896, in Tinchebray, a small inland town in the old French province of Normandy. The family soon moved, however, to the fishing port of Lorient, in Brittany, on the Atlantic coast of France. This seaside environment was particularly important later in the poet's life. When Breton first began to write in 1914, his highly imaginative lyrical poems expressed the wondrous abundance of nature and were often filled with images of sea life and other details evoking the maritime setting of his youth—which contrasted sharply with his life in Paris.

Breton was an only child, and his parents seemingly had an unusually strong influence on his personality. His father, who was a merchant, seems almost a prototype of the complacent, self-satisfied bourgeois that the Surrealists were later to attack as the epitome of the social conformity they rejected. Breton's mother, whom he described as straitlaced, puritanical, and harsh in her response to any suggestion of impropriety, must have also been responsible, to a large degree, for his later hatred of restraint and his provocative attitude toward anything he considered conventional.

Being the only child of a comfortably situated family, Breton had much attention lavished on him, and naturally, his parents had great ambitions for him. He attended school in Paris from 1907 until his graduation in 1912, entering the Sorbonne in 1913 to study medicine. This contact with medicine was also important for the later development of the poet and is reflected in Breton's diverse poetic vocabulary. Even more important, however, was the experience that resulted when Breton was sent to work at the neurological center of the hospital at Nantes during World War I instead of into combat. Breton's experiences as a medical assistant during the war—first at Nantes and later at the psychiatric center at Saint-Dizier, to which he was transferred in 1917—introduced the young, impressionable poet to the bizarre aberrations of mental illness.

During this period, Breton was exposed not only to the diverse forms of mental illness from which the soldiers suffered but also to the theories on which the practical measures used to treat them were based. Among the most important of these theories were those of Jean-Martin Charcot, Sigmund Freud, and Pierre Janet, each of which contributed an important element to the formulation of Breton's view of the operation, structure, and purpose of the human mind. From Charcot's work, Breton learned of the unlocking of the will through the use of hypnosis and saw some of the dramatic cures it was able to effect. From Freud's work, he learned about the existence of the unconscious, its role in determining mental health, and the method of dream interpretation by which one could reveal its secrets to the dreamer. From Janet's work, he learned about the existence of "psychic automatism" and the means by which it might be evoked—which eventually resulted in his own experiments with automatic writing.

These influences were reflected in three important ways in Breton's later work. First, they resulted in the two important prose experiments in automatic writing that he produced: *The Magnetic Fields*, written with Philippe Soupault, and *Poisson soluble*, which Breton created alone. The second product of his wartime experience was the novel *Nadja* (1928; English translation, 1960), which describes the encounter of an autobiographical persona with a mysterious woman who suffers a bizarre and debilitating psychosis. The third product of these influences was *L'Immaculée Conception*, a series of writings undertaken with Paul Éluard, with the purpose of simulating, in verbal form, the thought processes of various types of insanity.

Following the war, Breton came under the influence of Dadaism, which by then had moved its base of operation from Zurich to Paris. The heyday of Dada in Paris was brief, however, lasting from January of 1920 until July of 1923. In the meantime, beginning in May of 1921, Breton and some of his friends were forming a new group whose optimistic attitude toward life, experiments with new methods of literary composition, and increasingly systematic philosophical orientation was in marked contrast to Dada's attitude of nihilistic despair. Breton later called this period the intuitive phase of Surrealism, a phase that extended from May of 1921 until October of 1924, when the first *Manifesto of Surrealism* was published. The publication of this first manifesto established, in an explicit way, a new aesthetic and a profoundly optimistic, imaginative conception of the world which its author, Breton, named Surrealism. The intense period of Surrealist creative activity, which began at that time and continued unabated until the appearance of the *Second Manifesto of Surrealism* in 1930, Breton was later to call the reasoning phase of Surrealism. This period culminated in the appearance of *Communicating Vessels*, a series of lyrical philosophical discourses expressing in mature, fully developed form the central ideas of the Surrealist philosophy and aesthetic.

The period following 1930, the year of the second manifesto, was characterized by two developments. One of these was the Surrealists' increasing involvement with the

Communist International movement. The second development was, in a direct sense, an outgrowth of the first, for it was also during this period that Surrealism was disseminated on a worldwide scale and gained adherents outside Western Europe in many places where it was seen as the artistic concomitant of Marxist revolutionary philosophy. This period, which might be called, with some small injustice, the dogmatic phase of Surrealism, lasted until the outbreak of World War II. In 1941, Breton left France and lived for five years in New York. When he returned to Paris in 1946, Surrealism was effectively dead, although with those few friends of the original group who still remained, and with the growing support of countless other self-acknowledged "Surrealists" in many other countries where their dream had been carried, Breton lived on as the universally acknowledged magus of Surrealism until his death on September 28, 1966, in Paris.

ANALYSIS

André Breton's poetry forms a relatively small though important part of his total literary output, being dwarfed in quantity by his lengthy experiments in prose and his numerous polemical writings. His poetry, from the first published collection, *Mont de piété* (mount of piety), to his last major poetic work, *Ode to Charles Fourier*, shows a remarkable consistency of style. As a poet, Breton is best known for his remarkable imagery—which, at its best, expresses the powerful ability of the imagination to reconcile basic human drives and desires with the material conditions of reality and, at its worst, lapses into bizarre forms of irrationality that are incomprehensible to all but the poet himself.

In general terms, Breton's poetic imagery is characterized by comparisons that yoke together extremely disparate objects; by the sudden, sometimes violent shifting of context as the poet moves from one image to the next; and by an extremely indirect method of expressing comparisons between objects. It is these three qualities, above all, that give his poetic imagery the appearance of being spontaneous rather than deliberate. As critics have shown, however, much to Breton's credit as a poet, this initial impression is a misleading one.

Breton's imagery is reinforced by other prominent aspects of his style, one of which might be called devices of syntactic derangement. These devices range from the use of simple paradoxes involving logical and semantic contradictions, to syntactic ambiguity involving multiple or imprecise grammatical modification, to much more unsettling contradictions of reference—where the referent of a speech act is left unidentified, is deliberately misidentified, or is made ambiguous.

One other important element of Breton's style that helps support the dramatic effect of his poetic images on his readers is his diction, which is characterized by two principal traits. The first of these is the extremely wide range of his vocabulary, which frequently includes the use of words from anatomical, zoological, botanical, and technical contexts that are unfamiliar to most readers of poetry. The second important trait of his diction is the tendency to use words in specialized, atypical ways that emphasize (and often create) their figurative meanings over their denotations. These qualities have two important effects on Breton's work: The first helps make possible his imagery of violent contrasts, and the second is, to a large degree, responsible for the great difficulty his readers and translators encounter searching for paraphrasable or translatable meaning in his work.

Another element of Breton's style is his use of recurring themes and symbolic motifs, such as the revolver as a synecdochic image for rebellion or revolt of any kind. These recurring thematic and symbolic elements in Breton's work can frequently be used as contextual clues for interpreting his most difficult works.

The poetry of Breton expresses three key ideas—the liberating power of the imagination, the transformation of the material world into a utopian state, and the exploration of human potentiality through love—which recur, with increasing elaboration, throughout the course of his work and constitute the essence of his Surrealist vision.

POWER OF IMAGINATION

Breton's faith in the liberating power of the human imagination, although suggested and influenced by his contact with modern psychoanalytic thought, especially that of Freud on the operations of the unconscious, goes far beyond the notion of simply releasing the bound or "repressed" energies that is the therapeutic basis of psychoanalytic practice. For Breton, the unconscious is not an enclosed inner space, or reservoir, of trapped energy; it is, rather, the way out of the everyday world of material reality into the realm of the surreal. According to the Surrealists, this realm—where human reason and imagination no longer struggle against each other but function in harmony—is the ultimate reality, and each person's goal in life is to seek out continually the signs of this reality, which, when directly experienced, is capable of transforming the life of the person. Although Breton envisioned the realm of the surreal as accessible to all men who seek it, it was especially important for the artist, whose goal was to capture the fleeting traces of *le merveilleux* (the marvelous) in his writing.

The Surrealists recommended a number of different methods for attaining this experience. Two, in particular, are frequently used and referred to in Breton's work: the surrendering of the person to the *hasard objectif* ("objective chance") of the universe, and the evocation of the "primary processes" of the unconscious through such procedures as automatic writing. The first of these methods is illustrated well in "Au regard des divinités" ("In the Eyes of the Gods"), one of Breton's early poems from *Clair de terre* (the light of Earth):

> Shortly before midnight near the landing-stage
> If a dishevelled woman follows you, pay no attention.
> It's the blue. You need fear nothing of the blue.
> There'll be a tall blonde vase in a tree.

> The spire of the village of melted colors
> Will be your landmark. Take it easy,
> Remember. The dark geyser that hurls fern-tips
> Towards the sky greet
> Greets you.

This poem reads like, and in fact is intended to be, a set of instructions for encountering the marvelous through the technique of objective chance.

Breton's other primary technique for evoking the marvelous—using the unfettered association of ideas in the unconscious to produce automatic writing —is illustrated by "Au beau demi-jour" ("In the Lovely Half-light"), a poem from *L'Air de l'eau* (air of the water):

> In the lovely half-light of 1934
> The air was a splendid rose the colour of red mullet
> And the forest when I made ready to enter it
> Began with a tree that had cigarette-paper leaves
> For I was waiting for you. . . .

UTOPIAN IDEAL

Breton believed not only in the power of the creative imagination to transform the life of individuals but also in the possibility of transforming society itself into a Socialist utopia, and he came to believe that the Communist International movement was a means to that end. Breton's association with the Communist Party, which began about 1930, was an increasingly divisive force among the French Surrealists. Many who were willing to accept Surrealism's aesthetic and philosophical premises did not believe that this view of life could ever transform the material world of nations and societies. Breton saw this resistance against political involvement as an indication of insufficient commitment, while those who resisted engagement countered by emphasizing the restrictive nature of the Communist Party, its repressive disciplinary practices, and its hostility to artistic activity that did not directly further the interests of the party itself. Regardless of the problems it created for him, Breton never gave up this utopian faith, as the choice of subject for his last major poetic work, *Ode to Charles Fourier*, makes clear.

TRANSFORMATIVE POWER OF LOVE

The third key idea that informs Breton's poetry is one that, like his belief in the liberating power of the imagination, was shared by many of the Surrealists: the belief that romantic love was the means by which humans might establish an enduring link between the mundane world of material reality and the limitless, eternal world of surreality. At times, the mere presence of the beloved is enough to evoke such a response, and some of Breton's most moving poetry deals with this experience. The idea is expressed in two principal forms in Breton's love poetry. The first is the belief in woman as muse: The beloved becomes the source of contact with the realm of surreality, where, Breton's friend Paul Éluard (the greatest of the Surrealist love poets) wrote, "all transformations are possible." This belief is clearly expressed in two of Breton's best poems: the famous "catalog-poem" "Free Union," which celebrates the magical connection between the poet's beloved and the unspoiled world of nature, and "Fata Morgana," which celebrates the ecstatic elation of the poet at the advent of a new love. The second form taken by this belief in the magical power of love is the equation of poetic creation itself with sexual love, as in "Sur la route de San Romano" ("On the Road to San Romano"): "Poetry is made in a bed like love/ Its rumpled sheets are the dawn of things."

It was these three ideas—together with the support of countless writers, scattered across the world, who identified themselves with the Surrealist ideal—that sustained Breton throughout a career that lasted more than fifty years. Although Breton died in 1966, the beliefs that he helped to formulate and that he expressed so brilliantly in his own poetry continue to exist.

OTHER MAJOR WORKS

LONG FICTION: *Nadja*, 1928 (English translation, 1960).

NONFICTION: *Les Champs magnétiques*, 1921 (with Philippe Soupault; *The Magnetic Fields*, 1985); *Manifeste du surréalisme*, 1924 (*Manifesto of Surrealism*, 1969); *Les Pas perdus*, 1924; *Poisson soluble*, 1924; *Légitime Défense*, 1926; *Le Surréalisme et la peinture*, 1928, 1945, 1965; *L'Immaculée Conception*, 1930 (with Paul Éluard); *Second Manifeste du surréalisme*, 1930 (*Second Manifesto of Surrealism*, 1969); *Les Vases communicants*, 1932 (*Communicating Vessels*, 1990); *Point du jour*, 1934 (*Break of Day*, 1999); *Qu'est-ce que le surréalisme?*, 1934 (*What Is Surrealism?*, 1936); *L'Amour fou*, 1937 (*Mad Love*, 1987); *Prolégomènes à un troisième manifeste du surréalisme ou non*, 1942 (*Prolegomena to a Third Surrealist Manifesto or Not*, 1969); *Arcane 17*, 1944 (*Arcanum*, 1994); *Situation du surréalisme entre les deux guerres*, 1945; *Les Manifestes du surréalisme*, 1955 (*Manifestoes of Surrealism*, 1969); *Perspective cavalière*, 1970; *What Is Surrealism? Selected Writings*, 1978.

BIBLIOGRAPHY

Aspley, Keith. *Surrealism: The Road to the Absolute*. 3d ed. Chicago: University of Chicago Press, 1986. Updated with a new introduction. A critical history of Surrealist literature.

Balakian, Anna. *André Breton: Magus of Surrealism*. New York: Oxford University Press, 1971. A biography by an expert in Surrealist art and literature.

Benedikt, Michael. *The Poetry of Surrealism: An Anthology*. Boston: Little, Brown, 1975. With introduction, critical notes, and translations.

Breton, André. *Conversations: The Autobiography of Surrealism*. Translated and with an introduction by Mark Polizzotti. New York: Paragon House, 1993. Collection of interviews with Breton.

Carrouges, Michel. *André Breton and the Basic Concepts of Surrealism.* Tuscaloosa: University of Alabama Press, 1974. Biography and an introduction to Surrealism with bibliographic references.

Caws, Mary Ann. *André Breton.* Rev. ed. New York: Twayne, 1996. Caws provides practical analysis of individual works. The French is ably translated into readable English.

Petterson, James. *Poetry Proscribed: Twentieth-Century (Re)visions of the Trials of Poetry in France.* Lewisburg, Pa.: Bucknell University Press, 2008. Examines the relationship among poetry, politics, and culture in France, with a chapter on Breton.

Polizzotti, Mark. *Revolution of the Mind: The Life of André Breton.* New York: Farrar, Straus and Giroux, 1995. A thorough biography of the artist and poet highlighting his lifelong adherence to Surrealist principles even at the expense of personal relationships. With an extensive bibliography and index.

Steven E. Colburn

PAUL CELAN
Paul Antschel

Born: Czernowitz, Romania (now Chernivtsi, Ukraine); November 23, 1920
Died: Paris, France; April, 1970
Also known as: Paul Ancel

<small>PRINCIPAL POETRY</small>
Der Sand aus den Urnen, 1948
Mohn und Gedächtnis, 1952
Von Schwelle zu Schwelle, 1955
Gedichte: Eine Auswahl, 1959
Sprachgitter, 1959 (*Speech-Grille*, 1971)
Die Niemandsrose, 1963
Gedichte, 1966
Atemwende, 1967 (*Breathturn*, 1995)
Ausgewählte Gedichte: Zwei Reden, 1968
Fadensonnen, 1968 (*Threadsuns*, 2000)
Lichtzwang, 1970 (*Lightduress*, 2005)
Schneepart, 1971 (*Snow Part*, 2007)
Speech-Grille, and Selected Poems, 1971
Nineteen Poems, 1972
Selected Poems, 1972
Gedichte: In zwei Bänden, 1975 (2 volumes)
Zeitgehöft: Späte Gedichte aus dem Nachlass, 1976
Paul Celan: Poems, 1980 (revised as *Poems of Paul Celan*, 1988)
Gedichte, 1938-1944, 1985
Sixty-five Poems, 1985
Last Poems, 1986
Das Frühwerk, 1989
Gesammelte Werke in sieben Bänden, 2000 (7 volumes)
Glottal Stop: 101 Poems, 2000

<small>OTHER LITERARY FORMS</small>

The literary reputation of Paul Celan (TSEHL-on) rests exclusively on his poetry. His only piece of prose fiction, if indeed it can be so described, is "Gespräch im Gebirg" (1959), a very short autobiographical story with a religious theme. Celan also wrote an introductory essay for a book containing works by the painter Edgar Jené; this essay, entitled *Edgar Jené und der Traum vom Traume*, (1948; *Edgar Jené and the Dream About the Dream*, 1986), is an important early statement of Celan's aesthetic theory. Another, more oblique, statement of Celan's poetic theory is contained in his famous speech, "Der Meridian" (1960), given on his acceptance of the prestigious Georg Büchner Prize. (An English translation of this speech, "The Meridian," was published in the Winter, 1978, issue of *Chicago Review*.)

ACHIEVEMENTS

Paul Celan is considered an "inaccessible" poet by many critics and readers. This judgment, prompted by the difficulties Celan's poetry poses for would-be interpreters seeking traditional exegesis, is reinforced by the fact that Celan occupies an isolated position in modern German poetry. Sometimes aligned with Nelly Sachs, Ernst Meister, and the German Surrealists, Celan's work nevertheless stands apart from that of his contemporaries. A Jew whose outlook was shaped by his early experiences in Nazi-occupied Romania, Celan grew up virtually trilingual. The horror of his realization that he was, in spite of his childhood experiences and his later residence in France, a German poet was surely responsible in part for his almost obsessive concern with the possibilities and the limits of his poetic language. Celan's literary ancestors are Friedrich Hölderlin, Arthur Rimbaud, Stéphane Mallarmé, Rainer Maria Rilke, and the German expressionists, but even in his early poems his position as an outsider is manifest. Celan's poems, called Hermetic by some critics because of their resistance to traditional interpretation, can be viewed sometimes as intense and cryptic accounts of personal experience, sometimes as religious-philosophical discussions of Judaism, its tradition and its relation to Christianity. Many of his poems concern themselves with linguistic and poetic theory to the point where they cease to be poems in the traditional sense, losing all contact with the world of physical phenomena and turning into pure language, existing only for themselves. Such "pure" poems, increasingly frequent in Celan's later works, are largely responsible for the charge of inaccessibility that has been laid against him. Here the reader is faced with having to leave the dimension of conventional language use, where the poet uses language to communicate with his audience about subjects such as death or nature, and is forced to enter the dimension of metalanguage, as Harald Weinrich calls it, where language is used to discuss only language—that is, the *word* "death," and not death itself. Such poems are accessible only to readers who share with the poet the basic premises of an essentially linguistic poetic theory.

In spite of all this, much of Celan's poetry can be made accessible to the reader through focus on the personal elements in some poems, the Judaic themes in others, and by pointing out the biblical and literary references in yet another group.

BIOGRAPHY

Paul Celan was born Paul Ancel, or Antschel, the only child of Jewish parents, in Czernowitz, Romania (now Chernivtsi, Ukraine), in Bukovina, situated in the foothills of the Carpathian Mountains. This region had been under Austrian rule and thus contained a sizable German-speaking minority along with a mix of other nationalities and ethnic groups. In 1918, just two years before Celan's birth, following the collapse of the Austro-Hungarian Empire, Bukovina became part of Romania. Thus, Celan was reared in a region of great cultural and linguistic diversity, the tensions of which energized his poetry.

Little is known of Celan's early childhood, but he appears to have had a very close relationship with his mother and a less satisfying relationship with his father. Positive references to his mother abound in his poems, whereas his father is hardly mentioned. After receiving his high school diploma, the young Celan went to study medicine in France in 1938, but the war forced his return in the following year to Czernowitz, where he turned to the study of Romance languages and literature at the local university. In 1940, his hometown was annexed by the Soviet Union but was soon occupied by the Germans and their allies, who began to persecute and deport the Jewish population. Celan's parents were taken to a concentration camp, where they both died, while the young man remained hidden for some time and finally ended up in a forced-labor camp. These events left a permanent scar on Celan's memory, and it appears that he had strong feelings of guilt for having survived when his parents and so many of his friends and relatives were murdered. After Soviet troops reoccupied his hometown, he returned there for a short time and then moved to Bucharest, where he found work as an editor and a translator. In 1947, his first poems were published in a Romanian journal under the anagrammatic pen name Paul Celan. In the same year, he moved to Vienna, where he remained until 1948, when his first collection of poetry, *Der Sand aus den Urnen*, was published.

After moving to Paris in the same year, Celan began to frequent avant-garde circles and was received particularly well by the poet Yvan Goll and his wife. Unfortunately, this friendship soured after Goll's death in 1950, when Goll's wife, Claire, apparently jealous of Celan's growing reputation as a poet, accused him of having plagiarized from her husband. A bitter feud resulted, with many of the leading poets and critics in France and Germany taking sides. During this period, Celan also began his work as a literary translator, which was to be a major source of both income and poetic inspiration for the rest of his life. He translated from the French—notably the writings of Rimbaud, Paul Valéry, and Guillaume Apollinaire—as well as the poetry of William Shakespeare, Emily Dickinson, and Marianne Moore from the English and the works of Aleksandr Blok, Sergei Esenin, and Osip Mandelstam from the Russian.

In the following years, Celan married a French graphic artist, Gisèle Lestrange, and published his second volume of poetry, *Mohn und Gedächtnis* (poppy and memory), containing many poems from his first collection, *Der Sand aus den Urnen*, which he had withdrawn from circulation because of the large number of printing mistakes and editorial inaccuracies it contained. *Mohn und Gedächtnis* established his reputation as a poet, and most of his subsequent collections were awarded prestigious literary prizes.

Celan remained in Paris for the rest of his life, infrequently traveling to Germany. During his later years, he appears to have undergone many crises both in his personal and in his creative life (his feud with Claire Goll is only one such incident), and his friends agree that he became quarrelsome and felt persecuted by neo-Nazis, hostile publishers, and critics. His death in April of 1970, apparently by suicide—he drowned in the Seine—was the consequence of his having arrived, in his own judgment, at a personal and artistic dead end, although many critics have seen in his collections *Lightduress*, *Snow Part*, and *Zeitgehöft*, published post humously, the potential beginning of a new creative period.

ANALYSIS

Paul Celan's poetry can be viewed as an expressive attempt to cope with the past—his personal past as well as that of the Jewish people. Close friends of the poet state that Celan was unable to forget anything and that trivial incidents and cataclysmic events of the past for him had the same order of importance. Many of his poems contain references to the death camps, to his dead parents (particularly his mother), and to his changing attitude toward the Jewish religion and toward God. In his early collections, these themes are shaped into traditional poetic form—long, often rhymed lines, genitive metaphors, sensuous images—and the individual poems are accessible to conventional methods of interpretation. In his later collections, Celan employs increasingly sparse poetic means, such as one-word lines, neologisms, and images that resist traditional interpretive sense; their significance can often be intuited only by considering Celan's complete poetic opus, a fact that has persuaded many critics and readers that Celan's poems are nonsense, pure games with language rather than codified expressions of thoughts and feelings that can be deciphered by applying the appropriate key.

MOHN UND GEDÄCHTNIS

Mohn und Gedächtnis, Celan's first collection of poetry (discounting the withdrawn *Der Sand aus den Urnen*), was in many ways an attempt to break with the past. The title of the collection is an indication of the dominant theme of these poems, which stress the dichotomy of forgetting—one of the symbolic connotations of the poppy flower—and remembering, by which Celan expresses his wish to forget the past, both his own personal past and that of the Jewish race, and his painful inability to erase these experiences from his memory. Living in Paris, Celan believed that only by forgetting could he begin a new life—in a new country, with a non-Jewish French wife, and by a rejection of his past poetic efforts, as indicated by the withdrawal of his first collection.

Mohn und Gedächtnis is divided into four parts and contains a total of fifty-six poems. In the first part, "Der Sand aus den Urnen" ("Sand from the Urns"), Celan establishes the central theme of the collection: The poet "fills the urns of the past in the moldy-green house of oblivion" and is reminded by the white foliage of an aspen tree that his mother's hair was not allowed to turn white. Mixed with these reflections on personal losses are memories of sorrows and defeats inflicted on the Jewish people; references to the conquest of Judea by the Romans are meant to remind the reader of more recent atrocities committed by foreign conquerors.

The second part of *Mohn und Gedächtnis* is a single poem, "Todesfuge" ("Death Fugue"), Celan's most widely anthologized poem, responsible in no small part for establishing his reputation as one of the leading con temporary German poets. "Death Fugue" is a monologue by the victims of a concentration camp, evoking in vivid images the various atrocities associated with these camps. From the opening line, "Black milk of daybreak we drink it at sundown . . ."—one of the lines that Claire Goll suggested Celan had plagiarized from her husband—the poem passes on to descriptions of the cruel camp commander who plays with serpent-like whips, makes the inmates shovel their own graves, and sets his pack of dogs on them. From the resignation of the first lines, the poem builds to an emotional climax in the last stanza in which the horror of the cremation chambers is indicated by images such as "he grants us a grave in the air" and "death is a master from Germany." Although most critics have praised the poem, some have condemned Celan for what they interpret as an attempt at reconciliation between Germans and Jews in the last two lines of the poem. Others, however, notably Theodor Adorno, have attacked "Death Fugue" on the basis that it is "barbaric" to write beautiful poetry after, and particularly about, Auschwitz. A close reading of this long poem refutes the notion that Celan was inclined toward reconciliation with the Germans—his later work bears this out—and it is hard to imagine that any reader should feel anything but horror and pity for the anonymous speakers of the poem. The beautifully phrased images serve to increase the intensity of this horror rather than attempting to gloss it over. "Death Fugue" is both a great poem and one of the most impressive and lasting documents of the plight of the Jews.

"Auf Reisen" ("Travel"), the first poem of the third part of the collection, again indicates Celan's wish to leave the past behind and to start all over again in his "house in Paris." In other poems he makes reference to his wife, asking to be forgiven for having broken with his heritage and married a Gentile. As the title of the collection suggests, the poppy of oblivion is not strong enough to erase the memory of his dead mother, of his personal past, and of his racial heritage. In poems such as "Der Reisekamerad" ("The Traveling Companion") and "Zähle die Mandeln" ("Count the Almonds"), the optimistic view of "Travel" is retracted; in the former, the dead mother is evoked as the poet's constant travel companion, while in the latter, he acknowledges that he must always be counted among the "almonds." The almonds (*Mandeln*) represent the Jewish people and are an indirect reference also to the Russian Jewish poet Osip Mandelstam, whose work Celan had translated. The irreconcilable tension between the wish to forget and the inability to do so completely is further shown in "Corona," a poem referring to Rainer

Maria Rilke's "Herbsttag" ("Autumn Day"). Whereas the speaker of Rilke's poem resigns himself to the approaching hardships of winter, Celan converts Rilke's "Lord: it is time" into the rebellious "it is time that the stone condescended to bloom."

The poems in *Mohn und Gedächtnis* are not, for the most part, innovative in form or imagery, although the long dactylic lines and the flowery images of the first half begin to give way to greater economy of scope and metaphor in the later poems. There is a constant dialogue with a fictional "you" and repeated references to "night," "dream," "sleep," "wine," and "time," in keeping with the central theme of these poems. Celan's next collections show his continued attempts to break with the past, to move his life and his poetry to new levels.

Von Schwelle zu Schwelle

In *Von Schwelle zu Schwelle* (threshold to threshold), Celan abandoned his frequent references to the past; it is as if the poet—as the title, taken from a poem in *Mohn und Gedächtnis*, suggests—intended to cross over a threshold into a new realm. Images referring to his mother, to the persecution of the Jews, to his personal attitude toward God, and to his Jewish heritage are less frequent in this volume. Many German critics, reluctant to concentrate on Celan's treatment of the Holocaust, have remarked with some relief his turning away from this subject toward the problem of creativity, the possibilities of communication, and the limits of language. Indeed, if one follows most German critics, *Von Schwelle zu Schwelle* was the first step in the poet's development toward "metapoetry"—that is, poetry that no longer deals with traditional *materia poetica* but only with poetry itself. This new direction is demonstrated by the preponderance of terms such as "word" and "stone" (a symbol of speechlessness), replacing "dream," "autumn," and "time." For Celan, *Von Schwelle zu Schwelle* constituted a more radical attempt to start anew by no longer writing about—therefore no longer having to think about—experiences and memories that he had been unable to come to grips with in his earlier poems.

Speech-Grille

Speech-Grille is, as the title suggests, predominantly concerned with language. The thirty-three poems in this volume are among Celan's finest, as the enthusiastic critical reception confirmed. They are characterized by a remarkable discipline of expression, leading in many cases to a reduction of poetry to the bare essentials. Indeed, it is possible to see these poems as leading in the direction of complete silence. "Engführung" ("Stretto"), perhaps the finest poem in the collection and one of Celan's best, exemplifies this tendency even by its title, which is taken from musical theory and refers to the final section of a fugue. A long poem that alludes to "Death Fugue," it is stripped of the descriptive metaphors that characterized that masterpiece, such as the "grave in the air" and "the black milk of daybreak"; instead, experience is reduced to lines such as "Came,

came./ Came a word, came/ came through the night,/ wanted to shine, wanted to shine/ Ash./ Ash, ash./ Night."

DIE NIEMANDSROSE

Celan's attempt to leave the past behind in *Speech-Grille* was not completely successful; on the contrary, several poems in this collection express sorrow at the poet's detachment from his Jewish past and from his religion. It is therefore not surprising that Celan's next collection, *Die Niemandsrose* (the no-one's rose), was dedicated to Mandelstam, a victim of Joseph Stalin's persecutions in the 1930's. One of the first poems in this collection makes mention of the victims of the concentration camps: "There was earth inside them, and/they dug." Rather than concentrating on the horrors of camp existence, the poem discusses the possibility of believing in an omnipotent, benevolent God in the face of these atrocities; this theme is picked up again in "Zürich, zum Storchen" ("Zurich, the Stork Inn"), in which Celan reports on his meeting with the Jewish poet Nelly Sachs: "the talk was of your God, I spoke/ against him." Other poems contain references to his earlier work; the "house in Paris" is mentioned again, and autumn imagery, suggesting the memory of his mother, is used more frequently. Several other poems express Celan's renewed and final acceptance of his Jewish heritage but indicate his rejection of God, culminating in the blasphemous "Psalm," with its bitter tribute: "Praised be your name, no one."

LATER YEARS

Celan's poetry after *Die Niemandsrose* became almost inaccessible to the average reader. As the title *Breathturn* indicates, Celan wanted to go in entirely new directions. Most of the poems in Celan's last collections are very short; references to language and writing become more frequent, and striking, often grotesque, portmanteau words and other neologisms mix with images from his earlier poems. There are still references to Judaism, to an absent or cruel God, and—in a cryptic form—to personal experiences. In the posthumously published *Snow Part*, the reader can even detect allusions to the turbulent political events of 1968. The dominant feature of these last poems, however, is the almost obsessive attempt to make the language of poetry perform new, hitherto unimagined feats, to coerce words to yield truth that traditional poetic diction could not previously force through its "speech-grille." It appears that Celan finally despaired of ever being able to reach this new poetic dimension. The tone of his last poems was increasingly pessimistic, and his hopes, expressed in earlier poems, of finding "that ounce of truth deep inside delusion," gave way to silence in the face of the "obstructive tomorrow." It is the evidence of these last poems, more than any police reports, which make it a certainty that his drowning in the Seine in 1970 was not simply the result of an accident.

Celan's poetry can be understood only by grasping his existential dilemma after

World War II as a Jewish poet who had to create his poetry in the German language. Desperate to leave behind everything which would remind him of his own and his people's plight, he nevertheless discovered that the very use of the German language inevitably led him back to his past and made a new beginning impossible. Finally, the only escape he saw still open to him was to attempt to abandon completely the conventions of German lyric poetry and its language, to try to make his poetry express his innermost feelings and convictions without having to resort to traditional poetic diction and form. Weinrich suggests that Celan, like Mallarmé before him, was searching for the "absolute poem," a poem that the poet creates only as a rough sketch and that the reader then completes, using private experiences and ideas, possibly remembered pieces of other poems. If this is true, Celan must have ultimately considered his efforts a failure, both in terms of his poetic intentions and in his desire to come to terms with his personal and his Jewish past.

OTHER MAJOR WORKS

SHORT FICTION: "Gespräch im Gebirg," 1959.

NONFICTION: *Edgar Jené und der Traum vom Traume*, 1948 (*Edgar Jené and the Dream About the Dream*, 1986); *Collected Prose*, 1986.

TRANSLATIONS: *Der goldene Vorhang*, 1949 (of Jean Cocteau); *Bateau ivre/Das trunkene Schiff*, 1958 (of Arthur Rimbaud); *Gedichte*, 1959 (of Osip Mandelstam); *Die junge Parzel/La jeune Parque*, 1964 (of Paul Valéry); *Einundzwanzig Sonette*, 1967 (of William Shakespeare).

MISCELLANEOUS: *Prose Writings and Selected Poems*, 1977; *Selected Poems and Prose of Paul Celan*, 2001.

BIBLIOGRAPHY

Baer, Ulrich. *Remnants of Song: Trauma and the Experience of Modernity in Charles Baudelaire and Paul Celan*. Stanford, Calif.: Stanford University Press, 2000. Baer sees a basis for comparison of the nineteenth and the twentieth century poets. Bibliographical references, index.

Bernstein, Michael André. *Five Portraits: Modernity and the Imagination in Twentieth-Century German Writing*. Evanston, Ill.: Northwestern University Press, 2000. Compared with Celan are four other German poets and philosophers: Rainer Maria Rilke, Robert Musil, Martin Heidegger, and Walter Benjamin. Includes bibliographical references, index.

Chalfen, Israel. *Paul Celan*. New York: Persea Books, 1991. A biography of Celan's youth and early career. Includes bibliographical references.

Colin, Amy D. *Paul Celan: Holograms of Darkness*. Bloomington: Indiana University Press, 1991. An overview of Celan's cultural background as well as postmodernist textual analysis.

Del Caro, Adrian. *The Early Poetry of Paul Celan: In the Beginning Was the Word.* Baton Rouge: Louisiana State University Press, 1997. A detailed treatment of the early volumes *Mohn und Gedächtnis* (1952) and *Von Schwelle zu Schwelle* (1955).

Felstiner, John. *Paul Celan: Poet, Survivor, Jew.* 1995. Reprint. New Haven, Conn.: Yale University Press, 2001. Illuminates the rich biographical meaning behind much of Celan's spare, enigmatic verse. Includes bibliographical references, illustrations, map, index.

Hillard, Derek. *Poetry as Individuality: The Discourse of Observation in Paul Celan.* Lewisburg, Pa.: Bucknell University Press, 2009. An examination of individuality in the writings of Celan. Touches on philosophy and the psychology of knowledge.

Rosenthal, Bianca. *Pathways to Paul Celan.* New York: Peter Lang, 1995. An overview of the varied and often contradictory critical responses to the poet. Illustrated; includes bibliographical references, index.

Tobias, Rochelle. *The Discourse of Nature in the Poetry of Paul Celan: The Unnatural World.* Baltimore: The Johns Hopkins University Press, 2006. Provides critical analysis of Celan's poetry in terms of its relationship to the natural world.

Wolosky, Shira. *Language and Mysticism: The Negative Way of Language in Eliot, Beckett, and Celan.* Stanford, Calif.: Stanford University Press, 1995. A useful comparative study that helps to place Celan in context. Bibliographical references, index.

Franz G. Blaha

LUIS CERNUDA

Born: Seville, Spain; September 21, 1902
Died: Mexico City, Mexico; November 5, 1963

PRINCIPAL POETRY

Egloga, elegía, oda, 1927
Perfil del aire, 1927
Un río, un amor, 1929
Los placeres prohibidos, 1931
Donde habite el olvido, 1934
Invocaciones, 1935
La realidad y el deseo, 1936, 1940, 1958, 1964
Las nubes, 1940
Ocnos, 1942, 1949, 1964 (prose poems; English translation, 2004)
Como quien espera el alba, 1947
Variaciones sobre tema mexicano, 1952 (prose poems; *Variations on a Mexican Theme*, 2004)
Poemas para un cuerpo, 1957
Desolación de la quimera, 1962 (*Desolation of the Chimera: Last Poems*, 2009)
The Poetry of Luis Cernuda, 1971
Poesía completa, 1973
Selected Poems of Luis Cernuda, 1977
34 Poemas, 1998
Written in Water: The Prose Poems of Luis Cernuda, 2004 (includes *Ocnos* and *Variations on a Mexican Theme*)

OTHER LITERARY FORMS

Although Luis Cernuda (sur-NEW-dah) is best known for his poetry, he was also a prolific essayist and critic. He published several works in prose, three of which, devoted to criticism, appeared during his lifetime. In his *Estudios sobre poesía española contemporánea* (1957; studies on contemporary Spanish poetry), Cernuda analyzes the most important trends in Spanish poetry since the nineteenth century. He bestows upon Gustavo Adolfo Bécquer the distinction of having reawakened poetry after more than one hundred years of lethargy, and he lauds Miguel de Unamuno y Jugo as the most important Spanish poet of the twentieth century. Cernuda's *Pensamiento poético en la lírica inglesa (siglo XIX)* (1958; poetic thought in English lyricism), a study of the theory of poetry as practiced by nineteenth century British poets, reveals Cernuda's deep appreciation of and attachment to English verse of the Romantic and Victorian periods.

Many of Cernuda's essays and magazine and newspaper articles—which appeared originally in such publications as *Caracola, Litoral, Octubre, Cruz y raya, Heraldo de Madrid,* and *Insula*—have been collected in the two-volume *Poesía y literatura* (1960, 1964; poetry and literature) and in *Crítica, ensayos y evocaciones* (1970; criticism, essays, and evocations). *Variations on a Mexican Theme,* often referred to as poetic prose, is an affectionate reflection by the poet on the people of Mexico, their music, their art, their churches, and their poverty and misery. Mexico was the poet's adopted homeland, after some years in what he perceived to be alien environments, and he felt warmed by the Mexicans, their culture, and their climate, so reminiscent of his native Andalusia. *Ocnos* is a meditation on time, a prose poem that becomes the lyrical confession of a poet writing about himself and his art. Because it contains Cernuda's analysis of his work, this volume is a useful companion to his poetry. Cernuda also undertook the translation into Spanish of the poetry of Friedrich Hölderlin, Paul Éluard, William Wordsworth, and William Blake, as well as plays by William Shakespeare. He did not devote much effort to fiction, leaving behind only three short pieces: "El indolente" ("The Indolent One"), "El viento en la colina" ("The Wind on the Hill"), and "El sarao" (the dancing party), all published in the collection *Tres narraciones* (1948; three narratives).

ACHIEVEMENTS

While Luis Cernuda is recognized as an important member of the Generation of '27 (considered by some a second Spanish Golden Age), he did not receive during his lifetime the acclaim and recognition extended to some of his contemporaries, such as Federico García Lorca, Jorge Guillén, Rafael Alberti, and Vicente Aleixandre. Furthermore, Cernuda never enjoyed financial or professional security. His position as a self-exile—he never returned to Spain, even for brief periods, after 1938—might explain his lack of popularity during the 1930's and 1940's. In addition, his political sympathies (staunchly Republican), his open homosexuality, his reticence, and even the seemingly simple structure and language of his poetry were all factors that may have distanced him from an entire generation of readers. After his death, however, Cernuda's audience has been growing: A number of important critical studies have appeared, a complete edition of his poetry has been published, and a collection of many of his extant essays was issued in 1970—clear indications that Cernuda is being reappraised by a new generation of Spanish poets and critics.

However, as Carlos-Peregrín Otero has observed, it might still be premature to evaluate Cernuda's impact and his role as an innovator in Spanish letters. Cernuda displayed, first and foremost, a commitment to poetry and to the creative act. His work allowed him to express himself and served to sustain him. It was through his poetry that he came to understand himself and the world, and this understanding helped him endure the solitude and melancholy of his alienated and withdrawn existence. Through his writing, he was able to objectify his desire, his passion, and his love and to liberate himself in ways that his social persona never could. He also used his poetry to battle against his obsession with time and its relentless passage. These were the principal themes of Cernuda's works. He expressed them with increasing clarity and simplicity of language, yet, toward the end of his life, his work began to acquire the quiet, meditative tone of a man who is confident in the knowledge that his art, if nothing else, will escape decay.

BIOGRAPHY

Born to a comfortable middle-class family of Seville, Luis Cernuda y Bidón was the youngest of the three children of Bernardo Cernuda Bousa, a colonel of a regiment of engineers, and Amparo Bidón y Cuellar. In Cernuda's poem "La familia" ("The Family"), which appeared in *Como quien espera el alba* (like someone awaiting the dawn), the domestic environment of his youth is portrayed as grave, dark, and rigid like glass, "which everyone can break but no one bends." The poet does not reveal any warmth or affection for his parents or his two sisters. His parents, he adds, fed and clothed him, and even provided him with God and morality. They gave him all: life, which he had not asked for, and death, its inextricable companion. From an early age, Cernuda displayed a timidity and reticence which were to characterize his social interaction throughout his life.

Cernuda first began to appreciate poetry at the age of nine, when he came across some poems by Gustavo Adolfo Bécquer, the nineteenth century Romantic poet whose remains were transferred from Madrid to Seville for permanent interment in 1911, causing excitement among the residents of the city and renewed interest in the poet's work. After completing secondary school in a religious institution, Cernuda enrolled at the University of Seville to study law in 1919. He received his law degree in 1925 but never practiced. His most important experience during his university years was his contact with Pedro Salinas, the eminent poet whose first year as a professor at the university coincided with Cernuda's first year as a student. Their association—at first formal, impersonal, and restricted to the classroom—developed in the course of the next few years, as Salinas encouraged Cernuda and other students to pursue their poetic inclinations. Salinas recommended that Cernuda begin to read French authors, among them Charles Baudelaire, Stéphane Mallarmé, and André Gide. Gide's works helped Cernuda to confront and to reconcile himself to his homosexuality. Through the influence of Salinas, Cernuda was able to publish nine poems in the prestigious magazine *Revista de occidente* when he was only twenty-three. Two years later, in 1927, Cernuda published his first collection, *Perfil del aire* (air's profile). In spite of the coolness with which it was received, with one or two notable exceptions, Cernuda had determined to devote his life to writing, putting an end to any professional indecision he had felt earlier.

Upon the death of his mother in 1928—his father had died in 1920—Cernuda left Seville for good, traveling first to Málaga and then to Madrid, and meeting a number of the writers and poets who would be known as the Generation of '27, among them Manuel Altolaguirre and Emilio Prados (the editors of *Litoral*), Vicente Aleixandre, and Bernabé Fernández-Canivell (future director of the literary magazine *Caracola*, an outlet for Cernuda's poetry). He had met García Lorca in Seville in 1927. In the fall of 1928, through Pedro Salinas, Cernuda was offered an appointment as Spanish lecturer at the École Normale de Toulouse, a position that afforded the young poet the opportunity to spend some time in Paris. During his year in France, he immersed himself in the Surrealist movement and adopted a style and point of view to which he would adhere for the next four years.

The 1930's was a decade of steady productivity for Cernuda, marked by increasing recognition of his gifts among other writers of his generation. At the same time, it was a period of political instability that forced writers to take sides. Cernuda was a staunch supporter of the Spanish Republic and, for a brief period, around 1933, a member of the Communist Party, contributing several political articles to *Octubre*, a magazine edited by Rafael Alberti. In 1934, for a short time, he worked for Misiones Pedagógicas (pedagogic missions), an educational program sponsored by the Republican government to bring culture to remote areas of the country. Cernuda's job was to explain the great masterpieces of Spanish painting, presented to the audience in reproduction. Cernuda spent the first summer of the Spanish Civil War, in 1936, in Paris as a secretary to the Spanish ambassador to France, Alvaro de Albornoz, whose daughter Concha was a friend of Cernuda. Upon his return to Spain, Cernuda joined the Republican popular militia and fought in the Guadarrama. In the winter of 1938, he traveled to England to deliver a series of lectures arranged for him by the English writer Stanley Richardson. A few months later, while returning to Spain through France, Cernuda decided to go into exile permanently, first to Great Britain, where he taught in Surrey, Glasgow, Cambridge, and London, and then to the United States, where he arrived in the fall of 1947. His appointment as professor of Spanish literature at Mount Holyoke College, negotiated for Cernuda by Concha Albornoz, initiated the most stable and financially untroubled period of the poet's life. The New England climate and the isolation of the school, however, made Cernuda restless and caused him to explore the possibility of a teaching post at a university in Puerto Rico. In 1953, after several summers spent in the more hospitable Mexico, he resigned his tenure at Mount Holyoke and settled in Mexico, where he would remain—with only brief returns to the United States to teach at San Francisco State College and the University of California, Los Angeles—until his death from a heart attack in 1963. While in Mexico, he supported himself by his writing and by teaching several courses at the Universidad Autónoma in Mexico City.

ANALYSIS

In the case of Luis Cernuda, it is impossible to separate the poet from the man—his personality from his literary production. As much as Cernuda himself protested that he loathed the intrusion of the person in the poem, he, much more than most of his contemporaries, can be said to have revealed himself through his writing. He offered readers a glimpse of his poetic world from one window only, as Jenaro Talens states, and that window is open to the main character, who is frequently—if not always—Cernuda himself. As a consequence, his poetic production reflects his development as a man and his awareness of himself. This, in turn, tends to focus most analyses of his work along closely chronological lines, as his poetry evolves from the vague and dreamy musings of youth to the bitter acceptance of the relentlessness of time and the inevitability of death.

PERFIL DEL AIRE

Beginning with the first book of poems, *Perfil del aire*—published as a supplement to the magazine *Litoral* and edited by Manuel Altolaguirre and Emilio Prados in 1927—Cernuda embarked upon a journey of self-discovery. In this first collection, the youthful poet presents an indifferent, indolent attitude toward the world; he is there, but he dreams and is surrounded by emptiness. Dreams and walls protect him, provide him with a haven for his loneliness; there, he can savor his secret pleasures and his unfulfilled yearnings. This first major effort, retitled "Primeras poesías" and revised before reappearing in the first edition of *La realidad y el deseo* (reality and desire), was not well received. Cernuda was criticized sharply for imitating Jorge Guillén, and his production was judged unoriginal. More recent criticism, while acknowledging Cernuda's debt to Guillén, dismisses these charges as exaggerated, praising this early work for its fine sensibility and for the musical quality of its language.

EGLOGA, ELEGÍA, ODA

The negative reception of his first book encouraged Cernuda to withdraw, at least personally, from what he considered the literary mainstream and, by his own admission, "to wish to cultivate that which is criticized by others." He began work on a second collection, *Egloga, elegía, oda* (eclogue, elegy, ode), a series of four poems patterned after classical and neoclassical models, particularly the works of Garcilaso de la Vega, whose meter and rhyme Cernuda imitated deliberately. Some years later, reflecting on his development as a writer, Cernuda said that, while this second work had permitted him to experiment with classical themes and strophes, its style did not satisfy him, for he was unable to find what he loved in what he wrote. Nevertheless, in *Egloga, elegía, oda*, the poet was able to express more forcefully some of the feelings first introduced in *Perfil del aire*. Vague yearnings have become a compelling attraction to beauty in all its forms; the poet's need to satisfy his desires is confronted by the opposition of desire to such satisfaction. In this set of poems, he begins to remove his cloak of ennui, revealing a strong, sensuous nature. The pursuit of pleasure replaces indifference as the antidote for solitude and sadness. Desiring to express himself in a more daring fashion and to rebel against the constraints of bourgeois society, which misunderstood him and his sexuality, Cernuda gravitated toward the Surrealists. He read the works of Louis Aragon, André Breton, and Paul Éluard, whose poetry he translated into Spanish.

UN RÍO, UN AMOR AND LOS PLACERES PROHIBIDOS

Cernuda's Surrealist stage began, not coincidentally, with his year in France (1928-1929) and resulted in two important works, *Un río, un amor* (a river, a love) and *Los placeres prohibidos* (forbidden pleasures). The most notable technical characteristic of *Un río, un amor* is Cernuda's use of free verse, which was also being adopted during this period by other Spanish poets, such as Aleixandre, García Lorca, and Alberti. Freed of external constraints, Cernuda's verse nevertheless retained a strong sense of meter, and the rhythm of his lines was preserved through accentuation and cadence. He also made use of reiteration, anaphora, and anastrophe. From this period onward, Cernuda began to experiment with longer lines, although they seldom exceeded eleven syllables. In *Los placeres prohibidos*, Cernuda continued to discard technical conventions, alternating between verse and prose poems. Thematically, Surrealism provided Cernuda with the opportunity to liberate himself from social restrictions. Asserting his linguistic and stylistic freedom, he wrote of "night petrified by fists," "towers of fear," "iron flowers resounding like the chest of man," "tongue of darkness," and "empty eyes."

Toward the end of *Un río, un amor*, Cernuda intimates what is expressed openly in *Los placeres prohibidos*; he accepts his homosexuality and admits to being possessed by love. This love takes the form of passionate physical desire, rendered no less glorious and pure because of its carnality; only the outside world tarnishes this love with its opprobrium. In *Un río, un amor*, love produces an emptiness and a vacuum. Man is like a phantom, without direction; he is indifferent to the world, as if he were dead. In *Los placeres prohibidos*, however, love ceases to be the object of dreams; it becomes something real, the primary goal of man's desire, the motive behind all he does and feels: To give in to this love, without reservation, is man's purpose. Its attainment is nevertheless elusive—except for some fleeting moments—and contains an element of pain; herein lies the source of the solitude and the impotence of man.

DONDE HABITE EL OLVIDO

A third work published during this period, *Donde habite el olvido* (where oblivion dwells), closes out Cernuda's Surrealist phase. It was written after a failed love affair, one that the author naïvely had believed would last forever. This accounts for the bitterness of its tone, the poet's desire for death, and the harsh indictment of love, which, once it disappears, leaves nothing behind but the "remembrance of an oblivion." In the fourth poem of this collection, Cernuda retraces his personal history, as if it were a life already lived, replete with regrets and unfulfilled expectations. The first part of the poem exudes optimism, expansiveness, and anticipation, conveyed by the spring moon, the golden sea, and adolescent desire. The light, however, turns into shadows; the poet falls into darkness and is ultimately a living corpse.

LAS NUBES

With his next major publication, *Las nubes* (the clouds), Cernuda introduced two important new themes into his poetry: historical time, with its specific focus on Spain as the abandoned and beleaguered homeland, and humanity's spirituality and religiosity. Love, the recurring topic of much of Cernuda's work, plays virtually no role in this collection. In "Un español habla de su tierra" ("A Spaniard Speaks of His Homeland"), the poet writes nostalgically of the happy days of the past, before his land succumbed to the conquering Cains. The bitter days of the present find sustenance in the fond memories of years gone by, an idealized past that might someday be re-created, yet to which the poet cannot return. When that day comes, and his homeland is free, it will come looking for him—only to discover that death has come to call first. Ironically, as one critic has pointed out, this poem was prescient in its chronology. In "Impresión de destierre" ("Impression of Exile"), the dislocated narrator—then in London—overhears a fatigued voice announce the death of Spain; "'Spain?' he said. 'A name./ Spain has died. . . .'"

Las nubes also contains the clearest expression of Cernuda's views on traditional religion. While his poetic use of belief in the supernatural has been described as a type of pantheistic hedonism based on Mediterranean mythology, his spiritual quest included attempts to find answers in more traditional Christian imagery by positing the existence of a God through whom humanity can achieve love. Cernuda devoted four poems in this collection to the broad question of the existence of God: "La visita de Dios" ("God's Visit"), "Atardecer en la catedral" ("Dusk in the Cathedral"), "Lázaro" ("Lazarus"), and "La adoración de los magos" ("The Adoration of the Magi"). In the long poem "God's Visit," the protagonist, in a voice filled with anguish, confronts God with the terrible wreckage of what is now the speaker's country, the poet's paradise of years gone by, perhaps destroyed by the casual wave of his hand. As the last hope for renewal, the protagonist begs God to restore to the world beauty, truth, and justice; without these, he warns, God could be forgotten.

"THE ADORATION OF THE MAGI"

More firmly rooted in Christianity is the five-part poem "The Adoration of the Magi," in which Cernuda's debt to T. S. Eliot is clear. The poem opens with a meditation by Melchior on the existence of God, reaching the conclusion that if he himself is alive, God, too, might well exist. This knowledge does not fully satisfy Melchior. To reason the existence of God is not enough; some more evocative proof is needed. The second part of the poem, "Los reyes" ("The Kings"), presents the Magi, each with a distinctive voice which expresses the conflicting visions of a single character: Melchior the idealist, Gaspar the hedonist, and Balthasar the skeptic. Through their intertwined monologues, the pilgrim searches for proof of the existence of God. The next section, "Palinodia de la esperanza divina" ("Palinode of Divine Hope"), is perhaps the most inventive; in it, the author expresses the disenchantment and disappointment felt by the Magi upon arriving in Bethlehem after a long journey and finding nothing but a poor child, a life "just like our human one," after expecting "a god, a presence/ radiant and imperious, whose sight is grace." In the fourth part, "Sobre el tiempo pasado" ("On Time Past"), the protagonist is the old shepherd (Father Time?) who remembers a period in his youth, long past, when three wise men came to look at a newborn child. The old man, however, has no recollection of a god; how can a humble shepherd, whose knowledge of man is so lacking, have seen the gods? The poem closes with a short fifth part, "Epitafio" ("Epitaph"), wherein man, as searcher, is told that he once found the truth but did not recognize it; now he can console himself by living his life in this world, as a body, even though he cannot be free from misery.

PASSAGE OF TIME AS THEME

The publication of *Las nubes* marked a new beginning for Cernuda, the man and the poet. He had departed from Spain; he was approaching the age of forty—an age which, for a man who associated beauty with youth and joy with youthfulness, must have created much anxiety. His prospects for recognition in Spain had been shattered by political events. Cernuda responded to this situation by creating a protagonist with a distinct identity; he created the poet, whose role it was to substitute as the main character for the author and who would, when called upon, assume all responsibility for failure. Thus, Cernuda created what Phillip Silver calls his "personal myth" and entered into the mature stage of his poetic production. Poetry became a means to understand and preserve the past. The need to fulfill a grand passion was discarded; man must resign himself to a world that belongs to the gods, a world in which he cannot partake of paradise. If man can be made into a myth, however, his life will be eternal and his beauty everlasting. In poems such as "Noche del hombre y su demonio" ("A Man's Night and His Demon") and "Río vespertino" ("Evening River") from *Como quien espera el alba*, Cernuda expresses an attitude of acceptance, as if recounting a life already lived. He anticipates, without fear, the inevitability of death. There is but one small consolation: There is no ash without flame, no death without life. In the long poem "Apología pro vita sua" from the same collection, the poet gathers up all the suffering of his existence: his obsessions as a poet, the war, his agnosticism, and his need and hope for a personal, intimate God. From his bedside, the protagonist summons first his lovers to help illuminate his world growing dim, for "Is passion not the measure of human greatness . . . ?" He then calls in his friends to help him renounce the light. As in a confessional, he admits to regrets, but only for those sins which he has not had the opportunity or the strength to commit. He asserts that he has lived without God because he has not manifested himself to him and has not satisfied his incredulity. The protagonist maintains that to die, people do not need God; rather, God needs people in order to live. In an apparent contradiction, a few lines later, he asks God to fill his soul with the light that comes with eternity.

The past, that which has been, and the inevitable passage of time become the dominating theme of the remainder of Cernuda's poetic output. In his mature verses, he recounts his life and his loves with the pessimistic tone of one who knows that they will never come again. Splendor, beauty, passion, and joy are juxtaposed to solitude, old age, and death.

OTHER MAJOR WORKS

SHORT FICTION: *Tres narraciones*, 1948.

NONFICTION: *Estudios sobre poesía española cont emporánea*, 1957; *Pensamiento poético en la lírica inglesa (siglo XIX)*, 1958; *Poesía y literatura*, 1960, 1964 (2 volumes); *Crítica, ensayos y evocaciones*, 1970; *Prosa completa*, 1975.

BIBLIOGRAPHY

Harris, Derek. *Luis Cernuda: A Study of His Poetry*. London: Tamesis, 1973. A critical study of Cernuda's poetry. Includes bibliographic references.

_____. *Metal Butterflies and Poisonous Lights: The Language of Surrealism in Lorca, Alberti, Cernuda, and Aleixandre*. Anstruther, Fife, Scotland: La Sirena, 1998. An analysis of the use of surrealism in the poetry of Cernuda and other poets. Includes bibliographical references.

Jiménez-Fajardo, Salvador. *Luis Cernuda*. Boston: Twayne, 1978. An introductory biographical and critical analysis of selected works by Cernuda. Includes bibliographic references.

_____, ed. *The Word and the Mirror: Critical Essays on the Poetry of Luis Cernuda*. Rutherford, N.J.: Fairleigh Dickinson University Press, 1989. A collection of critical essays dealing with Cernuda's works.

McKinlay, Neil C. *The Poetry of Luis Cernuda: Order in a World of Chaos*. Rochester, N.Y.: Tamesis, 1999. A brief biographical and critical study. Includes bibliographical references and index.

Martin-Clark, Philip. *Art, Gender, and Sexuality: New Readings of Cernuda's Later Poetry*. Leeds, England: Maney, 2000. A critical interpretation of selected works by Cernuda. Includes bibliographical references and index.

Soufas, C. Christopher. *The Subject in Question: Early Contemporary Spanish Literature and Modernism*. Washington, D.C.: Catholic University of America Press, 2007. This general work on Spanish literature in the early twentieth century has a chapter looking at the themes of absence and experience in the poems of Cernuda and Rafael Alberti.

Clara Estow

AIMÉ CÉSAIRE

Born: Basse-Pointe, Martinique; June 26, 1913
Died: Fort-de-France, Martinique; April 17, 2008

PRINCIPAL POETRY

Cahier d'un retour au pays natal, 1939, 1947, 1956 (*Memorandum on My Martinique*, 1947; better known as *Return to My Native Land*, 1968)
Les Armes miraculeuses, 1946 (*Miraculous Weapons*, 1983)
Soleil cou coupé, 1948 (*Beheaded Sun*, 1983)
Corps perdu, 1950 (*Disembodied*, 1983)
Ferrements, 1960 (*Shackles*, 1983)
Cadastre, 1961 (revised editions of *Soleil cou coupé* and *Corps perdu*; *Cadastre: Poems*, 1973)
State of the Union, 1966 (includes abridged translation of *Miraculous Weapons* and *Shackles*)
Moi, Laminaire, 1982
Aimé Césaire: The Collected Poetry, 1983
Lyric and Dramatic Poetry, 1946-82, 1990
La poésie, 1994

OTHER LITERARY FORMS

Poet, dramatist, and essayist Aimé Césaire (say-ZEHR) is recognized not only for his poetry but also for his political and dramatic works. The first major poem he wrote, *Return to My Native Land*, set the tone and thematic precedence for his subsequent writings. *Tropiques*, a cultural magazine of which the poet was one of the principal founders, featured Césaire's own poems, which were reprinted in the Gallimard edition of *Miraculous Weapons* in 1946. As well as a vehicle for literary content, the magazine was used to arouse the cultural and political consciousness that would continue to mark Césaire's personality throughout his life.

Césaire's poetry attests his exceptional talent as an artist, and his polemical and historical works, *Discours sur le colonialisme* (1950; *Discourse on Colonialism*, 1972), born of the poet's disillusionment with the inferior role Martinique continued to play in its relations with France, and *Toussaint Louverture: La Révolution française et le problème coloniale* (1960), named after the black hero Toussaint-Louverture, who led the 1802-1803 revolution in Haiti, demonstrate the poet's effort to assail racism, colonialism, and the cultural alienation of blacks from all sides. He continued to explore the problems of the existence of blacks in the world and African culture, especially the issue of decolonization, in his drama—which is more accessible than his poetry.

His plays include *La Tragédie du Roi Christophe* (pr. 1963; *The Tragedy of King Christophe*, 1969), *Une Saison au Congo* (pb. 1966; *A Season in the Congo*, 1968), and a reworking of William Shakespeare's play *The Tempest* (pr. 1611) entitled *Une Tempête, d'après "La Tempête" de Shakespeare: Adaptation pour un théâtre nègre* (pr., pb. 1969; *A Tempest*, 1974).

ACHIEVEMENTS

Aimé Césaire's contribution to literature goes beyond his exceptional use of Surrealist techniques, his extraordinary mastery of the French language, and his attempt to articulate the inhumane effects of racism and colonialism. In 1982, he received the French Grand Prix National de la Poésie. By his example, Césaire helped to give impetus to the first great outpouring of written literature in Africa and the West Indies.

BIOGRAPHY

One of several children, Aimé Fernand David Césaire was born on June 26, 1913, in Basse-Pointe, Martinique; his father, Ferdnand, was a comptroller with the revenue service. Most of his childhood was spent in the midst of poverty, and as Césaire grew older, he became acutely aware of the oppressive conditions of the majority of the Martinicans. At the Lycée Schoelcher in Fort-de-France, he excelled in his studies, winning a scholarship to the Lycée Louis-le-Grand in Paris. Ironically, this sojourn in Paris paved the way for Césaire's political maturation.

His friendship with Léopold Senghor, whom he met at Louis-le-Grand, was instrumental in changing Césaire's view of Africa, which would serve time and again as a source of inspiration for him. Once he completed his studies, he returned to Martinique with his wife, Suzanne, whom he had married while he was a student at the École Normale Supérieure. They would have six children.

Césaire's return to Martinique, a journey he had envisioned in his first poem, was as significant as his departure. He (as well as his wife) enjoyed a brief teaching career (1940-1945) at his former *lycée* in Fort-de-France. As usual, Césaire left his mark, inspiring his students with his love of poetry and instilling in them an enthusiasm for learning. Like many of his black contemporaries, Césaire took on the dual role of artist and political leader. Elected mayor of Fort-de-France (1945) and deputy to the National Assembly in France (1946), Césaire worked diligently to improve the plight of the Martinicans. During his fourteen years in office in the National Assembly, he was a member of the French Communist Party. He left the party when he perceived its indifference to the particular interests of Martinique.

In 1957, Césaire founded the Martinican Progressive Party (Parti Progressiste Martiniquais), and despite his disillusionment, he never ceased to play an active role in shaping the political life of his homeland. He assumed the presidency of the local "regional council," but he retired from electoral politics entirely in 1993. Although he did not publish any new poetry after 1982, the collection of his work published in Paris in 1994 by the prestigious Seuil firm was a major event. Césaire died in Fort-de-France, Martinique, on April 17, 2008. Césaire remains the best-known writer of the West Indies.

ANALYSIS

Aimé Césaire arrived in France in 1931, at a time when Surrealism had already begun to dominate the literary scene. Instead of an ideology, this movement provided Césaire with the poetic vision and creative license to set his own creative Muse into action. Fleeing the oppressive poverty of his native Martinique, Césaire was ripe for the ideals put forth by the Surrealists. He was attracted, in particular, to the notion of *écriture automatique* (automatic writing) and the Freudian concept of the self, hidden in the recesses of the subconscious, waiting only for a propitious moment to reveal itself. Armed with these two concepts, Césaire destroyed the poems he had written previously and began writing his epic poem *Return to My Native Land*, which would eventually gain for him great fame. More significant, he adopted the methods of the Surrealists in the service of a truly revolutionary cause.

Thus, Césaire's sojourn in France, originally envisioned as an escape from the hopeless conditions in Martinique, resulted instead in his own cultural and political awakening. While pursuing his studies in Paris at the Lycée Louis-le-Grand, he met Senghor (who later became the first president of Senegal and one of Africa's greatest francophone writers). Thanks to their friendship, Césaire acquired a greater knowledge and appreciation of Africa. Together, they joined forces with Léon Damas, another young poet, to establish the journal *L'Étudiant noir*, which replaced a previous journal, *Légitime défense*, that had been silenced after its first publication. Thus, Césaire's cultural and political consciousness gradually began to take on a more concrete form. Before, racism and colonial exploitation were, in his perception, limited mainly to the geographical confines of the West Indies and, especially, to Martinique. Once in Paris, however, he began to realize that the suffering of blacks extended well beyond the boundaries of his homeland. For Césaire, Senghor, and Damas, the creation of *L'Étudiant noir* was an acknowledgment that blacks in the West Indies, Africa, and elsewhere underwent a common experience.

Although Césaire worked zealously to produce a poem that would express the range, depth, and complexity of his poetic vision, his efforts were not initially received with enthusiasm. The first publisher to whom he submitted *Return to My Native Land* refused to publish the poem. Césaire succeeded in having only excerpts from the poem published in the magazine *Volonté* in 1939. Consequently, both the poet and his work went unnoticed for the most part, but this did little to dampen his creative spirit. When Césaire finally returned to Martinique, where he founded the journal *Tropiques* with the aid of his wife, Suzanne Césaire; René Menil; and Aristide Maugée, he continued to bring to life his poetic inspirations. It was not, however, until Césaire met André Breton (who became aware of Césaire's poetic genius after having read, in *Tropiques*, the poems that make up *Miraculous Weapons*) that Césaire was reintroduced to France's reading public. Subsequent admiration of Césaire's work was not limited to writers or political figures. The 1950 deluxe edition of *Disembodied* contained thirty-two engravings by Pablo Picasso that richly illustrated the ten poems in the collection. The poetic genius that caught the attention of Breton continues to be recognized by Césaire's critics.

RETURN TO MY NATIVE LAND

In his preface to the first complete edition of Césaire's *Return to My Native Land*, Breton remarked that this poem represented the "greatest lyrical monument of the times." Indeed, Césaire's first major poem has left an indelible mark upon literature. Of all his works, *Return to My Native Land* is, by far, the most criticized, analyzed, and quoted.

If poetry allows the human spirit to liberate itself from the bonds of reason, as the Surrealists suggest, then it becomes quite clear why Césaire's first major work has such a strong autobiographical tone. The ever-present "I" calls attention to the poet's desire to become rooted once again in his history and culture. Thus, *Return to My Native Land*, a poem of revolt, self-awakening, and "engagement," represents, first and foremost, the poet's personal testimony. From the start, it recalls the town where Césaire grew up, an image that seems both to attract and to repel him. He vividly evokes the stagnant existence of black peasants in Martinique, trapped in poverty and despair, resigned and silent. The emphasis placed on the geographical isolation of the island reinforces, as well, the idea of cultural alienation from the African sources of the black people.

Césaire presents a distressing picture of the poverty in which he and his six brothers and sisters lived. His father's health was being destroyed by an unknown illness, and his mother spent her days and nights operating a Singer sewing machine to help provide the family's daily sustenance. However, poverty and illness were not the most tragic effects of colonialism and racism, for Césaire saw an entire race reduced to a state of intellectual and emotional apathy, convinced of their inability to build, to create, to take control of their own destiny. It was in response to this sense of apathy and self-contempt that Césaire developed the concept of negritude, emphasizing a very proud self-awareness of "blackness" and the distinctive qualities of black culture.

Césaire's recognition and acceptance of Martinique's history, which also represents his own as well, makes it possible for him to purge himself of his feelings of cultural inferiority and to begin his ascent toward a new sense of racial consciousness. From the abyss of despair there arises a magnificent cry of protest. In *Return to My Native Land*, Césaire undertakes what he envisions as a messianic mission: He becomes the voice of the downtrodden, the victims, the exploited, the oppressed—those who are unable to verbalize and articulate their own cry of protest. Critics often compare the poet to Christ, citing as examples the lines in which Césaire takes on himself the prejudices held against blacks. At one point, his account of the inhumanities suffered by blacks is reminiscent of the scourging of Christ. Césaire's acceptance of his Christ-like role strongly underscores the message of "engagement," the poet's role as a socially and politically committed artist.

SHACKLES

The themes and motifs found in Césaire's first major poem recur throughout his oeuvre. *Shackles*, published in 1960, explores the vicissitudes of the black experience in Martinique and the evolution of African culture. The title, which denotes the forging of iron, suggests the era of slavery. Césaire recaptures this brutal moment in black history in the title poem, which is replete with nautical expressions used to evoke the voyage of the slave ship. He uses this image to draw a comparison between the agony suffered by the slaves and the misery which plagues the lives of the Martinicans, "arrimés de cœurs lourds" (stowing heavy hearts). It is with this new generation of slaves, who are not necessarily physically bound by chains, that Césaire is primarily concerned.

The poet recognizes the need to reconcile the present with the past, heretofore rejected and denied, before there can be any real and permanent cultural revolution. Therein lies the salvation of Martinique, cut off physically and emotionally from its African roots. The past represents, in Césaire's words, an old "wound" which has never healed, an "unforgettable insult." Thus, Césaire, with other negritude writers, has finally been able to set the record straight, to place colonialism and slavery in their proper perspective. Like all the other sons and daughters of humanity, black people were not destined to be slaves for all time.

African independence has signaled the beginning of a new phase in the history of blacks. Suddenly, it became apparent that the masters of colonialism were not entirely invincible. This is a positive sign for Césaire, who sees in these events a confirmation of the latent force among blacks—a force needed to overcome years of inferiority and submission. His poem "Pour saluer le Tiers Monde" ("Salute to the Third World") is above all one of praise and exaltation. The poet feels an immense sense of pride in the advent of a new Africa. Césaire punctuates the text, several times, with the emphatic words "I see," calling attention to the fact that he is a witness to these changing times. The image Césaire presents of Africa, unexpectedly standing upright, contrasts, significantly, with his image of Martinique, made powerless by its somnolence. Césaire laments the lack of racial and cultural consciousness among the Martinicans and celebrates Africa, the maternal source of his people. Indeed, to some degree, Césaire places the burden of leadership for the West Indies on Africa. The poet depicts a symbolic ritual in which he covers his body with the soil of Africa in such a way as to infuse himself with its strength. It is important to note that Césaire's treatment of Africa in *Shackles* recalls his original theme of the "return to his native land," which signifies not only a physical journey but also a return to his African heritage.

While he grapples with the larger problems of Martinique's fate, Césaire continues to confront his personal dilemma as a committed artist. His situation is not a unique one; it is one he shares with the educated elite of all Third World nations. With this privileged status comes the awesome responsibility to represent the voice of the masses. In his public life, Césaire does this through his active involvement in the political affairs of Martinique. In the same way, his poetry reaffirms continually his message of racial consciousness and commitment. There is no art for art's sake in Césaire's work; style and content are so closely intertwined that it is virtually impossible to talk about one without the other.

In *Return to My Native Land*, Césaire refers to the creative power of words, a power that enables the individual to alter reality. Poetry has allowed the poet the freedom to manipulate and violate the French language in ways that would not have been possible in prose. Thus, the very texture of his language is political; his style is a declaration of independence, shattering conventions associated with the oppressors of his people.

Despite the thematic consistency that characterizes Césaire's oeuvre, a certain movement can be traced from *Return to My Native Land* to *Shackles*. The former deals with the necessity to affirm and reclaim the dignity of blacks. It was the product of a period of intense soul-searching for the poet, who had to overcome his own sense of cultural and racial inferiority. In *Shackles*, on the other hand, Césaire seeks to reconcile the ideals of negritude with the existing realities in the West Indies. The masses do not appear to be ready to take their destiny into their own hands, and Césaire has come to realize that the effects of years of silent resignation will be reversed only gradually. In all his works, however, Césaire has remained committed to his people, serving them as visionary, storyteller, historian, and poet.

OTHER MAJOR WORKS

PLAYS: *Et les chiens se taisaient*, pb. 1956; *La Tragédie du Roi Christophe*, pb. 1963 (*The Tragedy of King Christophe*, 1969); *Une Saison au Congo*, pb. 1966 (*A Season in the Congo*, 1968); *Une Tempête, d'après "La Tempête" de Shakespeare: Adaptation pour un théâtre nègre*, pr., pb. 1969 (*A Tempest*, 1974).

NONFICTION: *Discours sur le colonialisme*, 1950 (*Discourse on Colonialism*, 1972); *Toussaint Louverture: La Révolution française et le problème coloniale*, 1960.

MISCELLANEOUS: *Œuvres complètes*, 1976.

BIBLIOGRAPHY

Arnold, A. James. Introduction to *Césaire's Lyric and Dramatic Poetry, 1946-82*, by Aimé Césaire. Translated by Clayton Eshleman and Annette Smith. Charlottesville: University Press of Virginia, 1990. Provides a succinct introduction to Aimé Césaire's life and work. Offers critical observations that supplement and extend many of the readings in Arnold's important *Modernism and Negritude*.

_____. *Modernism and Negritude: The Poetry and Poetics of Aimé Césaire*. Cambridge, Mass.: Harvard University Press, 1981. This work is certainly the definitive study of Césaire's poetry and its relationship to both negritude and modernism. Highly readable and elegantly written.

Davis, Gregson. *Aimé Césaire*. New York: Cambridge University Press, 1997. A generally chronological examination of the evolution of Césaire's poetic and intellectual development and its connection to his aesthetics and politics.

Eshelman, Clayton, and Annette Smith. Introduction to *Aimé Césaire: The Collected Poetry*. Berkeley: University of California Press, 1983. In this illustrated collection of more than four hundred pages, Eshelman and Smith offer commentary on Césaire to accompany their translations of a selection of his poems for the English-language audience and students. Bibliographical references.

Figueroa, Victor. *Not at Home in One's Home: Caribbean Self-Fashioning in the Poetry of Luis Palés Matos, Aimé Césaire, and Derek Walcott*. Madison, N.J.: Fairleigh Dickinson University Press, 2009. Contains a chapter on Césaire's *Return to My Native Land* and describes Caribbean poetry.

Martin, Gerald, ed. *Men of Maize*. Pittsburgh, Pa.: University of Pittsburgh Press, 1993. A collection of essays by various authors relevant to Césaire, poetry as a genre, and Caribbean culture.

Munro, Martin. *Shaping and Reshaping the Caribbean: The Work of Aimé Césaire and René Depestre*. Leeds, England: Maney, 2000. Munro examines Caribbean literature through the works of Césaire and Depestre. Bibliography and index.

Pallister, Janis L. *Aimé Césaire*. New York: Twayne, 1991. Short biography and a critical analysis of Aimé Césaire's work and career. Includes bibliography and index.

Scharfman, Ronnie Leah. *Engagement and the Language of the Subject in the Poetry of Aimé Césaire*. Gainesville: University Press of Florida, 1987. This monograph addresses issues of race awareness and politics as well as literature. Bibliography, index.

Suk, Jeannie. *Postcolonial Paradoxes in French Caribbean Writing: Césaire, Glissant, Condé*. Oxford, England: Clarendon Press, 2001. This study of Caribbean writing includes analysis and discussion of the works of Césaire.

Cherie R. Maiden
Updated by Gordon Walters

RENÉ CHAR

Born: L'Île-en-Sorgue, France; June 14, 1907
Died: Paris, France; February 19, 1988

OTHER LITERARY FORMS

Like many French poets, René Char (shahr) wrote a great number of prose poems, and he is considered one of the finest practitioners in this genre since Charles Baudelaire and Arthur Rimbaud, by whom he was heavily influenced. These works are scattered throughout Char's poetry collections, suggesting that he does not distinguish the prose poem as a separate form. Char published several volumes of essays, including *Recherche de la base et du sommet* (1955; inquiry into the base and the summit) and *Sur la poésie* (1958; on poetry). He also contributed a number of prefaces, introductions, and catalogs for art shows, such as the 1973 Pablo Picasso exhibit in Avignon. Char's life-long interest in painting is reflected in essays on Georges Braque, Joan Miró, and other contemporary artists; he also was active in other arts, writing the scenario for the ballet *L'Abominable Homme des neiges* (pb. 1956; the abominable snowman), for example, and the play *Le Soleil des eaux* (pb. 1949). Char's work has been set to music by composer Pierre Boulez.

ACHIEVEMENTS

Early in his poetic career, René Char was deeply involved in Surrealism, coauthoring several works with Paul Éluard and André Breton and gaining some recognition for his work. Under that influence, he was encouraged in his taste for the fragment—the incomplete line and "broken" metaphor, which he called *le poème pulvérisé*. These Surrealist techniques led to his being identified with the movement but did not lead to serious individual recognition.

After World War II, Char dedicated his *Leaves of Hypnos* to Albert Camus, a fellow Resistance fighter, who called Char France's greatest living poet, praising his shift from the self-absorption of Surrealism to a more universal view. Char thereby became associated with the rising tide of existentialism and achieved recognition as a major poet. Char also is credited with achieving a new validation for the prose poem, which, though it had a long tradition in France, was still regarded as a stepchild of "real" poetry.

BIOGRAPHY

René-Émile Char was born on June 14, 1907, the son of Émile Char, a manufacturer, and Marie-Thérèse-Armand Rouget of Cavaillon. Char's father, who served as the mayor of L'Île-en-Sorgue, was the son of a ward of the state who had been given the name "Charlemagne," later shortened to "Char-Magne" and, eventually, to "Char." Char spent his childhood in L'Île-en-Sorgue in the Vaucluse region in the south of France. The Vaucluse has a lush landscape ringed with mountains, the beauty of which would later fill his poetry. It is also an area of diverse industries, and the young Char became familiar with men of many occupations, especially craftspeople, peasants, and Sorgue River fishermen. Their rugged independence helped to instill in him a lifelong love of freedom. The boy had begun his education in the public schools when his father died in 1918. He then continued to the *lycée* in Avignon (the closest large city) for his *baccalauréat*. In 1924, he spent some time in Tunisia, where he developed a distaste for colonialism. He returned to study briefly at the École-de-Commerce in Marseilles, leaving from 1927 to 1928 for artillery service in Nîmes. In 1928, he published his first book of poems, *Les Cloches sur le coeur*.

Char sent a copy of his second collection, *Arsenal*, to Éluard, the chief poet of Surrealism, in Paris. Éluard was impressed with Char's work and went to L'Île-en-Sorgue to meet him. They became lifelong friends, and Char moved to Paris, where Éluard introduced him to the leading figures of Surrealism, including Breton. Char cowrote the poem *Ralentir travaux* (works slowed down) with Éluard and Breton and helped found the periodical *La Surréalisme au service de la révolution*. In 1933, Char married Georgette Goldstein (they were divorced in 1949), and a year he later published *Le Marteau sans maître* (the hammer without a master). During the early 1930's, he resided sometimes in Paris, sometimes in L'Île-en-Sorgue, and made several trips to Spain.

By the mid-1930's, the political climate in Europe was changing, and Char broke with the Surrealists in 1934, as Éluard soon would, sensing a need for the kind of action hinted at in *Le Marteau sans maître*: the defense of the oppressed and the fight for justice. In 1935, Char accepted a job as manager of the chalk pits in Vaucluse, but he soon resigned. In 1936, he was seriously ill as a result of blood poisoning, and he spent a year—the same year the Spanish Civil War began—convalescing in Cannes. He published *Placard pour un chemin des écoliers* (sign for a bypath) and *Dehors la nuit est gouvernée* (somewhere night is ruled) in the late 1930's, both titles indicating his growing sense of commitment. As 1939 ended, Char found himself mobilized into the artillery in Alsace, where he fought until the French surrender.

Returning to L'Île-en-Sorgue, Char was suspected by the Vichy police of being a communist because of his association with Surrealism. He fled with Georgette to the Alps and there began his activities as a *maquisard* in the Armée Secrète. Using the name Captain Alexandre from 1943 to 1945, Char became the departmental commander of the Parachute Landing Division of the Second Region of the Forces Françaises Combattantes and deputy to the regional commander of the Free French operations network. He was wounded in combat against the Germans in June, 1944, and after being cared for by Resistance doctors, he continued to Algeria in July, 1944, in response to a summons from the North Africa Allied Council. Subsequently, he was parachuted into France and participated in the battles to liberate Provence. Demobilized in 1945, he received several decorations for his service, including the Croix de Guerre and the Médaille de la Résistance.

From 1939 to the liberation of France, Char did not publish any poetry. When *Seuls demeurant* (the only ones left) and *Leaves of Hypnos* appeared, he became famous. Georges Mounin's critique *Avez-vous lu Char?* (1947; Have you read Char?) praised Char's work and contributed to his success. Char again began to live part of each year in Paris and part in the Vaucluse; he did not, however, participate in the "official" literary life. He generally declined the honors offered to him, although he was made a Chevalier de la Légion d'Honneur and received the Prix des Critiques in 1966, and he argued that poetry should not be considered a means of making a living. He also stood apart from the partisan political involvements which entangled many French writers of the time— especially those who shared Char's leftist sympathies.

One of Char's closest friends was the novelist Albert Camus, who, like Char, linked literature with the struggle toward freedom and human dignity. Char also exchanged letters with the Russian poet and novelist Boris Pasternak and, beginning in 1955, kept in close contact with the German philosopher Martin Heidegger .

Throughout the 1950's and 1960's, the audience for Char's poetry grew, and he was translated into numerous foreign languages. After he became associated with Georges Braque in 1947, Char often published his poetry in beautiful editions, illustrated by celebrated contemporary artists such as Pablo Picasso, Nicolas de Stäel, Louis Broder, and Louis Fernandez. Char also illustrated his poetry himself. His interest in philosophy dominated his later poetry, and beginning in the 1950's, Char saw his role as poet as that of a commentator on society, a revolutionary in the service of humankind. He died in Paris on February 19, 1988.

ANALYSIS

Albert Camus once wrote that René Char's poetry was both ancient and new, subtle and simple, carrying both daytime and night: "In the brilliant landscape where Char was born, the sun . . . is something dark." Camus thus identified one of the predominant characteristics of Char's poetic method: the juxtaposition of opposites. According to critic Robert W. Greene, Char has rejected one of the fundamental concepts of Western thought: the Aristotelian principle that a thing cannot be anything other than what it is at one moment in time. Any poem working within different principles seems obscure and vaporous as Eastern religions which deny the reality of the world. Char, however, deeply admires the fragments of Heraclitus—who believed in the unity of opposites—and sets up oppositions throughout his poetry. Similar concepts can be found in earlier poetry influenced by Eastern thought, such as Ralph Waldo Emerson's "Brahma," in which the slayer is simultaneously the one who is slain. Char's rejection of the identity principle, however, has different implications in its twentieth century context. It reflects the linguistic, subjective philosophies developing in the late nineteenth and early twentieth centuries, and though Char has a tendency toward the fragmentary aphorism (possibly influenced by the fragments of Heraclitus), he grapples with modern problems in a specific way. Thus, as Camus rightly observed, Char's poetry is both "ancient and new."

"COMMUNE PRÉSENCE"

The concluding lines of Char's important early poem "Commune présence" are characteristic in their conjunction of opposites: "You have been created for extraordinary moments . . . Adjust yourself and disperse without regret." Here, a near-heroic proclamation of identity is immediately followed by a line advising assimilation. The following line, "According to a soft hardness," embodies yet another contradiction and illustrates Char's technique of opposing semantic units. It furthermore conveys Char's fundamental view of a world of unsynthesized opposites. Life is simultaneously total resistance and total acceptance. One is reminded of the existentialist assertions that whatever a person does is completely absurd, yet that it is necessary to act as if each moment had meaning. The final two lines of the poem contain a command: "Swarm the dust/ No one will decelerate your union." The penultimate line is a contradiction because a swarm of bees is similar to a cloud of dust only in appearance. Dust moves at random, each mote in its own direction; bees move in rough unison. Dust dissipates into nothingness; bees have a vital purpose. The final line promises that nothing can oppose the eventual union, however—the union that comes from an initial scattering. In political terms, one sees the allusion to humankind as a collection of individual, meaningless units (like dust), which can gain new meaning by union (like a swarm). All those meaningless units (bees, motes, people), added together, become meaning. Metaphorically, darkness becomes the sun.

SURREALIST PERIOD

Char's early association with Surrealism might be regarded as an influence in that direction, or it may be seen as a reflection of what Char already was reaching for in his work. As Camus wrote, "No doubt he did take part in Surrealism, but rather as an ally than as an adherent, and just long enough to discover that he could walk alone with more conviction." This is the general critical appraisal. Anna Balakian, however, asserts that Char carries on the tradition of Surrealism better than anyone else. As Char describes in *Le Poème pulvérisé*, he faces—like Breton and the others—"this rebellious and solitary world of contradictions" and cannot live without the image of the unknown before him. In this vast unknown, this world finally impossible to understand (hence the Surrealist's despair), one can only be an explorer, and poetry is the medium of exploration: words and meaning in conflict. Irrationality is crucial in setting aside the world of illusion and seeing beyond, to the more legitimate world of dreams. *The Nuptial Countenance* has been cited as exhibiting this trait in its mixing of objects that defy classification; it has many resemblances to the works of Breton and Éluard.

Critic Mechthild Cranston argues that Char took two important insights with him when he broke with Surrealism: He saw that the existing world order was in need of reexamination, along with the canons of art, and that violence and destruction would not solve the problems of his generation. The first idea remained with him throughout his career, in his commitment to the Resistance and in his generally leftist politics. The second, however, underwent modification. In Char's Surrealist period, he speaks of the need for violence, catastrophes, and crimes to help create a new concept of art. "Les Soleils chanteurs" mentions specific kinds of violence that will revitalize poetry. Char's poetry of this period is filled with images of chemicals, metals, and machinery, like the works of the Futurists, and has a similar purpose: to destroy the florid, false language of late Romanticism. Char's experience of the real—not metaphorical—violence of World War II changed his orientation. In his poetry published since the war, he abandoned the rhetoric of the Surrealists, achieving a new humility and seeking the simplicity of a child's vision.

LATER POETRY

Char's later poetry is also distinguished by its moral intensity, particularly its commitment to freedom. In Char's view, anything that inhibits human freedom is immoral. The poet's duty is to do battle continually against anything that would restrict humankind's ability to seek meaning. This includes any preconceived ideas, even the idea of liberty itself. One might see in this stance a combination of the didactic nature of Surrealism and the call to action and freedom in existentialism. Like the existentialists, Char attempts to re-create ethics for modern humanity, yet in doing so he invokes the mystery so important to Surrealist art. Thus, for Char, poetry is an existential stance, a becoming, an invitation to return to natural insights and to reject mechanical materialism.

OTHER MAJOR WORKS

PLAYS: *Claire: Théâtre de Verdure*, pb. 1949; *Le Soleil des eaux*, pb. 1949; *L'Abominable Homme des neiges*, pb. 1956 (ballet scenario); *Trois coups sous les arbres: Théâtre Saisonnier*, pb. 1967.

NONFICTION: *Recherche de la base et du sommet*, 1955; *Sur la poésie*, 1958.

MISCELLANEOUS: *En trente-trois morceaux*, 1956 (aphorisms).

BIBLIOGRAPHY

Caws, Mary Ann. *The Presence of René Char*. Princeton, N.J.: Princeton University Press, 1976. Critical interpretation of selected works by Char. Includes bibliographical references and index.

_____. *René Char*. Boston: Twayne, 1977. An introductory biography and critical interpretation of selected works by Char. Includes an index and a bibliography.

Eichbauer, Mary E. *Poetry's Self-Portrait: The Visual Arts as Mirror and Muse in René Char and John Ashbery*. New York: Peter Lang, 1992. An analysis of the relationship to visual art of the poetry of Char and Ashbery. Includes bibliographical references and index.

Lawler, James R. *René Char: The Myth and the Poem*. Princeton, N.J.: Princeton University Press, 1978. A critical analysis of Char's poetry. Includes bibliographic references.

Minahen, Charles D., ed. *Figuring Things: Char, Ponge, and Poetry in the Twentieth Century*. Lexington, Ky.: French Forum, 1994. A critical study and comparison of the works of Char and Francis Ponge. Includes bibliographic references.

Piore, Nancy Kline. *Lightning: The Poetry of René Char*. Boston: Northeastern University Press, 1981. A short critical study of selected poems. Includes an index and bibliography.

J. Madison Davis

JEAN COCTEAU

Born: Maisons-Laffitte, France; July 5, 1889
Died: Milly-la-Forêt, France; October 11, 1963

OTHER LITERARY FORMS

Jean Cocteau (kawk-TOH) was a formidable artist in many genres and very prolific.
Among his seven novels, little read today, the most important is *Les Enfants terribles*

Jean Cocteau
(National Archives)

(1929; *Enfants Terribles*, 1930, also known as *Children of the Game*). Among his many plays, some of the most notable are *Orphée* (pr. 1926; *Orpheus*, 1933), *La Voix humaine* (pr., pb. 1930; *The Human Voice*, 1951), *La Machine infernale* (pr., pb. 1934; *The Infernal Machine*, 1936), *Les Parents terribles* (pr., pb. 1938; *Intimate Relations*, 1952), and *La Machine à écrire* (pr., pb. 1941; *The Typewriter*, 1948). In the opinion of many critics, Cocteau's greatest achievements were in the cinema. His masterpieces—which he both wrote and directed—include *Le Sang d'un poète* (1930; *The Blood of a Poet*, 1949), *La Belle et la bête* (1946; *Beauty and the Beast*, 1947), *Les Parents terribles* (1948; *Intimate Relations*, 1952), *Les Enfants terribles* (1950), *Orphée* (1950; *Orpheus*, 1950), and *La Testament d'Orphée* (1959; *The Testament of Orpheus*, 1968). Cocteau also wrote scenarios for ballets by various composers, notably for Erik Satie's *Parade* (1917), for Darius Milhaud's *Le Boeuf sur le toit* (1920), and for *Les Mariés de la tour Eiffel* (1921; *The Wedding on the Eiffel Tower*, 1937), which had music by Les Six. Cocteau also collaborated on two opera-oratorios, *Odipus-Rex* (1927) with Igor Stravinsky, and *Antigone* (1922; English translation, 1961) with Arthur Honegger. Cocteau's nonfiction includes a variety of idiosyncratic autobiographical and critical works.

ACHIEVEMENTS

Jean Cocteau was one of the most remarkable figures in twentieth century art. Extremely versatile, he unified his diverse interests by seeing them as merely different aspects of *poésie: poésie de roman* (poetry of the novel), *poésie de théâtre* (poetry of the drama), *poésie cinématographique* (poetry of the film), and even *poésie graphique* (poetry of drawing). Curiously, with poetry as the metaphorical center of Cocteau's artistic achievement, critics are still uncomfortable with his accomplishments as a poet. Some consider him a central figure through whom the major currents of art in the early 1900's passed, while others regard him as a dilettante, interested only in stylishness and facile demonstrations of his considerable talents, lacking substance under the sparkling facade. Many of his contemporaries were uncertain of his importance because he remained always on the periphery of "serious" art. Looking back, however, it is clear that, at the very least, Cocteau's poetry is another brilliant aspect of one of the most versatile artistic minds of the century and that it has been underrated largely because of the difficulty in grasping Cocteau in all his variety.

BIOGRAPHY

Jean Cocteau was born in a prosperous suburb of Paris to Georges and Eugénie Lecomte Cocteau, a cultivated bourgeois couple who exposed Jean, his brother Paul, and their sister Marthe to the fine arts. When at their suburban home, the children played on the grounds of a nearby castle designed by François Mansart. When in Paris—Cocteau would always consider himself a Parisian above all—his family lived with his grandparents, whose house contained classical busts, vases, a painting by Eugène Delacroix, and drawings by Jean-Auguste-Dominique Ingres. Cocteau's grandfather was a cellist and would often be visited by the renowned violinist Pablo de Sarasate. Some of Cocteau's fondest memories of his early life were of trips to the circus, the ice palace, and the theater, especially the Comédie-Française. Years later, in his own drama, he would attempt to duplicate the lighting or brilliancy of theatrical events in his memory and would discover from lighting technicians that it had been technically impossible to do such things when he was a child. Time had increased the splendor of his memories, including those of the castle and of his grandparents' house. He thus began to perceive his own life as having mythological dimensions, as even his personal experiences had become exaggerated and distorted over time.

In 1899, Cocteau's father committed suicide as a result of financial problems. Cocteau became an indifferent student at the Petit Lycée Condorcet and, later, at the Grand Condorcet. Like many creative personalities, he found the institutional atmosphere oppressive. Besides having a weak constitution, which often led to legitimate absences, he was frequently truant. During his illnesses, he often had his German governess stitching doll clothes for his model theater. One of his closest childhood friends was Réné Rocher, later to become a director, who spent much time with Cocteau and his miniature theaters. After a trip with his mother to Venice, Cocteau began study for his baccalaureate, had his first love affair (with Madeleine Carlier, ten years his senior), and became more involved with the theater—meeting Edouard de Max, who acted opposite Sarah Bernhardt. Quite naturally, with all this to entertain him, Cocteau failed the examination.

On April 4, 1908, de Max sponsored a reading of Cocteau's poetry, by de Max, Rocher, and other prominent actors and actresses, at the Théâtre Fémina. Because the event was attended by many of the elite of Paris, including several leading literary critics, Cocteau became instantly well known. Subsequently, he became acquainted with such literary notables as Edmond Rostand, Marcel Proust, Charles-Pierre Péguy, Catulle Mendès, and Jules Lemaître. He became quite enamored of Comtesse Anna de Noailles and tried to write poetry like hers, with a refined sensibility and enhanced sensuality. He was one of three founders of a literary magazine, *Schéhérazade*, which was dedicated to poetry and music, and rented a room at the Hôtel Biron, where Auguste Rodin and his secretary, Rainer Maria Rilke, were also staying.

When Cocteau was introduced to the great impresario Sergei Diaghilev of the Ballets Russes, he begged Diaghilev to permit him to write ballets. Diaghilev eventually said "Étonne-moi!" ("Astonish me!"), and Cocteau took this injunction as an order to give shape to the rest of his life's work. His first ballet, *Le Dieu bleu* (1912), was not successful, though Diaghilev produced it for the coronation of George V. Convinced the music was at fault, Cocteau began to associate with Igor Stravinsky, living with him for a while. During this period, Cocteau was also trying to defend himself against the accusation of Henri Ghéon in the *Nouvelle Revue française*, who charged that he was an entirely derivative poet. Around 1914, Cocteau underwent what he called a "molting," breaking free of the influence of Rostand and the Comtesse de Noailles and moving toward his eventual association with Max Jacob and Guillaume Apollinaire.

As World War I broke out, Cocteau attempted to enlist but was rejected for health reasons. Illegally, he became an ambulance driver on the Belgian front, but after being discovered, he was sent back to Paris. These experiences would later form a large part of his novel *Thomas l'imposteur* (1923; *Thomas the Impostor*, 1925). Back in Paris, he met Amedeo Modigliani and Pablo Picasso and introduced the latter to Diaghilev, thereby creating the association that would produce Erik Satie's 1917 ballet *Parade*, with scenario by Cocteau, costumes and set by Picasso, and choreography by Léonide Massine. *Parade* created a scandal with its atonal music and extraordinary set and costumes. Only the presence of Apollinaire, in uniform and wearing a bandage over his head wound, kept the outraged spectators from attacking the creators of the ballet. Cocteau responded vigorously, attacking the musical influences of Claude Debussy, Richard Wagner, and Stravinsky and linking himself with the composers known as Les Six (Georges Auric, Louis Durey, Arthur Honegger, Darius Milhaud, Francis Poulenc, and Germaine Tailleferre).

In 1919, Cocteau met and fell in love with Raymond Radiguet, who was fifteen, handsome, and a poetic genius—or so Cocteau believed. Radiguet caused Cocteau to reevaluate his aesthetics and move toward a simpler, classic style; thus inspired, he found new energy and created a number of new works, including *Le Grand écart* (1923; *The Grand Écart*, 1925) and the volume of poems *Plain-Chant*. Radiguet, however, died of typhoid in December, 1923, and Cocteau was devastated. Diaghilev tried to shake Cocteau from his despair by taking him on a trip to Monte Carlo. The trip itself did little good, however, and the discovery of opium there proved to be Cocteau's only solace. His addiction eventually provoked his friends and family to persuade him to enter a sanatorium in 1925. There, he came under the influence of Jacques Maritain, the Catholic philosopher, who briefly restored Cocteau's faith in religion. He was able to pick up the pieces of this life and create such works as *L'Ange Heurtebise*, *Orpheus*, and *Children of the Game*. He even patched up his friendship with Stravinsky and wrote the words for Stravinsky's oratorio *Oedipus-Rex*.

In the 1930's, Cocteau seemed inexhaustible, even though he suffered a bout with typhoid in 1931. Plays, poems, songs, ballets, art criticism, and even a column for *Ce soir* poured forth from his pen. He took a trip around the world in imitation of Jules Verne's *Le Tour du monde en quatre-vingt jours* (1873; *Around the World in Eighty Days*, 1873). He became the manager of the bantamweight boxer Alphonse Theo Brown. Perhaps the most important of his activities during this period was his first attempt at *poésie cinématographique*, when he wrote and directed *The Blood of a Poet*.

Cocteau, always controversial, found himself caught between his artistic enemies and new political ones during the Nazi occupation of France. He was viciously attacked in the press. His play *The Typewriter* was banned. He never backed off, however, even when beaten by a group of French fascists for failing to salute the flag.

After the war, Cocteau found himself a "grand old man" of the artistic world, but he refused to rest on his laurels and continued arousing controversy. He traveled and wrote plays, journals, and films. He made recordings and designed frescoes for the city hall at Menton, the Chapel of St. Pierre at Villefranche-sur-Mer, the Chapel of Notre Dame in London, the Church of Saint Blaise-des-Simples in Milly-la-Forêt, and the Chapel of Notre-Dame-de-Jerusalem at Fréjus. He also designed fabrics, plates, and posters. He was made a member of the Royal Belgian Academy and the French Academy in 1955 and received an honorary doctorate of letters from Oxford University in 1956. He died on October 11, 1963, shortly after hearing of the death of his friend Edith Piaf.

ANALYSIS

Jean Cocteau's first three books of poetry enjoyed the kind of success that works that essentially flatter the prevailing literary establishment are prone to have. He was instantly praised and compared to various great poets, present and past, yet never aroused the outrage or bewilderment provoked by significant breakthroughs. Very much a salon poet and dandy, Cocteau had yet to discover his own voice. *La Lampe d'Aladin* contained poems dedicated to the various actors and actresses who had read them at Cocteau's "debut" in the Théâtre Fémina. Like much of the poetry of the early 1900's, the poems of this first volume seem self-serving, overly and insincerely emotional, and very immature, though occasionally some charming cleverness may emerge.

LE PRINCE FRIVOLE

Cocteau's second collection, *Le Prince frivole* (the frivolous prince), is little better than the first. Its title came to be applied to its author, and Cocteau would later refer to the book as elevating him to the "Prince du Ridicule." The creation of poetry here is still an amusing game. Cocteau rather dutifully insists on melancholy in many of the works, but it comes off as posing, even though it may be indicative of an indefinable feeling that all the praise he was receiving was undeserved.

LA DANSE DE SOPHOCLE

After the publication of *La Danse de Sophocle*, the inadequacy of Cocteau's artistic commitment was brought home to him in a review by Henri Ghéon in *Nouvelle Revue française* (André Gide may have had a hand in its authorship). Ghéon pointed out the derivative qualities of Cocteau's three books and implied that the poet was immature, frivolous, and greatly overestimated. Ghéon said that Cocteau was undeniably gifted but that he had not devoted himself to his gift. The review was more important in Cocteau's life than the book itself, though one can see in *La Danse de Sophocle* the beginning of Cocteau's lifelong interest in the eternal truths found in ancient Greek mythology and literature. The review provoked Cocteau to understand "that art and poetry aren't a game, but a descent into a mine, down toward the firedamp and danger."

LE CAP DE BONNE-ESPÉRANCE

Cocteau did not publish another collection of poetry until seven years later, after working for the Ballets Russes, associating with a more radical set of artists, and after his experiences in World War I. Later, when republishing his works, he ignored the earlier three books and dated his beginnings as a poet from *Le Cap de Bonne-Espérance* (the Cape of Good Hope), which was inspired by his association with the aviator Roland Garros. Garros would take Cocteau on daily flights from Villacoublay. He performed numerous acrobatics with Cocteau in the plane, and the poet was inspired by the sensation of flying and the view of Paris from the air. In 1918, after a remarkable escape from a German prison, Garros was shot down and killed. A proof copy of Cocteau's long poem dedicated to Garros was found in his cockpit. In the book, the airplane symbolizes the modern era: It frees humankind from earthly considerations, putting the pilot or passenger into a realm of new visions and solitude, where he can find his soul. At the same time, he faces death.

The poems in *Le Cap de Bonne-Espérance* are extremely sensual, despite the abstract element, and attempt to re-create the physical sensations of flying with fragmented lines and onomatopoeic vowels. These techniques were not original to Cocteau; the typographical effects had been used by Stéphane Mallarmé, Apollinaire, and Pierre Reverdy, and the *lettriste* effects by Pierre Albert-Birot. However, as Adrienne Monnier points out, it was daring of Cocteau to employ these still-radical devices. André Breton, among others, considered the collection not radical enough and had a sour expression the whole time Cocteau was reading it in Valentine Gross's apartment. Cocteau is said to have called his work old-fashioned, in an effort to charm Breton, but many see the reading as the beginning of Cocteau's long battle with the Surrealists. The book also provoked a letter from Proust, who gently asked whether it did not display a certain indiscriminate use of images.

DISCOURS DU GRAND SOMMEIL

Discours du grand sommeil (discourse of the great sleep) consists of eleven poems written between 1916 and 1918 and was inspired by Cocteau's experiences with the Fusiliers Marins, among whom he lived, illegally wearing the Marine uniform until discovered by an officer. A day after Cocteau was ejected from the front, most of the Fusiliers Marins were killed. Cocteau attempted in these poems to end once and for all his role as the "prince of frivolity." Though flippancy was always part of Cocteau's demeanor, he once asserted that it was the bourgeois way of dealing with catastrophe—that what appeared to be frivolity to others was actually Cocteau's way of dealing with his profound sadness. *Discours du grand sommeil*, writes Wallace Fowlie, is "a plunge downward," "a contact with the grim presence of death." The poems are quite effective in conveying the horror of war, of the exhausting marches, the screams of the dying, and the endless suffering. There is also an awakening sense of the soldier as symbolic of the tragedy of human existence and a movement toward a more classical style and attitude. The volume clearly points toward Cocteau's later aesthetic.

VOCABULAIRE

Vocabulaire also reveals a cleaner, purer style than that of Cocteau's youthful works yet still betrays the inordinate influence of the artistic movements of the war years, such as Dadaism, Futurism, Imagism, and cubism. Cocteau's fixation on certain images (such as snow turning to marble) is notable throughout his career. In this collection, the rose appears often, with obvious allusions to Pierre de Ronsard, in clear homage to French classicism. One finds Cocteau in search of himself, struggling as he had since the Ghéon review to achieve originality. The poems consist largely of philosophical speculations on the nature of change and the poet's role in metamorphosis. The endless flow of change is represented by the changes in clouds, aging, swans, the dissolution of salt statues, death, and snow. Cocteau's private mythology is fully developed here; several poems, such as "Tombeaux" (tombs) and "Oiseaux sont en neige" (birds are in snow), connect homosexuality to the themes of change and death. In these poems, Cocteau seems to be taking stock of his life, trying to find a direction and meaning to it.

POÉSIES, 1917-1920

Under Radiguet's influence, Cocteau was moving toward the tradition of French literature that employs the brief, clear, precise sentence. Cocteau renewed himself with this classicism and rediscovered the themes of classical antiquity. In *Poésies, 1917-1920*, Cocteau introduced a new set of topics, themes, and motifs, such as the clown, circus, angel, sailor, and athlete. Perhaps the most significant poem in the collection is "L'Ode à Picasso" (ode to Picasso), an attempt to grasp the complexity of the painter and artist whom Cocteau often watched at work for hours on end. The poem reveals Picasso as a man possessed by an inner fire, an embodiment of the concept, expressed by Socrates in Plato's *Iōn* (fourth century B.C.E.; *Ion*, 1804), of the madness of the poet. Painting, sculpture, film, and any other expression of art are therefore merely facets of the same thing: *poésie*. Cocteau sees in Picasso a man in constant contact with the Muses, free of mundane considerations. The poem expresses much of what Cocteau would attempt to be, would have the courage to be, after being inspired by Radiguet. The final poem of *Poésies, 1917-1920*, "Mouchoir" (handkerchief), bids farewell to influences of the past and sets the poet out on a voyage into the unknown. To be a poet is thus to move ahead relentlessly, to be uncertain of the results, to follow no one.

PLAIN-CHANT

Plain-Chant reveals in its title a further move toward simplification and, in Fowlie's view, is central to the work of Cocteau. It is classically metered and uses the imagery of Angel, Muse, and Death, symbolism that recurs in much of the rest of Cocteau's oeuvre. The Angel in this lyric poem is clearly Radiguet, and the poem expresses Cocteau's great love for him and also his fear of the death that will inevitably separate them. The Angel is his guide through the mysteries of poetic art and also his protector when the Muse leaves him or Death presses in on him. As Bettina Knapp has observed, however, Death becomes a restorative power, a bridge to another world: "He burrowed within and reached new depths of cognition, with beauty of form and classical restraint." The poem was also strangely prescient, as Radiguet died in 1923, emotionally shattering Cocteau.

OPÉRA

Cocteau's discovery of his identity as a poet under the guidance of Radiguet was not lost in his plummet into despair brought about by the young man's death. The collection *Opéra* mixes Cocteau's visions induced by opium with lucid language and precise control. Even in his agony, he rigorously adheres to a classical detachment, a coolness that enhances the feelings and mythological dimensions of the works. A blending of Christian and pagan mythology points toward Cocteau's extensive revising and adapting of works of classical mythology for the stage and film. "L'Ange heurtebise" in *Opéra* is usually thought to be one of Cocteau's most significant poems. It explores the question of angels, which he had discussed in an essay, *Le Secret professionnel* (1922). The poet is stuck on an earthly plane, struggling to understand a larger reality, while the Angel stands above. The Angel reappears in work after work of Cocteau, inspiring poets and urging them to look on the human predicament with detachment.

LATER YEARS

Cocteau did not cease writing poetry until his death, but most critics seem indifferent to the large number of his works after *Opéra*. Perhaps his work in film and prose detracted from his development in poetry, though Cocteau himself saw all his artistic works as facets of the same creative impulse: It was all poetry to him. His influence on the literary scene waned, perhaps because he had finally found his own unique path, and artists and critics found it difficult to categorize and thus assess the measure of Cocteau's achievement. His variety contributes to the difficulty of an overall assessment: He began each mature collection of poems as if he had only recently become a poet.

At the very least, Cocteau's poetry exhibits many of the primary traits of twentieth century poetry in its clean, precise form, its development of personal mythology, and its exploitation through adaptation of traditional mythological and literary themes. These traits are significant elements of the mainstream of modern poetry, and Cocteau is clearly in the middle of it.

OTHER MAJOR WORKS

LONG FICTION: *Le Potomak*, 1919; *Le Grand Écart*, 1923 (*The Grand Écart*, 1925); *Thomas l'imposteur*, 1923 (*Thomas the Impostor*, 1925); *Le Livre blanc*, 1928 (*The White Paper*, 1957); *Les Enfants terribles*, 1929 (*Enfants Terribles*, 1930; also known as *Children of the Game*); *Le Fantôme de Marseille*, 1933; *La Fin du Potomak*, 1939.

PLAYS: *Le Dieu bleu*, pr. 1912 (ballet scenario; with Frédéric de Madrazo); *Parade*, pr. 1917 (ballet scenario; music by Erik Satie, scenery by Pablo Picasso); *Le Boeuf sur le toit*, pr. 1920 (ballet scenario; music by Darius Milhaud, scenery by Raoul Dufy); *Le Gendarme incompris*, pr. 1921 (ballet scenario; with Raymond Radiguet; music by Francis Poulenc); *Les Mariés de la tour Eiffel*, pr. 1921 (ballet scenario; music by Les Six; *The Wedding on the Eiffel Tower*, 1937); *Antigone*, pr. 1922 (libretto; English translation, 1961); *Les Biches*, pr. 1924 (ballet scenario; music by Poulenc); *Les Fâcheux*, pr. 1924 (ballet scenario; music by George Auric); *Orphée*, pr. 1926 (*Orpheus*, 1933); *Oedipus-Rex*, pr. 1927, pb. 1928 (libretto; English translation, 1961); *La Voix humaine*, pr., pb. 1930 (*The Human Voice*, 1951); *La Machine infernale*, pr., pb. 1934 (*The Infernal Machine*, 1936); *L'École des veuves*, pr., pb. 1936; *Les Chevaliers de la table ronde*, pr., pb. 1937 (*The Knights of the Round Table*, 1955); *Les Parents terribles*, pr., pb. 1938 (*Intimate Relations*, 1952); *Les Monstres sacrés*, pr., pb. 1940 (*The Holy Terrors*, 1953); *La Machine à écrire*, pr., pb. 1941 (*The Typewriter*, 1948); *Renaud et Armide*, pr., pb. 1943; *L'Aigle à deux têtes*, pr., pb. 1946 (*The Eagle Has Two Heads*, 1946); *Le Jeune Homme et la mort*, pr. 1946 (ballet scenario; music by Johann Sebastian Bach); *Phèdre*, pr. 1950 (ballet scenario; music by Auric); *Bacchus*, pr. 1951 (English translation, 1955); *Théâtre complet*, 1957 (2 volumes); *Five Plays*, 1961; *L'Impromptu du Palais-Royal*, pr., pb. 1962; *The Infernal Machine, and Other Plays*, 1964.

SCREENPLAYS: *Le Sang d'un poète*, 1930 (*The Blood of a Poet*, 1949); *Le Baron fantôme*, 1943; *L'Éternel Retour*, 1943 (*The Eternal Return*, 1948); *L'Aigle à deux têtes*, 1946; *La Belle et la bête*, 1946 (*Beauty and the Beast*, 1947); *Ruy Blas*, 1947; *Les Parents terribles*, 1948 (*Intimate Relations*, 1952); *Les Enfants terribles*, 1950; *Orphée*, 1950 (*Orpheus*, 1950); *Le Testament d'Orphée*, 1959 (*The Testament of Orpheus*, 1968); *Thomas l'Imposteur*, 1965.

NONFICTION: *Le Coq et l'Arlequin*, 1918 (*Cock and Harlequin*, 1921); *Le Secret professionnel*, 1922; *Lettre à Jacques Maritain*, 1926 (*Art and Faith*, 1948); *Le Rappel à l'ordre*, 1926 (*A Call to Order*, 1926); *Opium: Journal d'une désintoxication*, 1930 (*Opium: Diary of a Cure*, 1932); *Essai de la critique indirecte*, 1932 (*The Lais Mystery: An Essay of Indirect Criticism*, 1936); *Portraits-souvenir, 1900-1914*, 1935 (*Paris Album*, 1956); *"La Belle et la bête": Journal d'un film*, 1946 (*"Beauty and the Beast": Journal of a Film*, 1950); *La Difficulté d'être*, 1947 (*The Difficulty of Being*, 1966); *Journal d'un inconnu*, 1952 (*The Hand of a Stranger*, 1956; also known as *Diary of an Unknown*, 1988); *The Journals of Jean Cocteau*, 1956; *Poésie critique*, 1960.

TRANSLATION: *Roméo et Juliette*, 1926 (of William Shakespeare's play).

BIBLIOGRAPHY

Crowson, Lydia. *The Esthetic of Jean Cocteau*. Hanover: University of New Hampshire Press, 1978. Chapters on Cocteau's milieu, the nature of the real, and the roles of myth, consciousness, and power. Includes introduction and bibliography. This work is for advanced students who have already consulted more introductory works.

Griffith, Alison Guest. *Jean Cocteau and the Performing Arts*. Irvine, Calif.: Severin Wunderman Museum, 1992. This museum catalog includes critical analysis of Cocteau's work as well as information on his contribution to the performing arts. Bibliography.

Knapp, Bettina L. *Jean Cocteau: Updated Edition*. Boston: Twayne, 1989. A thorough revision of Knapp's 1970 volume, which begins with her memory of her introduction to the writing. Knapp pursues both psychological and literary views of Cocteau's work, with chapters following a chronological approach. Includes separate chronology, notes, bibliography, and index.

Lowe, Romana N. *The Fictional Female: Sacrificial Rituals and Spectacles of Writing in Baudelaire, Zola, and Cocteau.* New York: Peter Lang, 1997. Highlights the sacrificial victim common in nineteenth and twentieth century French texts: women. Lowe traces structures and images of female sacrifice in the genres of poetry, novel, and theater with close readings of Baudelaire, Zola, and Cocteau.

Mauriès, Patrick. *Jean Cocteau.* Translated by Jane Brenton. London: Thames & Hudson, 1998. A brief but excellent biography of Cocteau illustrated with many photographs.

Peters, Arthur King, et al. *Jean Cocteau and the French Scene.* New York: Abbeville, 1984. Essays on Cocteau's biography, his life in Paris, his intellectual background, his view of realism, and his work in the theater and movies. Also contains a chronology, an index, and many illustrations and photographs.

Saul, Julie, ed. *Jean Cocteau: The Mirror and the Mask—A Photo-Biography.* Boston: D. R. Godine, 1992. This compilation from an exhibit celebrating the one-hundred-year anniversary of his birth, with an essay by Francis Steegmuller, provides insights into the life of Cocteau.

Selous, Trista. *Cocteau.* Paris: Centre Pompidou, 2003. A retrospective catalog compiled by the Centre Pompidou and the Montreal Museum that offers an illustrated review of Cocteau's creative output. It also includes seventeen essays on Cocteau's life and work.

Steegmuller, Francis. *Cocteau.* Boston: D. R. Godine, 1986. A major biography of Cocteau. Discusses his childhood, the influence of his mother, and fellow poets. Defines him as a "quick-change" artist with a propensity for constant self-invention, discarding old views and activities and assuming new roles or guises with remarkable facility. Twelve appendixes plus numerous illustrations. Includes bibliography, index.

Tsakiridou, Cornelia A., ed. *Reviewing Orpheus: Essays on the Cinema and Art of Jean Cocteau.* Lewisburg, Pa.: Bucknell University Press, 1997. Focuses on Cocteau's film work but is valuable for insight into his general artistry.

J. Madison Davis

ANDREI CODRESCU

Born: Sibiu, Romania; December 20, 1946
Also known as: Andrei Perlmutter; Andrei Steiu

PRINCIPAL POETRY

License to Carry a Gun, 1970
The History of the Growth of Heaven, 1971
Comrade Past and Mister Present, 1991
Belligerence, 1993
Alien Candor: Selected Poems, 1970-1995, 1996
Poezii Alese/Selected Poetry, 2000
It Was Today: New Poems by Andrei Codrescu, 2003
Jealous Witness: New Poems, 2008
The Forgiven Submarine, 2009 (with Ruxandra Cesereanu)

OTHER LITERARY FORMS

Andrei Codrescu (kah-DREHS-kew) has written novels, including *Messiah* (1999), *Casanova in Bohemia* (2002), and *Wakefield* (2004), and a collection of shorter pieces, *A Bar in Brooklyn: Novellas and Stories, 1970-1978* (1999). He wrote the screenplay for *Road Scholar: Coast to Coast Late in the Century* (1993), which won several awards, including a Peabody Award. He has published collections of essays, including *Zombifications: Essays from National Public Radio* (1994), *Hail Babylon! Looking for the American City at the End of the Millenium* (1998), *New Orleans, Mon Amour: Twenty Years of Writing from the City* (2006), and *The Posthuman Dada Guide: Tzara and Lenin Play Chess* (2009), and several memoir/travelogues, including *The Hole in the Flag: A Romanian Exile's Story of Return and Revolution* (1991) and *Ay Cuba! A Socio-Erotic Journey* (1999).

He founded and has served as editor for and contributor to the online journal *Exquisite Corpse: A Journal of Letters and Life*. He has also been a commentator on National Public Radio and a columnist for *Gambit Weekly*, a prize-winning alternative newspaper in New Orleans. He has translated the work of Lucian Blaga, a modern Romanian poet, and edited anthologies of material from *Exquisite Corpse*. He has also issued a number of audio tapes and compact discs.

ACHIEVEMENTS

Andrei Codrescu has received numerous awards and honors, including five National Endowment for the Arts Fellowships, the Big Table Poetry Award (1970), the A. D. Emmart Humanities Award (1982), Pushcart Prizes (1983, 2005), the General Electric

Foundation Poetry Award (1985), the Towson State University Literature Prize (1987), the American Civil Liberties Union Freedom of Speech Award (1995), the Mayor's Arts Award, New Orleans (1996), the Literature Prize of the Romanian Cultural Foundation, Bucharest (1996), the Lowell Thomas Gold Award for Excellence in Travel Journalism (2001), the Ovidius Prize for literature (2006), and the Romania Radio Cultural Award (2008). He was awarded honorary doctorates from Shenandoah College and the Massachussetts College of Art.

BIOGRAPHY

Born Andrei Perlmutter in 1946 in communist-controlled Transylvania, Andrei Codrescu first published under the name Andrei Steiu, chosen to conceal his Jewishness in that anti-Semitic milieu. He emigrated to the United States in 1966, living at first in Detroit, where he associated with the Detroit Artists Workshop, founded by John Sinclair, a well-known poet and social activist. At about this time, he began publishing poetry in Romania, using the name Codrescu. After a year, Codrescu moved to New York, linking up with the New York Beat poets, and began to publish in English. After publishing his first poetry book, *License to Carry a Gun*, he moved to San Francisco; seven years later, he moved to Baltimore and ultimately settled in New Orleans. He became a United States citizen in 1981. From 1984 to 2009, he was the MacCurdy Distinguished Professor at Louisiana State University. He has two children, Lucian and Tristan, from his first marriage to Alice Henderson. He later married Laura Cole.

ANALYSIS

Andrei Codrescu's work can be seen as combining two elements: Surrealism and the expressions of a flâneur, the gentleman stroller described by Charles Baudelaire, who comments on the urban scene of which he is a part. These converge to form a goal of intensified awareness of oneself and the environment. Codrescu is both detached and involved. His rejection of convention avoids the rage of the alienated and is paradoxically both softened and made more penetrating by humor.

JEALOUS WITNESS

In *Jealous Witness*, Codrescu's fascination with the urban milieu plays a central role. In the aftermath of Hurricane Katrina in 2005, he focused on New Orleans. In "Cleaning Ladies," he expresses his fear that an urban treasure is irremediably gone:

> they were cleansing storms
> katrina and rita
> they were cleaning women
> hired by the housing boom broom
> real estate real estate
> you kept rising like the water

> but the poor kept staying on
> in the days before the storms
> then came katrina and rita
> to finish what you began
> cleansing storms oh cleaning ladies
> making realtor dreams come true
> oh look over that rising sea
> I'll take the lobster and the vino
> see the shining shining city
> it's the new new orleans rising
> coin-operated by casinos

He alludes to the underclass, including artists, once protected and even nourished by the city's special social architecture but threatened by mercantile interests and then literally swept away by the storms, but he deftly avoids anger by the playfulness of "housing boom broom" and the personification of the storms as members of that underclass. With anger controlled, the bitter sarcasm of a shining city that has become a gambling arcade slices away crass unconcern for what has been lost.

This Surrealist flâneur has made the astonishing transition from marginalized outsider, foreigner and Jew, to academic insider and uncrowned laureate. That transition has not blunted his commitment to art as manifested both in his support of freshness and experimentation in poetry through *Exquisite Corpse* and in his rejoicing in beauty. In "The Incoming Sneeze or the Old Man's Nose," he writes:

> for you there is always beauty
> you can recognize by a whiff like a perfume in a crowd
> that's what your crooked nose is for

The reference to his Jewishness is as unmistakable as is the romantic tone, and so, presumably, is the reference, conscious or not, to Edmond Rostand's *Cyrano de Bergerac* (pr. 1897; English translation, 1898).

THE FORGIVEN SUBMARINE

In *The Forgiven Submarine*, Codrescu describes his exhilarating collaborative exploration of the unconscious with his coauthor, Ruxandra Cesereanu:

> the two divers were a shook-up pianist
> and a nearsighted drunk amerikan beatnik
> banding together for dives to great depths
> a pianist with hair from neverland and an amerikan
> with transylvanian moustaches sensitized by the
>   imminence of nothingness
> his head and armpits shaved one earring in his ear new
>   age aimlessness

gold chains jingling on his ankles setting the ocean
   foaming
and setting minds to work chewing the cud
ahoy there forgiven submarine
we are diving your way out of submerged and
   unadorned time

The deliberately unsettling Surrealism is softened with slang and self-mockery, and the ambition of "setting minds to work" made more palatable, as it were, by the homespun metaphor of "chewing the cud."

OTHER MAJOR WORKS

LONG FICTION: *The Repentance of Lorraine*, 1976; *The Blood Countess*, 1995; *Messiah*, 1999; *Casanova in Bohemia*, 2002; *Wakefield*, 2004.

SHORT FICTION: *A Bar in Brooklyn: Novellas and Stories, 1970-1978*, 1999.

SCREENPLAY: *Road Scholar: Coast to Coast Late in the Century*, 1993.

NONFICTION: *A Craving for Swan*, 1986; *Raised by Puppets Only to Be Killed by Research*, 1987; *The Disappearance of the Outside: A Manifesto for Escape*, 1990; *The Hole in the Flag: A Romanian Exile's Story of Return and Revolution*, 1991; *The Muse Is Always Half-Dressed in New Orleans*, 1993; *Road Scholar: Coast to Coast Late in the Century*, 1993; *Zombifications: Essays from National Public Radio*, 1994; *The Dog With the Chip in His Neck: Essays from NPR and Elsewhere*, 1996; *Hail Babylon! Looking for the American City at the End of the Millennium*, 1998; *Ay Cuba! A Socio-Erotic Journey*, 1999; *The Devil Never Sleeps, and Other Essays*, 2000; *An Involuntary Genius in America's Shoes (and What Happened Afterwards)*, 2001; *New Orleans, Mon Amour: Twenty Years of Writing from the City*, 2006; *The Posthuman Dada Guide: Tzara and Lenin Play Chess*, 2009.

TRANSLATION: *At the Court of Yearning*, 1989 (of Lucian Blaga).

EDITED TEXTS: *The Stiffest of the Corpse: An Exquisite Corpse Reader, 1983-1988*, 1988; *Thus Spake the Corpse: An Exquisite Corpse Reader, 1988-1998*, 1999.

BIBLIOGRAPHY

Codrescu, Andrei. "Andrei Codrescu Brings His Unique Take on America to Idaho." Interview by Anna Webb. *McClatchy-Tribune Business News*, February 13, 2007, p. 1. Codrescu discusses everything from leaving Romania, to being with the Beat poets, to Hurricane Katrina and the city of New Orleans in Louisiana. He says the United States is "momentarily occupied by zombies," but its "future is sound."

_____. "An Interview with Andrei Codrescu." Interview by Richard Collins. *Xavier Review* 20, no. 2 (2000): 13-18. The author talks about his writings and his life.

Collins, Richard. "Andrei Codrescu's Mioritic Space." *MELUS* 23, no. 3 (1998): 83-

101. Miorita, a ewe in a Romanian folk poem, warns the shepherd that he is about to be betrayed and murdered. The shepherd asks the ewe not to tell his mother that he was murdered but rather that he married the daughter of a king. So Miorita wanders, telling the tale of a wedding that never occurred. Lucian Blaga, the poet whose works Codrescu translated, defined a Mioritic space as a geography of the Romanian imagination.

Marin, Naomi. "The Rhetoric of Andrei Codrescu: A Reading in Exilic Fragmentation." In *Realms of Exile: Nomadism, Diasporas, and Eastern European Voices*, edited by Domnica Radulescu. Lanham, Md.: Lexington Books, 2002. Discussion of how Codrescu's status as an exile from his native land affects his writing.

Olson, Kirby. *Andrei Codrescu and the Myth of America*. Jefferson, N.C.: McFarland, 2005. Examines his poetry and essays and how they relate to Surrealism.

Ratner, Rochelle. Review of *It Was Today*. *Library Journal* 128, no. 13 (August, 2003): 88. Sees his poems falling into two types, everyday poems and those reflecting his experiences as an exile.

Alvin G. Burstein

GUNNAR EKELÖF

Born: Stockholm, Sweden; September 15, 1907
Died: Sigtuna, Sweden; March 16, 1968

OTHER LITERARY FORMS

In addition to more than ten volumes of poetry, Gunnar Ekelöf (AY-kuh-luhf) wrote four books of essays: *Promenader* (1941; walks), *Utflykter* (1947; excursions), *Blandade kort* (1957; a mixed deck), and *Lägga patience* (1969; playing solitaire). He also published four books of translations, mostly poetry, from French, German, English, Latin, and Persian: *Fransk surrealism* (1933; French Surrealism), *Hundra år modern fransk dikt* (1934; one hundred years of modern French poetry), *Valfrändskaper* (1960; chosen kinships), and *Glödande gåtor* (1966; a translation of Nelly Sachs's *Glühende Rätsel*). Since his death in 1968, there have appeared two books containing letters, the poet's annotations to some of his own works, and various other materials drawn from Ekelöf's notebooks and manuscripts: *En självbiografi* (1971; an autobiography), selected, edited, and with an introduction by the poet's wife and literary executor, Ingrid Ekelöf, and *En röst* (1973; a voice).

Achievements

Gunnar Ekelöf is widely recognized as the most original and influential Swedish poet of his generation. His reputation was well established in Scandinavia during his lifetime. Sweden honored him with many national literary prizes; the Danish Academy awarded him its Grand Prize for Poetry in 1964; and in 1966, the Scandinavian Council gave Ekelöf its prize for *Dīwān över fursten av Emgión* (Dīwān over the prince of Emgión). Although Ekelöf never completed his formal education, he was honored by academia. The University of Uppsala gave him an honorary degree in 1958, and in the same year, he was elected a member of the Swedish Academy. His contributions to Swedish literature were recognized: He expressed the voice of modernism and brought a new lyric tone to Swedish poetry. The concerns of Ekelöf's major poems are metaphysical and complex; to make them understood, Ekelöf continually tried to simplify poetic language. He pared away nonessentials—what he called "literary language"—until the tone of his poems became almost conversational. It is not, however, a casual voice that one encounters in the poems; it addresses the reader directly, intensely, and passionately. Scandinavians recognize this voice as belonging to a major poet, and many scholars believe that if Ekelöf had written in a language such as English, he would be regarded as a key international figure in the development of contemporary poetry.

Biography

Bengt Gunnar Ekelöf was born in Stockholm, Sweden, on September 15, 1907. His father, Gerhard Ekelöf, was a wealthy stockbroker, and Ekelöf grew up in big, finely furnished houses. Ekelöf's childhood, however, was not a happy one, despite his comfortable surroundings. His father had contracted syphilis, and his health was deteriorating when Ekelöf was a young boy. Before Ekelöf turned nine, his father died, and Ekelöf was sent away to boarding schools. When his mother, Valborg von Hedenberg, remarried several years later, Ekelöf felt rejected and homeless. Bengt Landgren and Reidar Ekner, the critics most familiar with Ekelöf's biography, point out that Ekelöf's relationship with his parents cultivated and reinforced his role as an "outsider." Ekelöf's failed love relationships—a 1932 marriage to Gunnel Bergström was dissolved after a few months, and an affair during 1933 and 1934 was broken off—reinforced Ekelöf's "outsider" perspective.

Ekelöf was particularly fascinated by two subjects as a student: music and Oriental mysticism. In 1926, he spent one semester at the London School of Oriental Studies, and in the next year, he began studies in Persian at the University of Uppsala in Sweden. Ekelöf was often sick as a student, and he never earned a degree, but his studies inspired a lifelong interest in Oriental mysticism and led to his discovery of Ibn el-Arabi's poetry, which moved Ekelöf to write his first poems. The attraction of mysticism for Ekelöf, so compelling when he was young, did not wane as he matured. Strains of mysticism can be found throughout his oeuvre, particularly in the last three collections of original work published before his death: *Dīwān över fursten av Emgión*, *Sagan om Fatumeh* (the tale of Fatumeh), and *Guide to the Underworld*.

In the late 1920's, Ekelöf moved to Paris to study music. Soon, however, his attention shifted from music to the problems of poetic language, as he struggled through an emotional breakdown to write many of the poems which appeared in his first book, *Sent på jorden* (late hour on Earth). After the publication of this initial volume, Ekelöf published new volumes every three or four years, becoming a popular as well as a critically acclaimed poet.

In 1943, Ekelöf married Gunhild Flodquist. Their marriage was dissolved in 1950, and in 1951, Ekelöf married Ingrid Flodquist, who became his literary executor after his death. A daughter, Suzanne, was born to them in 1952. As befitted a poet who sought to dissolve the boundaries of time and place, Ekelöf was a tireless traveler; in the last years of his life, he was increasingly drawn to the Middle East. His travels, particularly his 1965 trip to Istanbul, gave rise to the "eternal wanderers" of his later poetry. In 1968, he died of cancer of the throat. At Ekelöf's request, his ashes were placed in the ancient city of Sardis.

ANALYSIS

To discuss Gunnar Ekelöf's poetry is to discuss more than poetry: His books of poems also document evolving stages of Ekelöf's vision, the quest to resolve the great paradoxes of life and death and the boundaries of time. In his grappling with metaphysical questions, Ekelöf followed the path of the "contemporary mystic," in Eric Lindegren's words, and it is this quest which gives Ekelöf's poetry its distinctive character.

"EN OUTSIDERS VÄG"

In 1941, Ekelöf wrote an essay entitled "En outsiders väg" (an outsider's way), and readers have followed his lead in classifying Ekelöf's perspective as that of an "outsider." Certainly, the Byzantine and ancient Greek settings of his last books of poems are far removed from the life and landscape of his contemporary Sweden. One of the central themes in Ekelöf's poetry is the plight of the individual, both isolated and imprisoned within the conscious ego and subjective will of the "I" and "locked out" from all other people and things. The poet's first duty, Ekelöf has stated, is "to admit his unrelieved loneliness and meaninglessness in his wandering on the Earth." It is paradoxically this awareness, this outsider perspective, that allows the poet to create, for only then is the poet resigned enough to be uninhibited, to write truthfully—and thereby to be of some use to others. In typical Ekelöf fashion, total alienation and dejection are turned upside down to provide the starting point for genuine communication. Ekelöf never veers from his personal vision, his outsider's way, but at the same time, he never loses his audience. His personal vision is expressed with such uncompromising honesty and conviction that his private questions and dilemmas assume universal significance. Thus, however cryptic and arcane his verse becomes, it is never merely art for art's sake: "It is not art one makes/ But it is oneself."

SENT PÅ JORDEN

By analyzing Ekelöf's volumes of poetry chronologically, one can trace the development of his vision from the desperation and anguish expressed in his early poems to the integration of the individual and the unity of time in a cosmic oneness expressed in the Byzantine triptych. Although *Sent på jorden*, Ekelöf's first volume of poetry, did not receive a great deal of attention when it was published, it has been of enormous consequence for the development of Swedish poetry: *Sent på jorden* ushered in lyric modernism. Ekelöf composed the volume in Paris, supposedly while listening to recordings of Igor Stravinsky:

> I placed one word beside another and finally with a great deal of effort managed to construct a whole sentence. . . . It was the hidden meaning that I was seeking—a kind of *Alchemie du verbe*. . . . [P]oetry is this very tensioned-filled relationship between the words, between the lines, between the meanings.

Like the Surrealists and the Dadaists, Ekelöf sought to exploit the associative and suggestive power of words, but he was not content with mere verbal fireworks; he stressed the arrangement of the whole as he carefully placed "one word beside another."

Ekelöf has called *Sent på jorden* a "suicide book," and many of the poems in the volume express an anguished desperation. The persona of the poems is "dying in [his] own convulsions" as he violently struggles for expression and meaning: "crush the alphabet between your teeth." The persona's identity is ready to shatter as "nerves screech silently in the dying light." Locked up in a room, completely isolated from the outside world and even from the objects of the room itself, the persona can only chant: "I don't want to die, I don't want to die and cannot live . . . it's late on earth." Death offers a solution to the persona's desperation, an annihilation of the self. Thus, death is a tempting liberator, able to free the persona from imprisonment in ego. In "Cosmic Sleepwalker," however, the persona, rather than seeking self-annihilation, dreams of communion with a cosmic mother. The choices for the persona, then, are spelled out in "Apotheosis," the final poem of the collection: "Give me poison to die or dreams to live." The fragmented isolation of the individual, prisoner of the "I," is unbearable. In his first volume, then, Ekelöf defines one of his central themes. He also hints, however, at a resolution for the hysterical persona: a living cosmic oneness, where the individual is a part of a larger whole.

SURREALIST INFLUENCE

In 1934, the same year in which Ekelöf published *Dedikation*, he published a book of translations, *Hundra år modern fransk dikt*. The year before, in 1933, his translations of French Surrealist poems had been published in *Fransk surrealism*. Living in Paris in the late 1920's, Ekelöf was bound to feel the impulses of the various "isms" of the period, and many poems in his early volumes could be termed Surrealist. Ekelöf was attracted to the French Surrealists, particularly Robert Desnos, but ultimately found their methods contrived, artificial, and mechanical. On the title page of *Dedikation*, Ekelöf quotes a poet to whom he was more fundamentally drawn, Arthur Rimbaud: "I say: one must be a seer, one must make oneself a seer." In *Sent på jorden*, Ekelöf asked for "dreams to live," and Rimbaud offered a vision to synthesize life and dreams. Nevertheless, the "apotheosis" that Ekelöf sought in *Dedikation* failed; the glorified dream world of this volume later struck Ekelöf as false, and he rejected it. As Rabbe Enckell has pointed out, the romanticized images and prophetic voice in the volume seem an overcompensation for the desperate tone in *Sent på jorden*.

In *Sorgen och stjärnan* (sorrow and the star), the crucial problem remains the same: "One thing I've learned: reality kills! And something else: That no reality exists except this—that none exists!" In *Köp den blindes säng* (buy the blind one's song), the tone becomes calmer, though the perception is the same. The poet can, however, accept his condition, because it becomes a prerequisite for meaning. Ekelöf himself called *Köp den blindes säng* a transitional book; what he referred to as "the breakthrough" came with *Färjesång* (ferry song).

FÄRJESÅNG

The persona in *Färjesång* overcomes his desperation, assumes the role of the phoenix, and rises out of his ashes of anguish ready to "write it down." The tone is confident, at times assertive, and even lecturing: "In reality you are no one." The poet—who has experienced true vision—unmasks his readers and exposes the feeble self-deceptions they have invented to give significance and purpose to their lives. "Legal rights, human dignity, free will/ all of these are pictures painted with fear in reality's empty hall." Ekelöf asserts a new understanding of reality "beyond justice and injustice, beyond thesis and antithesis," a reality beyond individual personalities and perspectives. Exposing the meaninglessness of clichés and conventions of daily life, Ekelöf "surrenders" himself, "like the last rat on a sinking ship," in the hope of mystically uniting with all. The climax of the collection, the poem "Eufori" ("Euphoria"), clearly shows how Ekelöf's vision had evolved since the earlier volumes. The tone of the poem is calm. The persona is sitting in his garden, at peace with the natural world around him. The red evening glow, the moth, the candle, the aspen—all are pulsating with life, but in this transcendent moment, they pulsate with more than life: "All nature strong with love and death around you." The poet has a vision of the synthesis of life and death, of the individual consciousness and the awareness of all. In this poem, at least, the poet has an answer for himself and the reader: He can "sing of the only thing that reconciles/ the only practical, for all alike."

NON SERVIAM

The mood is much darker in *Non serviam*. In it the poet is estranged from the comforts of the welfare state: "Here, in the long, well-fed hours'/ overfurnished Sweden/ where everything is closed for draughts . . . it is cold to me." The ugly duckling, the odd one, "Svanen" ("The Swan"), surveys the "anemic blush over endless suburbs/ of identical houses." It is fall in this poem, the land laid waste with "worm-eaten cabbages and bare flowers." In a key poem of this collection, "Absentia animi," rotting mushrooms and tattered butterflies are omens of general oblivion. Echoing *Sent på jorden*, the poem repeats the refrain, "Meaningless. Unreal. Meaningless." The vision from *Färjesång* remains, however, although the intensity of the joyful tone is subdued:

> O deep down in me
> the eye of a black pearl reflects from its surface
> in happy half-consciousness
> the image of a cloud!
> Not a thing that exists
> It is something else
> It is in something existent
> but it does not exist
> It is something else
> O far far away
> in what is beyond is found
> something very near!

In "En Julinatt" ("A July Night"), a poem Ekelöf called central to the collection, the persona yearns for a prenatal state, suggesting "something else . . . beyond" as a state, or condition, of preconsciousness, before the intrusion of "I":

> Let me keep my world
> my prenatal world!
> Give me back my world!

> My world is a dark one
> but I will go home in the darkness
> through the grass, under the woods.

Despising the society and culture that produce "suburbs of identical houses," Ekelöf seems reconciled to the simple elements of nature. Like his predecessor, Edith Södergran, a Finno-Swedish poet he much admired, who declared that "the key to all secrets lies hidden in the raspberry patch," Ekelöf trusts nature's existence, concretely and as a revelation of "something else."

"A REALITY [DREAMED]"

In an essay published in 1941, Ekelöf wrote, "Kinship with the dead—or rather: the dead within one—is in many ways more alive than kinship with one's contemporaries, from whom one is separated by a thick layer of rhinoceros hide." The individual is alone—that is a central theme in Ekelöf's poetry—but teeming with life; the dead remain as integral parts of the individual's ego. In earlier volumes, Ekelöf had exposed the falsehoods of rational philosophies and denied their reality, but in "En verklighet [drömd]" ("A Reality [dreamed]"), from the collection *Om hösten* (in autumn), the poet's insight—somewhat akin to Ralph Waldo Emerson's "dream power"—enables him to construct a philosophy of life from his experience of nature. The persona overcomes all limitations, including time, space, and loneliness:

> every landscape, every shift in the landscape, contains
> all possible landscapes
> and this life contains all possible lives:
>
> .　.　.　.　.　.　.　.　.　.
>
> the peopled worlds,
> and the life of the unseen, and the dead.

THE 1940'S AND 1950'S

Critics agree that Ekelöf's poetry of the 1940's assured him a place as one of Sweden's greatest lyric poets. The concerns of the poetry are abstract, metaphysical, speculative. Most of the key poems of this period are longer lyrics, varying in tone from the explosiveness of *Färjesång* to the romantic, elegiac tone of *Om hösten*. The poems of the 1950's move in a different direction. Ekelöf simplified his style in an attempt to write depersonalized poetry, and the poems of this decade are generally short, simple lyrics about familiar objects and situations, pruned of all literary baggage to achieve what Ekelöf called "poetry of the factual," or antipoetry. The collections published in the 1950's also reveal a joking, absurd side of Ekelöf's vision. In contrast to the speculative, metaphysical poems of earlier volumes, many of these poems focus on the body: sexuality, eroticism, obscenity. If Ekelöf's antipoetry functions to balance the body-soul relationship by emphasizing feeling and existence here and now, as Pär Hellström's study of these volumes suggests, Ekelöf as seeker still permeates these collections. He continues as a solitary figure, affirming that "I do best alone at night," for then he can listen "to the talk of the eternal wanderers." Eternal wanderers, however, live an existence different from that of ordinary mortals, and many of these poems express a longing for death in the poet's desire to identify with and become a part of timeless existence. The poet's "self-reflecting waters" do not speak "of life but of Lethe's wave"; rebirth is to be found "in the swaddling cloth of death." This fascination with death, however, culminates in a turn toward life-giving uses of the past and tradition. Unable to exist in the isolation of his own ego, unable to accept the social alienation of his contemporary Sweden, Ekelöf turns to "ancient cities" to find his own "future." Thus, the publication of his next volume, *A Mölna Elegy*, marked a transition to the concerns that inform the trilogy that concluded his career.

A MÖLNA ELEGY

In his introductory notes to *A Mölna Elegy*, Ekelöf stated that the poem is concerned with "the relativity of the experience of time"; he hoped, he said, to capture a "traverse section of time, instead of a section lengthwise." In his attempt to analyze "the mood of a certain moment," Ekelöf revealed the complexity of consciousness. The life moment in *A Mölna Elegy* is a moment of mystical insight, with "time running wild" in the consciousness of the persona. The "I" comprises many personalities and undergoes many transformations as the present, past, and future are experienced as independent layers of consciousness. The life of the past—in the memory of the persona's relatives, for example—exists in the present, in the persona's consciousness, as well as in the lives of the dead. Any given moment, then, comprises images from a number of centuries and from various cultures and beliefs—from the past as well as the present. Demarcations of time and space are dissolved, borders between life and death eliminated. All existence is a unity: The reality "beyond" is all of it at once.

"I am of the opinion," Ekelöf once wrote, "that man carries humanity within himself, not only his father's and mother's inheritance but also his cousin's, his second cousins', and further, the animals', plants', and stones' inheritance." As Leif Sjöberg has so convincingly documented, the many "inheritances" which constitute the moment expressed in *A Mölna Elegy* are held together by the "I" of the poem—not only by means of his own observations, but also by means of dead relatives speaking through him, and through allusions to and quotations from dead poets. Ekelöf uses fragmentary allusions, many of them esoteric (such as authentic graffiti and inscriptions in Latin found on tombstones in Pompeii), and borrowings (for example, from Edith Södergran) to document a life and a piece of history. Ghosts, phantoms, spirits—the "dead ones"—still have a voice, and thus the past continues to live in the present, integral to the speaker's consciousness. People, things, and ideas can be fully comprehended only in the context of their connectedness to the past.

Ekelöf's 1965 trip to Istanbul, where he saw the Madonna icon of Vlachernes, inspired an outpouring of passionate lyrics. Poems came so quickly, Ekelöf wrote to a friend, that, "as far as I can understand, someone has written the poems with me as a medium. . . ." Within a few short months, Ekelöf composed the last three volumes he was to publish in his lifetime.

DĪWĀN ÖVER FURSTEN AV EMGIÓN

The Dīwān trilogy ranges from the Byzantine Middle Ages to an unspecified epoch in the Oriental (that is, Middle Eastern) world to classical antiquity and the Hellenic Age. In accepting the prize of the Scandinavian Council in 1966 for *Dīwān över fursten av Emgión*, Ekelöf stressed that these civilizations of the past can speak to modern times: "I have chosen Byzantium, long since lost, as a starting point from which I should be able to assail the present." His targets are "political decadence" and the "degradation" and "coldness" among persons he observes in modern life. These are familiar themes in Ekelöf's poetry, but they are given a particular intensity in the trilogy, an intensity derived from the controlled, pure passion they express.

In the Dīwān trilogy, Ekelöf has been able to concretize "something beyond" into a female figure, lover-daughter-sister, and finally an all-embracing mother figure. His vision can therefore be expressed in passionate love lyrics, or in what Bengt Landgren has termed "erotic mysticism." The persona in *Dīwān över fursten av Emgión* is captured in battle, imprisoned, tortured, and finally blinded. Locked in darkness, his only means of "escape" and survival is his ability to dream and to remember. The Ekelöf persona recognizes both God and the devil as "tyrants," as exponents of either/or, a world of duality he rejects. Love offers the persona an alternative to "the two locked in combat," a liberation from captivity in ego. The love for the mother figure allows a transition from life to death or the presence of death—or preconsciousness—in the present. The persona's dream power, or vision, enables him to "go home in the darkness" to that "prenatal world" Ekelöf called for in *Non serviam*. "Something else," something beyond, is now seen clearly as a "Mother to no man/ But who has breasts/ With milk for all."

SAGAN OM FATUMEH

The female persona in *Sagan om Fatumeh*, like the male persona in *Dīwān över fursten av Emgión*, suffers horribly. She is apparently deserted by the prince who has fathered her child. For a time she serves in a harem, but eventually she is thrown out on the street. As she becomes an old woman; she has to prostitute herself to survive. Nevertheless, her spirit is never crushed; her visions—the memories of her lover—sustain her. Fatumeh also sustains the prince, for she gives his "soul a shadow"; the love they feel for each other is their realization of the unity of all things, of the soul's awareness of the eternal Mother. Only something that exists can cast a "shadow": The soul exists in its expression of love, as felt between two people, and as a vision of the encompassing love of an Earth Mother. In Fatumeh's final meeting with her beloved, the mystic identification is realized as the lovers are effaced in a cosmic union.

GUIDE TO THE UNDERWORLD

Early in his career, in a poem published in *Färjesång*, Ekelöf described his "underworld":

> Each person is a world, peopled
> by blind creatures in dim revolt
> against the I, the kin, who rules them.
> In each soul thousands of souls are imprisoned,
> in each world thousands of worlds are hidden
> and these blind and lower worlds
> are real and living, though not full-born,
> as truly as I am real . . .

In *Guide to the Underworld*, the last volume of poetry he published before he died, Ekelöf is able to free these "blind creatures" because the "guide" is free of the ego. He has discovered that, "alone in the quiet night," he can escape the limitations of his own identity and "hover" in his visions, "weightless," "empty," "floating." Life and death, past and present, history and dreams converge and dissolve into each other. In a key poem, "The Devil's Sermon," the persona unites with the Virgin, or Eternal She, in an act of love. Thus, the persona merges with the universe and is one with the infinite. Ekelöf finally resolves the great paradox—he embraces a reality that is life and death at once:

> I wanted both
>
> The part of the whole as well as the whole
> And that this choice would involve no contradiction.

OTHER MAJOR WORKS

NONFICTION: *Promenader*, 1941; *Utflykter*, 1947; *Blandade kort*, 1957; *Verklighetsflykt*, 1958; *Lägga patience*, 1969; *Ensjälvbiografi*, 1971; *En röst*, 1973; *Modus Vivendi: Selected Prose*, 1996.

TRANSLATIONS: *Fransk surrealism*, 1933 (with Greta Knutsson-Tzara); *Hundra år modern fransk dikt*, 1934; *Valfrändskaper*, 1960; *Glödande gåtor*, 1966 (of Nelly Sachs's *Glühende Rätsel*).

MISCELLANEOUS: *Skrifter*, 1991-1993 (8 volumes; collected works).

BIBLIOGRAPHY

Adams, Ann-Charlotte Gavel. *Twentieth-Century Swedish Writers Before World War II*. Vol. 259 in *Dictionary of Literary Biography*. Detroit: Gale Group, 2002. Contains a biographical essay on Ekelöf that also analyzes his work.

Fioretos, Aris. "Now and Absence in the Early Ekelöf." *Scandinavian Studies* 62, no. 3 (Summer, 1990): 319. Analyzes the poetic techniques used in "Osynlig narvaro," the fourth entry in *Sent på jorden*.

Shideler, Ross. *Voices Under the Ground*. Berkeley: University of California Press, 1973. A critical study of Ekelöf's early poetry. Includes bibliographic references.

Sjöberg, Leif. *A Reader's Guide to Gunnar Ekelöf's "A Mölna Elegy."* New York: Twayne, 1973. A critical guide to *A Mölna Elegy*. Includes bibliographic references.

Thygesen, Erik. *Gunnar Ekelöf's Open-Form Poem, A Mölna Elegy*. Stockholm: Almqvist & Wiksell International, 1985. A critical study of *A Mölna Elegy*. Includes bibliographic references and an index.

C. L. Mossberg

PAUL ÉLUARD
Eugène Grindel

Born: Saint-Denis, France; December 14, 1895
Died: Charenton-le-Pont, France; November 18, 1952

PRINCIPAL POETRY

Le Devoir et l'inquiétude, 1917
Poèmes pour la paix, 1918
Les Animaux et leurs hommes, les hommes et leurs animaux, 1920
Les Nécessités de la vie et les conséquences des rêves, 1921
Mourir de ne pas mourir, 1924
Capitale de la douleur, 1926 (*Capital of Pain*, 1973)
L'Amour la poésie, 1929
À toute épreuve, 1930
La Vie immédiate, 1932
La Rose publique, 1934
Faciles, 1935
Thorns of Thunder: Selected Poems, 1936
Les Yeux fertiles, 1936
Les Mains libres, 1937
Donner à voir, 1939
Médieuses, 1939
Le Livre ouvert I, 1938-1940, 1940
Choix de poèmes, 1914-1941, 1941
Le Livre ouvert II, 1939-1941, 1942
Poésie et vérité, 1942 (*Poetry and Truth, 1942*, 1944)
Au rendez-vous allemand, 1944
En avril 1944: Paris respirait encore!, 1945
Le Dur Désir de durer, 1946 (*The Dour Desire to Endure*, 1950)
Poésie ininterrompue, 1946
Corps mémorable, 1947
Dignes de vivre, 1947
Le Livre ouvert, 1938-1944, 1947
Marc Chagall, 1947
Poèmes politiques, 1948
Premiers Poèmes (1913-1921), 1948
Une Leçon de morale, 1949 (*A Moral Lesson*, 2007)
Le Phénix, 1951

Poèmes, 1951

Tout dire, 1951

Poèmes pour tous, 1952

Les Derniers Poèmes d'amour de Paul Éluard, 1962 (*Last Love Poems of Paul Éluard*, 1980)

OTHER LITERARY FORMS

Paul Éluard (ay-LW AHR) wrote many critical essays explaining the theories of the Surrealist movement, in which he played so large a part, and delineating his personal aesthetic theories as well. These critical works include the various Surrealist manifestos (many coauthored with André Breton), *Avenir de la poésie* (1937), *Poésie involuntaire et poésie intentionelle* (1942), *À Pablo Picasso* (1944), *Picasso à Antibes* (1948), *Jacques Villon ou l'art glorieux* (1948) , *La Poésie du passé* (1951), *Anthologie des écrits sur l'art* (1952), and *Les Sentiers et routes de la poésie* (1952). Because the Surrealists were little interested in the limitations of genre, much of Éluard's poetic work falls into the category of the prose poem. His complete works are published in *Œuvres complètes* (1968). Some of his letters are published in *Lettres à Joe Bousquet* (1973).

ACHIEVEMENTS

Paul Éluard was, with Breton and Louis Aragon, a cofounder of Surrealism, one of the principal artistic movements of the twentieth century. Earlier, he had also been instrumental in the Dada movement. As one of the primary theoreticians of Surrealism, Éluard helped to outline its aesthetic concepts in a number of manifestos and illustrated its techniques in his huge output of poetry. He published more than seventy volumes of poetry in his lifetime, many of which reveal his ability to set aside Surrealist theories in favor of poetic effect. As a result, many critics have called him the most original of the Surrealist poets and the truest poet of the group. His love poetry in particular is singled out for praise. Eluard's *Capital of Pain*, *La Rose publique*, and *Les Yeux fertiles* are widely regarded as among the finest products of Surrealism in French poetry.

BIOGRAPHY

Paul Éluard was born Eugène Grindel on December 14, 1895, in Saint-Denis, a suburb of Paris. His background was strictly working-class—his father was a bookkeeper and his mother (from whom he took the name Éluard) a seamstress—and most of his early years were spent in the vicinity of factories in Saint-Denis and Aulnay-sous-Bois. Éluard was a good student at the École Communale, but later, when the Grindels moved to Paris and the boy was enrolled at the École Supérieure Colbert, his scholastic performance declined. His education was cut short by illness, and he was placed in a sanatorium in Davos, Switzerland, when he was sixteen. He returned to Paris two years later and almost immediately entered the army; his experiences in the trenches of World War

I crystallized his growing awareness of the suffering of humanity. Suffering from gangrene of the bronchi as a result of poison gas, Éluard spent more time in a sanatorium, reading much poetry, especially the works of Arthur Rimbaud, Lautréamont, and Charles Vildrac. He also read Percy Bysshe Shelley, Novalis, and Heraclitus of Ephesus, and he developed a special feeling for Walt Whitman, whose *Leaves of Grass* (1855) he read many times.

In 1917, Éluard published his first book of poetry, *Le Devoir et l'inquiétude*. The following year, his *Poèmes pour la paix* was published, and he met Jean Paulhan, "impresario of poets," who advanced his career. He also met Breton, Aragon, Tristan Tzara, Philippe Soupault, and Giorgio de Chirico—the writers and artists who would eventually become, with Éluard, the leading figures of the Surrealist movement. Surrealism, however, was preceded by Dada; Éluard, Breton, Aragon, Francis Picabia, Soupault, Marguerite Buffet, and others, according to Tzara, all took part in the public "debut" of Dada in January, 1920, at a matinee organized by *Littérature*, a Dadaist review. The spectacle caused an enormous uproar, and a week later, Éluard joined Breton, Soupault, and others in a public debate at the Université Populaire. Éluard began to publish a review called *Proverbe*, to which all the Dadaists contributed. Wrote Tzara, "It was chiefly a matter of contradicting logic and language."

As Dada moved toward the more rigorous Surrealism, Éluard's name appeared on various manifestos. His poetry changed as a result of his allegiance to Dada and Surrealism; under the influence of the Surrealists' enthusiasm for "automatic writing," his language became freer. He also developed friendships with some of the most influential artists of the time, including Pablo Picasso, Max Ernst, Salvador Dalí, and Joan Miró.

In 1917, Éluard married Gala (Elena Dimitievna Diakanova), whom he had met in Switzerland in 1912; they had a daughter, Cécile, in 1918. Gala turned her affections first toward the artist Max Ernst and later toward Salvador Dalì. Brokenhearted, Éluard disappeared without explanation in March, 1924. Rumors circulated that he had died. In fact, he had sailed on the first available ship out of Marseilles, beginning a mysterious seven-month voyage around the world. He was seen in Rome, Vienna, Prague, London, and Spain, and he visited such distant locales as Australia, New Zealand, the Antilles, Panama, Malaysia, Java, Sumatra, Ceylon, Indochina, and India.

On his return, Éluard once again enthusiastically threw himself into the Surrealist movement, becoming editor and director of the movement's reviews, *La Révolution surréaliste* and *La Surréalisme au service de la révolution*. Following Surrealist theories, he experimented in his poetry with verbal techniques, the free expression of the mind, and the relation between dream and reality. These inquiries led to *L'Immaculée Conception* (1930; *The Immaculate Conception*, 1990), which he wrote with Breton. That same year, he made a final break with Gala, having met Maria Benz (affectionately called Nusch), who was the subject of numerous works by Picasso. The publication of *Capital of Pain* had established Éluard as an important poet, and with *La Rose publique* and *Les Yeux fertiles*, he became the leading poet of Surrealism.

Éluard's world trip and his memories of proletarian life and of the war had made him sensitive to the political trends of the 1930's. These feelings came to the fore at the outbreak of the Spanish Civil War (1936-1939). The fascist armies in Spain seemed to Éluard the forerunners of a total destruction of the modern concept of freedom. In response, his poetry became more politically oriented. He wrote in *L'Évidence poétique* (1936) that "the time has come when poets have a right and a duty to maintain that they are profoundly involved in the lives of other men, in communal life." He became exasperated with the detachment of his Surrealist colleagues and separated from the group.

In 1939, Éluard once again found himself in the French army, and after the disastrous defeat, he courageously worked for the Resistance in Paris and Lozère, helping to found the weekly newspaper *Lettres Françaises*. He was constantly in danger of arrest, and he and Nusch, whom he had married in 1934, were forced to move every month to avoid the Gestapo. He joined the outlawed Communist Party in 1942 (he had been affiliated with it for nearly fifteen years). He used the pseudonyms Jean du Hault and Maurice Hervent, and the *maquis* circulated his poems underground. One poem, "Liberté," published in 1942 in the Nazi-denounced collection *Poetry and Truth, 1942*, which has been called one of the "consecrated texts of the Resistance." For a brief period, he was forced to hide in an asylum at Saint-Alban. He was deeply affected by the suffering of the inmates and the experience could be seen in his subsequent writings.

After the war, Éluard's life was shattered by the sudden death of Nusch. He sought a solution to his sorrow in his poetry and in extending his love to embrace all humankind. During this period, he was very active in the Communist Party, traveling to Italy, Yugoslavia, Greece, Poland, Switzerland, and the Soviet Union, which awarded him the International Peace Prize. In Mexico, attending the Congress of the World Council on Peace, he met Dominique Lemor, and his love for her did much to restore his moral vision. He married her in 1951, but a heart attack in September, 1952, weakened him, and he died of a stroke that November in his apartment overlooking the Bois de Vincennes, outside Paris.

ANALYSIS

Paul Éluard is regarded by many critics as Surrealism's greatest poet. Dubbed the Nurse of the Stars by Soupault, he was central to the movement from the beginning. Breton once answered the question What is Surrealism? by saying, "It is a splinter of the sparkling glass of Paul Éluard." It is therefore ironic that when Éluard's work is praised, its "non-Surrealistic" elements are generally singled out as having made his work better than that of the poets around him. Critics point out his permanent and universal themes, present even before the birth of Surrealism. He continually explores the themes of love, human suffering, and the struggle of the masses against hunger, slavery, and deprivation. His avoidance of shock and violence, employed programmatically by many of the

Surrealists, is also pointed out as evidence of his internal distance from the movement in which he played such a central role. Finally, unlike many of his fellow Surrealists, who regarded the world of dreams as a higher reality, sufficient unto itself, Éluard used dreams to interpret his experience: In his poetry, the dreamworld helps make the "real" world more comprehensible.

Nevertheless, Éluard's poetry can be understood only in the context of Surrealism. His works strongly reflect the Surrealist rejection of nineteenth century values, which had led not to the paradise promised by progressives of that century but to the abject horror of World War I. It was necessary, therefore, to reject the worldview that brought about the enslavement of the human imagination. The enemy was not only order but also the belief in order. Religion and science are both inherently limiting, the Surrealists argued, and fail to take account of the most fundamental element of existence: disorder.

When Éluard found a mystical revelation in six consecutive lines beginning with the letter *p* in Tzara's *Grains et issues* (1935), he was expressing the Surrealist faith in a truth beyond the surface of things, a truth that could be explored only through absolute freedom. Naturally, this freedom must exist in the political sphere as well, that Éluard, like a number of Surrealists, embraced an idealistic vision of communism is not surprising, given the context of the times. Communism preached the destruction of religion and of the bourgeoisie, and it was an avowed enemy of the fascism taking hold all over Europe in the 1920's and 1930's.

Above all, however, the Surrealists turned inward. Love, a privileged theme in their works, is treated as a means of altering consciousness, analogous in its effects to hallucinogenic drugs. Love becomes, paradoxically, both a way of escaping the world and the profoundest way of knowing it. Éluard adamantly holds that all real knowledge comes from love, and his finest poems express a longing for transcendence through sexual love.

"PREMIÈRE DU MONDE" AND "A WOMAN IN LOVE"

In Éluard's works, woman, as the object of love, is a mirror for which men reach; seeing themselves reflected there, they discover "surreality." Woman, in Éluard's poetry, is simultaneously a particular woman (Gala, Nusch, Dominique) and a universal woman, timeless, embodying womanhood and all women. She is a vision of light, and images of brightness, transcendence, and purity are associated with her. The poet, on the other hand, suffers in darkness, isolation, limitation, and impurity. He addresses her: "You who abolish forgetfulness, ignorance, and hope/ You who suppress absence and give me birth . . ./ You are pure, you are even purer than I." In "Première du monde" (from *Capital of Pain*), his woman is the first woman in the world. She is simultaneously held captive by the Earth and possessed by spirit. The light hides itself in her. She is a complex of wheels; she is grass in which one becomes lost; she resembles the stars; she takes upon herself a maze of fire. In another poem, he writes, "I love you for your wisdom that is not mine . . ./ For this immortal heart which I do not possess." In other poems, he relates the image of the mirror to the image of woman so that her eyes become mirrors and she plays a mirrorlike role. Woman is mirror is poetry is woman: Each reflects the other; each is the other. One sees this most strikingly in "L'Amoureuse" ("A Woman in Love," from *Mourir de ne pas mourir*), when the lover becomes one with the beloved: "She has the shape of my hands/ She has the color of my eyes/ She is swallowed in my shadow/ Like a stone against the sky."

SURREALIST INFLUENCES

Éluard's poetic vision of woman is representative of the constant shifting between opposites that characterizes his work. He moves between light and dark, despair and hope, mystery and knowledge. This subtle play between opposites is very much characteristic of Surrealism in general, but Éluard handles it with simple, direct language. Like many great writers dealing with enormously complex and difficult conceptions, Éluard simplifies his language, choosing ordinary words and rearranging them in extraordinary ways. One of his early short poems, "Enfermé, seul" (from *Les Nécessités de la vie et les conséquences des rêves*), illustrates his passionate simplicity: "Complete song/ The table to see, the chair to sit/ And the air to breathe./ To rest,/ Inevitable Idea,/ Complete song."

When Éluard is at his best, this plain language becomes exquisite, as in lines such as: "Dawn fallen like a shower"; "We were tired/ Of living in the ruins of sleep"; "The prism breathes with us"; "The fountain running and sweet and nude." Unlike traditional metaphors, which are based on logical resemblances between things, Éluard's metaphors come out of dreams, revealing the power of the mind to find meaning in "illogical" juxtapositions. The line "She is standing on my eyelids" from "A Woman in Love," for example, could be a literal transcription of a dream: Thus, the poet achieves expression of the previously inexpressible. Like Dalí's famous melting clocks, Éluard's images broaden the vision of the reader. This quality makes Éluard's poetry easy to grasp and yet extraordinarily difficult, immediately meaningful yet provoking endless reflection.

OTHER MAJOR WORKS

NONFICTION: *L'Immaculée Conception*, 1930 (with André Breton; *The Immaculate Conception*, 1990); *L'Évidence poétique*, 1936; *Avenir de la poésie*, 1937; *Poésie involuntaire et poésie intentionelle*, 1942; *À Pablo Picasso*, 1944; *Jacques Villon ou l'art glorieux*, 1948; *Picasso à Antibes*, 1948; *La Poésie du passé*, 1951; *Anthologie des écrits sur l'art*, 1952; *Les Sentiers et routes de la poésie*, 1952; *Lettres à Joe Bousquet*, 1973; *Letters to Gala*, 1989.

MISCELLANEOUS: *Œuvres complètes*, 1968.

BIBLIOGRAPHY

Caws, Mary Ann. *The Poetry of Dada and Surrealism: Aragon, Breton, Tzara, Éluard, and Desnos*. Princeton, N.J.: Princeton University Press, 1970. The chapter on Éluard is a very good analysis of Éluard's views on love and death as they emerge from the poet's continuous fascination with the ineffable that transcends the world of appearances.

————. *Surrealism*. New York: Phaidon, 2004. This art book format survey of Surrealism contains information on Éluard and other poets.

Gaitet, Pascale. "Éluard's Reactions, Poetic and Political to World War Two." *Literature and History* 2, no. 1 (1991): 24-43. Examines Éluard's shift from the destabilizing, antibourgeois doctrines espoused by the Surrealists toward a more conventional use of symbolism, reinforcing traditional values, and a unifying rhetoric during the Resistance era. Gaitet depicts Éluard's poetic output during this era as embracing a more utilitarian, propagandist function.

McNab, Robert. *Ghost Ships: A Surrealist Love Triangle*. New Haven, Conn.: Yale Press, 2004. Describes the love triangle among Max Ernst, Éluard, and Gala, as well as Éluard's disappearance and travels.

Meadwell, Kenneth W. "Paul Éluard." In *Modern French Poets*, edited by Jean-François Leroux. Vol. 258 in *Dictionary of Literary Biography*. Detroit: Gale, 2002. Provides an overview of the life and work of Éluard, with emphasis on collections and poems representing his literary evolution.

Montagu, Jemima. *The Surrealists: Revolutionaries in Art and Writing, 1919-1935*. London: Tate, 2002. This look at Surrealism in both literature and art contains a chapter on Éluard and Max Ernst.

Nugent, Robert. *Paul Éluard*. New York: Twayne, 1974. Approaches Éluard's poetry as the expression of the poet's solitude as well as humankind's solitude and includes a concise chronology and short bibliography of critical works.

Strauss, Jonathan. "Paul Éluard and the Origins of Visual Subjectivity." *Mosaic* 33, no. 2 (2000): 25-46. Offers close readings of passages taken from *Capital of Pain* to demonstrate Éluard's agile usage of the visual and his redefinition of subjectivity in terms of impossible images that can only be expressed through language. This tying of the sensuous to the abstract becomes the cornerstone of Éluard's attempt to create a new theory of subjectivity.

Watts, Philip. *Allegories of the Purge: How Literature Responded to the Postwar Trials of Writers and Intellectuals in France*. Stanford, Calif.: Stanford University Press, 1998. Chapter 4 examines Éluard's poetic output during the Occupation and the period of purge trials in France directly following the end of World War II to show that Éluard's shift from the linguistic and image play of his earlier writings to a strictly metered verse can be seen as a political act calling for the purge of collaborationist writers.

J. Madison Davis

ODYSSEUS ELYTIS
Odysseus Alepoudhelis

Born: Iraklion (also known as Heraklion), Crete; November 2, 1911
Died: Athens, Greece; March 18, 1996

OTHER LITERARY FORMS

Principally a poet, Odysseus Elytis (EH-lee-tees), in the eminently pictorial, ima-gistic, "architectural" nature of his verse, revealed his other, parallel propensity. Had he received any formal artistic education, he might have been a distinguished painter as well. As early as 1935, he produced a number of Surrealist collages; in 1966, he painted some thirty-odd gouaches, all but four of which he destroyed; and in the years from 1967 to 1974, the period of the dictatorship of the "colonels," he produced about forty remarkable collages, nineteen of which are reproduced in Ilías Petropoulous's book *Elytis, Moralis, Tsarouhis* (1974). Elytis's longstanding interest in the arts and his friendship with some of the most prominent modern artists in Greece and France have qualified him as an acute art critic as well.

Odysseus Elytis
(©The Nobel Foundation)

Elytis translated poets as varied as Le Comte de Lautreamont, Arthur Rimbaud, Pierre-Jean Jouve, Paul Éluard, Giuseppe Ungaretti, Federico García Lorca, and Vladimir Mayakovsky. Elytis's prose works include essays and monographs on sympathetic writers and painters. His most important work in prose, an invaluable companion to his poetry, is *Anihta hartia* (1974; *Open Papers*, 1995), a work of widely ranging, often aphoristic reflections, in which Elytis spoke extensively about his poetics and his development as a poet.

ACHIEVEMENTS

Odysseus Elytis's constantly renewed originality, his wise optimism, and his glorification of the Greek world in its physical and spiritual beauty have gradually won for him wide popularity and recognition as well as several distinctions, honors, and prizes— most notably the Nobel Prize in Literature in 1979. He won the National Poetry Prize in

1960 for *The Axion Esti* and the Order of the Phoenix in 1965. He was honored with several honorary doctorate degrees from institutions such as the University of Thessaloníki (1975), University of Paris (1980), and University of London (1981). In 1989, he was made a commander in the French Legion of Honor.

BIOGRAPHY

The offspring of a family originating on the island of Lesbos (or Mitilini), in the eastern Aegean, Odysseus Elytis was born Odysseus Alepoudhelis in Iráklion, Crete, in 1911, the sixth and last child of Panyiotis Alepoudhelis, a successful soap manufacturer, and Maria Vranas, of Byzantine extraction. In 1914, the family had settled permanently in Athens, where Elytis went to high school, but summers spent in Lesbos, Crete, and other Aegean islands provided him with what was to be his poetic world in terms of imagery, symbols, language, and cultural identity.

Elytis's early literary interests were given an outlet and direction through his chance discovery of the poetry of Paul Éluard in 1929. From 1930 to 1935, Elytis attended the law school of the University of Athens but never graduated. His meeting with the orthodox Surrealist poet Andreas Embirikos in 1935 decidedly enhanced his own Surrealist inclinations. That same year, Elytis published his first poems in the periodical *Nea Ghramata*, recently founded by the poet and critic Andréas Karandonis; under Karandonis's editorship, *Nea Ghramata* soon became the rallying center of the new poetry and prose in Greece. Elytis's first collection of poems, *Prosanatolizmi* (orientations), appeared in December, 1939.

Fascist Italy attacked Greece from Albania in 1940, and in 1940-1941, Elytis served as a second lieutenant on the Albanian front, where he almost perished in a military hospital from typhoid. During the Nazi occupation of Greece, his second book of poetry, *Ilios o protos, mazi me tis parallayies pano se mian ahtidha* (sun the first, together with variations on a sunbeam), was published, followed, soon after the liberation, by *Heroic and Elegiac Song for the Lost Second Lieutenant of the Albanian Campaign*. In 1945-1946, Elytis served as director of programming and broadcasting for the National Broadcasting System in Athens. From 1948 to 1952, Elytis lived in Paris, where he studied literature at the Sorbonne, and traveled in England, Switzerland, Italy, and Spain. During this period, he associated with André Breton, Éluard, Tristan Tzara, Pierre Jean Jouve, Henri Michaux, Ungaretti, Henri Matisse, Pablo Picasso, Alberto Giacometti, and Giorgio de Chirico. In 1950, Elytis was elected as a member of the International Union of Art Critics, and in 1953, after his return to Greece, he was elected to the Poetry Committee of the Group of Twelve, which annually awarded prizes for poetry. Elytis served once again as director of programming and broadcasting of the National Broadcasting System in Athens until 1954. From 1955 to 1956, he was on the governing board of the avant-garde Karolos Koun Art Theater, and from 1956 to 1958, he was president of the governing board of the Greek Ballet.

The publication of his two epoch-making books of verse, *The Axion Esti* and *Six and One Remorses for the Sky*, broke Elytis's poetic silence and won for him the National Poetry Prize in 1960. A selection from *The Axion Esti*, set to music by the composer Mikis Theodhorakis in 1964, brought the poet wide popularity.

In 1961, Elytis visited the United States for three months at the invitation of the State Department, and in 1962, he visited the Soviet Union on the invitation of its government. From 1965 to 1968, he was a member of the administrative board of the Greek National Theater.

In 1967, the government of Greece was toppled by a military coup. For the next seven years, the colonels (as the ruling junta was known) ruthlessly suppressed opposition to their regime, exercising severe censorship and otherwise curtailing civil rights. From 1969 to 1971, Elytis lived in France, primarily in Paris. Following his return to Greece, he published seven poetry books, including *The Monogram, The Sovereign Sun*, and *To fotodhendro ke i dhekati tetarti omorfia* (the light tree and the fourteenth beauty), as well as the prose work *Open Papers*. Elytis was awarded the Nobel Prize in Literature in 1979, and in 1980, he received an honorary doctorate from the Sorbonne. He died in Athens, Greece, on March 18, 1996.

ANALYSIS

The suicide of the Greek poet Kostas Karyotakis in 1928 may be said to have marked the end of an era in Greek poetry, which had long abided in Parnassianism, *poésie maudite*, Symbolism, and *poésie pure*. A spirit of discomfort, decadence, and despair prevailed, intensified by the military defeat suffered by Greece in Asia Minor in 1922. The year 1935 has generally been considered to mark the beginning of a great change in modern Greek poetry—a renaissance in which Odysseus Elytis, along with George Seferis and others, was most instrumental. Rejecting a tired traditionalism, these modernists invigorated Greek poetry by the adoption and creative assimilation of Western trends. The renaissance that they initiated is still flourishing; indeed, twentieth century Greek poetry is as rich as that of any nation in its time.

Adopting Surrealism as a liberating force with his extraordinary lyrical gifts, Elytis brought to Greek poetry a spirit of eternal youthfulness, beauty, purity, sanity, and erotic vigor. His inspiration sprung from nature, particularly from the Aegean archipelago, as well as from the Greek world throughout the centuries. At the same time, however, Elytis's mature vision was shaped by his experiences in World War II, which enriched and deepened his brilliant, careless, pictorial lyricism with historical awareness—an awareness of suffering as an essential and unavoidable part of life, which it is the poet's duty to recognize and transcend. A moderated Platonic idealism, earthly in its roots, characterized most of Elytis's work.

Elytis's early poetry broke new ground in Greek verse. Its youthful, optimistic freshness; genuine, powerful lyricism; and free Surrealistic associations, as well as the graceful richness of its imagery drawn from nature—all conspired to liberate Greek poetry from its Symbolist melancholy and despair. In Surrealism, Elytis found a force of sanity and purity, of liberating newness, but he quickly abandoned the automatism of Surrealist orthodoxy, choosing instead to subject the effusions of his unconscious to formal demands. Inspired by the Apollonian clarity of the Greek sunlight but also including its mystical, Dionysian essence, he thus accomplished an imaginative, creative assimilation, an acclimatization of the positive elements in Surrealism to the Greek world, its reality and spirit.

The physical elements of the Aegean archipelago, its landscapes and seascapes, provided Elytis with the material for a radiant, sun-drenched poetic realm, a setting in which adolescent youths learn of Eros as the all-mastering, all-penetrating, all-revealing, all-uniting procreative and inspiring force. Elytis identified humans with nature in terms of analogies existing between them: Nature is anthropomorphized in a joyful exchange that no deep sorrow dares to tint.

Throughout his long career, with its constant experimentation, inventive metamorphoses, renovations, and striking changes, Elytis remained faithful to certain fundamental beliefs concerning the objectives of his art:

> The lesson remains the same: it is sufficient to express that which we love, and this alone, with the fewest means at our disposal, yet in the most direct manner, that of poetry.

PROSANATOLIZMI

Elytis's first book, *Prosanatolizmi*, experimental in manner and form, features rhythmical free verse, gently sensual and mostly of imagery set in motion. Although this collection does not delve into thought and emotion, it contains some poems of exquisite beauty and power, including "Anniversary," "Ode to Santorini," "Marina of the Rocks," and "The Mad Pomegranate Tree," which won instant acclaim and lasting popularity, earning Elytis the title of the poet of the Aegean.

ILIOS O PROTOS, MAZI ME TIS PARALLAYIES PANO SE MIAN AHTIDHA

In Elytis's second book, *Ilios o protos, mazi me tis parallayies pano se mian ahtidha*, the idealized "countryside of open heart," the paradise of carefree and unaging youth, the world of an eternal present that ignores the past and hopes in the future, is more consciously mastered and revealed. This early collection demonstrates the poet's conscientious craftsmanship and sensitivity to the Greek language in all its expressive power, its visual and musical richness and beauty. A more thoughtful tone is apparent here as well.

THE AXION ESTI

The experience of the war, reflected in the long poem *Heroic and Elegiac Song for the Lost Second Lieutenant of the Albanian Campaign*, permanently altered Elytis's vision. Fourteen years passed between the publication of this wartime elegy and the appearance of Elytis's *The Axion Esti* (its title, meaning "worthy it is," appears in the liturgy of the Greek Orthodox Church as well as in several Byzantine hymns).

The Axion Esti may be viewed as the worldly equivalent of a Greek Orthodox mass, with its three parts corresponding to Christ's life, the Passion, and the Resurrection. The poem is not a Christian epic in the strict sense of the term; it is, however, much indebted to Byzantine hymnology. Its middle section consists of three types of poetic units corresponding to liturgical ones. Eighteen "psalms" alternate, in strictly mathematical, symmetrical order, with twelve "odes" and six "readings." The readings are objective, powerfully realistic prose accounts of representative scenes and episodes of the 1940's, while the psalms, in free verse, are lyrical and thoughtful reactions, and the odes are songlike in their various intricately metrical stanzas. On the whole, the poem is a tour de force in the technical variety of its forms and modes, in the richness of its language and imagery, and in its superbly conscious craftsmanship; it was on this poem in particular that the Swedish Academy bestowed its highest praise in awarding the Nobel Prize to Elytis. In this epic in lyric form, the poet of the impulsive unconscious presented a poetry that is described by Andreas Karandonis as "highly programmed, totally directed to a final goal, and measured in its every detail as if with a compass." Thematically, this epic may be said to have its first conception in Elytis's heroic elegy on the Albanian campaign, for it returns in part to the suffering and the heroism that he witnessed in the war, yet in its epic grandeur and technical variety, *The Axion Esti* widens to embrace the physical and spiritual identity of the Greek nation and the Hellenic world.

Of the three major sections of this poem, the first, "Genesis," is an imagistic and lyrical account of how light, the Aegean sunlight, defined the physical, ethical, spiritual, and psychological characteristics of the Greek world. Parallel to the growth of Greek culture and the Greek nation is the poet's own growth, for in him a personified sun, the divine creator, has its axis. This identification of the poet with the giver of life establishes the rhythm of the poem, which shifts constantly from the individual to the archetypal, from the microcosm to the macrocosm. The small world of Greece is identical with the "great world," as the "now" is with the "ever."

Following this account of the past, "The Passion"—the centerpiece of the poem, the longest, most stylistically varied, and most significant of the three sections— turns to the present, to the war decade (1940-1949), during which the "created world" is submitted to a major test of suffering. The third and last section, "Gloria," is highly lyrical and prophetic, earthy yet "meteoric," physical yet metaphysical. The disturbed and challenged world is waiting to be restored to its inherent beauty and worth as a "regained paradise," enriched by the lessons learned through hardship.

Speaking of the insistent "search for paradise" in his work, Elytis has remarked: "When I say 'paradise,' I do not conceive of it in the Christian sense. It is another world which is incorporated into our own, and it is our own fault that we are unable to grasp it."

Almost always connected with Elytis's notion of paradise are the "girls" ever present in his poetry, embodiments of beauty and inspirers of Eros, both physical and transcendental. Elytis's informing vision was described as a "solar metaphysics," the metaphysics of Greek sunlight. As Elytis remarked: "Europeans and Westerners always find mystery in obscurity, in the night, while we Greeks find it in light, which is for us an absolute. . . . *Limpidity* is probably the one element which dominates my poetry at present," where "behind a given thing something different can be seen."

TO FOTODHENDRO KE I DHEKATI TETARTI OMORFIA

Elytis's solar metaphysics found seminal expression in the collection entitled *To fotodhendro ke i dhekati tetarti omorfia*. These poems depict "the full miniature of a solar system, with the same tranquillity and the same air of eternity, the same perpetual motion in its separate constituent parts." The senses reach their "sanctity," becoming organs of poetic metaphysics and extensions of the spirit. In suggestive dreams, Elytis's "girls" became angelic phantoms, not earthly any more but inhabitants of a paradise that grows melancholy and mysterious. The "light tree" mentioned in the title, which Elytis once saw magically growing in the backyard of his childhood home, is symbolic of the light of life, of revelation and inspiration, of love and communion with the universe; when in his old age he returns in search of it, the tree is gone. In a series of nostalgic, intimate, imaginative recollections of his childhood and youth, he tried to recapture and decipher the meaning of his experience. These poems are apparently progressive stages in the day or week of his whole life, starting from a Palm Sunday morning, progressing to the sunset, then passing into night and the astral metaphysics of his old age. There, with mystical and occult insinuations, all opposites meet and are reconciled.

MARIA NEPHELE

A work that was later regarded to be the summa of Elytis's later writings, *Maria Nephele* was initially received by a hesitant public. As one critic noted, "some academicians and critics of the older generations still [wanted] to cling to the concept of the 'sun-drinking' Elytis . . . the monumental *Axion Esti*, so they [approached it] with cautious hesitation as an experimental and not-so-attractive creation of rather ephemeral value."

The issue lay with its radically different presentation. Whereas his earlier poems dealt with the almost timeless expression of the Greek reality that were not directly derived from actual events, *Maria Nephele* was based on a young woman he actually met. Moreover, unlike the women from his earlier work, the woman in Elytis's poem had changed to reflect the troubled times in which she lived, becoming a new manifestation of the eternal female. Maria stands opposed to the more traditional women figures of his early poems by serving as an attractive, liberated, restless, and even blasé representative of today's young woman. American youth radicalism hit its apex in the late 1960's, but it took another decade for its force to be felt in Greece. In *Maria Nephele*, the tensions produced from the radicalism interact with some more newly developed Greek cultural realities: increased cosmopolitanism (with its positive and negative aspects), technological advances, and concern with material possessions.

As one critic wrote, the urban Maria Nephele "is the offspring, not the sibling, of the women of Elytis's youth. Her setting is the polluted city, not the open country and its islands of purity and fresh air." The poem consists of the juxtaposed conversations of Maria Nephele, who represents the ideals of today's emerging woman, and Antifonitis, or the Responder, who stands for more traditional views. Maria forces the Responder to confront issues that he would rather ignore. Both characters are sophisticated and complex urbanites who express themselves in a wide range of styles, moods, idioms, and stanzaic forms.

OTHER MAJOR WORKS

NONFICTION: *O zoghrafos Theofilos*, 1973; *Anihta hartia*, 1974 (*Open Papers*, 1995); *I mayia tou Papadhiamandi*, 1976; *Anafora ston Andrea Embiríko*, 1978; *Ta dimosia ke ta idiotika*, 1990; *En lefko*, 1992; *Carte Blanche: Selected Writings*, 1999.

TRANSLATION: *Dhefteri ghrafi*, 1976 (of Arthur Rimbaud and others).

BIBLIOGRAPHY

Books Abroad. (Fall, 1975). A special issue devoted to Elytis, examing his life and works.

Bosnakis, Panayiotis. "*Ek tou plision*." *World Literature Today* 74, no. 1 (Winter, 2000): 211-212. A critical analysis of Elytis's posthumously published *Ek tou plision* (from close).

Decavalles, Andonis. *Odysseus Elytis: From the Golden to the Silver Poem*. New York: Pella, 1994. These seven essays analyze Elytis's work, interpreting his poetry as it transforms from the personal to the national.

Friar, Kimon. *Modern Greek Poetry: From Cavafis to Elytis*. New York: Simon & Schuster, 1973. Informative introduction, an essay on translation, and annotations to the poetry by the editor. Includes bibliography.

Glasgow, Eric. "Odysseus Elytis: In Memory of a Modern Greek Poet." *Contemporary Review* 270, no. 1572 (January, 1997): 33-34. A brief article written after the poet's death, remembering his life and works.

Hirst, Anthony. *God and the Poetic Ego: The Appropriation of Biblical and Liturgical Language in the Poetry of Palamas, Sikelianos, and Elytis*. New York: Peter Lang, 2004. Hirst examines the role of religion in the works of Elytis, Kōstēs Palamas, and Angelos Sikelianos.

Ivask, Ivar, ed. *Odysseus Elytis: Analogies of Light*. Norman: University of Oklahoma Press, 1981. A collection of critical essays on Elytis's work.

Andonis Decavalles
Updated by Sarah Hilbert

FEDERICO GARCÍA LORCA

Born: Fuentevaqueros, Spain; June 5, 1898
Died: Víznar, Spain; August 19, 1936

OTHER LITERARY FORMS

The publisher Aguilar of Madrid issued a one-volume edition of the works of Federico García Lorca (gahr-SEE-uh LAWR-kuh), compiled and annotated by Arturo del Hoyo, with a prologue by Jorge Guillén and an epilogue by Vicente Aleixandre. In addition to the poetry, it includes García Lorca's plays, of which the tragic rural trilogy *Bodas de sangre* (pr. 1933; *Blood Wedding*, 1939), *Yerma* (pr. 1934; English translation, 1941), and *La casa de Bernarda Alba* (pr., pb. 1945; *The House of Bernarda Alba*, 1947) are world famous and represent García Lorca's best achievement as a poet become director-playwright. To portray all the facets of García Lorca's artistic personality, the Aguilar edition also includes his first play, *El maleficio de la mariposa* (pr. 1920; *The Butterfly's Evil Spell*, 1963); an example of his puppet plays, *Los títeres de Cachiporra: La tragicomedia de don Cristóbal y la señá Rosita* (pr. 1937; *The Tragicomedy of Don Cristóbal and Doña Rosita*, 1955); selections from *Impresiones y paisajes* (1918; impressions and landscapes), García Lorca's first published prose works, in which his genius is already evident in the melancholic, impressionistic style used to describe his feelings and reactions to the Spanish landscape and Spanish life; several short prose pieces and dialogues; a number of lectures and speeches; a variety of representative letters to friends; texts of newspaper interviews; poems from the poet's book of suites; fifteen of his songs; and twenty-five of his drawings.

Although the Aguilar edition reflects a consummate artist, still missing from its pages are a number of other works: a five-act play, *El público* (fragment, pb. 1976; *The*

Audience, 1958), and the first part of a dramatic biblical trilogy titled "La destrucción de Sódoma" (wr. 1936; the destruction of Sodom), on which García Lorca was working at the time of his death. Lost are "Los sueños de mi prima Aurelia" (the dreams of my cousin Aurelia) and "La niña que riega la albahaca y el príncipe pregunton" (the girl who waters the sweet basil flower and the inquisitive prince), a puppet play presented in Granada on January 5, 1923. "El sacrificio de Ifigenia" (Iphigenia's sacrifice) and "La hermosa" (the beauty) are titles of two plays whose existence cannot be substantiated.

Reportedly, García Lorca also collected a group of poems titled "Sonetos del amor oscuro" (sonnets of dark love), the title suggesting to certain critics the poet's preference for intimate masculine relationships. Until the 1960's, most of the works evaluating García Lorca centered on the events of his life and death and were only interspersed with snatches of literary criticism. Since his death, thematic and stylistic studies by such noted scholars as Rafael Martínez Nadal, Gustavo Correa, Arturo Barea, Rupert C. Allen, and Richard L. Predmore have served to illuminate García Lorca's symbolic and metaphorical world.

ACHIEVEMENTS

The typically Spanish character of his plays and poetry, enhanced by rich and daring lyrical expression, have made Federico García Lorca one of the most universally recognized poets of the twentieth century. His tragic death in 1936 at the hands of the Falange, the Spanish Fascist Party, in the flower of his manhood and literary creativity, merely served to further his fame.

The first milestone of García Lorca's short but intense career was the publication of *The Gypsy Ballads of García Lorca*, which solidly established his reputation as a fine poet in the popular vein. His dark, brooding, foreboding ballads of Gypsy passion and death captured the imagination and hearts of Spaniards and foreigners, Andalusians and Galicians, illiterate farmers and college professors. Critics saw in García Lorca's poems the culmination of centuries of a rich and diverse Spanish lyric tradition. For example, Edwin Honig has noted that García Lorca's poetry took its inspiration from such diverse sources as the medieval Arabic-Andalusian art of amorous poetry; the early popular ballad; the Renaissance synthesis in Spain of classical traditions, as exemplified by the "conceptist" poetry of Luis de Góngora y Argote; and the *cante jondo*, or "deep song," of the Andalusian Gypsy.

Living in an era of vigorous cultural and literary activity, called by many Spain's second golden age, García Lorca clearly maintained his individuality. His innate charm and wit, his strong and passionate presence, his *duende*, or "soul," as a performer of Andalusian songs and ballads, and his captivating readings of his own poetry and plays drew the applause and friendship of equally talented writers and artists, such as Rafael Alberti, Pedro Salinas, Jorge Guillén, Vicente Aleixandre, Salvador Dalí, and Luis Buñuel.

The poet reached the peak of his popular success in the late 1920's. Both his *Songs* and *The Gypsy Ballads of García Lorca* were published to great critical acclaim. In the same period, he delivered two memorable lectures, the first at the *cante jondo* festival organized jointly with composer Manuel de Falla in Granada, and the second at the festival in honor of Góngora's tercentenary. His play *Mariana Pineda* (pr. 1927; English translation, 1950) was produced in Barcelona, and the following year he founded and published the literary journal *Gallo*. Despite these achievements, however, García Lorca suffered a grave spiritual crisis, to which he alludes in his correspondence but never really clarifies. This crisis led him to reevaluate his artistic output and turn to new experiences and modes of expression.

The result of García Lorca's soul-searching can be seen in his later works, especially *Poet in New York* and *Lament for the Death of a Bullfighter*. In the former, García Lorca fully unleashes his imagination in arabesques of metaphor that on first reading appear incomprehensible. *Poet in New York* is a difficult and frequently obscure work that has been viewed as a direct contrast to his earlier poetry. However, as Predmore has so painstakingly demonstrated, these poems extend rather than depart from García Lorca's established preference for ambiguous and antithetical symbolism.

The two threads that run throughout García Lorca's work are the themes of love and death: They lend a poetic logic and stability to what may otherwise appear chaotic and indecipherable. A study of these themes in García Lorca's poetry and plays reveals a gradual evolution from tragic premonition and foreboding, through vital passion repressed and frustrated by outside forces, to bitter resignation and death. Throughout his life, García Lorca's constant companion and friend was death. The poet Antonio Machado described this intimacy with death in his lament for García Lorca:

> He was seen walking with Her, alone,
> unafraid of her scythe.
>
> . . . .
>
> Today as yesterday, gypsy, my Death,
> how good to be with you, alone
> in these winds of Granada, of my Granada.

García Lorca's gift of imagination, his genius for metaphor and volatile imagery, and his innate sense of the tragic human condition make him one of the outstanding poets of the twentieth century. With his execution in Granada in 1936 at the outbreak of the Spanish Civil War, the frustrated personas of his poetry and plays, who so often ended their lives in senseless tragedy, materialized in his own person. In García Lorca, life became art and art became life. Combining the experience of two cultures, he addressed in both, the Andalusian and the American man's primal needs and fears within his own interior world.

BIOGRAPHY

Federico García Lorca was born on June 5, 1898, in Fuentevaqueros, in the province of Granada. His father, Don Federico García Rodríguez, was a well-to-do landowner, a solid rural citizen of good reputation. After his first wife died, Don Federico married Doña Vicenta Lorca Romero, an admired schoolteacher and a musician. García Lorca was very fond of his mother and believed that he inherited his intelligence and artistic bent from her and his passionate nature from his father. It was in the countryside of Granada that García Lorca's poetic sensibility took root, nourished by the meadows, the fields, the wild animals, the livestock, and the people of that land. His formative years were centered in the village, where he attended Mass with his mother and absorbed and committed to memory the colorful talk, the folktales, and the folk songs of the *vega* (fertile lowland) that would later find a rebirth in the metaphorical language of his poetry and plays.

In 1909, his family moved to Granada, and García Lorca enrolled in the College of the Sacred Heart to prepare for the university. This was the second crucial stage in his artistic development: Granada's historical and literary associations further enriched his cultural inheritance from the *vega* and modified it by adding an intellectual element. García Lorca wanted to be a musician and composer, but his father wanted him to study law. In 1915, he matriculated at the University of Granada, but he never was able to adapt completely to the regimentation of university studies, failing three courses, one of them in literature. During the same period, he continued his serious study of piano and composition with Don Antonio Segura. García Lorca frequented the cafés of Granada and became popular for his wit. In 1916 and 1917, García Lorca traveled throughout Castile, Léon, and Galicia with one of his professors from the university, who also encouraged him to write his first book, *Impresiones y paisajes*. He also came into contact with important people in the arts, among them Manuel de Falla, who shared García Lorca's interest in traditional folk themes, and Fernando de los Ríos, an important leader in educational and social reforms, who persuaded García Lorca's father to send his son to the University of Madrid.

In 1919, García Lorca arrived in Madrid, where he was to spend the next ten years at the famous Residencia de Estudiantes, in the company of Rafael Alberti, Jorge Guillén, Pedro Salinas, Gerardo Diego, Dámaso Alonso, Luis Cernuda, and Vicente Aleixandre. There García Lorca published his first collection of poems, *Libro de poemas*, and became involved with the philosophical and literary currents then in vogue. In 1922, García Lorca returned to Granada to conduct with Manuel de Falla a Festival of Cante Jondo.

The years from 1924 to 1928 were successful but troubled ones for García Lorca, marked by moments of elation followed by depression. During these years, García Lorca developed a close friendship with Salvador Dalí and spent several summers with the Dalí family at Cadaqués. He published his second book of poems, *Songs*, in 1927 and in that same year saw the premiere of *Mariana Pineda* in Barcelona and Madrid. In December of 1927, García Lorca participated in the famous Góngora tricentennial anniversary celebrations in Seville, where he delivered one of his most famous lectures, "The Poetic Image in Don Luis de Góngora." Gradually, García Lorca's fame spread, and his *The Gypsy Ballads of García Lorca* became the most widely read book of poems to appear in Spain since the publication of Gustavo Adolfo Bécquer's *Rimas* (*Poems*, 1891; better known as *The Rhymes*, 1898) in 1871. During the period from May to December of 1928, García Lorca suffered an emotional crisis that prompted him to leave Spain to accompany Fernando de los Ríos to New York. After spending nine months in the United States, a stay that included a visit to Vermont, García Lorca returned to Spain by way of Cuba with renewed interest and energy for his work. The clearest product of this visit was *Poet in New York*, one of his greatest books of poems, published four years after his death.

After his return to Madrid in 1930, García Lorca turned his focus increasingly to the dramatic. In 1932, under the auspices of the Republic's Ministry of Education, García Lorca founded La Barraca, a university theater whose aim was to bring the best classical plays to the provinces. In the same period, he saw the successful staging of *Blood Wedding* and *El amor de don Perlimplín con Belisa en su jardín* (pr. 1933; *The Love of Don Perlimplín for Belisa in His Garden*, 1941). His achievements in Spain were capped by another trip to the New World, this time to Argentina, where *Blood Wedding, Mariana Pineda*, and *La zapatera prodigiosa* (pr. 1930; *The Shoemaker's Prodigious Wife*, 1941) were staged and received with great enthusiasm. The years 1934 and 1935 saw the writing of the *Lament for the Death of a Bullfighter* and the premieres of at least four new plays. By 1936, García Lorca had decided to return to Granada for the celebration of his name day and also to bide his time until the political turmoil in Madrid abated. During his stay, the civil war broke out, and amid the fighting between the Nationalist and the Popular forces in Granada, García Lorca was detained and executed on August 19, 1936, in the outskirts of Víznar. His body was thrown into an unmarked grave.

ANALYSIS

In imagery that suggests an "equestrian leap" between two opposing worlds, Federico García Lorca embodies a dialectical vision of life, on one hand filled with an all-consuming love for humanity and nature and, on the other, cognizant of the "black torso of the Pharaoh," the blackness symbolizing an omnipresent death unredeemed by the possibility of immortality. The tension between these two irreconcilable forces lends a tautness as well as a mystery to much of his poetry.

"ELEGÍA A DOÑA JUANA LA LOCA"

A recurring theme throughout García Lorca's work that is expressive of this animating tension is that of thwarted love, repressed by society or simply by human destiny and ending inevitably in death. This obsession with unfulfilled dreams and with death is evident in the poet's first collection. In a moving elegy to the Castilian princess Juana la Loca titled "Elegía a doña Juana la Loca," García Lorca details in fifteen stanzas the lamentable fate of a woman driven to madness by her unrequited love for her husband, Felipe el Hermoso. Throughout the poem, García Lorca addresses her as a red carnation in a deep and desolate valley, to whom Death extended a bouquet of withered roses instead of flowers, verses, and pearl necklaces. Like other great tragic heroines of Spanish literature, such as Isabel de Segura and Melibea, and those of García Lorca's own creative imagination, she is a victim of fate.

The themes of violent passion and death, later more fully expressed in *The Gypsy Ballads of García Lorca*, are latent in the description of Juana as a princess of the red sunset, the color of blood and fire, whose passion is like the dagger, whose distaff is of iron, whose flax is of steel. Here, metallic substances are symbols of death; Juana lies in her coffin of lead, and within her skeleton, a heart broken into a thousand pieces speaks of her shattered dreams and frustrated life.

"BALLAD OF THE LITTLE SQUARE"

In contrast to the bleak symbolism of these works, children and their world interested and delighted García Lorca, and he futilely sought in their charm and innocence a respite from the anguish of existence. In another poem from his first collection, "Balada de la placeta" ("Ballad of the Little Square"), the poet is listening to children singing. In a playful dialogue, the children ask the poet what he feels in his red, thirsty mouth; he answers, "the taste of the bones of my big skull." The poet's consciousness of death's presence mars his contemplation of youthful fun. Although he might wish to lose himself in the child's world, he clearly recognizes in a later poem, "Gacela de la huida" ("Gacela of the Flight"), that the seeds of death are already sown behind that childish exterior: "No one who touching a newborn child can forget the motionless horse skulls." Still, he tries to reject the physical destruction, the putrefaction of death that he so vividly describes in "Gacela de la muerte oscura" ("Gacela of the Dark Death") and in the *Lament for the Death of a Bullfighter*.

"THE SONG OF THE HORSEMAN"

García Lorca was a master of the dramatic ballad, full of mystery, passion, and dark, sudden violence. His tools were simple words and objects culled from everyday living, which contrasted with and intensified the complex emotions underlying the verse. García Lorca's mastery of the ballad form is exemplified in "Canción de jinete" ("The Song of the Horseman"), from *Songs*. The horseman's destination is the distant city of Córdoba. Although he knows the roads well and his saddlebags are packed with olives, he fatalistically declares that he will never reach Córdoba. García Lorca never tells a story outright; he makes his audience do the work. Thus, Death is looking at the horseman from the towers of Córdoba, as he cries "Ay! How long the road! Ay! My valiant pony! Ay! That death should wait me before I reach Córdoba." How? Why? Who? Where? These questions are left to the imagination.

"SOMNAMBULE BALLAD"

It is through the figure of the Andalusian gypsy that García Lorca best conveys his personal vision of life. With his characteristic techniques of metaphorical suggestion and dramatic tension, enriched by an artist's palette of colors, García Lorca in *The Gypsy Ballads of García Lorca* treats his usual subject matter of love and death, passion and destruction, with great lyrical fantasy. The refrain "Green, how much I want you green" establishes the enchanted atmosphere of the famous "Romance sonambulo" ("Somnambule Ballad"), where everything possesses the greenish cast of an interior world: "Green wind, green flesh, green hair." The best known of García Lorca's ballads, it only implies the story behind the death of a pair of lovers: his the result of a wound that runs from his chest to his throat, hers from drowning in the sorrow of having waited for him so long in vain.

The themes of passion and violence are underscored by the theme of liberty, denied to the lovers by fate and a false social order. The gypsy girl's death is already intimated in the first stanza, where she is described as having a shadow on her waist, with green flesh, hair of green, and eyes of cold silver that cannot see. On a first reading, the two lines "The ship upon the sea/ and the horse in the mountain," which precede the description, seem to be a discordant and senseless addition to the narrative. To understand their function, the reader must see them in relation to the theme of liberty. Humans are imprisoned by their passions, by destiny, death, a sense of honor, and social institutions. In contrast, the images of the ship upon the sea and the horse on the mountain suggest total freedom. The horse, which in García Lorca's work often represents male virility, prefigures the gypsy's attainment of the freedom that is his by nature. The image of the ship, on the other hand, has a long tradition of symbolizing liberty, especially in the Romantic period; its interpretation here, as such, is logical and expected. The description of the stars as white frost and the mountain as a filching cat foreshadows the violence of the characters' deaths.

Thus, "Somnambule Ballad" offers a profusion of surrealistic and seemingly disconnected images governed by a vigorous inner logic. In this, it is representative of García Lorca's finest works. The repetition of key images—of green, cold silver, the moon, water, and the night—unifies the poem. The gypsy girl and the gypsy are together in death and cannot hear the pounding of the drunken civil guard on the door. Death has granted them freedom, and all is as it should be: "The ship upon the sea, and the horse on the mountain." Using the local color and ambience of gypsy life, García Lorca gives voice to his own frustrations and those of humanity in general. Fettered by passion, destiny, and social norms, humanity's only escape is through death.

POET IN NEW YORK

The strange poems of *Poet in New York* are the work of a mature poet. In New York, García Lorca, who had loved life in all its spontaneity, who had grieved over the death of gypsies, their instinctive and elemental passions suffocated, was confronted with the heartless, mechanized world of the urban metropolis. In *Poet in New York*, the gypsy is replaced by the black person, whose instinctive impulses and strengths are perverted by white civilization and whose repression and anguish is embodied in the figure of the great King of Harlem in a janitor's suit. The blood of three hundred crimson roses that stained the gypsy's shirt in "Somnambule Ballad" now flows from four million butchered ducks, five million hogs, two thousand doves , one million cows, one million lambs, and two million roosters.

The disrespect for life in this landscape of vomiting and urinating multitudes is portrayed in the death of a cat, within whose little paw, crushed by the automobile, García Lorca sees a world of broken rivers and unattainable distances. Alone, alienated, and frustrated in his endeavors, humans cannot appeal to anyone for help, not even the Church, which in its hypocrisy and heathen materialism betrays the true spirit of Christianity. The poet sees death and destruction everywhere. His own loneliness and alienation, described in "Asesinato" ("Murder"), recall the haunting words and melody of the *cante jondo*: "A pinprick to dive till it touches the roots of a cry."

LAMENT FOR THE DEATH OF A BULLFIGHTER

Considered by many to be García Lorca's supreme poetic achievement, *Lament for the Death of a Bullfighter* is the quintessence of the Spanish "tragic sense of life." In this lament, García Lorca incorporated aspects of a long poetic tradition and revitalized them through his own creativity. Based on a true incident, as were most of García Lorca's poems, the elegy was written on the death of his good friend Ignacio, an intellectual and a bullfighter, who was gored by a bull and died in August of 1934. The bullfight is elevated by García Lorca to a universal level, representing humanity's heroic struggle against death. Death, as always in García Lorca's poetry, emerges triumphant, yet the struggle is seen as courageous, graceful, meaningful.

The elegy is divided into four parts: "La cogida y la muerte" ("The Goring and the Death"), "La sangre derrameda" ("The Spilling of the Blood"), "Cuerpo presente" ("The Body Present"), and "Alma ansente" ("Absent Soul"). In general, the poem moves from the concrete to the abstract, from report to essay, from the specific to the general. Part 1 describes the events, the chaos, the confusion, the whole process of death in a series of images appealing to all the five senses. Phones jangle, the crowd is mad with grief, the bulls bellow, the wounds burn. What dominates is the incessant and doleful bell, reminding the poet, with each repetition of "at five o'clock in the afternoon," of the finality of death, worming its way into Ignacio's being, hammering its way into the public mind and into the poet's consciousness. The macabre sights and smells of death are detailed in all their colorful goriness: the white sheet, a pail of lime, snowy sweat, yellow iodine, green gangrene. Time ceases for Ignacio as all the clocks show five o'clock in the shadow of the afternoon. Refusing to look at Ignacio's blood in the sand, García Lorca vents his anger and frustration at seeing all that beauty, confidence, princeliness, strength of body and character, wit, and intelligence slowly seeping out as the moss and the grass open with sure fingers the flowers of Ignacio's skull.

The poet's initial reaction of shock and denial slowly softens into gradual acceptance. Using the slower Alexandrine meter in "The Body Present," García Lorca contemplates the form of Ignacio laid out on a sterile, gray, cold stone. The finality of death is seen in the sulphur yellow of Ignacio's face and in the rain entering his mouth in the stench-filled silence. García Lorca cannot offer immortality. He can only affirm that humankind must live bravely, and that death too will one day cease to exist. Hence, he tells Ignacio to sleep, fly, rest: Even the sea dies. Death, victorious, challenged only by the value of Ignacio's human experience, is dealt with in the last part. By autumn, the people will have forgotten Ignacio, robbed by death and time of the memory of his presence. Only those like the poet, who can look beyond, will immortalize him in song.

Lament for the Death of a Bullfighter expresses the fundamental attitude of the Spaniard toward death: One must gamble on life with great courage and heroism. Welcoming the dark angels of death, the "toques de bordón," or the black tones of the guitar, the poet is paradoxically affirming life. This is humanity's only consolation.

García Lorca's evolution as a poet was characterized throughout by this movement toward an all-encompassing death. Synthesizing a variety of themes and poetic styles and forms, García Lorca embodied, both in his life and in his verse, modern humans' struggle to find meaning in life despite the overwhelming reality of physical and spiritual death.

OTHER MAJOR WORKS

PLAYS: *El maleficio de la mariposa*, pr. 1920 (*The Butterfly's Evil Spell*, 1963); *Mariana Pineda*, pr. 1927 (English translation, 1950); *La doncella, el marinero y el estudiante*, pb. 1928 (*The Virgin, the Sailor, and the Student*, 1957); *El paseo de Buster Keaton*, pb. 1928 (*Buster Keaton's Promenade*, 1957); *La zapatera prodigiosa*, pr. 1930 (*The Shoemaker's Prodigious Wife*, 1941); *Bodas de sangre*, pr. 1933 (*Blood Wedding*, 1939); *El amor de don Perlimplín con Belisa en su jardín*, pr. 1933 (*The Love of Don Perlimplín for Belisa in His Garden*, 1941); *Yerma*, pr. 1934 (English translation, 1941); *Doña Rosita la soltera: O, El lenguaje de las flores*, pr. 1935 (*Doña Rosita the Spinster: Or, The Language of the Flowers*, 1941); *El retablillo de don Cristóbal*, pr. 1935 (*In the Frame of Don Cristóbal*, 1944); *Así que pasen cinco años*, pb. 1937, (wr. 1931; *When Five Years Pass*, 1941); *Los títeres de Cachiporra: La tragicomedia de don Cristóbal y la señá Rosita*, pr. 1937 (wr. 1928; *The Tragicomedy of Don Cristóbal and Doña Rosita*, 1955); *Quimera*, pb. 1938 (wr. 1928; *Chimera*, 1944); *La casa de*

Bernarda Alba, pr., pb. 1945 (wr. 1936; *The House of Bernarda Alba*, 1947); *El público*, pb. 1976 (wr. 1930, fragment; *The Audience*, 1958).

NONFICTION: *Impresiones y paisajes*, 1918; *Selected Letters*, 1983 (David Gershator, editor).

MISCELLANEOUS: *Obras completas*, 1938-1946 (8 volumes).

BIBLIOGRAPHY

Anderson, Reed. *Federico García Lorca*. London: Macmillan, 1984. Anderson's study focuses on García Lorca's dramatic art. The book has a fine overview of García Lorca's relationship to Spanish literature in general as well as insightful discussions of the early and mature dramas.

Binding, Paul. *Lorca: The Gay Imagination*. London: GMP, 1985. Binding's is a fine study focusing on García Lorca's work as it is an outgrowth of the poet's sexuality. Binding has a sympathetic sense of the modern temperament, and his readings, particularly of García Lorca's mature works, are excellent.

Bonaddio, Federico, ed. *A Companion to Federico García Lorca*. Woodbridge, Suffolk, England: Tamesis, 2008. Provides biographical information and critical analysis. Contains a chapter on poetry.

Delgado, Maria M. *Federico García Lorca*. New York: Routledge, 2007. A biography that looks at the life, politics, and mythology surrounding the poet and dramatist. Also looks at his legacy.

Gibson, Ian. *Federico García Lorca*. New York: Pantheon Books, 1989. A monumental biography that goes to the heart of García Lorca's genius with brilliant prose and telling anecdotes. Meticulously reconstructs the poet's periods in New York, Havana, and Buenos Aires. Vividly re-creates the café life of Spain in the 1930's and the artistic talents that were nurtured there. Evokes the landscapes of Granada, Almeria, Cuba, and Argentina celebrated in the poetry.

Johnston, David. *Federico García Lorca*. Bath, England: Absolute, 1998. Asserts that García Lorca is concerned with deconstructing the essentials of Spain's culture of difference. Claims that the poet's most radical ultimate intention was the deconstruction of a civilization and the redefinition of the individual's right to be, not through the language of ethics or of the law but in terms of a natural imperative.

Mayhew, Jonathan, ed. *Apocryphal Lorca: Translation, Parody, Kitsch*. Chicago: University of Chicago Press, 2009. Literary criticism of García Lorca's works. Mayhew contrasts the perception of the poet in the English-speaking world to that in the Spanish-speaking world. He notes the poet's legacy among American poets.

Morris, C. Brian. *Son of Andalusia: The Lyrical Landscapes of Federico García Lorca*. Nashville, Tenn.: Vanderbilt University Press, 1997. In six chapters and an epilogue, Morris identifies the presence of Andalusian legends, traditions, songs, and beliefs in García Lorca's life and works.

Sahuquillo, Angel. *Federico García Lorca and the Culture of Male Homosexuality*. Jefferson, N.C.: McFarland, 2007. Examines García Lorca's life and works from the perspective of his sexuality.

Stainton, Leslie. *Lorca: A Dream of Life*. New York: Farrar, Straus and Giroux, 1999. Stainton, an American scholar who lived in Spain for several years, writes of García Lorca's sexuality, his left-wing political views, and his artistic convictions. Her detailed account is strictly chronological. García Lorca's work is described but not analyzed.

Katherine Gyékényesi Gatto

GYULA ILLYÉS

Born: Rácegrespuszta, Hungary; November 2, 1902
Died: Budapest, Hungary; April 15, 1983

OTHER LITERARY FORMS

Although principally a poet, Gyula Illyés (IHL-yays) was also the author of significant prose and drama. Two of his most important prose works appeared in the 1930's: *Puszták népe* (1936; *People of the Puszta*, 1967), widely translated, is partly an autobiographical documentary and partly a sociography of Hungary's poverty-stricken peasantry; *Petőfi* (1936; English translation, 1973) is both a personal confession and a scholarly analysis of the great nineteenth century poet, Sándor Petőfi. Published late in Illyés's life, the essays collected in *Szellem és erőszak* (1978; spirit and violence), officially banned but published in the West in a facsimile edition, reflects his concern about the mistreatment of four million Hungarians living as minorities in countries neighboring Hungary. His principal plays deal with a search for lessons in Hungary's history.

Illyés also excelled as a translator of Louis Aragon, Ben Jonson, Robert Burns, Paul Éluard, Victor Hugo, Jean Racine, François Villon, and others; a collection of his translations was published in 1963 as *Nyitott ajtó* (open door).

ACHIEVEMENTS

Gyula Illyés is internationally recognized as one of the leading poets of the twentieth century. French poet and critic Alain Bosquet wrote about him: "Only three or four living poets have been able to identify themselves with the soul of the century. Their genius burns in the Hungarian poet Gyula Illyés." The International Biennale of Poets in Knokke-le-Zoute, Belgium, awarded him its Grand Prix in 1965, and the University of Vienna awarded him the Herder Prize in 1970. He received two literary prizes in France: the Ordre des Art et Lettres in 1974 and the Grand Prize in 1978 from the Société des Poètes Français. In 1981, he was awarded the Mondello literary prize in Italy. In 1969, he was elected vice president of the International PEN Club. In Hungary, among many other awards, he was three times the recipient of the Kossuth Prize.

Apart from the highest critical acclaim, Illyés achieved the status of a national poet and an intellectual leader in Hungary and in Europe. His unbending loyalty to the downtrodden and his contributions in clarifying the most important issues of his times earned him an extraordinary moral authority.

BIOGRAPHY

Gyula Illyés was born into a family of poor farm workers on one of the large estates of a wealthy aristocrat. His grandfather was a shepherd and his father a mechanic; the joint efforts of his relatives were needed to pay for his schooling in Budapest. At the end of World War I, the Austro-Hungarian monarchy collapsed, giving way to a liberal republic, which was taken over by a short-lived Communist regime. Illyés joined the Hungarian Red Army in 1919. After the old regime defeated the revolution, he fled to Vienna in 1920, then went to Berlin, and a year later to Paris. He attended the Sorbonne, studying literature and psychology, and he supported himself by tutoring and by working in a book bindery. His earliest poetry appeared in Hungarian émigré periodicals. During those years, he made the acquaintance of many young French poets, some of whom later became famous as Surrealists: Aragon, Éluard, and Tristan Tzara. In 1926, the political climate became more tolerant in Hungary, and Illyés returned. He worked as an office clerk and joined the circle connected with the avant-garde periodical

Dokumentum, edited by Lajos Kassák. Some of his early poems caught the eye of Mihály Babits, a leading poet and senior editor of the literary periodical *Nyugat*, and in a short time, Illyés became a regular contributor to that outstanding modern literary forum.

Illyés's first collection of poems was published in 1928, followed by twelve other books of poetry and prose, resulting in literary prizes as well as critical and popular recognition during the next ten years.

Another decisive event in Illyés's life is best described by him:

> I have arrived from Paris, being twenty-three-and-a-half years old. My new eyes saw a multitude of horrors when I looked around my birthplace. I had a deep and agonizing experience, I was outraged, shocked and moved immediately to action upon seeing the fate of my own people.

The result of this experience was *People of the Puszta*, a realistic personal account of the hardships and injustices that the poorest estate-servant peasants suffered. With this book, Illyés had joined the literary/political populist movement, which fought between the two world wars for the economic, social, educational, cultural, and political interests of the peasantry and, later, the working class as well.

In 1937, Illyés became one of the editors of *Nyugat*, and, after its cessation, he founded and edited its successor, *Magyar Csillag*. After World War II, Illyés was offered leading literary and political positions and edited the literary periodical *Válasz* from 1946 to 1949, but as the Stalinist Communist Party, with the help of the occupying Soviet army, enforced totalitarian control over the country, Illyés withdrew from public life. He continued to write, however, and his poems and plays created during these years of dictatorship address the issues of freedom, power, morality, and hope. His monumental poem *One Sentence on Tyranny*, written in the early 1950's but not published until 1956, was officially banned in Hungary; it became the emblem of the 1956 revolution. After the revolution was crushed by the Soviet army, Illyés went into passive resistance, not publishing anything until the government's release, in 1960, of most jailed writers.

In the 1960's and 1970's, Illyés published some thirty books, including poems, plays, reports, essays, and translations. In his old age, his themes became increasingly universal, and he died at the height of his creative powers, addressing issues of vital concern not only to his nation but also to humanity at large.

Analysis

Gyula Illyés's immense prestige and world renown were largely the result of his ability to integrate the philosophies and traditions of Eastern and Western Europe, the views and approaches of the rational intellectual and of the lyric dreamer, and the actions of *homo politicus* and *homo aestheticus*. In a 1968 interview, Illyés confided,

"With all the literary genres with which I experimented I wanted to serve one single cause: that of a unified people and the eradication of exploitation and misery. I always held literature to be only a tool." Five sentences later, however, he exclaimed, "I would forgo every single other work of mine for one poem! Poetry is my first, my primary experience and it has always remained that." André Frenaud has remarked of Illyés that he is a poet of diverse and even contradictory impulses: a poet who can be "violent and sardonic, who lacks neither visions coming from deep within, nor the moods of sensuality. He knows the cowardice of man and the courage needed for survival. He knows the past and interrogates the future."

Illyés began his literary career in the 1920's under the influence of Surrealism and Activism. He found his original style and tone at the end of the 1920's and the beginning of the 1930's. Lyric and epic qualities combined with precise, dry, objective descriptions (whose unimpassioned tone is occasionally heated by lyric fervor) determine the singular flavor of his poetry.

NEHÉZ FÖLD AND SARJÚRENDEK

Illyés's first book of poems, *Nehéz föld* (heavy earth), strongly reflects his intoxication with Surrealism and other Western trends. His next collection, *Sarjúrendek*, represents a turning point in his art; in this volume, Illyés turned toward populism and *engagé* realism, although he still retained many stylistic features of the avant-garde.

Illyés's tone became increasingly deep and bitter, his themes historical, and his style more and more intellectual during the 1930's and 1940's. In this period, he wrote many prose works, most of which reflected on historical, social, and political themes. He did not publish any significant collection of new poetry between 1947 and 1956. During this time of harsh political repression, he wrote historical dramas in which he sought to strengthen his people's national consciousness by the examples of great patriots of the past.

KÉZFOGÁSOK

Illyés's poetic silence ended in 1956 when he published a volume of poems titled *Kézfogások* (handshakes). This volume initiated another new phase for the poet: His style thereafter was more intellectual, contemplative, dramatic, and analytical. He never lost the lyric quality of his poetry, however, and the passionate lyricism of his tone makes the moral, ethical, and historical analysis of his poems of the next twenty-five years glow with relevance, immediacy, and urgency.

DŐLT VITORLA

A good example of this style is found in his collection *Dőlt vitorla* (tilted sail), published in 1965. This book contains a number of long poems—written in free verse—about his fellow writers and artists, amplifying their messages, identifying with their visions, and offering Illyés's conclusions. The volume also contains a number of prose poems. In his preface, Illyés gives his reasons for using this genre: He states that he wants "to find the most common everyday words to express the most complicated things.... To concentrate into a piece of creation all that is beautiful, good and true without glitter and pretention but with innovation and endurance."

Written in the middle 1960's to another writer, "Óda a törvényhozóhoz" ("Ode to the Lawmaker") analyzes the role of poets. The poet is "the chief researcher" who uncovers the future, "the progressive, the fighter, the ground breaker," a destroyer of surface appearances "who separates the bad from the good," who shows when the ugly is beautiful and when the virgin is a harlot. Such experimenters, such researchers, are the writers he celebrates: "They are the ones I profess as examples! They are the ones who signal the direction towards a tomorrow!" The tomorrow that these exemplary researcher-poets promote is one of pluralism and tolerance. In this poem, a passionate lyricist evokes a future that the rational intellectual already knows—a future that requires freedom combined with order. "Make laws, but living laws so that we [can] stay human." The poet demands recognition of shadings and nuances, of the "exception, which may be the rule tomorrow."

How can the individual relate to the modern powers of his world as well as realize his individual goals of freedom and humanity? The title poem of *Dőlt vitorla* offers a clue. "Look—when do mast and sail fly forward most triumphantly? When tilted lowest." The ancient Aesopian parable, about the reed that bows to the wind and survives while the proud oak tree breaks and dies, is given a new dimension in this poem: The boat flies forward while it heels low. The issue of relating to the ruling power structure—of surviving sometimes unbearable dictatorial pressures and of being able to realize oneself in spite of authoritarian inhumanities—has been a perennial problem in Hungary. Illyés's sailboat offers a possible solution to the dilemma of whether one should compromise or perish: It sways, bows, and bends, but using, instead of opposing, the forces of the wind, it dashes ahead.

ONE SENTENCE ON TYRANNY

Sometimes such a solution is not possible: The wind may be a killer hurricane. In totalitarian dictatorships, there is no escape. This is the conclusion reached by Illyés in *One Sentence on Tyranny*. This 183-line dramatic sentence is a thorough and horrifying analysis of the nature of such total oppression. Tyranny permeates every minute of every hour. It is present in a lover's embrace and a wife's goodbye kisses; it is present not only in the torture chambers but also in the nursery schools, the churches, the parliament, and the bridal bed; it is in everything, so that, finally, man becomes tyranny himself. He creates it, and it stinks and pours out of him; it looks at him from his mirror. Where there is tyranny, all is in vain. In Illyés's poem, the metaphors of Franz Kafka have become dehumanizing and annihilating realities.

STRENGTH AND WEAKNESS

The opportunity of people to be happy and free, to be able to fulfill themselves, should not depend on power or brute force. What chance do the weak have? Illyés the lyric poet and the concerned humanist is at his best when he redefines strength and weakness in several long poems written in the 1960's.

In "Ditirambus a nőkhöz" ("Dithyramb to Women "), he contrasts the hard, sharp, strong and proud forms of being with the fragile, yielding, and soft forms, and he finds the latter ones stronger: "Not the stones and not the metals, but grass, loess, sedge became the protest." Not the fortresses but the twig, wax, and pen have carried humans so far. Not the weapons and the kings but the clay, the fur, the hide have become the leaders. Not the armored soldiers storming to victory but the loins and breasts, the singing and the spinning, the everyday-working and humanity-protecting women have become the strongest. "Good" strength is defined here not as the strength of force, weight, uncompromising boldness, and pride, but as the strength of flexibility, endurance, resilience, beauty, and love. The contrast is masterfully woven not only between the forceful and softly enduring but also between the boastfully heroic and the gray, everyday, silent endeavor. As Illyés emphasizes in the concluding lines of another poem, "Hunyadi keze" ("The Hand of Hunyadi"): "Cowardly are the people who are protected by martyrs alone. Not heroic deeds but daily daring, everyday, minute-by-minute courage saves men and countries."

This motif of quiet everyday work and courage gives new dimensions to Illyés's theme of strength in weakness; it provides depth to the idea, further developed in "Az éden elvesztése" ("The Loss of Paradise"), a modern oratorio, a moral-political passion play about the chances of the average weak and powerless human individual to avoid the impending atomic cataclysm. After repudiating those who, because of naïveté, blind faith, fatalism, or determinism, accept the inevitability of an atomic war, Illyés argues with those who would capitulate to the threatening powers because of their feelings of weakness and powerlessness.

In his "Hymn of the Root," Illyés emphasizes that "Leaf and tree live according to what the root sends up to them to eat" and that "from the deepest depths comes everything that is good on this Earth." In a "Parable of the Stairs," he offers a concrete program of "everyday, minute-by-minute courage," by which the seemingly weak and powerless can win over the powerful, over dehumanization, over evil.

> Whenever we correct a mistake, that is a step. Whenever we dress a wound: one step. Whenever we reprimand a bossy person: one step. Whenever we do our job right without needing a reprimand: ten steps. To take a baby in one's arm, to say something nice to its mother. . . .

In the final lines of this oratorio, the prophet urges his people:

When the day of fury comes,
when the atom explodes,
on that final day,
before that terrible tomorrow,
people let us dare to do
the greatest deed:

. . . . . .

let us begin here, from the depths
by the strength of our faith,

. . . .

let us begin life anew.

OTHER MAJOR WORKS

LONG FICTION: *Hunok Párizsban*, 1946.

PLAYS: *Ozorai példa*, pb. 1952; *Fáklyaláng*, pb. 1953; *Dózsa György*, pb. 1956; *Malom a Séden*, pb. 1960; *Kegyenc*, pb. 1963; *Különc*, pb. 1963; *Tiszták*, pb. 1969; *Testvérek*, pb. 1972; *Sorsválasztók*, pb. 1982.

NONFICTION: *Petőfi*, 1936 (English translation, 1973); *Puszták népe*, 1936 (*People of the Puszta*, 1967); *Magyarok*, 1938; *Ebéd a kastélyban*, 1962; *Kháron ladikján*, 1969; *Hajszálgyökerek*, 1971; *Szellem és erőszak*, 1978; *Naplójegyzetek, 1977-1978*, 1991.

TRANSLATION: *Nyitott ajtó*, 1963 (of various poets).

BIBLIOGRAPHY

Berlind, Bruce. Introduction to *Charon's Ferry: Fifty Poems*, by Gyula Illyés. Evanston, Ill.: Northwestern University Press, 2000. Berlind's introduction to this work from the Writings from an Unbound Europe series, provides information on Illyés's life and his poetry.

Kolumbán, Nicholas, ed. *Turmoil in Hungary: An Anthology of Twentieth Century Hungarian Poetry*. St. Paul, Minn.: New Rivers Press, 1982. A collection of Hungarian poetry translated into English with commentary.

Serafin, Steven, ed. *Twentieth-Century Eastern European Writers: Third Series*. Vol. 215 in *Dictionary of Literary Biography*. Detroit: Gale Group, 1999. Contains a brief essay on Illyés.

Smith, William Jan. Introduction to *What You Have Almost Forgotten*, by Gyula Illyés. Willimantic, Conn.: Curbstone Press, 1999. The well-known poet provides a substantial introduction to Illyés and his poetry.

Tezla, Albert. *An Introductory Bibliography to the Study of Hungarian Literature*. Cambridge, Mass.: Harvard University Press, 1964. Contains publication information and some commentary on Illyés's work.

_____. *Hungarian Authors: A Bibliographical Handbook*. Cambridge, Mass.: Harvard University Press, 1970. Extension of *An Introductory Bibliography to the Study of Hungarian Literature*, and is to be used in conjunction with that work.

Károly Nagy

BOB KAUFMAN

Born: New Orleans, Louisiana; April 18, 1925
Died: San Francisco, California; January 12, 1986

PRINCIPAL POETRY

Solitudes Crowded with Loneliness, 1965
Golden Sardine, 1967
The Ancient Rain: Poems, 1956-1978, 1981
Cranial Guitar: Selected Poems, 1996

OTHER LITERARY FORMS

Bob Kaufman is known primarily for his poetry, but he was a contributing editor for *Beatitude*, a mimeographed literary magazine first published in San Francisco in 1959. Kaufman's poetry, which began as a form of oral literature, crosses over into theater because he was a San Francisco poet known for his spontaneous performances on the streets of the city and at the Co-existence Bagel Shop.

ACHIEVEMENTS

Bob Kaufman's "Bagel Shop Jazz" was nominated for the Guinness Prize for Poetry in 1961 and appeared in Volume 4 of *The Guinness Book of Poetry, 1959-1960* (1961). In 1979, Kaufman received a fellowship from the National Endowment for the Arts. His *Cranial Guitar* won a PEN Center USA West Poetry Award in 1997.

Because Kaufman applied the improvisational jazz style of saxophonist and composer Charlie Parker to poetry, Kaufman became known as the Original Bebop Man. In addition, because Kaufman followed the examples of Surrealism and Dadaism, creating extraordinarily imagistic combinations of words that eluded explication, some critics refer to Kaufman as the Black American Rimbaud. Although Kaufman made little effort to collect his writings, his poems still appear in major anthologies of African American and Beat generation writing. Both National Public Radio and the Public Broadcasting Service have produced programs on Kaufman.

BIOGRAPHY

Separating the legend of Robert Garnell Kaufman from the verifiable details of his life is a difficult task. Kaufman himself contributed to the development of his legend, and various biographical sources have recorded unverifiable information that has been reproduced in other sources.

The legend indicates that Kaufman's father was an orthodox Jew of German ancestry and his mother was a Catholic from Martinique who had some acquaintance with voodoo. Perhaps Kaufman's grandfather was partly Jewish, but Kaufman's siblings report that the New Orleans family was middle class and Catholic. His father, Joseph Kaufman, was a Pullman porter who worked on trains running between New Orleans and Chicago; his mother, Lillian, was a schoolteacher who made her book collection and piano important parts of the family home. The couple had thirteen children.

The legend suggests that Kaufman joined the United States Merchant Marine at age thirteen, traveled around the world numerous times, and developed his interest in literature when a shipmate influenced him and loaned him books. However, Kaufman probably did not enter the merchant marine until he was eighteen, and thereafter, he became an active member of the National Maritime Union. This union of merchant sailors faced federal review because it reputedly had ties to communist organizations, and Kaufman was one of two thousand sailors driven from the merchant marine because of his political views.

Kaufman moved to New York, where he studied for a time at the New School of Social Research and lived on the lower East Side. It was in New York that he met Allen Ginsberg and William Burroughs. Kaufman returned to San Francisco in 1958. Later that year, he married Eileen Singe.

Kaufman emerged as a literary artist in San Francisco in the late 1950's. *Abomunist Manifesto* was published as a broadside in 1959 by City Lights, and Kaufman's witty and innovative poem made him famous in the North Beach section of San Francisco. *Life* magazine (November 30, 1959) published Paul O'Neil's scathing report on the Beat generation, and a posed photo mocking Beatniks in their "pad" included Kaufman's broadside as an example of standard Beatnik reading. City Lights published two additional broadsides by Kaufman, *Does the Secret Mind Whisper?* and *Second April*. In 1960, Kenneth Tynan's *We Dissent*, a ninety-minute British television program included Kaufman among the featured Beatnik writers. Kaufman also was shown in Ron Rice's underground film *The Flower Thief* (1960), which dealt with the Beat generation in North Beach. As Kaufman became more flamboyant as a street poet in San Francisco, he came into conflict with the police and was often arrested and sometimes beaten. To be free of such treatment, he briefly went to New York, where he read poetry in Greenwich Village. He returned to San Francisco in 1963.

In 1965, New Directions published *Solitudes Crowded with Loneliness*, which included the broadsides and a selection of other poems. In 1967, City Lights published *Golden Sardine*, and in 1981, New Directions published *The Ancient Rain*.

The legend says that Kaufman took a vow of silence when John F. Kennedy was assassinated and maintained it until after the war in Vietnam ended. At a local gathering place, Kaufman is reported to have ended his silence in 1975 by reciting from T. S. Eliot's *Murder in the Cathedral* (pr., pb. 1935) and performing his own composition, "All Those Ships That Never Sailed."

Weakened by drug dependency and emphysema, Kaufman died in San Francisco in 1986. In tribute, a procession of artists, family members, and friends followed a New Orleans jazz band through the North Beach section of San Francisco to view the sites that Kaufman frequented during his career in poetry.

Through the collaboration of Eileen Kaufman (Kaufman's wife), Gerald Nicosia, and David Henderson, *Cranial Guitar*, a selection of poems by Kaufman, was published in 1996. Critical attention to Kaufman grew after its publication, and slowly critics began recognizing that categories such as Beat poet, jazz poet, and Surrealist poet only partially describe Kaufman.

ANALYSIS

As presented in Bob Kaufman's *Solitudes Crowded with Loneliness*, "Abomunist Manifesto" is a sequence of eleven parts. The title plays on *Manifest der Kommunistischen Partei* (1848; *The Communist Manifesto*, 1850) by Karl Marx and Friedrich Engels, but in the conversion of "com" to "abom," Kaufman calls attention to the world's focus on the A-bomb, or atomic bomb. The Abomunists contrast with communists and capitalists and have a modified language and special world perspective that Kaufman's manifesto humorously and provocatively discloses. For example, the Abomunists "vote against everyone by not voting for anyone." Never accepting candidacy, the Abomunists insist, "The only office Abomunists run for is the unemployment office." The worldview of the Abomunists is suggested in apparent contradictions: "Abomunists do not feel pain, no matter how much it hurts." Kaufman adds, "Laughter sounds orange at night, because/ reality is unrealizable while it exists."

Kaufman lends the sequence dramatic proportions when he indicates that the author is "Bomkauf," apparently a fusion of "Bomb" and "Kaufman" that humorously suggests the atomic bomb and the author's name, but also supplies a variation on *dummkopf*, a German word meaning idiot. Bomkauf extends the dramatic proportions of the poem when he indicates that "Further Notes," the third part in the sequence, is "taken from 'Abomunismus und Religion' by Tom Man," apparently a reference to Thomas Mann, and, for some readers, Tom Paine.

"Excerpts from the Lexicon Abomunon," the fifth part of the sequence, is a brief comical dictionary of Abomunist terms "compiled by BIMGO," or Bill Margolis, who, among others, collaborated with Kaufman on the editing of *Beatitude*, the mimeographed magazine in which "Abomunist Manifesto" first appeared. Kaufman's lexical game is shown in entries such as "Abomunize," which means "to carefully disorganize." An "Abomunasium" is a "place in which abomunastics occur, such as bars, coffee shops, USO's, juvenile homes, pads, etc."

The speakers in "Still Further Notes Dis- and Re-Garding Abomunism" include Bomkauf (with his associates, since he says "We"), who provides an introductory passage for five diary entries by Jesus from "the Live Sea Scrolls." The entries comically chronicle the last days of Jesus, who speaks in hipster language, complaining, "Barab-bas gets suspended sentence and I make the hill. What a drag. Well, that's poetry, and I've got to split now."

For "Abominist Rational Anthem," a sound poem that defies logical interpretation, Schroeder, the child pianist from the comic strip Peanuts, is cited as the composer of the music. "Abomunist Documents," which includes two pieces of eighteenth century cor-respondence, one written by Hancock (founding father John Hancock) and the other by Benedict (traitor Benedict Arnold), is material that, according to Bomkauf, was "*dis-covered during ceremonies at the Tomb of the Unknown Draftdodger.*"

The final entry in "Abomunist Manifesto" is "Abomnewscast . . . on the Hour . . . ," in which an unnamed newscaster presents comical headlines that refer to people, current events, and history. The newscast is "sponsored by your friendly neighborhood Abomunist." Kaufman satirizes society's quest for material gratification even as soci-ety stands on the brink of a nuclear apocalypse. The newscaster refers to a bomb shelter available in "decorator colors" with a "barbecue unit that runs on radioactivity." In a cemetery, one can acquire "split-level tombs." Norman Rockwell's charming interpre-tation of American life in "The Spelling Bee" becomes "The Lynching Bee" in the newscast, and the image is so American that the Daughters of the American Revolution give the work an award. The world spins forward with its population explosion, Cold War, arms race, and television programs, and the newscaster warns that the pending "emergency signal" will not be a drill. He advises, ". . . turn the TV off and get under it."

BAGEL SHOP JAZZ

Kaufman frequented the Co-existence Bagel Shop in San Francisco, and the shop became a forum for his presentations. In "Bagel Shop Jazz," Kaufman analyzes and de-scribes the "shadow people" and the "nightfall creatures" who populate the bagel shop and give it a special atmosphere. Among the people at the shop are "mulberry-eyed girls in black stockings." The girls are "love tinted" and "doomed," yet ". . . they fling their arrow legs/ To the heavens,/ Losing their doubts in the beat." There are also "angel guys" who have "synagogue eyes." These men are "world travelers on the forty-one bus" and they blend "jazz with paint talk." They are "lost in a dream world,/ Where time is told with a beat." In contrast to the guys and girls are "coffee-faced Ivy Leaguers, in Cambridge jackets." These men discuss "Bird and Diz and Miles" (jazz musicians Charlie "Bird" Parker, Dizzie Gillespie, and Miles Davis) and flash "cool hipster smiles" even as they hope that "the beat is really the truth."

Though the community of bagel-shop patrons poses no apparent threat, these people become "brief, beautiful shadows, burned on walls of night" because "the Guilty police arrive" and end the interaction the bagel shop encourages. The patrons are probably Abomunistic in their attitude, and society, as represented by the police, cannot tolerate their individuality and edginess.

THE ANCIENT RAIN

The title poem of *The Ancient Rain* is topical and prophetic, satirical and tender, as well as symbolic and surreal. A prose poem set in stanzas that often begin with the refrain "The Ancient Rain . . . ," Kaufman's "The Ancient Rain" honors the history of the United States and decries social injustice. The falling of the Ancient Rain is an apocalyptic event that strikes down evil and honors the righteous. The Ancient Rain has godlike powers: "The Ancient Rain is supreme and is aware of all things that have ever happened." Kaufman adds, "The Ancient Rain is the source of all things, the Ancient Rain knows all secrets, the Ancient Rain illuminates America." Kaufman foresees a destructive world war, but he also sees that the Ancient Rain will prevail over the war, giving righteous triumph to those who are just.

Among the heroes Kaufman names in the poem are Abraham Lincoln, George Washington, John F. Kennedy, Franklin Delano Roosevelt, Nathan Hale, Crispus Attucks, Hart Crane, Federico García Lorca, Ulysses S. Grant, John Brown, and Martin Luther King, Jr. Among the villains are George Custer, D. W. Griffith, the members of the Ku Klux Klan, Julius Caesar, Robert E. Lee, warmongers, and bigoted and hypocritical immigrants. Kaufman draws his greatest inspiration from Attucks, the black man who was the first to die in the American Revolution, and García Lorca, whose poetry lifted Kaufman into "crackling blueness" and led him to "seek out the great Sun of the Center."

BIBLIOGRAPHY

Anderson, T. J. *Notes to Make the Sound Come Right: Four Innovators of Jazz Poetry.* Fayetteville: University of Arkansas Press, 2004. Examines the jazz poetry of Bob Kaufman, as well as of Nathaniel Mackey, Stephen Jonas, and Jayne Cortez. Anderson provides overviews on jazz poetry as well as chapters on each of the poets. He studies Kaufman's appropriation of the rhythms and tones of jazz.

Christian, Barbara. "Whatever Happened to Bob Kaufman?" In *The Beats: Essays in Criticism*, edited by Lee Bartlett. Jefferson, N.C.: McFarland, 1981. Christian calls attention to social protest and jazz in Kaufman's work.

Damon, Maria. "'Unmeaning Jargon'/Uncanonized Beatitude: Bob Kaufman, Poet." In *The Dark End of the Street: Margins in American Vanguard Poetry*. Minneapolis: University of Minnesota Press, 1993. Examines the poetic works of Kaufman and the language he used.

_____, ed. "Bob Kaufman: Poet A Special Section." *Callaloo: A Journal of African American and African Arts and Letters* 25, no. 1 (Winter, 2002): 105-231. This special section in *Callaloo* presents articles on Kaufman by Aldon Lynn Nielsen, James Smethurst, Amor Kohli, Jeffrey Falla, Rod Hernandez, and Horace Coleman.

Henderson, David. Introduction to *Cranial Guitar*, by Bob Kaufman. Minneapolis: Coffee House Press, 1996. Henderson explains Kaufman's career and quotes extensively from a radio documentary on Kaufman.

Kohli, Amor. "Black Skins, Beat Masks: Bob Kaufman and the Blackness of Jazz." In *Reconstructing the Beats*. New York: Palgrave Macmillan, 2004. Kohli sees jazz performance as a means of protest.

Lawlor, William T. *"Cranial Guitar."* In *Masterplots II: African American Literature*, edited by Tyrone Williams. Rev. ed. Pasadena, Calif.: Salem Press, 2009. Provides in-depth analysis of *Cranial Guitar*, paying attention to themes and meanings. Also contains brief biography of Kaufman.

Thomas, Lorenzo. "'Communicating by Horns': Jazz and Redemption in the Poetry of the Beats and the Black Arts Movement." *African American Review* 26, no. 2 (1992): 291-299. Thomas draws a connection between jazz artists and rebellion against conformity.

Winans, A. D. "Bob Kaufman." *American Poetry Review* 29, no. 3 (May-June, 2000): 19-20. Winans offers a compact review of Kaufman's life.

William T. Lawlor

PABLO NERUDA
Neftalí Ricardo Reyes Basoalto

Born: Parral, Chile; July 12, 1904
Died: Santiago, Chile; September 23, 1973

PRINCIPAL POETRY

Crepusculario, 1923
Veinte poemas de amor y una canción desesperada, 1924 (*Twenty Love Poems and a Song of Despair*, 1969)
Tentativa del hombre infinito, 1926
El hondero entusiasta, 1933
Residencia en la tierra, 1933, 1935, 1947 (3 volumes; *Residence on Earth, and Other Poems*, 1946, 1973)
España en el corazón, 1937 (*Spain in the Heart*, 1946)
Alturas de Macchu Picchu, 1948 (*The Heights of Macchu Picchu*, 1966)
Canto general, 1950 (partial translation in *Let the Rail Splitter Awake, and Other Poems*, 1951; full translation as *Canto General*, 1991)
Los versos del capitán, 1952 (*The Captain's Verses*, 1972)
Odas elementales, 1954 (*The Elemental Odes*, 1961)
Las uvas y el viento, 1954
Nuevas odas elementales, 1956
Tercer libro de odas, 1957
Estravagario, 1958 (*Extravagaria*, 1972)
Cien sonetos de amor, 1959 (*One Hundred Love Sonnets*, 1986)
Navegaciones y regresos, 1959
Canción de gesta, 1960 (*Song of Protest*, 1976)
Cantos ceremoniales, 1961 (*Ceremonial Songs*, 1996)
Las piedras de Chile, 1961 (*The Stones of Chile*, 1986)
Plenos poderes, 1962 (*Fully Empowered*, 1975)
Memorial de Isla Negra, 1964 (5 volumes; *Isla Negra: A Notebook*, 1981)
Arte de pájaros, 1966 (*Art of Birds*, 1985)
Una casa en la arena, 1966 (*The House at Isla Negra: Prose Poems*, 1988)
La barcarola, 1967
Las manos del día, 1968
Aún, 1969 (*Still Another Day*, 1984)
Fin de mundo, 1969 (*World's End*, 2009)
La espada encendida, 1970
Las piedras del cielo, 1970 (*Stones of the Sky*, 1987)

Selected Poems, 1970
Geografía infructuosa, 1972
New Poems, 1968-1970, 1972
Incitación al Nixonicidio y alabanza de la revolución chilena, 1973 (*Incitement to Nixonicide and Praise of the Chilean Revolution*, 1979; also known as *A Call for the Destruction of Nixon and Praise for the Chilean Revolution*, 1980)
El mar y las campanas, 1973 (*The Sea and the Bells*, 1988)
La rosa separada, 1973 (*The Separate Rose*, 1985)
2000, 1974 (English translation, 1992)
El corazón amarillo, 1974 (*The Yellow Heart*, 1990)
Defectos escogidos, 1974
Elegía, 1974 (*Elegy*, 1983)
Jardín de invierno, 1974 (*Winter Garden*, 1986)
Libro de las preguntas, 1974 (*The Book of Questions*, 1991)
El mal y el malo, 1974
Pablo Neruda: Five Decades, a Selection (Poems, 1925-1970), 1974
El río invisible: Poesía y prosa de juventud, 1980
The Poetry of Pablo Neruda, 2003 (Ilan Stavans, editor)

OTHER LITERARY FORMS

Pablo Neruda (nay-REW-duh) was an essayist, translator, playwright, and novelist as well as a poet. His memoirs, *Confieso que he vivido: Memorias* (1974; *Memoirs*, 1977), are a lyric evocation of his entire life, its final pages written after the coup that overthrew Salvador Allende. Neruda's translations include works by Rainer Maria Rilke, William Shakespeare, and William Blake. The volume *Para nacer he nacido* (1978; *Passions and Impressions*, 1983) includes prose poems, travel impressions, and the speech that Neruda delivered on his acceptance of the Nobel Prize. He has written a novel, *El habitante y su esperanza* (1926); a poetic drama, *Fulgor y muerte de Joaquín Murieta* (pb. 1967; *Splendor and Death of Joaquin Murieta*, 1972); and essays on Shakespeare, Carlo Levi, Vladimir Mayakovsky, Paul Éluard, and Federico García Lorca, as well as several works of political concern.

ACHIEVEMENTS

Winner of the Nobel Prize in 1971, Pablo Neruda is one of the most widely read poets in the world today. His most popular book, *Twenty Love Poems and a Song of Despair*, has more than a million copies in print and, like much of his work, has been translated from Spanish into more than twenty languages. Neruda was so prolific a writer that nine of his collections of poems have been published posthumously.

Neruda's goal was to liberate Spanish poetry from the literary strictures of the nineteenth century and bring it into the twentieth century by returning verse to its popular

Pablo Neruda
(Library of Congress)

sources. In *Memoirs*, written just before his death, Neruda congratulates himself for having made poetry a respected profession through his discovery that his own aspirations are representative of those shared by men and women on three continents. Writing on the rugged coast of southern Chile, Neruda found passion and beauty in the harshness of a world that hardens its inhabitants, strengthening but sometimes silencing them. His purpose was to give others the voice they too often lacked.

BIOGRAPHY

Pablo Neruda was born Neftalí Ricardo Reyes Basoalto in the frontier town of Parral in the southern part of Chile on July 12, 1904. His mother died of tuberculosis a few days after his birth, and Neruda lived with his stepmother and father, a railroad conductor, in a tenement house with two other families. Hard work and an early introduction to literature and to the mysteries of manhood distinguished his first seventeen years. In school, the famous Chilean educator and poet Gabriela Mistral, herself a Nobel Prize winner, introduced the young Neruda to the great nineteenth century Russian novelists. In the fall of his sixteenth year, while he was assisting in the wheat harvest, a woman whom he was later unable to identify first introduced the young man to sex. A wide-ranging, voracious appetite for books and the wonders of love are memories to which Neruda continually returns in his work, as well as to the harsh Chilean landscape and the problems of survival that confronted his countrymen.

His father's determination that Neruda should have a profession took the young poet to Santiago, where he intended to study French literature at the university. He had learned French and English in Temuco from his neighbors, many of whom were immigrants. His affiliation as contributor to the journal *Claridad*, with the politically active student group Federación de Estudiantes, and the attractions of life in a large city, where Neruda quickly made friends with many influential people, served to expand his original plans. While living with the widow of a German novelist, Neruda tried repeatedly to gain access to the offices of the Ministry of External Affairs, hoping to obtain a diplomatic post in Europe. More important, he had begun to write his first serious poetry during his evenings alone in a boardinghouse at 513 Maruri Street.

Neruda's hatred of political oppression became firmly established when the students of a right-wing group attacked the officers of *Claridad* and the Santiago police freed the attackers and arrested the editors, one of whom died in jail. Thus, after a year and a half in Santiago, Neruda abandoned his university career and dramatically declared himself a poet and political activist, taking the pen name Pablo Neruda from the Czech writer Jan Neruda (1834-1891) to conceal his activities from his father.

In 1923, to publish his first book of poems, *Crepusculario*, Neruda sold his furniture and borrowed money from his friends; favorable critical reviews validated his decision. The similarity of his verse to that of the Uruguayan poet Sabat Erscaty forced Neruda to turn from inspirational and philosophical themes back to a more intimate poetry based on personal experience. The result in 1924 was *Twenty Love Poems and a Song of Despair*, Neruda's most popular book, in which he sings of the joy and pain of casual affairs with a student from Santiago and the girl he left in Temuco.

Neruda's abandonment of his university career to write for *Claridad* coincided with his moving to Valparaíso. The port city immediately won his favor. He had not abandoned his goal of a diplomatic post, and finally, through the influence of the Bianchi family, he succeeded in meeting the Minister of External Affairs, who was persuaded to allow Neruda to pick his post. Neruda chose the one city available about which he knew nothing: Rangoon, Burma (now Myanmar), then a province of India.

After a short stay in Burma, Neruda obtained a new post in Ceylon (now Sri Lanka), setting the pattern of his life for the next twenty-five years. During this period, Neruda was abroad most of the time, usually under the auspices of the Chilean government—although on occasion he would flee government arrest. Returning to Chile from the Far East, he was quickly off to Argentina, then to Spain (during the Spanish Civil War), then to France, where he had stopped en route to Rangoon and to which he returned a number of times. During the early years of World War II, Neruda held a diplomatic post in Mexico; he resigned in 1943 to return to Chile, where he became active in politics as a member of the Chilean Communist Party.

Neruda's Communist sympathies (which had their origin in the Spanish Civil War) hardened into an uncritical acceptance of Stalinism, which ill accorded with his genuine populist sentiments. He became a frequent visitor to the Eastern bloc in the 1950's and 1960's, even serving on the committee that met annually in Moscow to award the Lenin Peace Prize, which he himself had won in 1950.

From 1960 until his death in 1973, Neruda worked tirelessly, publishing sixteen books of poetry and giving conferences in Venezuela (1959), Eastern Europe (1960), Cuba (1960), the United States (1961, 1966, and 1972), Italy and France (1962), England (1965), Finland (1965), and the Soviet Union (1967). He was named president of the Chilean Writers Association, correspondent of the Department of Romance Languages of Yale University, doctor *honoris causa* at Oxford, and Nobel Prize winner in 1971. In 1969, he was nominated for the presidency of Chile; he rejected the nomination in favor of Salvador Allende, who named Neruda ambassador to France. Neruda's health, however, and his concern about a civil war in Chile, precipitated his return in 1973. His efforts to prevent a coup d'état proved fruitless, and Neruda died a few days after Allende. He had just finished his *Memoirs*, writing that he enjoyed a tranquil conscience and a restless intelligence, a contentment derived from having made poetry a profession from which he could earn an honest living. He had lived, he said, as "an omnivore of sentiments, beings, books, happenings and battles." He would "consume the earth and drink the sea."

ANALYSIS

Pablo Neruda stated in a prologue to one of four editions of *Caballo verde*, a literary review he had founded in 1935 with Manuel Altalaguirre, that the poetry he was seeking would contain the confused impurities that people leave on their tools as they wear them down with the sweat of their hands. He would make poems like buildings, permeated with smoke and garlic and flooded inside and out with the air of men and women who seem always present. Neruda advocated an impure poetry whose subject might be hatred, love, ugliness, or beauty. He sought to bring verse back from the exclusive conclave of select minorities to the turmoil from which words draw their vitality.

CREPUSCULARIO

Neruda's work is divided into three discernible periods, the turning points being the Spanish Civil War and his return to Chile in 1952 after three years of forced exile. During the first phase of his work, from 1923 to 1936, Neruda published six rather experimental collections of verse in which he achieved the poetic strength that carried him through four more decades and more than twenty books. He published *Crepusculario* himself in 1923 while a student at the University of Santiago. *Crepusculario* is a cautious collection of poems reflecting his reading of French poetry. Like the Latin American *Modernistas* who preceded him, he consciously adhered to classical forms and sought the ephemeral effects of musicality and color. The poem that perhaps best captures the message indicated by the title of the book is very brief: "My soul is an empty carousel in the evening light." All the poems in *Crepusculario* express Neruda's ennui and reveal his experimentation with the secondary qualities of language, its potential for the effects of music, painting, and sculpture.

There are several interesting indications of Neruda's future development in *Crepusculario* that distinguish it from similar derivative works. Neruda eventually came to see poetry as work, a profession no less than carpentry, brick masonry, or politics; this conception of poetry is anticipated in the poem "Inicial," in which he writes: "I have gone under Helios who watches me bleeding/ laboring in silence in my absent gardens." Further, in *Crepusculario*, Neruda occasionally breaks logical barriers in a manner that anticipates much of his later Surrealistic verse: "I close and close my lips but in trembling roses/ my voice comes untied, like water in the fountain." Nevertheless, *Crepusculario* is also characterized by a respect for tradition and a humorous familiarity with the sacred that Neruda later abandoned, only to rediscover them again in the third phase of his career, after 1952: "And the 'Our Father' gets lost in the middle of the night/ runs naked across his green lands/ and trembling with pleasure dives into the sea." Linked with this respect for his own traditions is an adulation of European culture, which he also abandoned in his second phase; Neruda did not, however, regain a regard for Western European culture in his mature years, rejecting it in favor of his own American authenticity: "When you are old, my darling (Ronsard has already told you)/ you will recall the verses I spoke to you."

In *Crepusculario*, the first stirrings of Neruda's particular contribution to Spanish poetry are evident—themes that in the early twentieth century were considered unpoetic, such as the ugliness of industrialized cities and the drudgery of bureaucracies. These intrusions of objective reality were the seeds from which his strongest poetry would grow; they reveal Neruda's capacity to empathize with the material world and give it a voice.

TWENTY LOVE POEMS AND A SONG OF DESPAIR

One year after the publication of *Crepusculario*, the collection *Twenty Love Poems and a Song of Despair* appeared. It would become the most widely read collection of poems in the Spanish-speaking world. In it, Neruda charts the course of a love affair from passionate attraction to despair and indifference. In these poems, Neruda sees the whole world in terms of the beloved:

> The vastness of pine groves, the sound of beating wings,
> the slow interplay of lights, a solitary bell,
> the evening falling into your eyes, my darling, and in you
> the earth sings.
> Love shadows and timbres your voice in the dying
>   echoing afternoon
> just as in those deep hours I have seen
> the field's wheat bend in the mouth of the wind.

Throughout these twenty poems, Neruda's intensity and directness of statement universalize his private experiences, establishing another constant in his work: the effort to create a community of feeling through the expression of common, universal experience.

TENTATIVA DEL HOMBRE INFINITO

In 1926, Neruda published *Tentativa del hombre infinito* (venture of infinite man), his most interesting work from a technical point of view. In this book-length poem, Neruda employed the "automatic writing" espoused by the Surrealists. The poem celebrates Neruda's discovery of the city at night and tests the capacity of his poetic idiom to sound the depths of his subconscious. Ignoring the conventions of sentence structure, syntax, and logic, Neruda fuses form and content.

The poem opens in the third person with a description of the poet asleep in the city of Santiago. It returns to the same image of the sleeping man and the hearth fires of the city three times, changing person from third to second to first, creating a circular or helical structure. The imagery defies conventional associations: "the moon blue spider creeps floods/ an emissary you were moving happily in the afternoon that was falling/ the dusk rolled in extinguishing flowers."

In the opening passages, Neruda explores the realm between wakefulness and sleep, addressing the night as his lover: "take my heart, cross it with your vast pulleys of silence/ when you surround sleep's animals, it's at your feet/ waiting to depart because you place it face to face with/ you, night of black helixes." In this realm between motive and act, Neruda's language refuses to acknowledge distinctions of tense: "a twenty-year-old holds to the frenetic reins, it is that he wanted to follow the night." Also, the limits that words draw between concepts disappear, and thoughts blend like watercolors: "star delayed between the heavy night the days with tall sails."

The poem is a voyage of exploration that leads to a number of discoveries. The poet discovers his own desperation: "the night like wine enters the tunnel/ savage wind, miner of the heavens, let's wail together." He discovers the vastness of the other: "in front of the inaccessible there passes by for you a limitless presence." He discovers his freedom: "prow, mast, leaf in the storm, an abandonment without hope of return impels you/ you show the way like crosses the dead." Most important, he discovers wonder: "the wind leaving its egg strikes my back/ great ships of glowing coals twist their green sails/ planets spin like bobbins." The abstract becomes concrete and hence tractable: "the heart of the world folds and stretches/ with the will of a column and the cold fury of feathers." He discovers his joy: "Hurricane night, my happiness bites your ink/ and exasperated, I hold back my heart which dances/ a dancer astonished in the heavy tides which make the dawn rise."

When the poet finds his beloved, he begins to acquire a more logical grasp of objective reality, but when he realizes that he is still dreaming, his joy becomes despair. He gradually awakens; his senses are assaulted by the smell of the timber of his house and the sound of rain falling, and he gazes through the windows at the sky. Interestingly, his dream visions do not abandon him at once but continue to determine his perceptions:

> birds appear like letters in the depths of the sky
> the dawn appears like the peelings of fruit
> the day is made of fire
> the sea is full of green rags which articulate I am the sea
> I am alone in a windowless room
> snails cover the walk
> and time is squared and immobile.

In this experimental work, Neruda mastered the art of tapping his subconscious for associative imagery. Although he never returned to the pure Surrealism of *Tentativa del hombre infinito*, it is the union of strikingly original and often surreal imagery with earthly realism that gives Neruda's mature poetry its distinctive character.

RESIDENCE ON EARTH, AND OTHER POEMS

In the poems of *Residence on Earth, and Other Poems*, Neruda first achieved that mature voice, free of any derivative qualities. One of the greatest poems in this collection, "Galope muerto" ("Dead Gallop"), was written in the same year as *Tentativa del hombre infinito*, 1925, although it was not published in book form until 1933. "Dead Gallop" sets the tone for the collection, in which Neruda repeatedly expresses a passionate desire to assimilate new experiences: "Everything is so fast, so living/ yet immobile, like a mad pulley spinning on itself." Many of the poems in *Residence on Earth, and Other Poems* begin in the same manner, recording those peripheral and secondary sensations that reside on the fringe of consciousness. They work toward the same end, resolving the new into understandable terms. As the poems come into focus, the reader participates in the poet's assimilation of his new world. For example, the significance of his vague memories of saying goodbye to a girl whom he had left in Chile gradually becomes clear in one poem:

> Dusty glances fallen to earth
> or silent leaves which bury themselves.
> Lightless metal in the void

and the suddenly dead day's departure.
On high hands the butterfly shines
its flight's light has no end.
You kept the light's wake of broken things
which the abandoned sun in the afternoon throws at the
    church steps.

Here, one can see Neruda's gift for surreal imagery without the programmatic irrationality and dislocation of the Surrealists.

In *Residence on Earth, and Other Poems*, too, there are magnificent catalogs in the manner of Walt Whitman: "the angel of sleep—the wind moving the wheat, the whistle of a train, a warm place in a bed, the opaque sound of a shadow which falls like a ray of light into infinity, a repetition of distances, a wine of uncertain vintage, the dusty passage of lowing cows."

Like Whitman, Neruda in *Residence on Earth, and Other Poems* opens Spanish poetry to the song of himself: "my symmetrical statue of twinned legs, rises to the stars each morning/ my exile's mouth bites meat and grapes/ my male arms and tattooed chest/ in which the hair penetrates like wire, my white face made for the sun's depth." He presents uncompromising statements of human sensuality; he descends into himself, discovers his authenticity, and begins to build a poetic vision that, although impure, is genuinely human. He manages in these sometimes brutal poems to reconcile the forces of destruction and creation that he had witnessed in India in the material world of buildings, work, people, food, weather, himself, and time.

Although Neruda never achieved a systematic and internally consistent poetic vision, the balance between resignation and celebration that informs *Residence on Earth, and Other Poems* suggests a philosophical acceptance of the world. "Tres cantos materiales" ("Three Material Songs"), "Entrada a la madera" ("Entrance to Wood"), "Apoges del apio" ("Apogee of Celery"), and "Estatuto del vino" ("Ordinance of Wine") were a breakthrough in this respect. In "Entrance to Wood," the poet gives voice to wood, which, though living, is material rather than spiritual. Neruda's discovery of matter is a revelation. He introduces himself into this living, material world as one commencing a funereal journey, carrying his sorrows with him in order to give this world the voice it lacks. His identification with matter alters his language so that the substantives become verbs: "Let us make fire, silence, and noise,/ let us burn, hush and bells."

In "Apogee of Celery," the poet personifies a humble vegetable, as he does later in *The Elemental Odes*. Neruda simply looks closely and with his imagination and humor reveals a personality—how the growth of celery reflects the flight of doves and the brilliance of lightning. In Spanish folklore, celery has humorous though obscene connotations which Neruda unflinchingly incorporates into his poem. The resultant images are bizarre yet perfectly descriptive. Celery tastes like lightning bugs. It knows wonderful secrets of the sea, whence it originates, but perversely insists on being eaten before revealing them.

Popular wisdom also finds its way into the poem "Ordinance of Wine." Neruda's discovery of the wonders of matter and of everyday experience led him to describe the Bacchanalian rites of drunkenness as laws, the inevitable steps of intoxication. In the classical tradition, Neruda compares wine to a pagan god: It opens the door on the melancholy gatherings of the dishonored and disheartened and drops its honey on the tables at the day's edge; in winter, it seeks refuge in bars; it transforms the world of the discouraged and overpowers them so that they sing, spend money freely, and accept the coarseness of one another's company joyfully. The celebrants' laughter turns to weeping over personal tragedies and past happiness, and their tears turn to anger when something falls, breaks, and abruptly ends the magic. Wine the angel turns into a winged Harpy taking flight, spilling the wine, which seeps through the ground in search of the mouths of the dead. Wine's statutes have thus been obeyed, and the visiting god departs.

In "Ordinance of Wine," "Apogee of Celery," and "Entrance to Wood," Neruda reestablished communion between humans and the material world in which they live and work. Since work was the destiny of most of his readers, Neruda directed much of his poetry to this reconciliation between the elemental and the social, seeking to reintroduce wonder into the world of the alienated worker.

Neruda was writing the last poems of *Residence on Earth, and Other Poems* in Madrid when the Spanish Civil War erupted. The catastrophe delayed the publication of the last book of the trilogy by twelve years. More important, the war confirmed Neruda's stance as a defender of oppressed peoples, of the poor. Suddenly, Neruda stopped singing the song of himself and began to direct his verse against the Nationalists besieging Madrid. The war inspired the collection of poems *Spain in the Heart*, a work as popular in Eastern Europe as is *Twenty Love Poems and a Song of Despair* in the West. These poems, such as Neruda's 1942 "Oda a Stalingrad" ("Ode to Stalingrad"), were finally published as part of *Residence on Earth, and Other Poems*. They were written from the defensive point of view of countries fighting against the threat of fascism. In them, the lyric element almost disappears before the onslaught of Neruda's political passion. Indeed, from 1937 to 1947, Neruda's poetry served the greater purpose of political activism and polemics:

> You probably want to know: And where are the lilies?
> the metaphysics covered with poppies?
> And the rain which often struck
> his words filling them
> with holes and birds?
> I'm going to tell you what has happened.
> I lived in a neighborhood in Madrid
> My house was called
> the House of Flowers . . .

And one evening everything was on fire
. . . Bandits with planes and with Moors
bandits with rings and duchesses
bandits with black friars giving blessings
came through the sky to kill children.

More than ten years had to pass before Neruda could reaffirm his art above political propaganda.

CANTO GENERAL

During the 1940's, Neruda worked by plan on his epic history of Latin America, *Canto General*. Beginning with a description of the geography, the flora, and the fauna of the continent, the book progresses from sketches of the heroes of the Inca and Aztec empires through descriptions of conquistadores, the heroes of the Wars of Independence, to the dictators and foreign adventurers in twentieth century Latin America. Neruda interprets the history of the continent as a struggle toward autonomy carried on by many different peoples who have suffered from one kind of oppression or another since the beginnings of their recorded history.

THE CAPTAIN'S VERSES

Neruda, however, did not disappear entirely from his work during these years. He anonymously published *The Captain's Verses* to celebrate falling in love with the woman with whom he would spend the rest of his life, Matilde Urrutia. Unlike his previous women, Matilde shared Neruda's origins among the poor of southern Chile as well as his aspirations. These poems are tender, passionate, and direct, free of the despair, melancholy, and disillusionment of *Twenty Love Poems and a Song of Despair* and of *Residence on Earth, and Other Poems*.

LAS UVAS Y EL VIENTO

While working in exile for the European Peace Party, Neruda recorded in *Las uvas y el viento* (the grapes and the wind) impressions of new friends and places, of conferences and renewed commitments made during his travels through Hungary, Poland, and Czechoslovakia. Neruda warmly remembers Prague, Berlin, Moscow, Capri, Madame Sun Yat-sen, Ilya Ehrenburg, Paul Éluard, Pablo Picasso, and the Turkish poet Nazim Hikmet. The most interesting works in the collection re-create Neruda's return to cities from which he had been absent for more than thirty years.

THE ELEMENTAL ODES

Neruda's travels through the East assured his fame. His fiftieth year signaled his return to Chile to fulfill the demand for his work that issued from three continents. In

1954, he built his house on Isla Negra with Matilde Urrutia and published the first of three remarkable collections, *The Elemental Odes*, followed by *Nuevas odas elementales* (new elemental odes) and *Tercer libro de odas* (third book of odes). In these books, Neruda returned to the discoveries made in the "Material Songs" of *Residence on Earth, and Other Poems*. In the odes, Neruda's poetry again gained ascendancy over politics, although Neruda never ignored his political responsibilities.

The elemental odes reflect no immediately apparent political concern other than to renew and fulfill the search for an impure poetry responsive to the wonder of the everyday world. Neruda writes that earlier poets, himself included, now cause him to laugh because they never see beyond themselves. Poetry traditionally deals only with poets' own feelings and experiences; those of other men and women hardly ever find expression in poetry. The personality of objects, of the material world, never finds a singer, except among writers such as Neruda, who are also workers. Neruda's new purpose is to maintain his anonymity, because now "there are no mysterious shadows/ everyone speaks to me about their families, their work, and what wonderful things they do!"

In the elemental odes, Neruda learns to accept and celebrate the common gift of happiness, "as necessary as the earth, as sustaining as hearth fires, as pure as bread, as musical as water." He urges people to recognize the gifts they already possess. He sings of such humble things as eel stew, in which the flavors of the Chilean land and sea mix to make a paradise for the palate. Against those who envy his work and its unpretentious message of common humanity, Neruda responds that a simple poetry open to common people will live after him because it is as unafraid and healthy as a milkmaid in whose laughter there are enough teeth to ruin the hopes of the envious.

Indeed, the language of the elemental odes is very simple and direct, but, because Neruda writes these poems in such brief, internally rhyming lines, he draws attention to the natural beauty of his Spanish, the measured rhythm of clauses, the symmetry of sentence structure, and the solid virtues of an everyday vocabulary. In the tradition of classical Spanish realism, the elemental odes require neither the magic of verbal pyrotechnics nor incursions into the subconscious to achieve a fullness of poetic vision.

LATER WORK

After the collection *Extravagaria*—in which Neruda redirected his attention inward again, resolving questions of his own mortality and the prospect of never again seeing places and people dear to him—the poet's production doubled to the rate of two lengthy books of poems every year. In response partly to the demand for his work, partly to his increased passion for writing, Neruda's books during the last decade of his life were often carefully planned and systematic. *Navegaciones y regresos* (navigations and returns) alternates a recounting of his travels with odes inspired by remarkable people, places, and events. *One Hundred Love Sonnets* collects one hundred rough-hewn sonnets of love to Matilde Urrutia. *Isla Negra* is an autobiography in verse. *Art of Birds* is a poetic ornithological guide to Chile. *Stones of the Sky, Ceremonial Songs, Fully Empowered*, and *The House at Isla Negra* are all-inclusive, totally unsystematic collections unified by Neruda's bold style, a style that wanders aimlessly and confidently like a powerful river cutting designs in stone. *Las manos del día* (the hands of the day) and *La espada encendida* (the sword ignited), written between 1968 and 1970, attest Neruda's responsiveness to new threats against freedom. *Geografía infructuosa* (unfruitful geography) signals Neruda's return again to contemplate the rugged coast of Chile. As Neruda remarks in his *Memoirs* concerning his last decade of work, he gradually developed into a poet with the primitive style characteristic of the monolithic sculptures of Oceania: "I began with the refinements of Praxiteles and end with the massive ruggedness of the statues of Easter Island."

OTHER MAJOR WORKS

LONG FICTION: *El habitante y su esperanza*, 1926.

PLAYS: *Romeo y Juliet*, pb. 1964 (translation of William Shakespeare); *Fulgor y muerte de Joaquín Murieta*, pb. 1967 (*Splendor and Death of Joaquin Murieta*, 1972).

NONFICTION: *Anillos*, 1926 (with Tomás Lago); *Viajes*, 1955; *Comiendo en Hungría*, 1968; *Cartas de amor*, 1974 (letters); *Confieso que he vivido: Memorias*, 1974 (*Memoirs*, 1977); *Lo mejor de Anatole France*, 1976; *Cartas a Laura*, 1978 (letters); *Para nacer he nacido*, 1978 (*Passions and Impressions*, 1983); *Correspondencia durante "Residencia en la tierra,"* 1980 (letters; with Héctor Eandi).

BIBLIOGRAPHY

Agosin, Marjorie. *Pablo Neruda*. Translated by Lorraine Roses. Boston: Twayne, 1986. A basic critical biography of Neruda.

Dawes, Greg. *Verses Against the Darkness: Pablo Neruda's Poetry and Politics*. Lewisburg, Pa.: Bucknell University Press, 2006. Dawes examines how Neruda's poetry was affected by his political views during the Cold War. Examines the moral realism in "España en el corazon" (*Spain in the Heart*).

Feinstein, Adam. *Pablo Neruda: A Passion for Life*. New York: Bloomsbury, 2004. The first authoritative English-language biography of the poet's life. Thoroughly researched and indexed.

Longo, Teresa, ed. *Pablo Neruda and the U.S. Culture Industry*. New York: Routledge, 2002. A collection of essays examining the process by which Neruda's poetry was translated into English and the impact of its dissemination on American and Latino culture.

Méndez-Ramírez, Hugo. *Neruda's Ekphrastic Experience: Mural Art and "Canto General."* Lewisburg, Pa.: Bucknell University Press, 1999. This research focuses on the interplay between verbal and visual elements in Neruda's masterpiece *Canto General*. It demonstrates how mural art, especially that practiced in Mexico, became the source for Neruda's ekphrastic desire, in which his verbal art paints visual elements.

Nolan, James. *Poet-Chief: The Native American Poetics of Walt Whitman and Pablo Neruda*. Albuquerque: University of New Mexico Press, 1994. A comparative study of Whitman and Neruda, and the influence on them of both the theme of Native American culture and the practice of oral poetry.

Sayers Pedén, Margaret. Introduction to *Selected Odes of Pablo Neruda*, by Pablo Neruda. Translated by Sayers Pedén. Berkeley: University of California Press, 2000. Sayers Pedén is among the most highly regarded translators of Latin American poetry. Here her introduction to the translations in this bilingual edition constitutes an excellent critical study as well as providing biographical and bibliographical information.

Teitelboim, Volodia. *Neruda: A Personal Biography*. Translated by Beverly J. DeLong-Tonelli. Austin: University of Texas Press, 1991. A biography written by a close friend and fellow political exile.

Wilson, Jason. *A Companion to Pablo Neruda: Evaluating Neruda's Poetry*. Rochester, N.Y.: Tamesis, 2008. Wilson provides a guidebook to Neruda's numerous poetical works, furthering the readers' understanding.

Woodbridge, Hensley Charles. *Pablo Neruda: An Annotated Bibliography of Biographical and Critical Studies*. New York: Garland, 1988. Reflects the growing interest in Neruda following the translations of his works into English in the 1970's.

Kenneth A. Stackhouse

PIERRE REVERDY

Born: Narbonne, France; September 13, 1889
Died: Solesmes, France; June 17, 1960

OTHER LITERARY FORMS

Pierre Reverdy (ruh-VEHR-dee) worked extensively in other forms besides poetry. He wrote two novels and many stories and published collections of prose poems. Most of these are in a Surrealist vein, mixing experimentation in language with personal and unconscious reflection. As an editor of an avant-garde review, Reverdy also contributed important theoretical statements on cubism and avant-garde literary practice. Later in his career, he published several volumes of reminiscences, including sensitive reevaluations of the work of his near contemporaries, including Guillaume Apollinaire.

ACHIEVEMENTS

Pierre Reverdy is one of the most central and influential writers in the tradition of twentieth century avant-garde poetry. Already well established in terms of both his

Pierre Reverdy

work and his theoretical stance by the mid-1910's, Reverdy exerted considerable influence over the Dada and Surrealist movements, with which he was both officially and informally affiliated.

Reverdy's firm conviction was in a nonmimetic , nontraditional form of artistic expression. The art he championed and practiced would create a reality of its own rather than mirror a preexisting reality. In this way, the language of poetry would be cut loose from restraining conventions of meter, syntax, and punctuation in order to be able to explore the emotion generated by the poetic image.

In connection with the avant-garde artists of cubism, Dada, and Surrealism, Reverdy's formulations helped to break down the traditional models of artistic creation that then held firm sway in France. Reverdy's firm conviction was that artistic creation precedes aesthetic theory. All the concrete means at an artist's disposal constitute his aesthetic formation.

Along with Apollinaire, his slightly older contemporary, Reverdy became a central figure and example for a whole generation of French poets generally grouped under the Surrealist heading. His having been translated into English by a range of American poets from Kenneth Rexroth to John Ashbery shows the importance of his work to the modern American tradition as well.

BIOGRAPHY

Pierre Reverdy was born on September 13, 1889, in Narbonne, France, a city in the Languedoc region. The son and grandson of sculptors and artisans in wood carving, he grew up with this practical skill in addition to his formal studies. The Languedoc region at the turn of the century was an especially volatile region, witnessing the last major peasant uprising in modern French history.

After completing his schooling in Narbonne and nearby Toulouse, Reverdy moved to Paris in 1910, where he lived on and off for the rest of his life. Although exempted from military service, he volunteered at the outbreak of World War I, saw combat service, and was discharged in 1916. By profession a typesetter, Reverdy also worked as the director of the review *Nord-Sud*, which he founded in 1917.

From 1910 to 1926, Reverdy worked in close contact with almost all the important artists of his time. He had especially close relationships with Pablo Picasso and Juan Gris, both of whom contributed illustrations to collections of his verse. As the editor of an influential review, he had close contact with and strong influence on the writers who were to form the Dada and Surrealist movements. Already an avant-garde poet and theorist of some prominence by the late 1910's, Reverdy was often invoked along with Apollinaire as one of the precursors of Surrealism. He collaborated with the early Surrealist efforts and continued his loose affiliation even after a formal break in 1926.

That year saw Reverdy's conversion to a mystic Catholicism. From then until his death in 1960, his life became more detached from the quotidian, and he spent much of his time at the Abbey of Solesmes, where he died.

ANALYSIS

In an early statement on cubism, Pierre Reverdy declaimed that a new epoch was beginning, one in which "one creates works that, by detaching themselves from life, enter back into it because they have an existence of their own." In addition to attacking mimetic standards of reproduction, or representation of reality, he also called for a renunciation of punctuation and a freeing of syntax in the writing of poetry. Rather than being something fixed according to rules, for Reverdy, syntax was "a medium of literary creation." Changing the rules of literary expression carried with it a change in ideas of representation. For Reverdy, the poetic image was solely responsible to the discovery of emotional truth.

From 1915 to 1922, Reverdy produced many volumes of poetry. The avant-garde called for an overturning of literary conventions, and Reverdy contributed with his own explosion of creative activity. In addition to editing the influential review *Nord-Sud*, he used his experience as an engraver and typesetter to publish books, including his own. The list of artists who contributed the illustrations to these volumes of poetry by Reverdy reads like a Who's Who of the art world of the time: Gris, Picasso, André Derain, Henri Matisse, Georges Braque, among others. Reverdy's work, along with that of Apollinaire, was cited as the guiding force for Surrealism by André Breton in his *Manifestes du surréalisme* (1962; *Manifestoes of Surrealism*, 1969).

Reverdy's early work achieves an extreme detachment from mimetic standards and literary conventions that allows for the images to stand forth as though seen shockingly for the first time. The last two lines from "Sur le Talus" (on the talus), published in 1918, show this extreme detachment: "L'eau monte comme une poussière/ Le silence ferme la nuit" (The water rises like dust/ Silence shuts the night). There can be no question here of establishing a realistic context for these images. Rather, one is cast back on the weight of emotion that they carry and that must thus guide their interpretation. Reflections off water may appear to rise in various settings, though perhaps particularly at twilight. The dust points to a particular kind of aridity that may be primarily an emotional state. The sudden transition from an (implied) twilight to an abrupt nightfall undercuts any kind of conventional emotional presentation. The quick cut is a measure perhaps of the individual's lack of control over external phenomena and, by extension, inner feelings as well.

"CARREFOUR"

Much of Reverdy's early work is based on just such an imagistic depiction of interior states, with a strong element of detachment from reality and a certain resulting confusion or overlapping. The force of emotion is clearly there, but to pin it down to a particular situation or persona proves difficult because any such certainty is constantly being undercut by the quick transitions between images. The complete suppression of punctuation as well as a certain freedom of syntax as one moves from line to line are clearly tools that Reverdy developed to increase the level of logical disjunction in his poetry. At times, however, this disjunction in the logical progression of word and image gives way to a resolution. The short poem "Carrefour" (crossroad) sets up a surreal image sequence:

> De l'air
> De la lumière
> Un rayon sur le bord du verre
> Ma main déçue n'attrape rien

> Air
> Light
> A ray on the edge of the glass
> My disappointed hand holds nothing

Here the elements are invoked, and then two images, one of an inanimate object and one the hand of the speaker. From this atmosphere of mystery and disjunction, the poem's conclusion moves to a fairly well-defined emotional statement:

> Enfin tout seul j'aurai vécu
> Jusqu'au dernier matin
> Sans qu'un mot m'indiquât quel fut le bon chemin

> After all I will have lived all alone
> Until the last morning
> Without a single word that might have shown me
> which was the right way

Here, as in many of Reverdy's poems, the emotion evoked is a kind of diffused sadness. The solitary individual is probably meant to stand for an aspect of the human condition, alone in a confrontation with an unknown destiny.

"GUERRE"

Reverdy saw military duty during World War I, and it may well be that this experience muted the youthful enthusiasm that pervades his earliest works. It may also be the case that Reverdy, while espousing radical measures in literary practice, still was caught in the kind of bittersweet ethos that characterizes fin de siècle writers generally. Whatever the case may be, there is no question that Reverdy wrote some of the most affecting war poems in the French language. One of the most direct is titled simply "Guerre" (war). Running through a series of disjointed, if coherent, images, Reverdy toward the end of the poem approaches direct statement, when the speaker says:

> Et la figure attristée
> Visage des visages
> La mort passe sur le chemin

> And the saddened figure
> Visage of visages
> Death passes along the road

Close to a medieval allegorizing of death, this figure also incorporates a fascination with the effect of the gaze. One's face is revealing of one's emotion because of the way one looks—the distillation of the phenomenon into a general characteristic is a strong term to describe death. If this image is strong, the poem's ending is more forceful still:

> Mais quel autre poids que celui de ton corps
> as-tu jeté dans la balance
> Tout froid dans le fossé
> Il dort sans plus rêver

> But what other weight than that of your body
> have you thrown in the balance
> All cold in the ditch
> He sleeps no longer to dream

Philosophers have questioned whether the idea of death is properly an idea, since strictly speaking, it has no content. Caught between viewing another's death from the outside and facing one's own death, which one can never know, death is a supreme mystery of human existence. Reverdy in these lines seems to cross the line between the exterior, objective view of another's death and the unknowable, subjective experience of the individual. This is what he means by the emotion communicated through the poetic image.

Despite a continued tendency toward the surreal image in Reverdy's work, these poems in *Sources du vent* (sources of the wind) also represent the first major collection of poems after Reverdy's conversion to a mystic Catholicism in 1926. Increasingly, his poetry of the postconversion period tends toward an introjection of the conflicts raised through the poetic image. While a tone of lingering sadness had always been present from the earliest work, in these poems, the atmosphere of sadness and loss moves to the center of the poet's concerns. Unlike the conservative Christian poets Charles-Pierre Péguy and Paul Claudel, the content of the poems is never directly religious. Rather, a mood of quietism seems to become more prominent in the collections of poems after the conversion. A concurrent falling off in the level of production also takes place. After 1930, Reverdy publishes only two more individual collections of verse, along with two collected volumes and works in other forms. After 1949, for the last twelve years of his life, the heretofore prolific Reverdy apparently ceased to write altogether.

"MÉMOIRE"

The poem "Mémoire" (memory) from *Pierres blanches* (white stones), shows this mood of increasing resignation in the face of worldly events. The poem invokes a "she," someone who has left or is going to leave, but then, in apparent reference to the title, says there will still be someone:

> Quand nous serons partis là-bas derrière
> Il y aura encore ici quelqu'un
> Pour nous attendre
> Et nous entendre
>
> When we will have gone over there behind
> There will still be someone
> To wait for us
> And to understand us

The positive mood of these lines, however, is undercut by the poem's ending: "Un seul ami/ L'ombre que nous avons laissée sous l'arbre et qui s'ennuie" ("A single friend/ The shadow we have left beneath a tree and who's getting bored"). The impersonality tending toward a universal statement that was present in Reverdy's early work here seems to work toward an effacement of the individual personality. If memory can be imaged as a bored shadow left beneath a tree, the significance of the individual seems tenuous at best. The emotion generated through the poetic image here seems to be one of sadness and extreme resignation.

The interpretation of a poet's work through biography must always be a hazy enterprise, all the more so in a poet such as Reverdy, whose life directly enters into his work not at all. In a general sense, then, the course of his poetic life and production might be said to mirror the course of French literary life generally. The enthusiasm of the avant-garde literary and artistic movements in Europe generally in the early years of the twentieth century saw a reaction in the post-World War I years toward an art that questioned societal assumptions. Dada and Surrealism can be seen in terms of this large movement, and Reverdy's work as an example. The coherence of the Surrealist movement in turn breaks down in the late 1920's and early 1930's with the split coming over what political allegiance the Surrealist artists should take, according to its leaders. Reverdy's personal religious convictions cause him to cease active involvement with the movement altogether. It is a measure of his status as a strong precursor to the movement that he is not attacked directly by the more politically motivated leaders of Surrealism.

"MAIN-MORTE"

With the extreme politicization of the Surrealist movement in the late 1930's, even some of the most dedicated younger adherents to Surrealism cut their formal ties with the movement. René Char is an example. The young Yves Bonnefoy is an example of a poet with early leanings toward Surrealism who in the late 1940's moved more in the direction of a poetry expressive of essential philosophical and human truths. It might be possible, in like manner, to trace Reverdy's increasing distance from Surrealism as a movement to some kind of similar feelings that have been more openly expressed by his younger contemporaries. His collection *Plein Verre* (full glass) does indeed move more toward the mode of longer, contemplative poems, still in the atmosphere of sadness and resignation to life. The end of "Main-Morte" (dead-hand) shows this well:

> Entre l'aveu confus et le lien du mystère
> Les mots silencieux qui tendent leur filet
> Dans tous les coins de cette chambre noire
> Où ton ombre ni moi n'aurons jamais dormi
>
> Between the confused vow and the tie of mystery
> The silent words which offer their net
> In every corner of this black room
> Where your shadow nor I will have ever slept

Even the highly suggestive early lyrics do not contain quite the level of hovering mystery and intricate emotional states offered in these lines. One may well wonder if the "you" invoked here even refers to a person or whether it might be a quasi-human interior presence such as that invoked in the later poems of Wallace Stevens (such as "Final Soliloquy of the Interior Paramour"). The weight of the images in the direction of silence lends to this whole utterance an aura of high seriousness.

"ENFIN"

The last poem in *Plein Verre*, titled "Enfin" (at last), also ends with a statement hinting at a highly serious attitude. The speaker states:

> À travers la poitrine nue
> Là
> Ma clarière
> Avec tout ce qui descend du ciel
> Devenir un autre
> À ras de terre
>
> By means of the naked breast
> There
> My clearing
> Along with all that descends from the sky
> To become an other
> At earth level

More and more in the later poems, a level of ethical statement seems to emerge. Whereas the early poems introduce strange and startling images in an apparently almost random fashion, the images here seem to be coordinated by an overall hierarchy of values, personal and religious. The naked breast at the beginning of this passage thus could refer to the lone individual, perhaps alone with his or her conscience. This is in contrast to something which descends from the sky, an almost unavoidably religious image. The wish "To become an other/ At earth level" might then be interpreted as the fervent desire of an extremely devoted individual to attain a higher level of piety here on earth.

LE CHANT DES MORTS

The extended sequence, *Le Chant des morts* (the song of the dead), composed in 1944-1948 and published in 1948 as part of the collected volume *Main d'œuvre* (work made by hand), presents an extended meditation on the emotional inner scene of war-devastated France. In this sequence, as in his earlier poems on World War I that drew on his direct experience of the horrors of war, Reverdy uses a diction stripped bare of rhetoric, preferring instead the direct, poignant images of death and suffering. Death in these poems is both inescapable and horrible, or as he calls it: "la mort entêtée/ La mort vorace" ("stubborn death/ Voracious death"). As a strong countermovement to the implacable march of death, there is also a tenacious clinging to life. As the poet says: "C'est la faim/ C'est l'ardeur de vivre qui dirigent/ La peur de perdre" ("It is hunger/ It is the ardor to live that guide/ The fear of losing"). The poet of the inner conscience in these poems confronts the essential subject of his deepest meditations: the conscious adoption of his authentic attitude toward death.

The ultimate renunciation of poetry that characterizes the last years of Reverdy's life is preceded by an exploration of the subject most suited to representing death (remembering Sigmund Freud)—that is, silence.

"Et Maintenant"

The poem that Reverdy seems to have chosen to come at the end of his collected poems, titled "Et Maintenant" (and now), ends with a poignant image of silence: "Tous les fils dénoués au delà des saisons reprennent leur tour et leur ton sur le fond sombre du silence" ("All the unknotted threads beyond the seasons regain their trace and their tone against the somber background of silence"). Reverdy here seems to hint at what lies beyond poetic expression in several senses. His entire ethos of poetic creation has been consistently based on an act of communication with the reader. Thus, the threads he refers to here could well represent the threads of intention and emotion that his readers follow in his poetry to achieve an experience of that emotion themselves, or to discover an analogous emotional experience in their own memory or personal background. He might also be hinting at those threads of intention and emotion that led beyond the limitations of individual life in a reunification with a divine creator. In the former interpretation, the background of silence would be that silence which precedes the poetic utterance or act of communication, as well as the silence after the act of communication or once the poet has ceased to write. In the religious interpretation, the background of silence would be that nothingness or nonbeing out of which the divine creation takes place and which, in turn, has the capability of incorporating silence or nonbeing into self, a religious attitude of a return to the creator even in the face of one's own personal death.

Legacy

Reverdy is a complex and fascinating figure in the history of French poetry in the first half of the twentieth century. He was a committed avant-garde artist in the years directly preceding, during, and following World War I; his outpouring of poetry and aesthetic statements made him one of the most significant precursors to the movements of Dada and Surrealism. Though his formal affiliation with the Surrealist movement was of brief duration, his example of using the poetic image to communicate emotion is central to everything for which Surrealism stood. The extreme respect shown to his work by other poets and artists confirms his importance as a creative innovator. Reverdy, in turn, paid respectful homage to his poet and artist contemporaries a stance that shows his ongoing intellectual commitment to the importance of art and literature in human terms, despite his personal isolation and quietism toward the end of his life. The poems from the end of his career that bear the weight of a continued meditation on death are a moving commentary on that from which language emerges and into which it returns: silence.

OTHER MAJOR WORKS

LONG FICTION: *Le Voleur de Talan*, 1917; *La Peau de l'homme*, 1926.
SHORT FICTION: *Risques et périls*, 1930.
NONFICTION: *Self Defence*, 1919; *Le Gant de crin*, 1927; *Le Livre de mon bord*, 1948; *Cette émotion appellée poésie: Écrits sur la poésie, 1932-1960*, 1975; *Nord-Sud, Self Defence, et autres écrits sur l'art et la poésie*, 1975; *Note éternelle du présent*, 1975.

BIBLIOGRAPHY

Greene, Robert W. *The Poetic Theory of Pierre Reverdy*. 1967. Reprint. San Bernardino, Calif.: Borgo Press, 1990. An analysis of Reverdy's work in poetic theory.

Pap, Jennifer. "Transforming the Horizon: Reverdy's World War I." *Modern Language Review* 101, no. 4 (October, 2006): 966-978. Pap examines the theme of war in Reverdy's works, noting that although he favored an art that followed its own aims, he did treat the war in his poetry.

Rizzuto, Anthony. *Style and Theme in Reverdy's "Les Ardoises du toit."* Tuscaloosa: University of Alabama Press, 1971. Rizzuto's critical study of one of Reverdy's poetic works. Includes bibliographic references.

Rothwell, Andrew. *Textual Spaces: The Poetry of Pierre Reverdy*. Atlanta: Rodopi, 1989. A critical analysis of Reverdy's works. Includes bibliographic references.

Schroeder, Jean. *Pierre Reverdy*. Boston: Twayne, 1981. An introductory biography and critical study of selected works by Reverdy. Includes an index and bibliographic references.

Sweet, David LeHardy. *Savage Sight/Constructed Noise: Poetic Adaptations of Painterly Techniques in the French and American Avant-gardes*. Chapel Hill: Department of Romance Languages, University of North Carolina, 2003. The poetry of experimental poets Reverdy, Guillaume Apollinaire, André Breton, Frank O'Hara, and John Ashbery is examined for the poets' use of painterly techniques.

Peter Baker

JAMES TATE

Born: Kansas City, Missouri; December 8, 1943

OTHER LITERARY FORMS

James Tate is known primarily as a poet, although he has produced some fiction and nonfiction.

ACHIEVEMENTS

James Tate came onto the literary scene at the age of twenty-three, when his first full-length manuscript of poems, *The Lost Pilot*, was selected for publication in the prestigious Yale Younger Poets Series by Yale University Press. Other works, long and short, followed, and Tate became editor of the *Dickinson Review* in 1967. He has also served as an associate editor at Pym-Randall Press and Barn Dream Press (small presses located in Cambridge, Massachusetts) and as a consultant to the Coordinating Council of Literary Magazines. For two years running, in 1968 and 1969, and again in 1980, he received writing fellowships from the National Endowment for the Arts. In 1972, he was the Phi Beta Kappa poet at Brown University. He won a National Institute of Arts and Letters Award in 1974, followed two years later by a Guggenheim Fellowship. He was awarded the Pulitzer Prize in poetry in 1992 for *Selected Poems*. In 1994, he was honored with a National Book Award for *Worshipful Company of Fletchers*, and in 1995 with a Wallace Stevens Award from the American Academy of Poets. He edited *The Best American Poetry, 1997* (1997), and his poems have been included in many editions of the anthology. He became a member of the American Academy of Arts and Letters in 2004 and served as chancellor for the Academy of American Poets from 2001 to 2007.

Tate has established himself as a formidable exponent of literary surrealism of a peculiarly American kind. His work has garnered the praise of many academic critics and journal reviewers; his poetry has appeared across the gamut of magazines in North America and England and has influenced the style of many young writers.

BIOGRAPHY

James Vincent Tate was born in Kansas City, Missouri, in 1943. He began college study at the University of Missouri in Columbia and finished his B.A. at Kansas State College in Pittsburg, Kansas, in 1965. He entered the Writers' Workshop at the University of Iowa and received an M.F.A. in poetry in 1967. In 1966, Tate began teaching creative writing and literature courses at the University of Iowa (1966-1967), the University of California, Berkeley (1967-1968), Columbia University (1969-1971), and Emerson College in Boston (poet-in-residence, 1970-1971). He joined the regular teaching faculty at the University of Massachusetts at Amherst in 1971, where he would remain except for short periods of residence in such places as Sweden, Ireland, and Spain.

ANALYSIS

There are two kinds of poets in the world: those who grow with age and alter style, outlook, and argument over the years, and those who burst onto the scene fully fledged and polish what is in essence an unchanging perception of life throughout their careers. James Tate is of the second sort; his stunning appearance in his first major book, *The Lost Pilot*, set the pattern for all he would write over the succeeding decades. The poetry of *Distance from Loved Ones* is a richer, denser, more masterful execution of the style and themes he set for himself as a young man.

Variation for Tate is a subtle thing; beneath the variances of style and diction lies a core of subjects and emotions that are constant in his poetry: loss of relations, the quixotic world of appearances, and a violent underworld of emotion waiting to erupt through the crevices of the mundane. The central theme running throughout Tate's canon is the desire to shatter superficial experience, to break through the sterility of suburban life and drown it in erotic passion. His characters languish from unfulfilled longings; the objects he contemplates are all prisoners of definition and stereotype; life is a desert of routine expectation waiting to blow up from the forces of liberated imagination, whimsy, outrage, and humor.

Tate joins a long line of midwestern writers who fought in their writing against the domestic tedium of their region. Theodore Dreiser set the pattern of the rebellious midwestern writer in his novels about youths trapped in the social coils of work, poverty, and loveless marriages; Sherwood Anderson paved the way of modernist writers through his depictions of the sterile sanity of small-town life in his novel *Winesburg, Ohio: A Group of Tales of Ohio Small Town Life* (1919). F. Scott Fitzgerald and Ernest Hemingway explored the unrealizable dreams of their characters, who had escaped only partway from their families and bleak pasts. Poets of the Midwest, including T. S. Eliot, Ezra Pound, and Carl Sandburg, emphasized realistic detail in their unflinching reports of what had gone wrong in American society in their time.

THE LOST PILOT

The Lost Pilot joins this tradition of harsh assessments of midwestern life; the argument itself is a rather somber account of a young man's loneliness, despair, and feelings of isolation. "The End of the Line," from the middle section of the book, is emblematic of the themes treated in the poems. "We plan our love's rejuvenation/ one last time," the speaker comments, but the jaunty tone of the piece breaks down as he admits that the relationship has gone sour for good. The poems acutely examine the meaning of relationships, the risk of loving someone, and the desolation at losing a father or lover through unexplained accident or fatal whim. This instability lying at the heart of emotion makes everything else around him equally shimmering and unreal.

Tate's use of surrealist language, the dreamy, irrational figures and images that define his view of things, is derived from European and South American writing of the twentieth century. The original motives of Surrealism sprang from the devastations of war and the corruption of the state. For Tate, though, the corruption lies somewhere else: in the incapacity of human beings to face their dilemmas honestly, to admit that the heart is wild, immoral, anarchic, or that life is essentially a reality beyond the grasp of moral principles. For Tate, the American situation is the opposite of war-torn Europe or politically corrupt South America. The American scene is too stable, too ordered and domesticated; underneath the neat appearances of reality lies a universe of chaotic energies waiting to spring back. To that degree, one may casually link Tate's vision to the horrific suspense of Stephen King's novels or to the wounded idealism of Tom Wolfe and Hunter Thompson. In each of these writers lives a certain purity of taste for the natural world and for the lost values of a pastoral and Edenic past that modernity has outraged and insulted.

To love in Tate's poetry is to tap into this hidden volcano of irrationality, to tease its powers awake. Most often, his lovers quake at the first sign of wilderness in their emotions and drift back to the safety of their homely, selfish worlds. To fall in love is to touch nature directly and to break through to the other side of reality. This sentiment is expressed at the close of *The Lost Pilot* when Tate writes, "I am falling, falling/ falling in love, and desire to leave this place." The place he desires to leave is that parched desert of convention where all of his characters languish.

The poetry of this first collection generates a kind of philosophical earthquake in its brief descriptions, debunking the moral fictions of an ordered life through the riotous outpouring of illogical imagery. This is a poetry of emotional purgings, of discreet, Janovian primal screams into the bedroom mirror.

The Lost Pilot is grounded by its title poem, an elegy combining a son's wit, fantasy, and tears over the death of his father in World War II. The phrase itself is instructive; a pilot is one who finds his way through dark skies. The father as lost pilot compounds the son's forlornness; here is a father who has disappeared, a guide without compass who leaves his son behind in a dull, seemingly trackless void. The reader learns in the poem that the son keeps an annual vigil and looks up to see his father orbiting overhead—a curious, droll, and yet appropriate image for the son's grief. Another poem, written to the boy's mother, commemorates Father's Day in an ironic reference to the missing father. A careful look at all the poems reveals the image of the missing father in each of them: He haunts the world as a peculiar absence of love, as when lovers leave the poet, or emotion goes rank and sour.

In the closing poem, "Today I Am Falling," even the title suggests something of Tate's humor in poetry: The falling has no object, but in the text, the reader finds that the falling is toward love, which in turn leads only to the desire to escape. The place the speaker is trying to reach is a "sodium pentothal landscape," a place of lost memories aroused by the intravenous intake of a "truth serum" once used in psychotherapy. That landscape lies behind repression and emotional stagnation, its "bud about to break open." The trembling surface of Tate's language here and elsewhere is that effort to break through the false appearance of things, the dull veneer of human convention concealing passion and the energy of nature.

However, for a poet trying to break through, the early poems are terse, carefully worked miniatures that technically belie their purpose. Tate prefers a short, three-line stanza as his measure, with a varying line of between five and six syllables, usually end-stopped—that is, punctuated with a comma-length pause or ended with a period. The flow of speech often requires enjambment, the running through of one line to the next, but not in the free-verse fashion of breaking lines arbitrarily at prepositions, adjectives, and nouns after the manner of prose. Instead, Tate makes sure his phrases are well-defined rhythmically before cutting to the next line. If he carries the rhythm through to the next line, or allows it to leap over a stanza break, usually he has found some emphatic word to terminate the line before he does so.

The poems on the page look slightly cramped and compressed, as if the thinking were squeezed down to an essence of protest. The poetry written by Tate's contemporaries is expansive, even sprawling by comparison. Few poets took the medium to these limits of compression, and when they did, they were freer with the pattern of line and accent. One may speculate that Tate's statements are intended as whispers in tight places—quick, emergency pleas to the reader or to himself. However they are intended, the language is uniformly limpid, purified, the hesitation revised out of each smoothly cresting phrase. There is high finish in the wording and phrasing, which may at times work against the sense of emotional torment Tate wants to convey.

Thumbing through the pages of *The Lost Pilot*, one is struck by the contradiction between polished execution and troubled content. The move in poetry after 1945 was to incorporate into the linguistic and prosodic structure of the poem the movement of emotion tracked by the meaning of words. The poem should come apart in sympathy with, or in representation of, the emotional disarray of the speaker, and the language of the poem should involve the detritus of spent or erupting emotion in its configuration. Distillation of language down to an essence was in some ways a Christian aesthetic carried over into "closed" or traditional poetics—a sense of language as having a spiritual inner text that the poet pared down to achieve communication with the soul. The throwing up of verbal dross and trivia into the language stream of lyric after 1945 was an effort to join "soul music" with the blunt, earthy matter of nature; hence the languorous and wayward course of much lyric energy in the postmodern era. In Tate, however, and in a contingent of southern male poets who came of age with him, one finds uniformly tidy and balanced typographical structures that avoid technical deformation.

Tate's aesthetic tradition, which includes Wallace Stevens, Robert Frost, the European Symbolists, and the Deep Image movement of Robert Bly and James Wright, rejected a projective aesthetic that would incorporate the turmoil of mind into the finished artwork. That distinction between content and execution may have proved over the years to be confining to the range of Tate's subject matter and stylistic virtuosity. There is the hint of a technical repression of feeling in this mode of terse lyric, of funneling into sparse and smoothly patterned verses the chaos of longing and rage intended by the poems. The risk one takes in keeping to this method of writing is that emotional diversity may be diluted by the repetition of lyric forms.

Through the succession of Tate's later books, the poem does not change its technical strategy except to grow in size: Stanza and line are fleshed out, articulation is fuller and more sonorous, and rhythm has greater sweep, but the poet set his stylistic signature in *The Lost Pilot*, and the rules he gave himself were essentially unalterable thereafter. The burden on readers is to pay keen attention to content against a background of similar, even uniform measures, to make out with sympathetic attention the varying inner world that has been systematized in repetitive lyrical patterns. The burden on Tate is to risk everything on the line itself, to dazzle, compel, and sweep away the reader on the force of an image, a powerful phrase, the stunning resolution of a whole poem on a single word.

THE OBLIVION HA-HA

In *The Oblivion Ha-Ha*, a three-stanza poem, "The Pet Deer," works on the principle of the single line holding the poem aloft. Stanza 1 is purely functional exposition, given in limpid phrases; stanza 2 sets up the conflict implied in the deer's realizing that it is a kind of centaur in love with a human girl; and stanza 3 builds slowly toward the closing line, revealing that the girl is unaware of "what/ the deer dreams or desires." Here repression is located in an animal, a deft reversal of Tate's usual argument. The girl is placid, lovely, unaffected in her sexual allure; the deer is the captive soul unable to break out and satisfy desire.

The poem hangs by the thread of its final line along with the touches in several other phrases, but in sum, it works on the plainness of its exposition, its setup of an incident, which it transforms by a single lyric thrust of insight. This is Symbolist methodology given an American stamp by Tate's withholding the intellectual and ideological motives of the lyric act. In Symbolist poetry, almost any incident will reveal the poet's own psyche, which he will have expressed referentially through an object, animal, or character.

The deer is, by the twists of psychic projection in this poem, the poet himself, the girl a combination of lovers longed for and lost. The art of the poem is to raise the ordinary theme of repression and longing to a degree of generality that turns experience into fable, myth, or even allegory. Too broad a stroke, and the delicate suggestibility of language collapses; too little said, and the poem remains a mere fragment of thought without affect.

"Here is my heart,/ I don't know what to do with it," Tate writes in "Plea Based on a Sentence from a Letter Received by the Indiana State Welfare Department." The line expresses succinctly the theme of *The Oblivion Ha-Ha*. The title has confused critics; it is usually taken to mean a kind of maniacal laughter in the face of a bitter world. However, a secondary definition of "ha-ha" is a garden enclosure, usually of hedge or earthwork, separating one small planting bed from surrounding ground. In early Roman gardens, a raised inner court often supported a small statue of Adonis, a chthonic god of fertility; in modern times, gazebos and small terraces take the same role as the Adonis mound. Curiously, the garden meaning of the word, derived from French, bears the same hyphen as the first meaning. Tate's conceit may be that one laughs helplessly at sight of the enclosed Eden, thus doubling the meanings into one trope.

That inner garden reserve, perhaps, is the point of the title, an inner garden that is shut in or inaccessibly remote and psychological, but rooted in the familiar world of human senses. The oblivion ha-ha is the soul, the secret inner self in its own mound of earth, which the poems try to capture.

In "The Salute," a man dreams about a black widow spider whom he loves; yet he "completely misunderstood" her "little language." The secret soul is located on one side or another of broken relationships; lovers who try to reach across the distance confront either the sorrows of the deer or the suicidal love of this dreamer, willing to mate with a spider who kills her lovers. "Nobody gets what he wants," Tate writes in "Consumed," which closes on this characteristic remark about a lover: "You are the stranger/ who gets stranger by the hour." Another poem on parents, "Leaving Mother Waiting for Father," returns to the theme of loss, with the speaker leaving his doll-like, decrepit mother leaning against a hotel, as he goes off into the world an adult orphan.

ABSENCES

In every case, Tate creates a portrait of an isolated heart longing for relation and failing to achieve it. The world that denies love to his characters is superficially intact, but beneath appearance it festers with neurotic passion and chaos. It is no wonder, therefore, that he would write a book called *Absences*. In it, Tate experiments with a looser style; prose poems appear in section 3, while long poems occupy section 2. The title poem and "Cycle of Dust" are sequential works that have more diffuse imagery and lack the point of surprise perfected in the short lyric.

The interesting turn in *Absences* is in the image-making itself; it focuses on characters who dismantle themselves, or try to disappear, in their blind effort to cross over to the "other" side of reality. These figures do not quite make it; they practice escaping from the blind literalism of things but end up dismantling only their defined selves. They do not reach Paradise. The shift to decomposing this part of reality marks Tate's decision to alter the lyric path he was on. From here onward, Tate drops the Edenic or pastoral ideal altogether and concentrates instead on exploding the empirical world of sense and definition. Experience itself will be his target.

Put another way, in *Absences* and beyond, one-half of the metaphoric principle of his poetry drops away, the ideal and hidden dimension of vision. What remains is the imploding and decaying half of reality, the objects metaphor dwells on to hint at possibilities in the dream world. There are only the objects themselves now, deformed, fragmentary, increasingly meaningless as the stuff of lyric. More and more, Tate will imply the end of such language: There is still the need to escape, to break out of reality into the other world, but references to the other world by image or suggestion are rare. His poems dwell on the disappearance of reality itself, its decomposition into fantasy and paradox. In "Harm Alarm," the second poem of *Absences*, a man fearfully examines his street, decides that all harm lies "in a cradle/ across the ocean," and resumes his walk after observing that his "other" self should "just about awake now" as the source of that harm. The divided self splits evenly between dream and waking, serene emptiness and conflicted, wounded life. Pain abounds as the defining attribute of consciousness; the pin functions as a motif in a number of these poems.

There is little or no plot, and no organization to narrate the flow of language. The poems accumulate around the thematic abstraction of reality's own breakup. That means that individual lines and sentences have the burden of forming the book. Reading Tate, one looks for lines, images, and stunning metaphors as the point of poetry. There is no structural principle embodying language or visionary argument. Tate's assumption is that reality is dead, and the surreal lyric depicts that through its own formlessness and its occasional glimpses into magic through a phrase or word. Another position would hold that the poem itself is an object of nature, an expression of creative principles. Tate's metaphysic, however, is still linked with the Christian view that meaning derives from a spiritual source outside nature. These poems, strange and irrational as they are, are secularized forms of prayer, beseeching an "outside" for grace and succor.

These matters are summed up in "Wait for Me," when he writes, "A dream of life a dream of birth/ a dream of moving/ from one world into another// All night dismantling the synapses/ unplugging the veins and arteries." The rest of the poem is about the dissolving self, the fading consciousness, as the reader continues to watch, in this world, with him. The tone is not far removed from the self-abnegating fervor of the medieval martyr, whose longing to purify life and join God is merely the extreme of Tate's lyrics of self-abandonment. "I hear a laugh swim up/ from the part of myself/ I've killed," he writes in "Delicate Riders," in which the reader sees that it is the spiritual self that has died out in the contemporary desert of materialism. "I who have no home have no destination either," he writes in "The Boy." "One bone against another,/ I carve what I carve/ to be rid of myself by morning/ by deep dreams disintegrated."

Tate's feud with reality is that it has no soul; it is the broken world of modern, spiritless philosophy. What remains is the memory of soul in magical lyricism, which surveys the fallen world and discovers fading glimmers of spirit in paradox, accidental juxtaposition, chaotic series, and the like.

VIPER JAZZ

This mordant perspective on the world is the subject of his next major book, *Viper Jazz*, published in the Wesleyan Poetry Program series (Wesleyan University Press) in 1976. In it, Tate reins in the experimentalism of *Absences* and writes in short, stanzaic lyrics and prose poems on the theme of "worlds refused by worlds." A man goes crazy with his obsessions in "Many Problems," his suffering soul dying on "the boneyard of vegetables/ the whole world is built on." In "Read the Great Poets," the couch allows "the spirit to leave/ the broken body and wander at will" through "this great dull life."

In "Blank-Stare Encounter," the speaker blurts out a new imperative, "I want to start a new religion," but the dead world's "blank stare drags me along." The point is, however, that no "new religion" is forthcoming from Tate. Midway through *Viper Jazz*, one begins to feel a withdrawal from that premise and the setting in of a reductive new attitude that is partly resignation and partly a return to the chattier, amusing voice of early lyrics. There is a quality here of stand-up comedian, the one-liner gag writer who keeps his audience off balance by surrealist turns.

RIVEN DOGGERIES

From *Viper Jazz* to the following book, *Riven Doggeries*, one notes with misgivings a certain carelessness in the work; the language is flimsy, form is lazily sketched in, and poems turn on anecdote and coincidence, sometimes without the clinching phrase to energize them. The theme for much of *Riven Doggeries* is travel, both actual and in the mind, the feverish transport into and out of reality as the locus of mere existence. By now it is obvious that there is no Paradise opening through the mist; instead, Tate's style hardens into a parody of the real world, a burlesque of the poet's daily life to which the shreds of a previous idealism still cling. "We are all members/ of Nature's alphabet. But we wanted more," he writes in "Nature Poem: Demanding Stiff Sentences," a pun-laced and well-crafted lyric tucked into the middle of the book. However, such reminders of his romantic principles do not make up for his lax writing.

As a sign that the verse poem may be wearing out here, Tate turns increasingly to the prose poem as miniature short story and frame for the fantasized speech he is using. In "Missionwork," part 3 of *Riven Doggeries*, the language is dense and humorous again, and self-mocking. "It's a sickness, this desire to fly," he notes. Here too the ideal slips away in a dozen forms, from fireflies to dogs—the dog is an essential motif of the absconding spirit throughout the book, the "rivening" of the title.

The prose poem, used here with skill, crept into poetry and has become a standard form in the American repertoire. Beginning with the French poet Charles Baudelaire's *Petits Poèmes en prose* (1869; also known as *Le Spleen de Paris*; *Poems in Prose*, 1905, also known as *Paris Spleen, 1869*, 1947), an early experiment in the mode, poets have discovered its use as a form of fantasizing meditation, but without the rhythmic intimacy or precision required in verse. Prose is borderless, a more "submerged" form of writing in that line breaks and phrasings are no longer functions of intense feeling or ideation. A poet's prose makes the presumption of being literal, often somber self-analysis, just as fantasy and the absurd slowly decompose the argument. The trick is to construct an elaborate ruse of confidentiality that is undone the moment the next improbable detail is sprung on the reader's belief, crushing it. Some writers, including Tate and his friend Charles Simic, compound the irony by going past the point of disbelief to reestablish partial credibility.

CONSTANT DEFENDER

Beginning with *Riven Doggeries*, Tate is trying to find ways to open the poem, to spread out its intricate patterns and create more space for rambling monologue and humorous asides. He directs his efforts at colloquializing his verse speech, which begins to take effect in *Constant Defender*. Here a well-balanced fantasy mixes with verse compression, though the clinching phrase is often muted in the process. The dialectic between spiritual ideals and the morbidity of the real take subtler form, as in "Tall Trees by Still Waters," where "the actual world was pretending again,/ no, not pretending, imagining an episode/ of unbelievable cruelty, involving invalids."

The self of these poems is more harried, beaten down, and Kafkaesque than in previous books. One detects the wearing down of the idealist in such poetry, intimated in the title—the wearying vigilance of the "constant defender" of his beliefs. The theme running throughout is of abandoned houses to which the speaker returns forlornly, disillusioned once more at cruelty and indifference. In "Tell Them Was Here," the "I" intentionally omitted, the poem ends, "Started to leave,// turned, scratched out my name—/ then wrote it back again." A darker look at self occurs in "Lousy in Center Field," a wonderful poem with dazzling imagery that remarks, "I'm frozen once again/ in an attitude of unfortunate/ interior crumbling mouseholes." He is the ballplayer who has lost all interest in catching the ball, which flies over him in a cobwebbed sky.

The landscape is filling up with the dead souls of the modern city. This theme, though tentative and sketchy in *Constant Defender*, becomes pronounced in *Reckoner* and *Distance from Loved Ones*. Both continue the breezier, conversational style that set in with *Constant Defender*. The poems work as accumulations of one-line observations, some pithy, some empty, with here and there a humorous turn or a startling image to enliven the pace of what are often tedious aggregates of lines. One poem flows into the next in these books, in which a manic speaker seems desperate to keep up his chatter against a growing sense of loss in his life.

RECKONER

Reckoner mixes prose poems and lyric or narrative verse; the tone shifts slightly from one to the other, but Tate has turned his attention away from the formality and finish of individual poems to the sense of words running together across boundaries to create a metatextual whole. The poems no longer hold up as unique, intricately structured maps of thought; their titles and shapes on the page maintain a certain ghost of formality over which the content leaps. The resulting flow of commentary creates the impression of a speaker's feverish avoidance of some impending tragedy. Even the humor is shrill, worn out, the emotions exhausted by frenetic articulation. The jokes and grotesque exaggeration have an almost menacing insistence; the reader has come upon their formulas many times before in Tate.

Many of the poems open on the same frenetic tempo, with fully punctuated sentences lined up as stanzas, as in "The Flithering Ignominy of Baba Ganoosh," which begins,

> He played the bongo drums and dated infant actresses.
> His signature still glitters in all the most exhausted hotels.
> He has positive contempt for rain, for chattering.
> His sofa was designed by a butcher.

This is the sort of shtick Henny Youngman made famous, the one-liner that waits for guffaws or the drummer's rim shot in the background. A pace of this kind wears out humor and begins arousing other emotions by its drugged repetition. Poem after poem renounces the minutiae of the waking world, as some other, darker voice hints that the underlying hidden world has sealed itself for good. The speaker is someone left behind, unable to imagine the possibility of regaining what he somewhere calls the "parallel world." "I've been feeling so cooped up in this hotel," begins a prose poem, "Magazines," where banter goes on for a page without resolution, without argument, without premise even, but for this dejection that pervades all of *Reckoner.*

DISTANCE FROM LOVED ONES

In *Distance from Loved Ones*, the pace does not slacken, but the theme of universal death gathers emphasis and becomes a central motif, with many references to death, the dying, and the already deceased who are memories of the speakers. There are now "citizens of the deep," as the speaker remarks in the opening poem, "Quabbin Reservoir," while he alone kills time along the shore as the last of the living voices. Other ghosts are portrayed, as in "Peggy in the Twilight," who "spent half of each day trying to wake up, and/ the other half preparing for sleep."

Tate's characters in *Distance from Loved Ones* keep lonely vigils among the dead; their voices have turned to memory. Many of the poems are variations on the elegy, the very form with which *The Lost Pilot* began. The poems' characters, variations on that youthful speaker who awaited his father's orbital return each birthday, live futile, empty lives waiting to join the dead around them. They have no purpose in life; their only defense against remorse is their disjunctive humor, their ability to disconnect the tedious logic of their world and playfully deconstruct their own identities.

In "How Happy We Were," one of these loners notes that his vision of eternity included "a few of the little angels/ whose sole job it is to fake weeping for people like us." Crowds in America practice "dead mall worship," he writes in "Beaucoup Vets," and in "Anatomy," a beautiful girl studies anatomy and continually cries. The others "know she is dying inside." In "Taxidermy," "Everything is dead anyway." In a sense, the death of the father in Tate's first book has spread out over his many books to encompass the world; the memory of the dead father created a glimmering afterlife Tate never could bring into sharp focus or make the basis of a sustaining vision. His poetry began as elegy and has built a vast edifice of language to exhaust the content of that emotion.

WORSHIPFUL COMPANY OF FLETCHERS

The title of National Book Award winner *Worshipful Company of Fletchers* refers to the ancient guild of arrow makers. The tone shifts to the sort of dark humor of Paul Auster's novels, particularly his dystopian fantasy *In the Country of Last Things* (1987). In that book and in Tate's later poetry, one finds a deepening sense of gloom over the future of cities, and something of the mordant tone of the poet Leonard Cohen's lyric, "the future is murder," and of Don DeLillo's wry assessment, "The future is crowds." For Tate, the city is fast becoming a barren landscape of parentless people, those without fathers who accept routine merely because it distracts them from desperate loneliness and a sense of futility.

In the title poem, a small boy, Tate's alter ego, is confronted by the older poet, who notes that he "lives at the edge of the woods" and that it is "still not clear to me where he really lives." The "really" underscores the ironic tone of the story: In Tate's world, no one appears to be living in reality; rather, one escapes from reality by means of fantasy and self-delusion. The speaker goes on to note that "he'd live with animals if they'd take him in," and thus withdraw altogether from an untrustworthy community of adults. The woods are still poet Frost's place of retreat, where the mind may heal itself from the woes of this world, and William Wordsworth's woods, where innocence may live unviolated by the evils of city life. At the "edge" of the woods, however, one is neither protected by the animals nor free of adult corruptions, and the boy's vaguely orphaned state permits Tate to expand on his identity as the picture of Everyman groping for relationships, loath to accept the meager terms of existence he might find in his suburban neighborhood.

The poems are still page-length lyrical narratives or commentaries, nearly all of which are composed in Tate's wry, drily surreal style, which derives part of its voice from the matter-of-fact tone of Frost, who depicts a life of drudging and narrow-mindedness from which he tries to escape by remembering his childhood and by proposing outrageous questions to his dowdy neighbors. Tate grows out of the same rebellious nature set against uneventful lives, whose language has leapt beyond mere representation of events to fracture common sense by shifting to different subjects without transition or logical connectives.

In this sense, Tate has moved all his strategies from his previous books into a single thrust of reasoning aimed at the disenchanted world of adulthood and its mundane circumstances. He is the confirmed orphan living without benefit of a father's counsel or affection, who finds others laboring without joy and merely using up their mortal span. His defense against this empty materialism is to bend logic by allowing dreams and the anarchy of the unconscious to erupt at will. Tate's definition of the orphan soul is that it is without membranes between a rational self and its fortified ego, on one hand, and the great swampy interiors of one's dream self and the night world of longings and unfulfilled love, on the other.

In page after page of this and succeeding books, the poems report events from a slightly cracked perspective. The company of fletchers who feather arrow shafts take their work seriously, though their product belongs mainly to the fantasy lives of boys who look for their roots in myth and folklore and wilderness landscapes, like the orphan in the title poem. By means of his fractured accounts of daily life, Tate creates a Norman Rockwell painting of ordinary America in which the certainties in the background—small houses and neat little roads—peel away from the surface to reveal some other landscape that the soul longs for and cannot reach. Tate's humor is laced with bitterness and disillusionment that he could not grow up normally after losing a father in the war when he was an infant.

Some other, more difficult motive is at play in this and the books to come: a desire to so muddle the usual progress of lyric argument as to make each word an unpredictable event, thus preventing the reader from feeling as if the language could be anticipated and thus ignored. The poem becomes resistant to being read, to being predicted or interrupted by the reader's own wandering thoughts. Average poems have about them what the poet Charles Bernstein calls "absorptiveness," or a kind of senseless spongy believability in which readers even forget that what they are reading is a poem or that there is any alternative reality to the thing being read. The "anti-absorptive" work of art is so fashioned as to make the reader aware of its every word as if it were a physical object, not a convenient screen of illusion in which to lose one's self. Tate's thinly veiled surrealism is enough to make the reader uncomfortable, slightly puzzled, and on guard against all the rug pulling in the average Tate lyric. In the last poem of this volume, "Happy as the Day Is Long," the fallen world of mere reality is itemized:

> I take the long walk up the staircase to my secret room.
> Today's big news: they found Amelia Earhart's shoe, size 9.
> 1992: Charlie Christian is bebopping at Minton's in 1941.
> Today, the presidential primaries have failed us once again.
> We'll look for our excitement elsewhere, in the last snow
> that is falling, in tomorrow's Gospel Concert in Springfield.
> It's a good day to be a cat and just sleep.

SHROUD OF THE GNOME

Shroud of the Gnome opens with the poem "Where Do Babies Come From?," the perennial question of growing youngsters to their parents, which receives this jaundiced report about hapless orphans forced into hard labor:

> Many are from the Maldives,
> southwest of India, and must begin
> collecting shells immediately.
> The larger ones may prefer coconuts.
> Survivors move from island to island
> hopping over one another and never
> looking back. After the typhoons
> have had their pick, and the birds of prey
> have finished with theirs, the remaining few
> must build boats.

Other poems move into poet Stevens's tropical landscape of cockatiels and sunny rooms, only to find reality equally dismembered in Tate's world. If reality is Tate's target, he snips at its ligaments with surgical scissors in this volume, keeping up the pretense that his form of chatter has rails under it, when in fact it races off its track from line to line, silently mocking the flimsy laws of grammar and veracity on which most conversation is based. Tate is a metaphysical satirist, a comedian of the laws of verisimilitude, who finds everything floating on illusory foundations. Hence, his poems read like idle chitchat after dinner among half-educated well-meaning suburbanites, whose generalities and clichés allow readers to glimpse the quicksand on which reality has built its world.

Shrouds are winding sheets of the dead, and gnomes are out of fairy tales; the title doubles the references to a world at the edge of consciousness, where gnomes have died but live on in some other dimension to haunt us. Reality has excluded them, but the mere act of juxtaposing items creates a nonsense argument in which things happen in spite of one's attempts to "make sense" of life. This "cut up" method, invented by the novelist William Burroughs, is used here with drier, but more telling, effect. Here is how the method works in the title poem,

> And what amazes me is that none of our modern inventions
> surprise or interest him, even a little. I tell him
> it is time he got his booster shots, but then
> I realize I have no power over him whatsoever.
> He becomes increasingly light footed until I lose sight
> of him downtown between the federal building and
> the post office. A registered nurse is taking her
> coffee break. I myself needed a break, so I sat down
> next to her at the counter. "Don't mind me," I said,
> "I'm just a hungry little gnostic in need of a sandwich."

The "gnostic" may be a clue to the subversive logic of Tate's entire canon, for gnostic wisdom is based on intuitive glimpses into mysteries independent of the senses or the logic of empiricism. The gnostic believes in other worlds and their power to merge with our own sensory experience. Tate's speaker is often confronting those who have no alternative world to draw from, making his own "gnostic" processes seem disjointed and absurd, as in the poem, "Same as You":

> I put my pants on one day at a time.
> Then I hop around in circles hobbledehoy.
> A projectile of some sort pokes me,
> in the eye—I think it's a bird
> or a flying pyramid that resembles a bird.

Memoir of the Hawk

In *Memoir of the Hawk*, Tate covers a widening range of subjects that include a young woman's desire to see a "blue antelope," in the closing poem, and after removing her clothes in a park she begins to see them moving "like angels" toward her. The situation is a page torn from Eugène Ionesco's Surrealist one-act play *Rhinocéros* (pr., pb. 1959; *Rhinoceros*, 1959), although without the menacing suggestion of fascism's contagious spirit. This "antelope" is a creature of innocence longed for by a woman and a man who both lie naked as if to return to childhood and visionary experience. The poem, like so many others before it, is a testament to Tate's enduring ability to find new expressions for a lifelong antidote to the sorrows of aging and the burden of the merely material world, made orthodox long ago as the logical view of things. He has challenged this view by drawing on the literature of rebellion from Romanticism to Surrealism to make the case that other worlds are sandwiched between the objects of reality and signify a multitude of possibilities excluded by an official grammar of experience.

LOST RIVER

In *Lost River*, Tate has assembled twenty narrative-like poems that emphasize a sense of people being disconnected from the human experience. Although Tate opens the collection with "The Memories of Fish," he appears to funnel the poems through the title poem "Lost River." The speaker in "Lost River" details his journey with his wife to a legendary village, where they anticipate purchasing a pterodactyl wing from a man. When they are detoured to a deserted store, the couple unexpectedly encounters an old man, who coincidentally has a pterodactyl wing and offers it to them, free of charge. Tate's preference to juxtapose the real with the surreal resonates in "Lost River" and is particularly effective in illustrating how people lose touch with the human experience. Moreover, Tate's desire to show people who are incapable of allowing the human experience to penetrate them is authenticated through the speaker's detached perspective. The poem concludes with the couple accepting the generous gift and continuing their journey. Tate's depiction of the couple's being oblivious to any deeper meaning of their encounter with the old man shows the blind motivation with which people may attempt to seek fulfilment. While traditional connoisseurs of poetry may feel disconnected because of the nontraditional themes conveyed and forms employed in poems such as "Lost River," Tate's modern-day style does more to free the reader's intellect than it does to paralyze it. Because of his use of free-verse forms that emulate the often satirical characteristics of the novella, Tate's poetry could plausibly be likened to the fiction of Flannery O'Connor in that both are unparalleled in their ability to merge the mundane aspects of life with situations that mirror the mysterious and absurd aspects of life.

Several other works in the collection involve unusual encounters with animals, which illustrate a sense of disconnect to nature. For example, "Never Enough Darts" shows a bear invading a town as if it were in its natural habitat. Although the townspeople are described as longing to reconnect with nature, their desire is contingent on maintaining an adequate food supply. In "It Happens Like This," Tate offers a fantasy-like narrative as he depicts a goat befriending a man. The narrative concludes with an image of the goat and the man walking off into unknown territory. While "Never Enough Darts" implies how a society becomes blind to its self-serving wants, "It Happens Like This" suggests that humankind can function as a partner with nature rather than try to dominate it. The fact that these eclectic works are assembled in a collection with "lost" in its title reinforces Tate's poetic vision, which aims to portray the ways in which a society can lose control of its moral compass.

RETURN TO THE CITY OF WHITE DONKEYS

Return to the City of White Donkeys contains more than one hundred works. As a whole, the collection explores feelings of otherworldliness, and Tate continues to employ his technique of conveying a narrative through free-verse poetry. The title poem, "Return to the City of White Donkeys," may surprise some readers because although the "city of white donkeys" is an underground world populated by albino donkeys and alien-like people, the city is not an uninviting place. Tate's description of these colorless life-forms suggests that this underground world has not been tainted by situations that often mar the human condition. The narrative unfolds through the dialogue between the speaker and his lifelong friend, who claims to be a native of the underground world. The irony of the narrative is that the speaker's friend paints a bleak picture of the lives of the inhabitants of this underground world, who live in mud houses and subsist on indigenous harvests; however, these alien-like people experience the same range of emotions that humans experience—happiness, love, and sadness. That Tate depicts an undesirable underground world as a world to be preferred underscores one of his constant themes—accepting what may be possible versus what is probable.

THE GHOST SOLDIERS

The Ghost Soldiers contains more than ninety poems that embody many of the topics and themes of Tate's previous publications, such as the disillusionment and isolation that people experience when life fails to live up to the ideas longed for by one's heart. Written in Tate's signature narrative-like style, the title poem explores how a society forgets the sacrifices made by those who have lost their lives in battle. The speaker opens the poem by describing his journey to a downtown Memorial Day parade. Tate injects a mournful tone through images of disabled veterans standing along a route crowded with silent townspeople. He portrays the townspeople as feeling insulted by the fact that none of the town's soldiers has returned home alive, and in this way, he underscores the dehumanizing effect on even those people who do not have firsthand experience of deadly combat war zones.

OTHER MAJOR WORKS
    LONG FICTION: *Lucky Darryl*, 1977 (with Bill Knott).
    SHORT FICTION: *Hottentot's Ossuary*, 1974; *Dreams of a Robot Dancing Bee: Forty-four Stories*, 2002.
    NONFICTION: *The Route as Briefed*, 1999.
    EDITED TEXT: *The Best American Poetry, 1997*, 1997.

BIBLIOGRAPHY

Harms, James. "Clarity Instead of Order: The Practice of Postmodernism in the Poetry of James Tate." In *A Poetry Criticism Reader*, edited by Jerry Harp and Jan Weissmiller. Iowa City: University of Iowa Press, 2006. Examines Tate's poetry and what characterizes it as postmodern poetry. Says Tate's poems "exist in that nether region which is redolent of dreams but saturated with reality."

Henry, Brian, ed. *On James Tate*. Ann Arbor: University of Michigan Press, 2004. Contains essays on Tate's poetry, including his use of the prose poem, and numerous reviews of his works, from early to late.

McDaniel, Craig. "James Tate's Secret Co-Pilot." *New England Review* 23, no. 2 (Spring, 2002): 55-74. Examines Tate's development as a poet in relationship to Fyodor Dostoevski's prose and how it influenced "The Lost Pilot."

Revell, Donald. "The Lost Pilot." In *Masterplots II: Poetry Series*, edited by Philip K. Jason. Rev. ed. Pasadena, Calif.: Salem Press, 2002. Contains an in-depth analysis of the poem.

Rosen, R. D. "James Tate and Sidney Goldfarb and the Inexhaustible Nature of the Murmur." In *American Poetry Since 1960: Some Critical Perspectives*, edited by Robert B. Shaw. Cheshire, England: Carcanet Press, 1973. Argues that both Tate and Goldfarb belong to a generation that uses poetry to escape from the postwar age; their writing, notes Rosen, is that of moral outlaws.

Tate, James. *The Route as Briefed*. Ann Arbor: University of Michigan Press, 1999. Collects Tate's interviews, essays, and occasional writings; he comments on his composing method and fields questions from various interviewers about the peculiar nature of his lyric arguments, his influences, and the like.

Upton, Lee. *The Muse of Abandonment: Origin, Identity, Mastery in Five American Poets*. London: Associated University Presses, 1998. A critical study of the works of five twentieth century American poets, including Tate, and their points of view on alienation, power, and identity. Includes bibliographical references and index.

Paul Christensen
Updated by Theresa E. Dozier

TRISTAN TZARA
Sami Rosenstock

Born: Moineşti, Romania; April 4, 1896
Died: Paris, France; December 24, 1963

PRINCIPAL POETRY

La Première Aventure céleste de Monsieur Antipyrine, 1916
Vingt-cinq Poèmes, 1918
Cinéma calendrier du coeur abstrait, 1920
De nos oiseaux, 1923
Indicateur des chemins de coeur, 1928
L'Arbre des voyageurs, 1930
L'Homme approximatif, 1931 (*Approximate Man, and Other Writings*, 1973)
Où boivent les loups, 1932
L'Antitête, 1933
Primele Poème, 1934 (English translation, 1976)
Grains et issues, 1935
La Deuxième Aventure céleste de Monsieur Antipyrine, 1938 (wr. 1917)
Midis gagnés, 1939
Une Route seul soleil, 1944
Entre-temps, 1946
Le Signe de vie, 1946
Terre sur terre, 1946
Morceaux choisis, 1947
Phases, 1949
Sans coup férir, 1949
De mémoire d'homme, 1950
Parler seul, 1950
Le Poids du monde, 1951
La Première main, 1952
La Face intérieure, 1953
À haute flamme, 1955
La Bonne heure, 1955
Miennes, 1955
Le Temps naissant, 1955
Le Fruit permis, 1956 (wr. 1946)
Frère bois, 1957
La Rose et le chien, 1958

De la coupe aux lèvres, 1961
Juste présent, 1961
Selected Poems, 1975

OTHER LITERARY FORMS

Although the largest part of the work of Tristan Tzara (TSAH-rah) consists of a vast body of poetry—filling more than thirty volumes—he did experiment with drama, publishing three plays during his lifetime: *Le Coeur à gaz* (pb. 1946; *The Gas Heart*, 1964), *Mouchoir de nuages* (pb. 1924; *Handkerchief of Clouds*, 1972), and *La Fuite* (pb. 1947; the flight). His important polemical writings appeared in two collections: *Sept Manifestes Dada* (1924; *Seven Dada Manifestos*, 1977) and *Le Surréalisme et l'après-guerre* (1947; Surrealism and the postwar period). Much of Tzara's critical and occasional writing, which is substantial in volume, remains unpublished, including book-length works on François Rabelais and François Villon, while the published portion includes *Lampisteries* (1963; English translation, 1977), *Picasso et la poésie* (1953; Picasso and poetry), *L'Art Océanien* (1951; the art of Oceania), and *L'Égypte face à face* (1954).

ACHIEVEMENTS

Tristan Tzara's importance as a literary figure of international reputation rests primarily on his relationship to the Dada movement. Of all the avant-garde movements that challenged the traditional foundations of artistic value and judgment at the beginning of the present century, Dada was, by consensus, the most radical and disturbing. In retrospect, the Dada aesthetic, which was first formed and expressed in Zurich about 1916, seems to have been a fairly direct response to World War I; the Dadaists themselves suggest as much in many of their works during this period.

The harsh, confrontational nature of Dada is notorious, and Tzara was one of the most provocative of all the Dadaists. In his 1930 essay, "Memoirs of Dadaism," Tzara describes one of his own contributions to the first Dada soiree in Paris, on January 23, 1920, in which he read a newspaper while a bell rang. This attitude of deliberate confrontation with the conventional, rational expectations of the audience—to which the Dadaists juxtaposed their illogical, satirical productions—is defended by Tzara in his most famous polemical work, "Manifeste Dada 1918" ("Dada Manifesto 1918"), in which he asserts the meaninglessness of Dada and its refusal to offer a road to truth.

To escape the machinery of human rationality, the Dadaists substituted a faith in spontaneity, incorporating the incongruous and accidental into their works. Even the name by which the Dadaists called themselves was chosen rather arbitrarily. According to most accounts (although this report is subject to intense difference of opinion among Dadaists), it was Tzara himself who chose the word *dada*, in February of 1916, by opening a French dictionary to a randomly selected entry.

Tzara's achievements are not limited solely to his leadership in the Dada movement.

Until recently , Tzara's later work—which is more optimistic in tone and more controlled in technique—has been overshadowed by his more violent and sensational work from the Dada period. It is now becoming apparent to many readers and critics that the Surrealist phase of Tzara's work, the little-known work of his post-Surrealist phase , and his early pre-Dada work in Romanian, are equally important in considering his contribution to modern literature. In the 1970's and 1980's, largely through the work of editors and translators such as Mary Ann Caws, Henrí Behar, and Sasa Paná, this work became more readily available.

BIOGRAPHY

Tristan Tzara, whose real name was Sami Rosenstock, was born on April 4, 1896, in Moineşti, a small town in the province of Bǎcǎu, in northeastern Romania. His parents were Jewish, his father a prosperous merchant. Tzara first attended school in Moineşti, where Romanian was spoken, but later, when he was sent to Bucharest for his secondary education, he attended schools where instruction was also given in French. In addition to languages, Tzara studied mathematics and music. Following his graduation in 1913, he attended the University of Bucharest for a year, taking courses in mathematics and philosophy.

It was during this adolescent period, between 1911 and 1915, that all Tzara's Romanian poems were written. His first published poems appeared in 1912 in *Simbolul*, a short-lived Symbolist review that he helped to edit. These first four poems were signed with the pseudonym S. Samyro. The subsequent poems in Romanian that Tzara published during this period were often signed simply "Tristan" or "Tzara," and it was not until near the end of this period, in 1915, that the first Romanian poem signed "Tristan Tzara" appeared.

In the fall of 1915, Tzara went to Zurich, in neutral Switzerland, where he became involved with a group of writers and artists—including Hugo Ball, Richard Huelsenbeck, Marcel Janco, and Hans Arp—who were in the process of forming an artistic movement soon to be called Dada. This period, between Tzara's arrival in Zurich in the fall of 1915 and February of 1916, was the germinating period of the Dada movement. The Dadaists' first public announcement of the birth of a new movement in the arts took place at the Cabaret Voltaire on the evening of February 5, 1916—the occasion of the first of many such Dada soirees. These entertainments included presentations such as "simultaneous poems," which confronted the audience with a chaotic barrage of words made incomprehensible by the din; recitations of "pure sound-poems," often made up of African-sounding nonsense syllables and recited by a chorus of masked dancers; satirical plays that accused and insulted the audience; and, always, the ceaseless manifestos promoting the Dada revolt against conformity. Tzara's work during this period was written almost entirely in French, and from this time on he used that language exclusively for his literary productions.

As the activities of the Zurich Dadaists gradually attracted notice in other countries, especially Germany and France, Tzara's own fame as an artist spread to an increasingly larger audience. The spread of Dada's fame from Zurich to other centers of avant-garde activity in Europe was aided by the journal *Dada*, edited by Tzara and featuring many of his most provocative works. Although this journal lasted only through five issues, it did draw the attention of Guillaume Apollinaire in Paris, and through him the devoted admiration of André Breton, who was later to be one of the leaders of the Surrealist movement. At Breton's urging, Tzara left Zurich shortly after the Armistice was declared, arriving in Paris in December of 1919.

For a short period between January of 1920, when the first public Dada performance in Paris was held, and May of 1921, when Breton broke his association with Tzara to assume the leadership of the developing Surrealist movement, Breton and Tzara organized an increasingly outrageous series of activities that frequently resulted in public spectacles. Following Breton's break with the Dada group, Tzara continued to stage public performances in Paris for a time, collaborating with those who remained loyal to the Dada revolt. By July of 1923, however, when the performance of his play *The Gas Heart* was disrupted by a Surrealist counter demonstration, even Tzara regretfully admitted that Dada was effectively dead, a victim of its own destructive impulses. Tzara gave up the Dada ideal reluctantly and continued to oppose the Surrealists until 1929, when he joined the Paris Surrealist group, accepting Breton's leadership. Tzara's resumption of activities with Breton's group was also accompanied by an increasing move toward political engagement.

The same year that he joined the Surrealists, Tzara visited the Soviet Union, and the following year, in 1930, the Surrealists indicated their dedication to the Communist International by changing the name of their own journal, *La Révolution surréaliste*, to *Le Surréalisme au service de la révolution*. For Tzara, this political commitment seemed to be a natural outgrowth of his initial revolt, for, as he wrote later in *Le Surréalisme et l'après-guerre*: "Dada was born . . . from the deep feeling that man . . . must affirm his supremacy over notions emptied of all human substance, over dead objects and ill-gotten gains."

In 1935, Tzara broke with the Surrealists to devote himself entirely to the work of the Communist Party, which he officially joined at this time. From 1935 to 1937, he was involved in assisting the Republican forces in the Spanish Civil War, salvaging art treasures and serving on the Committee for the Defense of Culture. This political engagement continued during World War II, with Tzara serving in the French Resistance, all the time continuing to publish his work, despite widespread censorship, under the pseudonym T. Tristan. In 1946 and 1947, he delivered the lectures that make up *Le Surréalisme et l'après-guerre*, in which he made his controversial assessment of Surrealism's failure to influence Europe effectively between the wars. In 1955, Tzara published *À haute flamme* (at full flame), a long poetic reminiscence in which he reviewed the stages of his lifelong revolt and reaffirmed his revolutionary aesthetic. Tzara continued to affirm the authenticity of his position until his death in Paris at the age of sixty-seven, a victim of lung cancer.

ANALYSIS

Whatever else Tristan Tzara was—Dada instigator and polemicist, marginal Surrealist, Communist activist, or Romanian expatriate—his great skill as a poet is abundantly apparent. At his death, Tzara left behind a vast body of poems, extremely diverse in style, content, and tone. Important features of his work are his innovations in poetic technique and his development of a highly unified system of symbolic imagery. The first of these features includes the use of pure sound elements, descriptive ideophones, expressive typography, enjambment that creates complex syntactic ambiguities, and multiple viewpoints resulting in a confusing confluence of speaking voices. The second important feature includes such elements as Tzara's use of recurring verbal motifs and refrains, ironic juxtapositions, and recurring image clusters.

Tzara's earliest period extends from 1911 to 1915 and includes all the poetry he wrote in his native Romanian. Until recently, little attention has been given to Tzara's Romanian poetry. Several Romanian critics have noted the decisive but unacknowledged influence on Tzara of the Romanian poet Urmuz (1883-1923), virtually unknown in the West, who anticipated the strategies of Dada and Surrealism. Much of Tzara's early work, however, is relatively traditional in technique, although it must be remembered that this period represents his poetic apprenticeship and that the poems were written when he was between the ages of fifteen and nineteen. The poetry of this period often displays a curiously ambivalent tone, mixing a detached ironic perspective—which is sometimes gently sarcastic and at other times bitterly resentful—with an uncritically sentimental nostalgia for the past. In some of the poems, one of these two moods dominates, as in Tzara's bitterly ironic treatment of war's destructive effect on the innocence of youth in "The Storm and the Deserter's Song" and "Song of War," or the romantic lyricism of such highly sentimental idylls on nature as "Elegy for the Coming of Winter" and "Evening Comes."

PRIMELE POÈME

The most successful poems of this period—later collected as *Primele Poème*—are those which mix nostalgia with irony, encompassing both attitudes within a single poem. The best example of this type of poem is "Sunday," whose conventional images of leisurely activities that occupy the inhabitants of a town on the Sabbath are contrasted with the bitter reflections of the alienated poet-speaker who observes the scene. The scene seems idyllic enough at first, presenting images of domestic tranquillity. Then the reflecting consciousness of the alienated speaker intrudes, introducing images that contrast darkly with and shatter the apparently false impression he himself has just created.

Into the scene of comfortable regularity, three new and disturbing elements appear: the inescapable presence of death in wartime, the helplessness of parents to protect their children from danger, and the futility of art stagnated by Decadence.

VINGT-CINQ POÈMES

This mixture of sentimental lyricism with ironic detachment is developed to an even greater degree in Tzara's first collection of poems in French, *Vingt-cinq Poèmes* (twenty-five poems), a collection that, although published after he had already arrived in Zurich, still resembles in technique and content the early Romanian poems. In "Petite Ville en Sibérie" ("Little Town in Siberia"), there are a number of new elements, the most important of which are Tzara's use of typography for expressive purposes, the complex syntactic ambiguity created by enjambment, the rich confluence of narrative voices, and the appearance of images employing illogical juxtapositions of objects and qualities:

> a blue light which flattens us together on the ceiling
> it's as always comrade
> like a label of infernal doors pasted on a medicine bottle
> it's the calm house tremble my friend

This disorienting confluence of voices is deliberate, and it evokes in the reader a futile desire to resolve the collage (based on the random conjunction of several separate discourses) into a meaningful and purposeful poetic statement.

DE NOS OISEAUX

In Tzara's second period—extending from 1916 until 1924—he produced the Dadaist works which brought him international fame. To the collage technique developed in *Vingt-cinq Poèmes*, the poems that make up *De nos oiseaux* (of our birds)—the major collection from this period—introduce several innovations, including pure sound elements such as African- sounding nonsense words, repeated phrases, descriptive ideophones, use of multiple typefaces, and catalogs of discrete, separable images piled one upon the other. Tzara's collage technique has become more radical in these poems, for instead of simply using the juxtaposition of speaking voices for creating ironic detachment, in the Dada poems the narrative itself breaks down entirely into a chaotic barrage of discontinuous fragments that often seem to lack any discursive sense. These features are readily apparent in "La Mort de Guillaume Apollinaire" ("The Death of Guillaume Apollinaire") and "Les Saltimbanques" ("The Circus Performers"), two of the best poems from *De nos oiseaux*.

"THE DEATH OF GUILLAUME APOLLINAIRE"

In his Dadaist elegy for Apollinaire, Tzara begins with a series of propositions that not only establish the resigned mood of the speaker but also express the feeling of disorder created in the reader by the poem itself. A simple admission of man's inability to comprehend his situation in the world is followed by a series of images that seem designed to convey the disparity the speaker senses between a world which is unresponsive to human needs (the unfortunate death of Apollinaire at such an early age is no doubt one aspect of this) and a world in which he could feel comfortable (and presumably learn to accept the death of his beloved friend):

> if snow fell upward
> if the sun rose in our houses in the middle of the night
> just to keep us warm
> and the trees hung upsidedown with their crowns . . .
> if birds came down to us to find reflections of
>   themselves
> in those peaceful lakes lying just above our heads
> THEN WE MIGHT UNDERSTAND
> that death could be a beautiful long voyage
> and a permanent vacation from flesh from structures
>   systems and skeletons

The images of this poem constitute a particularly good illustration of Tzara's developing symbolic system. Although the images of snow falling upward, the sun rising at night, trees hanging upside down, and birds coming to earth at first appear unrelated to one another, they are actually related in two ways. First, Tzara is describing processes within the totality of nature which give evidence that "nature is organized in its totality." Humanity's sorrow over the inescapable cycles of life and death, of joy and suffering, is caused by a failure to understand that humans, too, are a part of this totality. Second, Tzara's images suggest that if one's perspective could only be reversed, one would see the reality of things properly. This method of presenting arguments in nondiscursive, imagistic terms was one of Tzara's primary poetic accomplishments, and the uses to which he put it in this elegy for Apollinaire were later expanded and developed in the epic scope of his masterpiece, *Approximate Man, and Other Writings*.

"THE CIRCUS PERFORMERS"

"The Circus Performers" illustrates Tzara's increasing use of pure sound elements in his work. The images of this poem attempt to capture the exciting rhythms of the circus performance that Tzara is describing. In the opening vignette of the poem, in what seems at first an illogical sequence of statements, Tzara merges the expanding and contracting rhythm of the verses with his characteristic use of imagery to convey thought in analogical, nondiscursive terms. Describing a ventriloquist's act, Tzara uses an image that links "brains," "balloons," and "words." In this image, "brains" seems to be a metonymic substitution for ideas or thoughts—that which is expressed by "words."

Here the brains themselves are inflating and deflating, as are the balloons. What is the unstated analogical relation between the two? These words are treated like the words and thoughts of comic-strip characters—where words are enclosed in the "balloons" that represent mental space in newspaper cartoons. To help the reader more easily identify the analogy, Tzara has included an explanatory aside, enclosed in parentheses. A second example of Tzara's use of sound in this poem is the presence of "ideophones"— words that imitate the sounds of the actions they describe. Pure sound images devoid of abstract meaning are scattered throughout the poem.

APPROXIMATE MAN, AND OTHER WRITINGS

By all standards of judgment, *Approximate Man, and Other Writings*, a long epic in nineteen sections, is Tzara's greatest poem. It was Tzara's most sustained effort, its composition and extensive revisions occupying the poet between 1925 and 1931, the year that the final version appeared. Another important characteristic of the work is its epic scope, for *Approximate Man, and Other Writings* was Tzara's attempt to discover the causes of modern humanity's spiritual malaise, drawing on all the technical resources he had developed up to the time of its composition. The most important feature of the poem, however, is its systematic presentation of Tzara's revolutionary ideology, which had begun to reflect, in a guarded form, the utopian vision of Surrealism.

Approximate Man, and Other Writings is about the intrusion of disorder into modern life, and it focuses on the effects of this disorder on the individual. Throughout the poem, Tzara makes it clear that what he is describing is a general disorder or sickness, not a personal crisis. This is one of the key ideas that is constantly repeated in the form of a refrain: "approximate man like me like you reader and like the others/ heap of noisy flesh and echoes of conscience/ complete in the only element of choice your name." The most important aspect of the poem's theme is Tzara's diagnosis of the causes of this debilitating universal sickness, since this indicates in a striking way his newly found attitude of commitment.

The first cause of humanity's sickness is the very condition of being "approximate." Uncertain, changeable, or lacking commitment to any cause that might improve the world in which he lives, Approximate Man wanders aimlessly. For Tzara, the lost key for curing the sickness is commitment, as Tzara himself declared his commitment to the work of the Communist Party in 1935, shortly after the completion of this poem.

Humanity's sickness arises not only from inauthentic relationships with others but also from an exploitative attitude toward nature—an attitude encouraged by the development of modern technology. In Tzara's view, this modern belief in humanity's preeminent importance in the universe is a mistaken one, as is evident in "The Death of Guillaume Apollinaire," and such vanity contributes to the spiritual sickness of humankind.

Tzara finds a third cause of humanity's spiritual sickness in humans' increasing reliance on the products of their own alienated consciousness, especially reason and language. In *Approximate Man, and Other Writings*, Tzara's efforts to describe this solipsistic entrapment of humans by their own systems gives rise to many striking images, as in the following passages: "vapor on the cold glass you block your own image from your/ sight/ tall and insignificant among the glazed frost jewels/ of the landscape" and "I think of the warmth spun by the word/ around its center the dream called ourselves." These images argue that human reason is like a mirror in which the reflection is clouded by the observer's physical presence, and that human language is like a silken cocoon that insulates people from the external world of reality. Both reason and language, originally created to assist humans, have become debased, and to attain a more accurate picture of the world, humans must learn to rely on instinct and imagination. These three ideas, which find their fullest expression in *Approximate Man, and Other Writings*, form the basis of Tzara's mature poetic vision and constitute the most sustained expression of his critique of the modern sensibility.

OTHER MAJOR WORKS

PLAYS: *Mouchoir de nuages*, pb. 1924 (*Handkerchief of Clouds*, 1972); *Le Coeur à gaz*, pb. 1946 (wr. 1921; *The Gas Heart*, 1964); *La Fuite*, pb. 1947.

NONFICTION: *Sept Manifestes Dada*, 1924 (wr. 1917-1918; *Seven Dada Manifestos*, 1977); *Le Surréalisme et l'après-guerre*, 1947; *L'Art Océanien*, 1951; *Picasso et la poésie*, 1953; *L'Égypte face à face*, 1954; *Lampisteries*, 1963 (English translation, 1977).

MISCELLANEOUS: *Œuvres complètes*, 1975-1991 (6 volumes).

BIBLIOGRAPHY

Browning, Gordon Frederick. *Tristan Tzara: The Genesis of the Dada Poem: Or, From Dada to Aa*. Stuttgart, Germany: Akademischer Verlag Heinz, 1979. A critical study of Tzara's Dada poems. Includes bibliographical references.

Caws, Mary Ann. Introduction to *Approximate Man, and Other Writings*, by Tristan Tzara. Translated by Mary Ann Caws. Detroit: Wayne State University Press, 1973. This book is an excellent selection of English translations of Tzara's poetry, and the introduction provides a helpful guide to each phase of his work.

_____, ed. *Surrealist Painters and Poets: An Anthology*. Cambridge, Mass.: MIT Press, 2001. Contains translations of several prose pieces by Tzara as well as works by many of his contemporaries, providing an overview of the context in which he operated. Includes many illustrations.

Forcer, Stephen. *Modernist Song: The Poetry of Tristan Tzara*. Leeds, England: Legenda, 2006. Traces Tzara's development and changing poetry from his early works to publications in the 1950's.

Marcus, Greil. *Lipstick Traces: A Secret History of the Twentieth Century*. 1989. 20th anniversary ed. Cambridge, Mass.: Belknap Press, 2009. A highly original and accessible study of nihilistic movements in art, music, and literature, from Dada to punk rock. Tzara is only one of many figures discussed here, but this book deserves mention because of its broad historical scope and excellent analysis of the relationship between popular culture and the avant-garde.

Motherwell, Robert, and Jack D. Flam, eds. *The Dada Painters and Poets: An Anthology.* 2d ed. Cambridge, Mass.: Harvard University Press, 1989. A collection of Dada documents including journals, reviews, and manifestos that hold valuable biographical and historical details of the life and work of Tzara.

Peterson, Elmer. *Tristan Tzara: Dada and Surrational Theorist.* New Brunswick, N.J.: Rutgers University Press, 1971. A study of Tzara's aesthetics. Includes bibliographical references.

Richter, Hans. *Dada: Art and Anti-Art.* New York: Thames & Hudson, 1997. Through selections from key manifestos and other documents of the time, Richter records Dada's history, from its beginnings in wartime Zurich to its collapse in the Paris of the 1920's.

Sandqvist, Tom. *Dada East: The Romanians of Cabaret Voltaire.* Cambridge, Mass.: MIT Press, 2006. Looks at Dadaism in Romania, where Tzara was born.

Steven E. Colburn

CÉSAR VALLEJO

Born: Santiago de Chuco, Peru; March 16, 1892
Died: Paris, France; April 15, 1938

PRINCIPAL POETRY

Los heraldos negros, 1918 (*The Black Heralds*, 1990)
Trilce, 1922 (English translation, 1973)
España, aparta de mí este cáliz, 1939 (*Spain, Take This Cup from Me*, 1974)
Poemas en prosa, 1939 (*Prose Poems*, 1978)
Poemas humanos, 1939 (*Human Poems*, 1968)
Obra poética completa, 1968
César Vallejo: The Complete Posthumous Poetry, 1978
Poesía completa, 1978
Selected Poems, 1981
The Complete Poetry: A Bilingual Edition, 2007 (Clayton Eshleman, editor)

OTHER LITERARY FORMS

César Vallejo (vah-YAY-hoh) wrote fiction, plays, and essays, as well as lyric poetry, although his achievement as a poet far outstrips that in any other genre. His short stories—many of them extremely brief—may be found in *Escalas melografiadas* (1923; musical scales). A longer short story, "Fabla salvaje" (1923; primitive parlance), is a tragic idyll of two rustic lovers, and *Hacia el reino de los Sciris* (1967; toward the kingdom of the Sciris) is set in the time of the Incas. *El tungsteno* (1931; *Tungsten*, 1988), is a proletarian novel with an Andean setting that was written in 1931, the year Vallejo joined the Communist Party. Another story, *Paco Yunque* (1969), is about the mistreatment of a servant's son by a classmate who happens to be the master's son.

Vallejo became interested in the theater around 1930, but he destroyed his first play, "Mampar." Three others, *Entre las dos orillas corre el río* (pb. 1979; the river flows between two banks); *Lock-Out* (pb. 1979), and *Colacho hermanos: O, presidentes de América* (pb. 1979; Colacho brothers), never published during the poet's lifetime, are now available in *Teatro completo* (1979; complete theatrical work). His long essay, *Rusia en 1931: Reflexiones al pie del Kremlin* (1931; reissued in 1965), was followed by *Rusia ante el segundo plan quinquenal* (1965); *Contra el secreto profesional* (1973); and *El arte y la revolución* (1973). His master's thesis, *El romanticismo en la poesía castellana*, was published in 1954.

ACHIEVEMENTS

Finding an authentic language in which to write has always represented a fundamental problem for Latin American writers, since it became evident that the language inherited from the Spanish conquerors could not match Latin American reality. The problem of finding such a language goes hand in hand with that of forging a separate cultural identity. An important attempt at renovating poetic language was made by the Spanish American *Modernistas* around the turn of the century, but their verse forms, imagery, and often exotic subject matter were also becoming obsolete by the time César Vallejo reached maturity. It was thus up to him and his contemporaries to find a language that could deal with contemporary concerns involving war, depression, isolation, and alienation. Although hardly recognized in his lifetime, Vallejo did more than perhaps any other poet of his generation to provide an idiom that would at once reflect the Spanish tradition, his own Peruvian heritage, and the contemporary world. Aware of his heritage from Spain's great writers of the past, he blended traditional poetic vocabulary and tropes with homely Peruvian idioms and even the language of children. Where the result was still inadequate, he made up new words, changed the function of old ones, and incorporated a lexicon never before seen in poetry, often savaging poetic convention.

Vallejo's gradual conversion to Marxism and Communism is of great interest to those attempting to understand how collectivist ideals may shape poetry. The evolution of his ideology continues to be studied intensively by many individuals committed to bettering the conditions of poverty and alienation about which Vallejo wrote so eloquently—conditions that still exist in Latin America and other parts of the world. His unflinchingly honest search for both linguistic and moral solutions to the existential anguish of modern human beings gives his poems universal validity, while their density and complexity challenge critics of the most antithetical modes.

BIOGRAPHY

César Abraham Vallejo was born in Santiago de Chuco, a primitive "city" of some fourteen thousand inhabitants in Peru's northern mountains that could only be reached by a rail trip and then several days ride on mule or horseback. Both of his grandfathers had been Spanish priests and both of his grandmothers native Peruvians of Chimu Indian stock. His parents were literate and of modest means; his father was a notary who became a subprefect in the district. Francisco de Paula Vallejo and María de los Santos Mendoza were an upright and religious pair whose marriage produced twelve offspring and who were already middle-aged when their youngest child, César, was born. In his writings, Vallejo was often to remember the security and warmth of his childhood home—games with three of his older siblings, and particularly with his mother, who might have been especially indulgent with her sensitive youngest child.

At age thirteen, Vallejo left Santiago de Chuco to attend high school in Huamachuco, another mountain village, where he received an introduction to literature and began scribbling verses. Economic difficulties prevented him from continuing the university studies that he had begun in the larger coastal cities of Trujillo and Lima in 1911. The young man first went to work in a nearby tungsten mine—an experience that he would later draw upon for his Socialist Realist novel *Tungsten*—and then on a coastal sugar plantation. While there, he observed the tightly structured hierarchy that kept workers in misery while the middle class, to which he himself belonged, served the needs of the elite. In 1913, he returned to the University of Trujillo and graduated two years later, having written a master's thesis titled *El romanticismo en la poesía castellana*. For the next few years, he studied law in Trujillo, supporting himself by becoming a first-grade teacher. One of his pupils, Ciro Alegría, later to become an important novelist, described Vallejo in those days as lean, sallow, solemn, and dark skinned, with abundant straight black hair worn somewhat long, brilliant dark eyes, a gentle manner, and an air of sadness.

During these years, Vallejo became familiar with the writings of Ralph Waldo Emerson, José Rodó, Friedrich Nietzsche, Miguel de Unamuno y Jugo, Walt Whitman, and Juan Ramón Jiménez. Vallejo also read the poems of two of the leading Spanish American *Modernistas*, Rubén Darío and Julio Herrera y Reissig, as well as those of Peruvian poets of the day. Vallejo declaimed his own poems—mostly occasional verse—at various public ceremonies, and some of them appeared in Trujillo's newspapers. Critical reception of them ranged from the cool to the hostile, since they were considered to be exaggerated and strange in that highly traditional ambience. Vallejo fell in love with a young Trujillo girl, Zoila Rosa Cuadro, the subject of several poems included in *The Black Heralds*. The breakup of this relationship provided one motive for his departure, after he had obtained a law degree, for Lima in 1918. There he found a position teaching in one of the best elementary schools and began to put the finishing touches on his first volume of poems.

Vallejo was soon in love with the sister-in-law of one of his colleagues, a woman identified only as "Otilia." A number of the *Trilce* poems, which he was writing at the time, deal with this affair. It ended when the poet refused to marry the woman, resulting in the loss of his job. This crisis was compounded by the death of his mother, a symbol of stability whose loss made him feel like an orphan. For some time, Vallejo had thought of going to Paris, but he decided to return first to his childhood home in Santiago de Chuco. During a national holiday, he was falsely accused of having been the instigator of a civil disturbance and was later seized and imprisoned for 112 days despite the public protests of many Peruvian intellectuals. The experience affected him profoundly, and the poems that he wrote about it (later published in *Trilce*) testify to the feeling of solidarity with the oppressed that he voiced for the first time. While in prison, he also wrote a number of the sketches to appear in *Escalas melografiadas*. In 1923, he sailed for Europe, never again to return to Peru.

While Vallejo's days in Lima had often been marked by personal problems, in Paris, he experienced actual penury, sometimes being forced to sleep in the subway. Eventually, he found employment in a press agency but only after a serious illness. He began to contribute articles to Lima newspapers, made friends with a number of avant-garde artists, and journeyed several times to Spain, where he was awarded a grant for further study. Increasingly concerned with injustice in the world, he made his first trip to Russia in 1928 with the intention of staying. Instead, he returned within three weeks, living soon afterward with a Frenchwoman, Georgette de Philippart, who was later to become his wife. With some money that had come to her, the pair set out on a tour by train through Eastern Europe, spending two weeks in Moscow and returning by way of Rome. As Vallejo's enthusiasm for Marxism became increasingly apparent in his newspaper articles, he found them no longer welcome in Lima, and in 1930, he was ordered to leave France because of his political activity. Once again in Spain, he wrote several plays and the novel *Tungsten* and published *Rusia en 1931*, the only one of his books to sell well. No publisher could be found for several other works. After a third and final visit to Russia as a delegate to the International Congress of Writers, he wrote *Rusia ante el segundo plan quinquenal* (Russia facing the second five-year plan) and officially joined the Communist Party.

In 1932, Vallejo was permitted to return to Paris, where he tried unsuccessfully to publish some new poems. In 1936, the Spanish Civil War broke out, and Vallejo became an active supporter of the Republic, traveling to Barcelona and Madrid to attend the Second International Congress for the Defense of Culture. He visited the battlefront and learned at first hand of the horrors suffered by the Spanish people in the war. Returning to Paris for the last time, he poured his feelings into his last work, *Spain, Take This Cup from Me*. In March, 1938, he became ill. Doctors were unable to diagnose his illness, and Vallejo died a month later on Good Friday, the day before the troops of Francisco Franco won a decisive victory in Spain.

ANALYSIS

One of the unique qualities of César Vallejo's poetry—one that makes his work almost impossible to confuse with that of any other poet writing in the Spanish language—is his ability to speak with the voice and sensibility of a child, whether as an individual orphaned by the breakup of a family or as a symbol of deprived and alienated human beings everywhere. Always, however, this child's voice, full of expectation and hope, is implicitly counterposed by the adult's ironic awareness of change and despair. Inseparable from these elements is the poet's forging of a language capable of reflecting the register and the peculiarly elliptical reasoning of a child and, at the same time, revealing the Hermetic complexity of the adult intellectual's quest for security in the form of truth. The poetry that is Vallejo's own answer to these problems is some of the most poignant and original ever produced.

THE BLACK HERALDS

The lines of Vallejo's subsequent development are already evident in his first volume, *The Black Heralds*, a collection of sixty-nine poems grouped under various subtitles. As critics have observed, many of these poems reflect his involvement with Romantic and *Modernista* poetry. They are conspicuous in many cases for their descriptions of idyllic scenes in a manner that juxtaposes words of the Peruvian Sierra and the vocabulary of Symbolism, including religious and erotic elements. Vallejo did not emphasize rhyme and rhythm to the extent that some *Modernistas* did, but most of these early poems are framed in verse forms favored by the latter, such as the Alexandrine sonnet and the *silva*. While demonstrating his impressive mastery of styles already worked out by others, he was also finding his own voice.

This originality is perhaps most evident in the last group of poems in *The Black Heralds*, titled "Canciones de Hogar" ("Home Songs"), poems dealing with the beginning of Vallejo's sense of orphanhood. In "A mi hermano Miguel in memoriam" ("To My Brother Miguel in Memoriam"), the poet relives a moment of the childhood game of hide-and-seek that he used to play with his "twin heart." Speaking to his brother, Vallejo announces his own presence in the part of the family home from which one of the two always ran away to hide from the other. He goes on to remind his playmate of one day on which the latter went away to hide, sad instead of laughing as he usually was, and could not be found again. The poem ends with a request to the brother to please come out so as not to worry "mama." It is remarkable in that past and present alternate from one line to the next. The language of childhood, as well as the poet's assumed presence at the site of the events, lends a dramatic immediacy to the scene. At the same time, the language used in the descriptive passages is clearly that of the adult who is now the poet. Yet in the last verse, the adult chooses to accept literally the explanation that the brother has remained in hiding and may finally respond and come out, which would presumably alleviate the mother's anxiety and make everything right once more. The knowledge that the poet is unable (or refuses) to face the permanent alteration of his past may elicit feelings of tragic pathos in the reader.

"Los pasos lejanos" ("The Distant Steps") recalls the poet's childhood home in which his parents, now aged, are alone—the father sleeping and the mother walking in the orchards. Here, the only bitterness is that of the poet himself, because he is now far away from them. He in turn is haunted by a vision of his parents as two old, white, and bent roads along which his heart walks. In "Enereida," he imagines that his father has died, leading to a regression in time so that the father can once again laugh at his small children, including the poet himself, who is again a schoolboy under the tutelage of the village priest.

Many of the poems in *The Black Heralds* deal with existential themes. While religious imagery is pervasive, it is apparent that the poet employs it to describe profane experiences. Jean Franco has shown that in speaking of "the soul's Christs" and "Marías who leave" and of Communions and Passions, Vallejo trivializes religious language rather than attempting to inflate the importance of his own experiences by describing them in religious terms. As well as having lost the security and plenitude of his childhood home, the poet has lost the childhood faith that enabled him to refer in words to the infinite.

In the title poem, "Los heraldos negros" ("The Black Heralds"), Vallejo laments life's hard blows, harder sometimes than humans can stand. He concludes that these blows come from the hatred of God, that they may be the black heralds sent by Death. In "Los dados eternos" ("The Eternal Dice"), God is a gambler throwing dice and may as easily cast death as life. In fact, Earth itself is his die. Now worn to roundness, it will come to rest only within the sepulchre. Profane love is all that is left; while the beloved may now be pure, she will not continue to be so if she yields to the poet's erotic impulses. Love thus becomes "a sinning Christ," because humankind's nature is irrevocably physical. Several poems allude to the poet's ideal of redeeming himself through brotherly love, a thematic constant in Vallejo's work, yet such redemption becomes difficult if not impossible if a person is lonely and alienated. In "Agape," the poet speaks of being alone and forgotten and of having been unable therefore to "die" for his brother. "La cena miserable" ("The Wretched Supper") tells of the enigma of existence in which humans are seen, as in "Agape," as waiting endlessly for spiritual nurture, or at least for some answer concerning the meaning of life. Here, God becomes no more than a "black spoon" full of bitter human essence, even less able than humans to provide needed answers. The lives of humans are thus meaningless, since they are always separated from what they most desire—whether this be the fullness of the past, physical love, God's love, or brotherly love.

Even in the poems most laden with the trappings of *Modernismo*, Vallejo provides unusual images. In "El poeta a su amada" ("The Poet to His Beloved"), he suggests that his kiss is "two curved branches" on which his beloved has been "crucified." Religious imagery is used with such frequency that it sometimes verges on parody, and critics agree that in playing with language in this way Vallejo is seeking to highlight its essential ambiguity, something he continues to do in *Trilce* and *Human Poems*, even while totally abandoning the imagery of *Modernismo*. Such stripping away of excess baggage is already visible in *The Black Heralds*. Antitheses, oxymorons, and occasional neologisms are also to be noted. While the great majority of the poems are elegantly correct in terms of syntax—in marked contrast to what is to become the norm in *Trilce*—there are some instances of linguistic experimentation, as when nouns are used as adjectives. In "The Distant Steps," for example, the mother is described as being "so soft, so wing, so departure, so love." Another device favored by the poet in all his later poems—enumeration—is also present. Finally, traditional patterns of meter and rhyme are abandoned in "Home Songs," with the poetic emotion being allowed to determine the form.

TRILCE

Despite these formal adumbrations and although *The Black Heralds* is not a particularly transparent work, there is little in it to prepare the reader for the destruction of language in the Hermetic density of *Trilce*, which came along only three years later. These were difficult years for the poet, in which he lost his mother, separated from Otilia, and spent what he was later to refer to as the gravest moments of his life in the Trujillo jail. All the anguish of these events was poured into the seventy-seven free-verse poems of his second major work. If he suffered existentially in *The Black Heralds* and expressed this suffering in writing, it was done with respect for traditional verse forms and sentence structure, which hinted at an order beyond the chaos of the poet's interior world. In *Trilce*, this order falls. Language, on which "logical assumptions" about the world are based, is used in such a way as to reveal its hollowness: It, too, is cut loose and orphaned. Abrupt shifts from one metaphorical sphere to another make the poems' internal logic often problematic.

A hint of what is to come is given in the title, a neologism usually taken to be a hybrid of *tres* (three) and *dulce* (sweet), an interpretation that is in accord with the poet's concern about the ideal number expressed in several poems. It is not known, however, what, if any, concrete meaning the poet had in mind when he coined the word; it has become a puzzle for readers and critics to solve. It is notable that in "interpreting" the *Trilce* poems, critics often work out explications that seem internally consistent but that turn out to be related to a system diametrically opposed to the explication and system of some other critic. It is possible, however, to say with certainty that these poems deal with a struggle to do something, bridge something, and say something. Physical limits such as the human body, time, space, and numbers often render the struggle futile.

Two of the thematic sets of *Trilce* for which it is easiest to establish concrete referents are those dealing with the poet-as-child and those dealing with his imprisonment. In poem III, the poet once again speaks in the voice of a child left at home by the adults of the family. It is getting dark, and he asks when the grown-ups will be back, adding that "Mama said she wouldn't be gone long." In the third stanza, an ironic double vision of years full of agonizing memories intrudes. As in "To My Brother Miguel in Memoriam," the poet chooses to retain the child's faith, urging his brothers and sisters to be good and obey in letter and spirit the instructions left by the mother. In the end, it is seen that the "leaving" is without remedy, a function of time itself; it eventually results in the poet's complete solitude without even the comfort of his siblings. In poem XXIII, the mother, the only symbol of total plenitude, is seen as the "warm oven" of the cookies described as "rich hosts of time." The nourishment provided by the mother was given freely and naturally, taken away from no one and given without the child's being obliged. Still, the process of nurturing leads to growing up and to individuation and alienation. Several poems mythicize the process of birth but shift so abruptly to demythicize human existence that the result is at first humorous. In poem XLVII, a candle is lighted to protect the mother while she gives birth, along with another for the babe who, God willing, will grow up to be bishop, pope, saint, "or perhaps only a columnary headache." Later, in *Human Poems*, there is a Word Incarnate whose bones agree in number and gender as it sinks into the bathtub ("Lomo de las sagradas escrituras"/"Spine of the Scriptures").

In poem XVIII, the poet surveys the four walls of the cell, implacably closed. He calls up a vision of the "loving keeper of innumerable keys," the mother, who would liberate him if she could. He imagines the two longer walls as mothers and the shorter ones as the children each of them is leading by the hand. The poet is alone with only his two hands, struggling to find a third to help him in his useless adulthood. In poem LVIII, the solid walls of the cell seem to bend at the corners, suggesting that the poet is dozing as a series of jumbled thoughts produce scenes in his mind that follow no easy logical principle of association. The poet sees himself helping the naked and the ragged, then dismounting from a panting horse that he also attempts to help. The cell is now liquid, and he becomes aware of the companions who may be worse off than he. Guilt suddenly overwhelms him, and he is moved to promise to laugh no more when his mother arises early to pray for the sick, the poor, and the prisoners. He also promises to treat his little friends better at play, in both word and deed. The cell is now boundless gas, growing as it condenses. Ambiguously, at the end, he poses the question, "Who stumbles outside?" The openness of the poem is similar to that of many others in *Trilce*, and it is difficult to say what kind of threat to the poet's resolutions is posed by the figure outside. Again, the poetic voice has become that of a child seeking to make all that is wrong in the world right once more by promising to be "a good boy." Of course, he is not a child at all, as the figure outside may be intended to remind both him and the reader. The result is once again a remarkable note of pathos tinged with poignant irony.

Many of *Trilce*'s poems deal with physical love and even the sexual act itself. "Two" seems to be the ideal number, but "two" has "propensities of trinity." Clearly, the poet has no wish to bring a child into the world, and sex becomes merely an act of organs that provides no solution to anything. While the poet seems to appreciate the maternal acts performed by his lover, he fails to find any transcendental satisfaction in the physical relationship, even though he is sad when it is over.

An important theme that emerges in *Trilce* and is developed more fully in *Human Poems* and *Spain, Take This Cup from Me* is that of the body as text. In poem LXV, the house to which the poet returns in Santiago seems to be his mother's body. Parts of the body—the back, face, shoulder, eyes, hands, lips, eyelashes, bones, feet, knees, fingers, heart, arms, breasts, soles of the feet, eyelids, ears, ribs—appear in poem after poem, reminding the reader of human and earthly functions and the limitations of human beings.

In many ways, *Trilce* resembles the poetry of such avant-garde movements as Surrealism, Ultraism, and Creationism in the boldness of its images, its unconventional vocabulary, and its experimentation with graphics. Vallejo did have very limited exposure to some of this poetry after he reached Lima; his critics, however, generally agree that *Trilce* was produced independently. While Vallejo may have been encouraged to experiment by his knowledge of European literary currents, his work coincides with them as an original contribution.

HUMAN POEMS

As far as is known, the poems after *Trilce* were written in Europe; with very few exceptions, none was published until 1939, a year after the poet's death, when they appeared under the title *Human Poems*. While Vallejo's life in Peru was far from affluent, it must have seemed easy in comparison with the years in Paris, where he often barely subsisted and suffered several illnesses. In addition, while he did see a new edition of *Trilce* published through the intervention of friends in 1931 and his *Rusia en 1931* did go into three editions during his lifetime, he could never count on having his writings accepted for publication.

Human Poems, considered separately from *Spain, Take This Cup from Me*, is far from being a homogeneous volume, and its final configuration might have been different had it been Vallejo who prepared the final edition rather than his widow. Generally speaking, the poems that it includes deal with ontological anguish whose cause seems related to physical suffering, the passage of time, and the impossibility of believing that life has any meaning. In fact, *Human Poems* examines suffering and pain, with their corollaries, poverty, hunger, illness, and death, with a thoroughness that few other works can match. At times, the anguish seems to belong only to the poet, now not only the orphan of *Trilce* but alienated from other people as well. In "Altura y pelos" ("Height and Hair"), the poet poses questions: "Who doesn't own a blue suit?/ Who doesn't eat lunch and board the streetcar . . . ?/ Who is not called Carlos or any other thing?/ Who to the kitty doesn't say kitty kitty?" The final answer given is "Aie? I who alone was solely born." At least two kinds of irony seem to be involved here. The activities mentioned are obviously trivial, but neither is it easy to be alone. In the well-known "Los nueve monstruos" ("The Nine Monsters"), the poet laments the abundance of pain in the world: "Never, human men/ was there so *much* pain in the chest, in the lapel, in the wallet/ in the glass, in the butcher-shop, in arithmetic!" and "never/ . . . did the migraine extract so much forehead from the forehead!" Pain drives people crazy "in the movies,/ nails us into the gramophones,/ denails us in bed . . ." The poem concludes that the "Secretary of Health" can do nothing because there is simply "too much to do."

"The Nine Monsters" is representative of several features of *Human Poems*. The language is extremely concrete, denoting things that are inseparable from everyday existence. Much of the poem consists of lists, continuing a device for which the poet had already shown a disposition in his first work. Finally, the logic of the systems represented by the items named is hard to pin down, so that it is somewhat reminiscent of child logic in its eccentricity. Again and again, Vallejo's remarkable sensibility is demonstrated beyond any preciosity or mere posturing.

One reason for the poet's alienation is that he sees people as engaged in trivial occupations and as being hardly more advanced on the evolutionary scale than pachyderms or kangaroos, whereas he himself aspires to rise above his limitations. In "Intensidad y altura" ("Intensity and Height"), he tells of his desire to write being stifled by his feeling "like a puma," so that he might as well go and eat grass. He concludes, "let's go, raven, and fecundate your rook." He thus sees himself condemned not to rise above the purely mundane. Religion offers no hope at all. In "Acaba de pasar el que vendrá . . ." ("He Has Just Passed By, the One Who Will Come . . ."), the poet suggests that "the one who will come"—presumably the Messiah—has already passed by but has changed nothing, being as vague and ineffectually human as anyone else.

While the majority of these posthumously published poems convey utter despair, not all of them do. Although the exact dates of their composition are generally unknown, it is natural to associate those that demonstrate growing concern for others with Vallejo's conversion to Marxist thought and eventually to Communism. In "Considerando en frío . . ." ("Considering Coldly . . ."), speaking as an attorney at a trial, the poetic voice first summarizes the problems and weaknesses of humanity (he "is sad, coughs and, nevertheless,/ takes pleasure in his reddened chest/ . . . he is a gloomy mammal and combs his hair . . .") Then, however, he announces his love for humanity. Denying it immediately, he nevertheless concludes, "I signal him,/ he comes,/ I embrace him, moved./ So what! Moved . . . Moved. . . ." Compassion thus nullifies "objectivity." In "La rueda del hambriento" ("The Hungry Man's Wheel"), the poet speaks as a man so miserable that his own organs are pulled out of him through his mouth. He begs only for a stone on which to sit and a little bread. Apparently ignored, aware that he is being importunate, he continues to ask, disoriented and hardly able to recognize his own body. In "Traspié entre dos estrellas" ("Stumble Between Two Stars"), the poet expresses pity for the wretched but goes on to parody bitterly Christ's Sermon on the Mount ("Beloved be the one with bedbugs,/ the one who wears a torn shoe in the rain"), ending with a "beloved" for one thing and then for its opposite, as if calling special attention to the emptiness of mere words. It is possible to say that in these poems the orphan has finally recognized that he is not alone in his orphanhood.

SPAIN, TAKE THIS CUP FROM ME

Although first published as part of *Human Poems*, *Spain, Take This Cup from Me* actually forms a separate, unified work very different in tone from the majority of the other posthumous poems—a tone of hope, although, especially in the title poem, the poet seems to suspect that the cause he has believed in so passionately may be lost. In this poem, perhaps the last that Vallejo wrote, the orphan—now all human children—has found a mother. This mother is Spain, symbol of a new revolutionary order in which oppression may be ended. The children are urged not to let their mother die; nevertheless, even should this happen, they have a recourse: to continue struggling and to go out and find a new mother.

Another contrast is found in the odes to several heroes of the Civil War. Whereas, in *Human Poems*, humans are captives of their bodies and hardly more intelligent than the lower animals, *Spain, Take This Cup from Me* finds people capable of true transcendence through solidarity with others and the will to fight injustice. A number of poems commemorate the battles of the war: Talavera, Guernica, Málaga. Spain thus becomes a text—a book that sprouts from the bodies of an anonymous soldier. The poet insists again and again that he himself is nothing, that his stature is "tiny," and that his actions rather than his words constitute the real text. This may be seen to represent a greatly evolved negation of poetic authority, first seen in *The Black Heralds* with the repeated cry, "I don't know!"

Nevertheless, *Spain, Take This Cup from Me* rings with a biblical tone, and the poet sometimes sounds like a prophet. James Higgins has pointed out certain images that recall the Passion of Christ and the New Jerusalem, although religious terminology, as in all Vallejo's poetry, is applied to humans rather than to divinity. While Vallejo continues to use techniques of enumeration—which are often chaotic—and to use concrete nouns (including many referring to the body), he also employs abstract terms such as peace, hope, martyrdom, harmony, eternity, and greatness. The sense of garments, utensils, and the body's organs stifling the soul is gone and is replaced by limitless space. In Vallejo's longest poem, "Himno a los voluntarios de la República" ("Hymn to the Volunteers for the Republic"), a panegyric note is struck.

One of Vallejo's most immediately accessible poems, "Masa" ("Mass"), tells almost a parable of a dead combatant who was asked by one man not to die, then by two, and finally by millions. The corpse kept dying until surrounded by all the inhabitants of Earth. The corpse, moved, sat up and embraced the first man and then began to walk. The simplicity of the story and of its narration recalls the child's voice in *Trilce*, promising to cease tormenting his playmates in order to atone for the world's guilt. In this piece, as well as in all Vallejo's last group of poems, however, the irony is gone.

POETIC CYCLE

It is thus possible to see the completion of a cycle in the four works. Disillusionment grows in *The Black Heralds*, and then alienation works its way into the language itself in *Trilce*. *Human Poems* is somewhat less Hermetic than *Trilce*, but life is an anguished nightmare in which the soul is constrained by the ever-present body that seems to be always wracked with pain. Only in *Spain, Take This Cup from Me*, with the realization that men are brothers who can end their common alienation and suffering by collective action, does the poet regain his lost faith and embark upon a positive course. The orphan relocates the lost mother, whom he now sees to be the mother of all, since all men are brothers. The true significance of Vallejo's poetry, however, surely lies in his honesty in questioning all established rules of poetic expression, as well as the tradition of poetic authority, in order to put poetry fully in touch with the existential prison house of twentieth century humanity.

OTHER MAJOR WORKS

LONG FICTION: *Fábula salvaje*, 1923 (novella); *El tungsteno*, 1931 (*Tungsten*, 1988).

SHORT FICTION: *Escalas melografiadas*, 1923; *Hacia el reino de los Sciris*, 1967; *Paco Yunque*, 1969.

PLAYS: *Colacho hermanos: O, presidentes de América*, pb. 1979; *Entre las dos orillas corre el río*, pb. 1979; *La piedra cansada*, pb. 1979; *Lock-Out*, pb. 1979; *Teatro completo*, 1979.

NONFICTION: *Rusia en 1931: Reflexiones al pie del Kremlin*, 1931, 1965; *El romanticismo en la poesía castellana*, 1954; *Rusia ante el segundo plan quinquenal*, 1965; *Contra el secreto profesional*, 1973; *El arte y la revolución*, 1973.

BIBLIOGRAPHY

Britton, R. K. "Love, Alienation, and the Absurd: Three Principal Themes in César Vallejo's *Trilce*." *Modern Language Review* 87 (July, 1992): 603-615. Demonstrates how Vallejo's poetry expresses the anguished conviction that humankind is simply a form of animal life subject to the laws of a random, absurd universe.

Dove, Patrick. *The Catastrophe of Modernity: Tragedy and the Nation in Latin American Literature*. Lewisburg, Pa.: Bucknell University Press, 2004. This discussion of the theme of modernity as a catastrophe contains a chapter on Vallejo's *Trilce*.

Hart, Stephen M. *Stumbling Between Forty-six Stars: Essays on César Vallejo*. London: Centre of César Vallejo Studies, 2007. A collection of essays on various aspects of the poet.

Hart, Stephen M., and Jorge Cornejo Polar. *César Vallejo: A Critical Bibliography of Research*. Rochester, N.Y.: Boydell and Brewer, 2002. A bibliography collecting works of Vallejo. Invaluable for researchers.

Hedrick, Tace Megan. "Mi andina y dulce Rita: Women, Indigenism, and the Avant-Garde in César Vallejo." In *Primitivism and Identity in Latin America: Essays on Art, Literature, and Culture*, edited by Erik Camayd-Freixas and José Eduardo González. Tucson: University of Arizona Press, 2000. Relates the indigenism of "Dead Idylls" from *The Black Heralds* to the "avant-garde concerns and practices" of *Trilce*, often considered Vallejo's most brilliant work.

Higgins, James. *The Poet in Peru: Alienation and the Quest for a Super-Reality*. Liverpool, England: Cairns, 1982. Contains a good overview of the main themes of Vallejo's poetry.

Lambie, George. "Poetry and Politics: The Spanish Civil War Poetry of César Vallejo." *Bulletin of Hispanic Studies* 69, no. 2 (April, 1992): 153-170. Analyzes the presence of faith and Marxism in *Spain, Take This Cup from Me*.

Niebylski, Dianna C. *The Poem on the Edge of the Word: The Limits of Language and the Uses of Silence in the Poetry of Mallarmé, Rilke, and Vallejo*. New York: Peter

Lang, 1993. In the context of the language "crisis" of modern poetry and the poet's dilemma in choosing language or silence, Niebylski examines the themes of time and death in Vallejo's *Human Poems*.

Sharman, Adam, ed. *The Poetry and Poetics of César Vallejo: The Fourth Angle of the Circle*. Lewiston, N.Y.: Edwin Mellen Press, 1997. Collection of essays examining Vallejo's work from the perspectives of Marxism, history, the theme of the absent mother, and postcolonial theory.

Lee Hunt Dowling

CHECKLIST FOR EXPLICATING A POEM

I. The Initial Readings

A. Before reading the poem, the reader should:
  1. Notice its form and length.
  2. Consider the title, determining, if possible, whether it might function as an allusion, symbol, or poetic image.
  3. Notice the date of composition or publication, and identify the general era of the poet.

B. The poem should be read intuitively and emotionally and be allowed to "happen" as much as possible.

C. In order to establish the rhythmic flow, the poem should be reread. A note should be made as to where the irregular spots (if any) are located.

II. Explicating the Poem

A. *Dramatic situation.* Studying the poem line by line helps the reader discover the dramatic situation. All elements of the dramatic situation are interrelated and should be viewed as reflecting and affecting one another. The dramatic situation serves a particular function in the poem, adding realism, surrealism, or absurdity; drawing attention to certain parts of the poem; and changing to reinforce other aspects of the poem. All points should be considered. The following questions are particularly helpful to ask in determining dramatic situation:
  1. What, if any, is the narrative action in the poem?
  2. How many personae appear in the poem? What part do they take in the action?
  3. What is the relationship between characters?
  4. What is the setting (time and location) of the poem?

B. *Point of view.* An understanding of the poem's point of view is a major step toward comprehending the poet's intended meaning. The reader should ask:
  1. Who is the speaker? Is he or she addressing someone else or the reader?
  2. Is the narrator able to understand or see everything happening to him or her, or does the reader know things that the narrator does not?
  3. Is the narrator reliable?
  4. Do point of view and dramatic situation seem consistent? If not, the inconsistencies may provide clues to the poem's meaning.

C. *Images and metaphors.* Images and metaphors are often the most intricately crafted vehicles of the poem for relaying the poet's message. Realizing that the images and metaphors work in harmony with the dramatic situation and point of view will help the reader to see the poem as a whole, rather than as disassociated elements.

1. The reader should identify the concrete images (that is, those that are formed from objects that can be touched, smelled, seen, felt, or tasted). Is the image projected by the poet consistent with the physical object?
2. If the image is abstract, or so different from natural imagery that it cannot be associated with a real object, then what are the properties of the image?
3. To what extent is the reader asked to form his or her own images?
4. Is any image repeated in the poem? If so, how has it been changed? Is there a controlling image?
5. Are any images compared to each other? Do they reinforce one another?
6. Is there any difference between the way the reader perceives the image and the way the narrator sees it?
7. What seems to be the narrator's or persona's attitude toward the image?

D. *Words.* Every substantial word in a poem may have more than one intended meaning, as used by the author. Because of this, the reader should look up many of these words in the dictionary and:

1. Note all definitions that have the slightest connection with the poem.
2. Note any changes in syntactical patterns in the poem.
3. In particular, note those words that could possibly function as symbols or allusions, and refer to any appropriate sources for further information.

E. *Meter, rhyme, structure, and tone.* In scanning the poem, all elements of prosody should be noted by the reader. These elements are often used by a poet to manipulate the reader's emotions, and therefore they should be examined closely to arrive at the poet's specific intention.

1. Does the basic meter follow a traditional pattern such as those found in nursery rhymes or folk songs?
2. Are there any variations in the base meter? Such changes or substitutions are important thematically and should be identified.
3. Are the rhyme schemes traditional or innovative, and what might their form mean to the poem?
4. What devices has the poet used to create sound patterns (such as assonance and alliteration)?
5. Is the stanza form a traditional or innovative one?
6. If the poem is composed of verse paragraphs rather than stanzas, how do they affect the progression of the poem?

7. After examining the above elements, is the resultant tone of the poem casual or formal, pleasant, harsh, emotional, authoritative?

F. *Historical context.* The reader should attempt to place the poem into historical context, checking on events at the time of composition. Archaic language, expressions, images, or symbols should also be looked up.

G. *Themes and motifs.* By seeing the poem as a composite of emotion, intellect, craftsmanship, and tradition, the reader should be able to determine the themes and motifs (smaller recurring ideas) presented in the work. He or she should ask the following questions to help pinpoint these main ideas:
1. Is the poet trying to advocate social, moral, or religious change?
2. Does the poet seem sure of his or her position?
3. Does the poem appeal primarily to the emotions, to the intellect, or to both?
4. Is the poem relying on any particular devices for effect (such as imagery, allusion, paradox, hyperbole, or irony)?

BIBLIOGRAPHY

GENERAL REFERENCE SOURCES

BIOGRAPHICAL SOURCES

Colby, Vineta, ed. *World Authors, 1975-1980*. Wilson Authors Series. New York: H. W. Wilson, 1985.

_____. *World Authors, 1980-1985*. Wilson Authors Series. New York: H. W. Wilson, 1991.

_____. *World Authors, 1985-1990*. Wilson Authors Series. New York: H. W. Wilson, 1995.

Cyclopedia of World Authors. 4th rev. ed. 5 vols. Pasadena, Calif.: Salem Press, 2003.

Dictionary of Literary Biography. 254 vols. Detroit: Gale Research, 1978-   .

International Who's Who in Poetry and Poets' Encyclopaedia. Cambridge, England: International Biographical Centre, 1993.

Seymour-Smith, Martin, and Andrew C. Kimmens, eds. *World Authors, 1900-1950*. Wilson Authors Series. 4 vols. New York: H. W. Wilson, 1996.

Thompson, Clifford, ed. *World Authors, 1990-1995*. Wilson Authors Series. New York: H. W. Wilson, 1999.

Wakeman, John, ed. *World Authors, 1950-1970*. New York: H. W. Wilson, 1975.

_____. *World Authors, 1970-1975*. Wilson Authors Series. New York: H. W. Wilson, 1991.

Willhardt, Mark, and Alan Michael Parker, eds. *Who's Who in Twentieth Century World Poetry*. New York: Routledge, 2000.

CRITICISM

Brooks, Cleanth, and Robert Penn Warren. *Understanding Poetry*. 4th ed. Reprint. Fort Worth, Tex.: Heinle & Heinle, 2003.

Classical and Medieval Literature Criticism. Detroit: Gale Research, 1988-   .

Contemporary Literary Criticism. Detroit: Gale Research, 1973-   .

Day, Gary. *Literary Criticism: A New History*. Edinburgh, Scotland: Edinburgh University Press, 2008.

Draper, James P., ed. *World Literature Criticism 1500 to the Present: A Selection of Major Authors from Gale's Literary Criticism Series*. 6 vols. Detroit: Gale Research, 1992.

Habib, M. A. R. *A History of Literary Criticism: From Plato to the Present*. Malden, Mass.: Wiley-Blackwell, 2005.

Jason, Philip K., ed. *Masterplots II: Poetry Series, Revised Edition*. 8 vols. Pasadena, Calif.: Salem Press, 2002.

Lodge, David, and Nigel Wood. *Modern Criticism and Theory*. 3d ed. New York: Longman, 2008.

Magill, Frank N., ed. *Magill's Bibliography of Literary Criticism*. 4 vols. Englewood Cliffs, N.J.: Salem Press, 1979.

MLA International Bibliography. New York: Modern Language Association of America, 1922-   .

Nineteenth-Century Literature Criticism. Detroit: Gale Research, 1981-   .

Twentieth-Century Literary Criticism. Detroit: Gale Research, 1978-   .

Vedder, Polly, ed. *World Literature Criticism Supplement: A Selection of Major Authors from Gale's Literary Criticism Series*. 2 vols. Detroit: Gale Research, 1997.

Young, Robyn V., ed. *Poetry Criticism: Excerpts from Criticism of the Works of the Most Significant and Widely Studied Poets of World Literature*. 29 vols. Detroit: Gale Research, 1991.

POETRY DICTIONARIES AND HANDBOOKS

Carey, Gary, and Mary Ellen Snodgrass. *A Multicultural Dictionary of Literary Terms*. Jefferson, N.C.: McFarland, 1999.

Deutsch, Babette. *Poetry Handbook: A Dictionary of Terms*. 4th ed. New York: Funk & Wagnalls, 1974.

Drury, John. *The Poetry Dictionary*. Cincinnati, Ohio: Story Press, 1995.

Kinzie, Mary. *A Poet's Guide to Poetry*. Chicago: University of Chicago Press, 1999.

Lennard, John. *The Poetry Handbook: A Guide to Reading Poetry for Pleasure and Practical Criticism*. New York: Oxford University Press, 1996.

Matterson, Stephen, and Darryl Jones. *Studying Poetry*. New York: Oxford University Press, 2000.

Packard, William. *The Poet's Dictionary: A Handbook of Prosody and Poetic Devices*. New York: Harper & Row, 1989.

Preminger, Alex, et al., eds. *The New Princeton Encyclopedia of Poetry and Poetics*. 3d rev. ed. Princeton, N.J.: Princeton University Press, 1993.

Shipley, Joseph Twadell, ed. *Dictionary of World Literary Terms, Forms, Technique, Criticism*. Rev. ed. Boston: George Allen and Unwin, 1979.

INDEXES OF PRIMARY WORKS

Frankovich, Nicholas, ed. *The Columbia Granger's Index to Poetry in Anthologies*. 11th ed. New York: Columbia University Press, 1997.

_____. *The Columbia Granger's Index to Poetry in Collected and Selected Works*. New York: Columbia University Press, 1997.

Guy, Patricia. *A Women's Poetry Index*. Phoenix, Ariz.: Oryx Press, 1985.

Hazen, Edith P., ed. *Columbia Granger's Index to Poetry*. 10th ed. New York: Columbia University Press, 1994.

Hoffman, Herbert H., and Rita Ludwig Hoffman, comps. *International Index to Re-corded Poetry*. New York: H. W. Wilson, 1983.

Kline, Victoria. *Last Lines: An Index to the Last Lines of Poetry*. 2 vols. Vol. 1, *Last Line Index, Title Index*; Vol. 2, *Author Index, Keyword Index*. New York: Facts On File, 1991.

Marcan, Peter. *Poetry Themes: A Bibliographical Index to Subject Anthologies and Re-lated Criticisms in the English Language, 1875-1975*. Hamden, Conn.: Linnet Books, 1977.

Poem Finder. Great Neck, N.Y.: Roth, 2000.

POETICS, POETIC FORMS, AND GENRES

Attridge, Derek. *Poetic Rhythm: An Introduction*. New York: Cambridge University Press, 1995.

Brogan, T. V. F. *Verseform: A Comparative Bibliography*. Baltimore: Johns Hopkins University Press, 1989.

Fussell, Paul. *Poetic Meter and Poetic Form*. Rev. ed. New York: McGraw-Hill, 1979.

Hollander, John. *Rhyme's Reason*. 3d ed. New Haven, Conn.: Yale University Press, 2001.

Jackson, Guida M. *Traditional Epics: A Literary Companion*. New York: Oxford University Press, 1995.

Padgett, Ron, ed. *The Teachers and Writers Handbook of Poetic Forms*. 2d ed. New York: Teachers & Writers Collaborative, 2000.

Pinsky, Robert. *The Sounds of Poetry: A Brief Guide*. New York: Farrar, Straus and Giroux, 1998.

Preminger, Alex, and T. V. F. Brogan, eds. *New Princeton Encyclopedia of Poetry and Poetics*. 3d ed. Princeton, N.J.: Princeton University Press, 1993.

Spiller, Michael R. G. *The Sonnet Sequence: A Study of Its Strategies*. Studies in Literary Themes and Genres 13. New York: Twayne, 1997.

Turco, Lewis. *The New Book of Forms: A Handbook of Poetics*. Hanover, N.H.: University Press of New England, 1986.

Williams, Miller. *Patterns of Poetry: An Encyclopedia of Forms*. Baton Rouge: Louisiana State University Press, 1986.

Maura Ives

Updated by Tracy Irons-Georges

GUIDE TO ONLINE RESOURCES

WEB SITES

The following sites were visited by the editors of Salem Press in 2010. Because URLs frequently change, the accuracy of these addresses cannot be guaranteed; however, long-standing sites, such as those of colleges and universities, national organizations, and government agencies, generally maintain links when their sites are moved.

Academy of American Poets

http://www.poets.org

The mission of the Academy of American Poets is to "support American poets at all stages of their careers and to foster the appreciation of contemporary poetry." The academy's comprehensive Web site features information on poetic schools and movements; a Poetic Forms Database; an Online Poetry Classroom, with educator and teaching resources; an index of poets and poems; essays and interviews; general Web resources; links for further study; and more.

Contemporary British Writers

http://www.contemporarywriters.com/authors

Created by the British Council, this site offers profiles of living writers of the United Kingdom, the Republic of Ireland, and the Commonwealth. Information includes biographies, bibliographies, critical reviews, and news about literary prizes. Photographs are also featured. Users can search the site by author, genre, nationality, gender, publisher, book title, date of publication, and prize name and date.

LiteraryHistory.com

http://www.literaryhistory.com

This site is an excellent source of academic, scholarly, and critical literature about eighteenth, nineteenth, and twentieth century American and English writers. It provides individual pages for twentieth century literature and alphabetical lists of authors that link to articles, reviews, overviews, excerpts of works, teaching guides, podcasts, and other materials.

Literary Resources on the Net

http://andromeda.rutgers.edu/~jlynch/Lit

Jack Lynch of Rutgers University maintains this extensive collection of links to Web sites that are useful to researchers, including numerous sites about American and English literature. This collection is a good place to begin online research about poetry, as it

links to other sites with broad ranges of literary topics. The site is organized chronologically, with separate pages about twentieth century British and Irish literature. It also has
separate pages providing links to Web sites about American literature and to women's
literature and feminism.

LitWeb
http://litweb.net

LitWeb provides biographies of hundreds of world authors throughout history that
can be accessed through an alphabetical listing. The pages about each writer contain a
list of his or her works, suggestions for further reading, and illustrations. The site also
offers information about past and present winners of major literary prizes.

The Modern Word: Authors of the Libyrinth
http://www.themodernword.com/authors.html

The Modern Word site, although somewhat haphazard in its organization, provides a
great deal of critical information about writers. The "Authors of the Libyrinth" page is
very useful, linking author names to essays about them and other resources. The section
of the page headed "The Scriptorium" presents "an index of pages featuring writers who
have pushed the edges of their medium, combining literary talent with a sense of experimentation to produce some remarkable works of modern literature."

Outline of American Literature
http://www.america.gov/publications/books/outline-of-american-literature.html

This page of the America.gov site provides access to an electronic version of the ten-
chapter volume *Outline of American Literature*, a historical overview of poetry and
prose from colonial times to the present published by the Bureau of International Information Programs of the U.S. Department of State.

Poetry Foundation
http://www.poetryfoundation.org

The Poetry Foundation, publisher of *Poetry* magazine, is an independent literary organization. Its Web site offers links to essays; news; events; online poetry resources,
such as blogs, organizations, publications, and references and research; a glossary of literary terms; and a Learning Lab that includes poem guides and essays on poetics.

Poet's Corner
http://theotherpages.org/poems

The Poet's Corner, one of the oldest text resources on the Web, provides access to
about seven thousand works of poetry by several hundred different poets from around
the world. Indexes are arranged and searchable by title, name of poet, or subject. The

site also offers its own resources, including "Faces of the Poets"—a gallery of portraits—and "Lives of the Poets"—a growing collection of biographies.

Representative Poetry Online
http://rpo.library.utoronto.ca

This award-winning resource site, maintained by Ian Lancashire of the Department
of English at the University of Toronto in Canada, has several thousand English-
language poems by hundreds of poets. The collection is searchable by poet's name, title
of work, first line of a poem, and keyword. The site also includes a time line, a glossary,
essays, an extensive bibliography, and countless links organized by country and by
subject.

Voice of the Shuttle
http://vos.ucsb.edu

One of the most complete and authoritative places for online information about literature, Voice of the Shuttle is maintained by professors and students in the English Department at the University of California, Santa Barbara. The site provides countless
links to electronic books, academic journals, literary association Web sites, sites created
by university professors, and many other resources.

Voices from the Gaps
http://voices.cla.umn.edu/

Voices from the Gaps is a site of the English Department at the University of Minnesota, dedicated to providing resources on the study of women artists of color, including
writers. The site features a comprehensive index searchable by name, and it provides
biographical information on each writer or artist and other resources for further study.

ELECTRONIC DATABASES

*Electronic databases usually do not have their own URLs. Instead, public, college, and
university libraries subscribe to these databases, provide links to them on their Web
sites, and make them available to library card holders or other specified patrons. Readers can visit library Web sites or ask reference librarians to check on availability.*

Canadian Literary Centre

Produced by EBSCO, the Canadian Literary Centre database contains full-text content from ECW Press, a Toronto-based publisher, including the titles in the publisher's
Canadian fiction studies, Canadian biography, and Canadian writers and their works series; *ECW's Biographical Guide to Canadian Novelists*; and *George Woodcock's Intro-*

duction to Canadian Fiction. Author biographies, essays and literary criticism, and book reviews are among the database's offerings.

Literary Reference Center

EBSCO's Literary Reference Center (LRC) is a comprehensive full-text database designed primarily to help high school and undergraduate students in English and the humanities with homework and research assignments about literature. The database contains massive amounts of information from reference works, books, literary journals, and other materials, including more than 31,000 plot summaries, synopses, and overviews of literary works; almost 100,000 essays and articles of literary criticism; about 140,000 author biographies; more than 605,000 book reviews; and more than 5,200 author interviews. It contains the entire contents of Salem Press's MagillOnLiterature Plus. Users can retrieve information by browsing a list of authors' names or titles of literary works; they can also use an advanced search engine to access information by numerous categories, including author name, gender, cultural identity, national identity, and the years in which he or she lived, or by literary title, character, locale, genre, and publication date. The Literary Reference Center also features a literary-historical time line, an encyclopedia of literature, and a glossary of literary terms.

MagillOnLiterature Plus

MagillOnLiterature Plus is a comprehensive, integrated literature database produced by Salem Press and available on the EBSCOhost platform. The database contains the full text of essays in Salem's many literature-related reference works, including *Masterplots, Cyclopedia of World Authors, Cyclopedia of Literary Characters, Cyclopedia of Literary Places, Critical Survey of Poetry, Critical Survey of Long Fiction, Critical Survey of Short Fiction, World Philosophers and Their Works, Magill's Literary Annual,* and *Magill's Book Reviews.* Among its contents are articles on more than 35,000 literary works and more than 8,500 poets, writers, dramatists, essayists, and philosophers; more than 1,000 images; and a glossary of more than 1,300 literary terms. The biographical essays include lists of authors' works and secondary bibliographies, and hundreds of overview essays examine and discuss literary genres, time periods, and national literatures.

Rebecca Kuzins; updated by Desiree Dreeuws

GEOGRAPHICAL INDEX

CATEGORY INDEX

SUBJECT INDEX